EVIDENCE OF INSANITY

PUBLISHED BY LULU PUBLISHING

Copyright@2010 by Carol Piner
All rights reserved. Published in the United States by
Lulu Publishing

Manufactured in the United States of America
First Edition
ISBN 978-0-557-38693-2

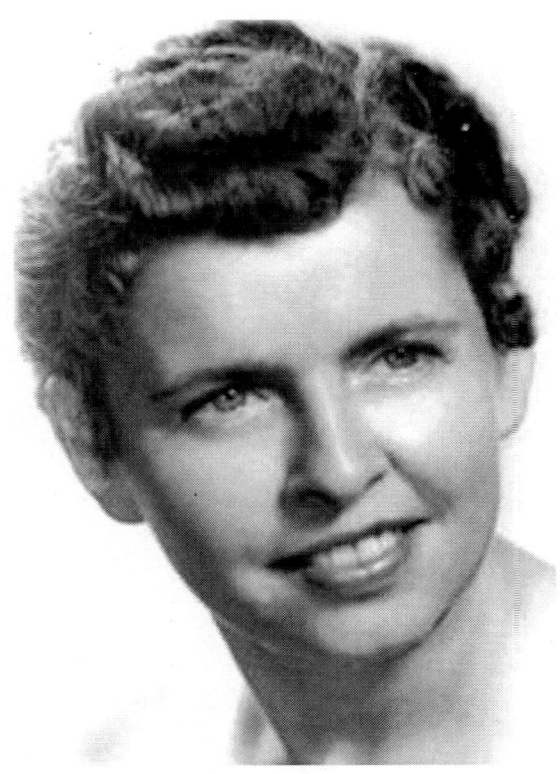

This book is dedicated to my Mama, also known as the hell cat. The woman who taught me to laugh and feel free to "have at it" if I felt the need to. At the same time, she allowed me to be the crazy ass fool I am.

...Evidence of Insanity...

    I am not sure when I realized it was there. I think I got it with my gene job. Hey, not my fault. Hell, it was all around me. Why fight it? Maybe give it a chance to grow like it was a vine. Sure felt like one.

    All I knew was it made me lucky. When God decided to pop my ass into some unknowing womb, like bread in a toaster, He gave me a gift. When I popped out seven months later, He had made me Mama's child.

ONE HOPPED UP FEMALE

    I thought of him as Big Daddy, not because he was, but because he was stupid enough to think he was. I called her Big Mama because she knew how to be one. She was only five feet three inches tall, but the lady could take up a whole lot of room. "Feisty" was not the word for her. She was way more than that. She'd get your heart beating going so hard you'd get a nervous stomach, and you wouldn't know if you were going to throw up right on the spot or what. Mama'd do it for fun and giggles. This cranked up lady was not boring..not for a second. I worshiped her. I wanted to be just like her. A kick ass kind of woman. I heard her before I ever saw her. Me? I was a fetus so I'm not really sure about much. All I could do was listen.

    Once I was a baby, I realized there were people who were in front of what I would later come to realize were eyeballs. While going through the unique process of getting to know my fingers and toes, I slowly started paying attention to whoever the hell this person was that seemed to buzz around me a lot. I didn't know what I was doing to warrant so much focus from the monster with long hair, but as long as it didn't piss me off, I would go along with it. Genius here, huh? I didn't remember if it was the Mama creature or the Daddy thing who first did something to get my attention, but let me tell you this, I felt the impact. You know, the whatever somebody did that got you looking at them funny for the very first time. You would stop all that babbling and stare at them like they had lost their minds. Then you realized all those sounds are actually directed at you. What in the world could they want? I tried getting some of the Mama and Daddy responses going back at them. Aha! They were happy if I made certain noises. Then they would go away and leave me alone. I was so smart I even knew which noise was which. That was cool. I paid attention for the first time instead of just laying there letting my head loll around from boredom. I don't know why, but I couldn't hold the damn thing up. You noticed I also learned to cuss, but I didn't want to talk yet, so nobody knew but me. Cool.

    I went from a fetus, to a baby, to a walking, talking pain in the ass to Mama. Eventually, I could dress myself and pretend to brush my teeth. That was about five, right? Who knew? Those early memories..what joy they brought. One memory was the fondest recollection of my very own parental nightmares. We were all in the kitchen. Specifically, the kitchen at the Eagles Nest, a home we lived in for awhile on Thirtieth Street located in a small Southern coastal town in North Carolina. It was game on time. I remember all five of us kids would be in full battle stance, gathering weapons, while Mama had Daddy up against the wall and was scratching his eyes out the best she could. Whap! Whap! Mama could slap you so fast you couldn't slap back and that would really piss you off. Daddy didn't have a chance. You can't even imagine the amount of screeching the woman could do while she banged his head up side the kitchen wall. You know how the cops make a lot of noise to confuse you. She did that before they ever thought of it. Screeching and hollering at her highest level, Mama finally got hold of his hair. That counted. That was known as control. They can't teach this stuff in college.

Grabbing that head of hair was one of Mama's finest gifts to my childhood. I would be running back and forth, hooting and hollering, trying to make as much noise as she was, waiting for the mane event. I would be getting into the mood of it all when Mama would take him by his pride and joy; that seven inch long, white tressy treasure of his. I knew she was ready to kick ass when she got him by the hair. She knew he was not about to fight back because he knew damn well he was going to lose some of it if he moved. If he did, she yanked, and Daddy wasn't willing to lose one more strand than the good Lord took. Mama would ride it for all it was worth. She'd carry on like an Indian in an old western. My fab Mama always took him to that point of no return, eased up and then went back at him again.

She would be banging away at him, screaming at the top of her lungs, the five of us standing there with our shoulders up around our ears in sweet anticipation chanting, "yes, yes! Git 'im, Mama, git 'im." We weren't ready to lunge at him yet because she was still winning. Mama wasn't at her worst until she felt him try to act like a man. It got its ugliest when the tide started to turn. If he started to lay one hand on her, all five of us were ready and we'd cover him like molasses. We'd get right into the fray. We were like trained dogs, but like most dogs, having a good time wagging our tails, puffing and drooling. Whining for more. Waiting for that signal to close in on him.

All he had accomplished up to now was a plaintive little "now, Anna". I've heard that a time in my life as he tried to settle her butt down. Mama didn't settle down until she expended the exact amount of rage she thought she could get away with. She could get as much damn rage going as she damn well pleased, like she had it in a bucket with no bottom. I felt all of us start to ease up a little, tails wagging a little slower. We were all thinking, come on, Mama, get back into this thing. Don't let us down now. I was watching everybody, peeking for all the different emotions on their faces. It never crossed my mind to think about what mine looked like, but I would venture to guess it bordered on ecstasy. You see, I just loved it when she took him apart. There aren't enough loves to go around to describe how much I loved it. One, she was good at it; two, he always deserved it; three, this was when life in the household got really good. Nothing, absolutely nothing, got better than this.

Genius that I am, I picked up on it first. She was getting ready to blow. I'd be jumping, beating my fists against my head, hollering, "Blow, Mama, blow! Come on, you can do it!" Running back and forth, arms a 'swinging, pushing and shoving the other kids to get them riled up. I hold the world record for instigating. Its good for them. Gets them motivated. On a good day, major damage could occur. My favorite time of all.

Like I said, she had him up against the wall doing the head banging thing when he finally got the nerve to attempt to take a stand. He started that huffing and puffing thing that made him look so stupid. His face got red and fatter like a pissed off balloon. The air would get so tight and thick, you figured every one of us would be having trouble breathing normal. You could hear little, short gasps coming from us like we were all dying..but it was really loud when it was times five. We could have launched our very own air balloon, just like Daddy's, right there in the room. Daddy would start to inflate. I guess his manhood had finally found a foothold. Mama wasn't going to have any of it. She started coming apart at all the seams, lots of seams, and was egging him on. The hell cat would put that little bitty index finger right in his face..wiggle it a little with that little "buster, come on if you've got the nerve gesture." Made him mad, it did. It would really piss him off. Really, really piss him off. Lord God Almighty, was I having fun or what? I couldn't make anymore noise than I already was because I didn't want to divert their attention from whatever violence they longed to partake of next. That was more important than anything. So, I was stuck wriggling around on the floor about ready to pee myself. I was rooting for fireworks.

Dying to jump in there to make things worse. No doubt about whose kid I was. Mama's little volcano job had been completely exhausted. She was ready to move on to better things. When she cocked that eye at him, it was time for lift off.

Daddy was inflating, like I said. Mama saw it coming and was daring him to even take one more breath in this lifetime. Teeny was tensing. Everybody was primed and ready to go. We were so excited we were on our tip toes, tilting back and forth towards whomever was hollering loudest. He took a weak swing at her. Didn't he? Was that a swing? Didn't look like a swing to me. Feeble, you know. We all looked at each other. Hell, it was good enough for us. Let's call it a swing even though it was more like a pale, limp fish hanging off the end of his wrist. All hell broke loose. I hit the floor again. I was ducking blows and screaming encouragement to everybody all at the same time. The kids piled on him like he was a ladder. I hit him low because I was still on the floor laughing. I had my legs held together as tight as I could so I wouldn't pee myself. Its distracting. My job was to get him wobbling. Hell, if I could get him off his feet, he'd be a goner. I was also at that level because I was still short, so it was about as high as I could go. I was biting his ankles but he wouldn't fall. But he didn't mind swiping at me like I was a mosquito. Teeny got him at the highest point, though he really wanted to take Mama down. MaryBeth was holding onto his waistline, whining about getting along. Crystal was totally bewildered by who's doing what, not to mention why. Jimmy was tap dancing and running back and forth pulling for both sides, because he wasn't sure which way it was going to go. Finally, finally it happened. Mama whacked Daddy so hard he bounced off the wall. Twice. Twice was a double header. Ten for Mama, zero for Daddy. The wall had served its purpose for today. Its not there to hold up the house, it is there to give Daddy something to crack into that is really, really hard. You don't want a wall with any give in it.

Right along with the sound of him rebounding off the wall, I was whooping and screaming in joy like you wouldn't believe. Most people never have a chance to make this much noise in their whole damn lives and we got to do it every other day. Then, everybody stopped dead..we tensed. We suddenly realized that Mama had pretty much run the violence phase, so she went into her next mode. All five feet three inches tall, one hundred ten pounds of her seemed to grow upward and outward.

We went into Phase II, in spite of my major disappointment and whining for Mama to hit him one more time. Smack him or something, but it was over. Time for the trip to the water. Damn.

If you were from down South, and grew up in a family like mine, you knew what a trip to the water meant. Mama did not merely toss Daddy's clothes into the yard. No sir, not her. She had to take us, burdened with his whole damn wardrobe, down to the water. Across other people's yards, no less, so the whole damn town would know what Daddy had done. Then, we'd throw them in. Everybody knew when Daddy was messing around with other women long before us but we pretended we were the first to know. They came out of their houses and watched us go by like we were the train that went through town. They'd snicker because they knew he was going to have to find a clothing store somewhere. We only seemed to sell fish in this damn town. The reason the man would need to buy new clothes was so Mama would have something to throw away next time. There would be a next time. Bank on it. She told us it was to get that "whore stench" out of the house. Ew.

There we were. Like a precious little duck family on the way to the shore. Mama would lead the way while we ran along behind, sharing in our little warm togetherness way. What you could call the righteous Public Humiliation of Big Daddy. Worked for me. You could call it public humiliation, but you have to give a shit to be humiliated and neither of these folks understood that concept. We kids were past struggling to understand when other people said "Weren't you humiliated?" Hell, no. I'd be jumping up and down with my right arm pumping. Hey, you only have one life so I think you should enjoy it. Gimme a reason to throw his clothes out..gimme. Great grits!!

At the edge of the water it looked like a baptism of sorts. Only it was the clothes burbling as they went down, not us. Daddy would not be following, of course. He would be back at the Eagles Nest either trying to figure out if this was the worse it got or was she going to come back and get real mad. Then again, he could have been trying to figure out how much this latest tart was going to cost him in new clothes. If he didn't just drive down main street with them, it would be so much cheaper. He had a five year old who sat him down and tried to explain it to him. He could have chosen to take them to church with him. So many tough decisions in life. The first pew? Stupid.

I think he would have been disappointed if he knew his clothes just sank. He wasn't God and they didn't stand up for him. Puffed up jerk. He probably thought they reared straight up like a battleship before they went down, flags a'flying. After all, he was Somebody. Yeah, he's somebody. An idiot without the savant. I am not going to tell you his real name. Sure I am. Teen. Winner there, huh?

Well, too bad Chad. They just sank. Down they went and we'd head back to the house clothesless, with Mama leading the way. Righteous indignation aglow. The filthy other woman's smell on those clothes are outta here. I wasn't going to ask her if she had smelled his car lately. That was not her perfume, fellas. Of course, the five of us were not being silent. We were young-un's so we were screaming and carrying on like headless chickens. Good times. Teeny would be yelling about how he didn't know how a woman could shame her man like that. Piss on him. MaryBeth would be going on relentlessly about how we should act like family. Weren't we? Who, other than a family would act like this? Crystal would be trying to be a part of it all. Jimmy would have just about figured that Mama was gonna win this one. She always did. He just never caught on to it. Me, I was having the time of my life doing spins and cartwheels; flinging my tiny self all over the place, 'cause I knew it was nitty gritty time. Now, the full fledged power play could go into effect. In front of God and everybody, and I mean everybody, Mama cut Daddy off. Mama did these things very publicly and very, very loudly. She was like a foghorn on crack when she cut him off. She didn't do this in the house. The street worked just fine for her. For Anna, it was like turning off a spigot. He was not going to get anywhere near her sweetness any time soon. What is that, by the way? Am I supposed to know that at five years old? Whatever. The bad boy had been running on her again. He'd never learn.

For the record, we did not consider this domestic violence so I don't want to hear any crap from anybody. I didn't anyway. If this was violence, it was my thing. This was just a hellaciously good time. Didn't everybody live like that? We figured it was how everybody brought their kids up. Now I wonder, if not, why not? Worked for me.

Let me introduce you more clearly to the children, of which I was the baby. Teeny, my oldest brother, was primed for his oldest brother routine; being smarter than anyone else in the history of the universe. MaryBeth was raring to start controlling everybody's life down to the finest detail and was only slightly less dominating than Mama. Crystal was completely oblivious that this could be a life or death situation but satisfied that it wasn't her role to figure it out. Jimmy was a favorite sibling of mine at the time. He was being Jimmy..nothing, nowhere, like an amoeba. Basically shapeless, meaningless but everybody's favorite. Translated that meant he was not going to take any stand whatsoever. No how, no way, until it progressed enough for him to be able to judge the winner. Then, he'd jump in like he'd been rooting for them all along. Ergo, the favorite. As a rule, he wasn't very smart, but he could do a world class suck up. For him, that was about as clever as he got. He always got on my nerves. Always. I had heard boys had things called balls. Hell, I'd seen his. Maybe they just malfunctioned or something. Then, there was me. Little Callie. Everybody's little sugar pie. Yeah, right. I was young, and still somewhat stupid, but it was ok with everybody. Five kids in six years and people wondered why Mama was mad all the time. I'd a sure been mad.

    This little example of a day out of the life drew a picture. I was capable of seeing things clearly at a very young age. I had a picture in my mind of some things that went on even before I was born. I think I had picked up on all this through osmosis or something. Imagine that. I guess that's why I didn't think everything was my fault like so many dorky kids. "Did I cause it, mommy?" Good grief. I think that when Mama was pregnant with me, I got an inkling of what was going on. All that adrenaline and all that emotion she could churn up, and there would be little old me inside her belly, all tucked up tight, churning right along with her. Fists pumping. Rooting for her, of course. She was the home team, so to speak. I know I came out ready for it. I know it was going on the day I was born. I didn't have a squashed head for nothing. Oh, did I mention I didn't need gas? I had some.

BUD DIXON'S TEXACO STATION

    In the South, men didn't hide their goings on. They stuck it right out there for everybody to see like it was a poster on the wall. If they didn't do it right in front of everybody, then nobody would know and they wouldn't be so very, very special. Morehead would have to dry up and blow away from nothing to talk about.

That was our biggest industry. Talk. Low down, dirty, mean mouth kind of talking. Of course, it was all true, but let's forget that for a moment and move on. Not only was it the low down, dirty stuff, it mattered that everybody know. Small town people understand that. Move down here and you'd figure it out quick enough unless you're ignorant. Women and children weren't supposed to pass judgment on the gods. The men hadn't figured out that God wasn't born in Morehead. Nonetheless, the women and children weren't supposed to say anything when the men did their running. I didn't agree. I wanted to get in on the fighting even while in the womb. Unfortunately, up to then, I'd pretty much had to keep my mouth shut, since it didn't work so I tried being a nice womb tenant. I have to admit, I was fed up with being quiet. I wanted in on the some of this fine action. I'd already been in that womb for seven months and I wanted out. It was all Daddy's fault that Mama got so torn up on the day I was born. He was running on her even then. Now, remember I was not born yet so I get a little relief from the facts here.

    I knew Morehead was the kind of slow-walking, slow-talking kind of lazy Southern town that had railroad tracks running right down the middle of main street. There was your normal good side of the tracks and bad side of the tracks, but the tracks didn't have much to do with it this time. It was more a directional thing. In this case, it mattered more that one side went west and one side went east. Mama was going east in Uncle Robert's car since she didn't have her own car. Only the men gods got a car. Daddy was going west in that big, British racing green Cadillac with the black convertible top. A fine automobile for a fine man. A big dick car. There was another woman in his car when he pulled into Bud Dixon's Texaco for gas. Mama came leisurely down Arendell Street headed for town when she saw him standing at the pump. She saw the other woman, too. I felt the adrenalin start to flow. At that moment, what he was, was a sitting dead duck with a blonde in the car. I think seven months is long enough to wait for a shit storm, don't you? You ask and the Lord will provide.

    Mama decided to get involved with this little gas filling tryst going on at Bud Dixon's Texaco. She had a tendency not only to act out what she thought but throw a fit at the same time. I felt I had missed this rodeo long enough. She was mad and I was kicking. Hell, she probably didn't even know I existed, but I like to think she knew I was on her side from day one. This, people, became day one. Good enough for me. I was stomping and kicking, ready to unload this damn rope stuck to my stomach.

Bud Dixon got the honor for this soon to be interesting show of shows. As I mentioned, when Mama saw Daddy and his lady friend at into Bud Dixon's, she didn't keep going until she got to the next intersection to turn around. Oh no, hell no. Fire breathing, ass kicking Anna yanked that steering wheel hard to the left and k-damn bam. She went airborne when she hit those railroad tracks, landed on the east side, aimed that car for a direct hit and rammed Daddy's car while he was obliviously pumping away. Maybe he was whistling a little tune. Who knows? Who cares? Mama jumped out of her car, squirmed through the back window of Daddy's Cadillac and started hell beating "that other woman" from over the front seat. She was out for blood. Either Daddy's or the whore's, who was being picky? Daddy would be lucky if Mama didn't toss his Cadillac in the water while she was at it since it had that stench in it she was so adverse to.

Striving to save his pumps before they went up in flames, Bud Dixon ran into his station to call the police while Daddy was trying to decide if he was pissed enough about her ramming his sweet baby car to really take her on. You gotta think these things through sometimes. While Daddy was trying as hard as he could to form an intelligent thought, Mama was still pummeling the helpless female. You'll have to forgive me, I never got her name. I was a fetus at the time.

Mama was in the back, reaching over the front seat to get to the blond. Hair pulling, teeth biting woman fighting. Pandemonium in it's finest form. Wade was the local police and it wasn't but a minute before he showed up. People ate it up when Mama caught Daddy. They knew she would put on a great show for them. A wide open female of the finest kind. Wade only had to see the two cars meeting at the hip and he was up and out of his patrol car in a shot trying to pull Mama off the female without killing me. Wade and Bud got Mama into the front seat of the patrol car and put Daddy and the undoubtedly bleached, thunderstruck and well into learning about Anna, the Hun, blonde in the back seat and they all headed for Swansboro, the county line, about thirty minutes away. Mama continued to lean over the seat, squashing me while raising hell and fists as Daddy fended her off as best he could. I am sure people could hear it for miles.

I could hear it from where ever the hell I was. When we got there, Wade was hollering at the blonde to get out of Carteret County and never come back. Showing that good police stuff. After all, he's Mama's nephew, not Daddy's. Kinfolk means a lot down here. Everybody's related, but that's another story. Wade probably started smirking and grinning when he got the call.

Wade jumped out of the squad car, ran around to the back door, and got the blond out of the car. We left her standing, dazed, on the side of he road. She probably wouldn't go back to church with MY Daddy. I'm sure Bud Dixon had gotten on the phone to my Uncle Charlie as soon as Wade pulled into the gas station, telling Uncle Charlie to go get her. Charlie was not going to let a good blonde go to waste. If he didn't go, I'm sure Bud could find somebody who would.

Mama had nothing to do now except go for the silver. Hair, that is. Daddy's. Seven months pregnant, she was half over the front seat grabbing him and pulling for all she was worth and then wham, bam, her water broke. Wade flew down the highway to get her to the hospital as fast as he could before she could mess up his squad car any worse than it was. When she got to the hospital, I was practically waiting for her. There I was. Immediately. All three pounds, four ounces of perfect seven month me. Output number 5. She told me later she thought she had gas until she was five months pregnant. I guess she thought that was funny, but to me it was meaningful and prophetic. You could say that I was almost born at a gas station. Symbolic, having a little gas myself at the time. Hence, it should be considered poetic that my birthday is forever linked with a gas station in my mind. Jimmy ended up nine months older than me instead of twelve. I ended up a Scorpio instead of a Sagittarius. Its not my fault I'm bitchy. Apparently, Daddy didn't like me from the beginning. I must have come out already thinking he was an ass. He changed my damn name before I ever got to have my first bowel movement. But the real reason he didn't like me was he blamed me for what happened next. She had him neutered. Yee-ha..

Before I go on, I must admit I did not come out perfect. I had twenty/two hundred vision in both eyes. One was correctable while the other just kinda visited. Mama wore size 5 shoes. She took me home from the hospital in her shoe box. You could say I was short even then.

THE EAGLES NEST

The house that we had so much fun in was called the Eagles Nest. Because it had one. I learned a lot about family dynamics there. Plus, I really loved that place. It had an aura about it that somehow smacked of a lot of living having gone on there. We sure added to the list. It was a big, rambling house one block from the water with a large empty lot next door. Fire ants owned that lot, but they let us play on it so they could feast on our blood. They would crawl in our ears when we fell and feed on our brains. I still wonder how smart I could have been had we moved somewhere else. Whatever. Standing in the front yard, you could see a tall, wide, pure white house with two stories. It had columns, like in Savannah. There was a porch on the first and second levels that went from one end of the house to the other. From the second level you could you look out at the Intracoastal Waterway that flowed past Morehead and Beaufort on the way to Florida. There was a porch on the first floor with two rocking chairs, but we didn't spend much time there because you couldn't see the water. Not to mention, we liked hanging off the second level porch and holding each other over the rails where it was good and dangerous. The house was white because most houses in this area with a water view are. Why is that? When you came in the front door, you had a large living area in front of you and the infamous kitchen, location of the better battles, was to your right. In front of you was the natural wood winding staircase leading from the first floor to the second. Think of me as a small Scarlet O'Hara. A grimy at all times Scarlet, but her nonetheless.

For someone who must have been only two feet tall, the staircase was a mountain to be climbed. The bannister rail was sleek, polished wood with one long curve as you neared the top, then there was a landing leading to the left and right with bedrooms on both sides. That bannister rail was mine to conquer. My only reason for existence was so I could slide down it. I would go down it headfirst from the top to the bottom floor with my hands at my sides. Holding on was cheating. My rules. The turn was a bitch and I would often crash and burn on a landing, depending on how far I got down it before I fell off. I mean burn literally. It was very descriptive of my face and elbows most of the time. Very rarely would I be lucky enough to land on the stair side. Most of the time I would fall all the way down to the floor. By the way, that was a hell of a drop down. It was far enough for me to figure out how stupid this game was. Not one to give up, though, the goal was to make that turn and start to speed toward the bottom of the staircase without using my hands. Sped right up, too. Of course, the day finally arrived when I challenged myself right into massive migraines. I came sliding down and made the turn with my hands still against my sides. Did I mention the hard wooden ball at the bottom of the bannister rail? I came up on that ball flying a hundred miles an hour. I always figured whoever designed the staircase hated kids and put it there to kill them. The ball from hell. Wouldn't you know I failed the required hand trick test? The one where I put my hands up just before I got to the ball to stop myself. That was supposed to be the point when I would throw my hands up to save myself from banging my skull into the solid wood ball and survive with my brains intact. Instead, I went headfirst into said ball. It didn't budge. The ball, that is. My skull did plenty of budging. It caved in. The ball became a part of my head, and then it shattered. The head, that is. Damn, that hurt.

   Your first reaction as a kid was like wow. Who'd a thought there was that much blood in a head? It was better than science class. Up to then, you thought all those ears and eyeballs took up most of the room. Nope, mostly blood. For all I knew, blood and brains were the same thing. Something fell out. My second reaction was Mama was going to be really pissed about all that blood on the hardwood floor and it's never ending ability to absorb anything I could spill on it. My third reaction was to pray. As that gray stuff came over my eyes, I couldn't see anymore. Then everything went black. I quit worrying about it. I think that was God's idea. Until I came to. Talk about the headache of a lifetime. My body came off the floor, but my head took it's sweet, Southern time. It had all day and Lord knows, the rest of me wasn't going anywhere without it. I figured as long as the eyeballs were still with me, the rest of the garbage in my head could stay on the floor. Giving in to an unsuccessful first attempt, I laid back down to wait for everything to come back together. I was flat out on the floor, miserable, covered in my own blood (gross) and suddenly, there was Mama. One inch from my only working eyeball. Hellfire running through her. I thought for a second I had survived but when she let loose on me, I knew for sure I had died and gone to hell. She mopped with one hand and popped my head with the other. She wanted me to see how much trouble I was in. I got it. I healed eventually, but I still wonder how much intellect I spilled on that floor. I coulda been smarter than I am but for that. Go figure.

Jimmy's favorite thing at the Eagles Nest was sleep walking. He would sleep walk right out the bedroom door on the second floor, without Teeny hearing him, tiptoe down the staircase, and run off to the beach. I always thought he was in training for when he became a teenager and would crawl out the window on purpose. I also wondered how many times we found him coming and how many times we found him going. Mama, not being ignorant, chose to challenge the sleep walking excuse, so she began locking him in his room when he went to bed. Consequently, he went out the second floor window and climbed down a trellis. Asleep. Right. She knew what he was doing. Mama and I went to the trellis and removed some of the nails holding it to the house. Giggling at the thought of what was to come. Finally, one night, while Jimmy was climbing down it, it separated from the house. The big boy crashed, bounced back up and down a few times, just for fun and games, and then thudded to the green, green grass. I heard when the trellis separated so I had my head out my window giving me the opportunity to watch his bounce and thud. I half believed he was sleep walking until then. I realized he was just an awake walking idiot. But, it shows how easy it is to stop someone from sleepwalking if you're serious. Put 'em on the second floor, lock 'em in, open the window. That'll teach 'em. Shows how much time Mama's kids spent with our faces pushed through the back of our heads.

ANYBODY SEE A GHOST?

With our house, for free, we had our very own ghost. It belonged to all of us. Ghosts are cool. I didn't think so at first, but I learned. Once I got to know him, I named him Wilson. He brought us together, so to speak. It became something to get excited about other than walk to the water and toss clothes out. Our Wilson provided unique entertainment.

In the house, if you came up the stairs and took a right, you would pass a bathroom. Next you would go straight into the room where we three girls slept. Crystal was the first to see him. Bummer. She slept to the right of the doorway. MaryBeth was on the far wall, and I was on the wall heading back to the door. Jimmy and Teeny were down the hall on the right and Mama and Daddy were on the left.

    Crystal started screaming one night, but we didn't take her too seriously. We were unusually used to screaming at any time day or night. We simply absorbed the sound like a rag, then ignored it. Not a huge ticket puncher there. Crystal didn't come right out at first and say she saw a ghost. No one would have believed her. I wouldn't set myself up for something like that with this circus crowd, either. But, she kept bawling and saying she saw something. MaryBeth and I didn't see anything for a couple of weeks, but that was because every time Crystal started to scream, we'd close our eyes. Smart, huh? Real detectives. Two Sherlock Stupid Holmes in the making. I'm pretty sure MaryBeth was the next to see it, because I wasn't opening my eyes for anybody. If I didn't recognize the voice, I wouldn't even come up for air. MaryBeth also got credit for calling it a ghost. I'm convinced, this wouldn't have happened if I hadn't left my brains on the living room floor. She not only had the guts to be the first to call it a ghost, she could describe it. I was the last of the girls to see it. When I finally did see it, I was dumbfounded because you actually could SEE IT. Shape and all. It would come in the door while we were lying there like frightened rabbits. If rabbits did the fetal position, that is. We didn't dare get up and leave be ause Daddy did not want to deal with this so we were trapped by who to be afraid of most and Daddy won hands down. It would float in and out. Really. The legs wouldn't be moving, but the shape itself was moving. The entity itself was on the move without any body parts causing it. Weird. You could see arms and legs, torso and the head, and unexpectedly, it wore a hat. And a uniform. Swear to God. I night I hollered, "Hey, Wilson."

    Wilson looked like a policeman or a serviceman. We were only seventeen miles from the largest marine corp airbase in the US. in one direction and forty miles from another in the other direction. It could have been a milkman or postman. Who knew? He would come in and sort of float to the right, toward Crystal. It came across her wall, it passed MaryBeth's wall, then mine and went out the door. It wasn't quick or slow, just smooth. Slow motion, but not dragging. No moaning or anything like that, unfortunately or I might have figured out it was a dead person sooner. Real quiet, he was. You notice I've said "he". It was not a female, because it was clearly a he. He didn't say hi. Everybody saw it before he was shot.

Early on we screamed mostly at each other, because it didn't seem to bother him. Sometimes we screamed just to practice for everyday life and the ghost had nothing to do with it. I did anyway. I was intrigued by it because he acted like he had somewhere to go. We would scream real quick when we first saw it and shut up fast, embarrassed. Mama wouldn't have screamed. She never did. By then, everyone had seen it and it was time for us to get blase' about it all. Continental, you know. Like everybody had one. He became one of the family to everybody but Daddy and Teeny. Teeny made the first strike against him. Nerd ball.

I said earlier that Wilson seemed to have somewhere to go. Apparently, it was the bathroom. Gross thought, huh? A ghost sitting there, taking a dump in the same toilet you sit on. Yuk. However, that is where it would head when it left our room. Not really wanting to be trapped in a bathroom with a ghost, Teeny decided to mount his attack while it was in our room. Right over MaryBeth's head. One night he came into the room with a knife he had carved by hand. A knife of unusual beauty; all smooth and shellacked. Maybe 9" of blade and 5" of handle. It was a beautiful creation plus it was his pride and joy. He carried it around with him on his belt and considered himself armed. Had that strut in his walk, you know? He strutted in, but then he hid under MaryBeth's bed, like a coward. I am sure he thought it was strategy. Wilson was dead, Teeny. Get with it. I was really hoping it would go under the bed after him. I'd pay good money to see that. If I'd had any.

We waited for it to show, which it did faithfully every evening after that first night. You could count on it. Same time, same place, same routine. When Wilson came in, we automatically fetaled. Is that a word? He came in slowly, then started going around the wall. Teeny jumped up, you know, like he was going to surprise it or something and slung that beautiful knife at the ghost. The ghost kept gliding, nice and slow. Doing it's ghost thing while Teeny's knife stayed right where it stuck. We were having conniptions. At least, I was. You think back and you wonder what had been in Teeny's head? Did he plan to kill it or just maim it? Did he think he would impale it and there it would be, stuck to the wall? Good God Almighty! And if either of those notions were in his head, what did he think he would do with it then? Filet it like a fish? I would think a ghost moving away from you was a lot easier to deal with than one stuck on your damned wall, for Christ's sake. But that's just me. If he wants it as a poster, let him stick it to his own damn wall. How long did he plan to let it suffer while hanging there? At least in his mind it would be hanging there. I think I loved these people. I'm not sure. He was the oldest of us and you would think he should have been smarter than that by then. I knew it wouldn't work for much longer but, at the time, it was more fun laughing at him than trying to train him. These people were a hoot a minute.

You might not be surprised to find out the knife went right through it? Duh! It was still stuck a full inch into the wall. Teeny was speechless, and Teeny speechless was a delight to behold. Of course, the baton was immediately passed to Daddy. His first born had failed. What irony. What creativity. He used a gun. I think God looked down when he created this crew of brainless homo sapiens and decided he hadn't had a chance to screw around since knocking off the dinosaurs, so he'd play with us. Have a snicker or two.

Daddy did the same thing Teeny did. Like son, like father? Who thought of these awful things? I couldn't handle all the fun I was having. Quietly, mind you, lest the evil force, Daddy, turn on me. There Daddy was one night, in a crouch. Getting in an offensive position to tackle something that wasn't even real. Up to now, it had only hurt Teeny's pride. Daddy's was in for a pounding. Wilson came in, waltzed around the walls and went out. He was a whole lot less dangerous that the menfolk who were focused on it's destruction. Wilson meandered down the landing and sauntered in it's nice ghostly way into the bathroom. Without knocking, Daddy charged after it. Bellowing. Attila the idiot. I don't know how you see it, but for me, this was the way to grow up. Who could have it any better? The way I looked at it was, I didn't know what a ghost goes into the bathroom for and I didn't wanta find out. But that was just me.

For a minute, we had one of those pregnant pauses. We didn't hear anything outta that bathroom. It only lasted a second because I was going nuts and Mama was hanging onto me trying to hold me back. I wanta see, I wanta seeeeeee. All of a sudden a shotgun blast went off. A shotgun, guys, in a bathroom. Do you know how loud that can be? Whoeee! Daddy shot a ghost in the bathroom, Daddy shot a ghost in the bathroom! Sing it out loud. I laughed so hard I fell down. Then, Daddy came running out, white as a ghost, you might say. Damn near ran over me. Jimmy ran in when Daddy ran out. No doubt looking for whatever a shot ghost looked like. What a circus. What a family. What a life. The only thing Daddy accomplished was Mama got a new bathroom and we got a glimpse of a head with nothing but air in it, and I'm not talking about the ghost.

So, since we couldn't kill it (again), we shared the house with our new friend. Hell, I'd rather have a Wilson for my father than a Teen. Who wouldn't? Daddy, however, was grumpier than ever. It could have been because he made an absolute ass of himself in front of babies smarter than he was. Those of us with brains enjoyed his humiliation, anyway. However, Teeny went into the kind of battle he was better at. This time with research. He found out a mailman lived there years before. He had been in uniform on the porch on the second level and accidently killed himself cleaning his rifle. He had slept in our room. We received no updates from Tenny about the ghost's need to go to the bathroom, but I let that pass. Mama and Daddy thought seriously about moving. To me, you gotta be seriously crazy to move out of a house that has a ghost. I decided we were special. God had sent someone down to screw with us. What was wrong with that? Didn't they get it? Hello-o-o-o?

EVIL ABOUNDS

When I was about seven years old, on one of those so called lazy, hazy, crazy days of summer, I was out on the empty lot owned by the previously mentioned cannibals, the fire ants. It was where we played football because it was big enough for us to really get in trouble. I was having one of those hot, sweaty days with nothing to do blues, lying on my back, thinking about nothing. My favorite thing. I was also in my favorite outfit, a space suit. It wasn't really a space suit but that's what they come up with at Christmas to add flavor to boring gifts. They pack it up differently, put a bow on it, and call it something other than what it really is and get away with it because its Christmas. Otherwise, its just a baseball uniform with boots. On the other hand, if Mama said it was a space suit, it was a space suit. The box said so, too. If you thought it was anything else, you'd keep your mouth shut if you were half smart. Of course, nobody ever said Jimmy was smart. He told her it was just a baseball uniform with boots. He learned. No space suit for him. Treasure your gifts, don't question them, dickhead.

Lying there, I was watching a tiger butterfly flitter around me. The whole area drew a lot of butterflies. No big deal. I wasn't attempting to commune with nature or anything like that. I wasn't old enough. But, it was real peaceful and quiet. A shadow suddenly blocked my sunlight and when I looked up, Daddy was standing there, looming over me. I can't remember ever liking that jerkwad. No matter how young, even as a fetus, I don't think I liked him. Every time he came around me, I got real quiet and kept my one good eye on him, trolling with his movement, like you would if he were a snake. Which he was. I wasn't afraid of him like Marybeth and Crystal were. I watched my back. I knew I made him nervous because he couldn't get reactions out of me or make me cry. I just watched him and kept my mouth shut. He liked to try to do things to make me mad or sad or do something just to piss me off. He knew I had been watching the butterfly, so he reached down, not a word was said, and snatched the butterfly out of the air by it's wings. He took a pin off my hat, excuse me, space helmet, and pinned the butterfly to the hat, close to my right ear. It was still alive and struggling. He watched me a minute to see if I was going to cry or something. When all I did was give him what I hoped was an evil eye, he cussed me and stalked off.

I hung around a few minutes, not wanting anyone to see how far out my bottom lip was sticking. Man, I was pissed. Not hurt, furious. What a useless human being he was. He not only didn't care about anybody, he didn't care about anything except running on Mama. I got up, walked into the house and headed for the kitchen where it seemed Mama spent all her time. When I got there, I got right in front of her and stood there looking at her, bottom lip and all. Daddy was half sprawled over the kitchen table cramming a piece of chicken down his gullet. I had a tight knot of bitterness in my throat that I couldn't swallow. I didn't say a word. I just glared at Mama, willing her to look down at me. When she did, she saw the butterfly, never doubting how it got pinned to my hat. She calmly reached down and unpinned it. It was dead by then because there was no struggling coming from it. She looked me straight in the eye, turned and quietly dropped it in the trash. Her way of telling me to do something about something I could do something about and leave what I had no control over to her fine, competent hands. I was too young, too small. She, however, was tall enough to walk over to the kitchen table where Daddy was still feeding his face and whack him so hard he almost fell out of the chair. Not a word was said. But, it put a big grin on my face. And I let him see it. Fart face. Then I went outside and threw my hat onto the seat of his car to make sure he understood I knew I had the female lion on my side. He didn't need any more reasons to get cut off, believe me. Let him wonder why it was there. The, I found some fresh dog poop and smeared it on the accelerator of his car. Maybe he'd think it was a little reminder not to screw with me. Kept the boots.

    I mentioned the unfortunate fact that my bottom lip stuck out when I pouted. Why can't you pout without looking like you were a baby? Mama loved that lip, though. When I'd pout too much, she'd grab my bottom lip and drag me around the room. Damn, she was fast. I couldn't unpout fast enough to avoid her. She loved it. It was a game to her. It was also a life lesson. I figured my job was to keep my damn lips from where they didn't belong. Namely, in Mama's hands. There were times I barely smiled around her when she was feeling feisty for fear she might grab me and mop the floor with me. She'd done it before, damn it. Lip-grabbing was a sport to her.

    Another warm, togetherness family time for us was when Teeny gathered together almost all the kids so he could shoot them. Notice the way I slipped "almost" in there. Not me, boy. For some reason I never understood, they liked me. Go figure. Maybe it was because I laughed a lot and they didn't know it was at them. Jr's frustration at the continuing breakdown of the family had been growing like a fungus. You could practically see it when he growled. He got meaner and meaner and madder and madder. Its not like his attitude helped. He was real smart, but taciturn and rude, to say the least. He said he wanted to save us all, but apparently he really wanted to kill us. We all knew when this whole family dynamic thing ended, it would not be pretty. He was handling it worse than anybody. He was coming on fourteen and fluctuated between being really funny, horny and being a snob, too good for the rest of us. He was knee deep in the "I'm an alpha male" bull. He got scary when he was mad. One of those bookish types that could go off on you.

I don't know what set him off. I'd been outside playing with the ants. When I walked in the door, there stood Teeny with his B.B. rifle. Oops. I thought seriously about wandering the hell back outside because lined up against the wall was Jimmy, Crystal and MaryBeth. Mama wasn't home. Good thing, he'd would have kept shooting until he killed her, for sure. Sometimes I couldn't figure out how I got stuck with these people. I decided it was not time to wonder about life, just save myself. I sidled up t to him. Me and Teeny, together..forever, you know. He was pointing the rifle at them, all pissed off. Sometimes you simply could not reason with him. This was one of those times. I wanted to ask him what he was thinking. I was truly curious, but I figured the timing might make him swing that B.B. gun my way. I decided I didn't want to draw attention to myself. It was clear he simply felt like shooting them. Not a bad idea. Ok, go for it. It was reassuring to be standing next to him with him acting like I was an okay kind of guy..not included in the "them" category. I was smart enough to know if he didn't tell me to get up against the wall, I just might make it. What I really didn't expect was for him to do it. But he did. Shot 'em all. Bam, Bam, Bam. I jumped a foot in the air. Scared me speechless. Lord Almightly, Teenie. You did it. Shazamm.

Jesus, what a crowd. He shot Jimmy on the hand, and Crystal in the left eye right near her tear duct, I really hated that. He got MaryBeth on the side of her head. I wondered if he aimed or simply let loose. They were all lucky, except Crystal, that it was just a pellet gun. Her tear duct took umbrage, as they say, to a pellet being shot at it. I guess they thought it probably wouldn't hurt. It must have for all the carrying on. Nothing was done about it, of course. All the racket died instantly when Mama got home. After that everybody soft pedaled it like an unfortunate accident had happened to all three of them at once. Right. Crystal said she got something in her eye. Lord knows, we didn't want Mama to find out the truth. She would have finished us off. There wasn't too much blood to clean up, anyway. All in a day. Hey, if the floor was ok, what's the harm, huh? Better than a barbecue.

We called it the Eagles Nest because it had one between the roof and chimney. House had spirit. In more ways than one.

BEACHING INSTEAD OF BITCHING

So you don't get maudlin about it all, there were other hot and spicy times. Living in Morehead was like being split between two totally diverse worlds and cultures. When it was cold enough to shrink something I am too young to talk about, I was stuck in the land of the fishing village. Not a college sport, mind you. You can't be too stupid to fish. I know. People who had never met me would recognize me. It seemed there wasn't a soul in sight that wasn't kin to me. People would walk up to me and say "Aren't you a Piner?" How did they know? Was there a sign on my forehead or butt or something? I hated to go out the front door. It was like opening a book and everybody but me had read it. However, when that warm, precious sun from God came out around May, I was transported to paradise. Good news was I only had to go two miles. There was piss and vinegar everywhere on the beach. Attitude. To get away from all the Morehead grunts, I had the beach. All the boomers from the South in the 60's remember Billy Stewart sang a song called "Summertime... and the living is easy." He'd still be alive if he hadn't believed it. He did a concert at the Pavilion. You would get on your knees and thank God for the Pavilion if you had ever been there. Then he smoked dope and ran right into a bridge abutment. Head first. Damn shame. But that's what life's about Down East. If you die, at least you knew you had a good time because good times were everywhere and everybody was having them. You didn't move to the land of the hazy sun for career choices. It was about doing the least you could get away with. Beginning in May, suddenly there was nobody on your ass. They were not only not on your ass, they were nowhere in sight. "They" were those things made in the parent format. What a great way to grow up and how awful to ever grow away from it. There was nothing worse than having to say you grew up and became normal. God awful thought. Why would you want to go do something like that? Not me, boy. I intend to stay a whack job all my living life.

My first real memory of the beach was a of a place called the Idle Hour. For short and curly, this was in the late fifties, and just a touch of the early sixties. It was owned by the Coopers who owned everything that God didn't claim first. But, they were really nice people. I remember Alfred Cooper with fondness. Something I did not have in great quantities, by the way. I didn't think they were kin because they had money. Pots and pots and pots of money. They didn't know how to act, but then who did? Good folks, and somewhat decent hearts in spite of it all. On Saturday nights way back then, the women would frilly up to go out. Prom dress kind of frilling. Mama was always known as "pretty little Anna." Even the women called her that, so you know it had to be true. Everybody knew she was a spitfire female and relished in it as long as it wasn't directed at their butts. She was good-looking with cold black hair and the blue eyes of an angel. The black hair had blue highlights the color of her eyes. The hair was an "oh my" kind of hair. Wondrously thick hair and deep blue eyes that sparkled. Mesmerizing. I got her ears, I think. I got her height coupled with Daddy's face color and of all things, I looked like him, not her. Don't tell me there's a God. He wouldn't be that treacherous. If I had looked like Granny, it would have led me to bloody wrists. Go figure. It all worked on her, didn't with me. She also could be as much a lady as anyone who had ever been in high society. I tried to pull off the acting like a lady thing, but she didn't have to act. She could be the best lady in the house. Let's not get caught up in thinking she was sweet. That's carrying the cow too far.

She had breasts, too. Used them all up on Marybeth and Crystal. She really felt bad that I didn't get 'em. Where did I go wrong? They talked about how proportionate I was like that was going to make me feel better. Men turn around and stare at "proportionate"? Right. They can't even spell it. But, they would stare at Mama and wanted her to know it. They ran their eyes up and down that delectable little package like she was fudge ripple ice cream. She was witty and had what people snidely call a biting, sarcastic humor. Back you right up she would. I know she would hate to hear me say this, but damned if I didn't love it. My kinda female. Smart, sassy. Men loved her. Ate her right up. I worshiped her. She could do no wrong. The worse she acted, the harder I laughed. Well, I knew she did wrong, but I didn't give a damn. She had more balls than any man in the room and they knew it. When she got dressed up on Saturday night, there was no doubt in my mind why the men wanted her. She was a hot, sassy cat and she could give lessons on flirting. She didn't wear tight clothes or too much makeup or anything like that She'd just cut those eyes at the men from across those beautiful shoulders and they would be willing to get in the boat, pilot Daddy out to the

Big Rock and throw him over board. She licked it up like it was milk. Hot flame kinda woman. She could also throw her hip out of joint on purpose. Gross.

    Mama and Daddy could rock and roll like something off Dancing with the Stars. Believe me, these two knew the moves. When we went to the Idle Hour, she would get on the floor to put on a show. She didn't know how not to. And how she loved to dance. She didn't give me breasts, but she taught me to love to dance. She would dance every song, never tiring. I have been like her ever since. Daddy would be right there with her. Mangy tomcat that he was, he wouldn't even be interested in anybody else when Mama hit the dance floor. Remember Lady and the Tramp? That was them. But, to give him credit nobody but Daddy could touch her when it came to dancing. They were magic together on those Saturday nights at the Idle Hour. Her in her gorgeous dress, Daddy in his best suit. The Idle Hour had something for everybody. It had a bowling alley, arcade and a spinning ball over the dance floor. Unbelievably noisy, but when Mama was on that dance floor, or I was for that matter, you never knew anything else was going on. The music was early fifties and sixties black soul music. The Blue Notes, the Ink Spots, Laverne Baker with her "Bop ting a ling, you handsome thing, I'd like to get next to you. Do wa ditty, you look so pretty, you thrill me through and through." It was wonderful. We had the dance called the jitterbug. I was good at it. We did the Charleston, too; only wide open just for fun. We only did the Charleston when you couldn't do anything else to the song because we were die hard jitterbuggers.

    I was about six years old when I started going out with them on Saturday nights and it went on for years. Mama wanted me with her and she knew I wanted to be there. When we got there, she would plant me on a bar stool. Now, you shut up, old fogies. It was more fun than sitting home with a sibling who'd beat me up. Alfred Cooper would keep me entertained while she put Daddy through his paces and worked all the guys into a frenzy. We'd spend all evening under that spun silver spinning ball. It would light up the dance floor like fireworks were going off. It was like we were in New York. Mama and Daddy would dance and the ball would light them up like they were in a fairy tale. They could dance to anything. They even had rhythm when they slow danced. Grinding kind of moving. Nasty stuff. Shouldn't been seen by innocent eyes. They could do anything they made up their minds to. The jitterbug, the Charleston, the Tango..anything. If it was a dance that took moving, they owned it. Forget about going home in time to get the little one to sleep. We never left until two or three in the morning. Why would you hurry home from that? If we had, next thing you know we'd be in the kitchen slugging it out. Dancing together was the only thing they did that didn't involve fast slaps to the side of the face.

    She'd dress me up, too. Only time I acted like a girl instead of a tomboy. Every third song or so, Ray Willis, Max Graff or Uncle Charlie would come get me and I would boogie right along with them. Dance just like Mama did, full out. They called me the fastest feet in the east. "Little Darling", "White Cliffs of Dover", "Let the Little Girl Dance", "Handy Man". "Dance with me, Henry, all night Baby. Dance with me, Henry, I don't mean maybe," and of course, "Anna". I had rhythm. Got it from her. Couldn't sing at all, but my feet were right there with the music of the times. California music could drop into the ocean for all we cared. This was Southern soul. Often, Mama would stop and watch me dance. I was primed for all that love and laughter in her eyes. I wish time had stopped right then. People always remembered me when I danced. Could have been because I was about a foot and a half shorter than the average dwarf.

    Their favorite dance was also my favorite. Fast dancing. She would cut loose. Feet flying, head back, laughing. Every man in the place would start moving when Mama got going. Making love to the dance floor. Daddy was so proud that he got to go home with her. He'd always get that male, peacock strut thing going. Daddy ended up planting many a black eye on Marines who didn't understand that a woman could act like that and not be on stage taking dollar bills down her bodice. Jitterbugging kept them going. It kept them in love and married. Until all us young'uns came along, got old enough to get in trouble, and got in their way. Mama put us first. Even dancing can't withstand that kind of pressure. It was the only time I ever knew them when they were really in sync; completely together and happy. She liked flirting and he liked her doing it, because she was going home with him. If he behaved.

    With the dancing, we might have lived through it all But, it was not to be. Mama just had too many kids. It went downhill like a plane flying off a mountain with no landing strip. As a family, we landed hard and crashed. Given that, it took awhile for the unraveling to work it's way to her ability to cope.

After the head banging, sleepwalking, Wilson and our getting older, Mama had more and more crap on her hands. Things started to get even worse. It could have been because, as kids, our mouths were in constant motion. She probably wished we could just deafen her and get it over with. Between us and Daddy, there was a constant air of fear, distrust and deep, deep anger in the air all the time. He was mad because she put us first. Frick and Frack were fighting all the time. The man finally started to wear a hat, he'd lost so much hair. We were carting clothes down to the water so often we were sick of it. I didn't know what a stench was anyway. I think he had a hidden stash of clothes somewhere so it didn't bother him anymore. Which, of course, bothered her. We were all flying at each other and chewing off body parts if we could like rabid dogs hungry for a piece of anybody with our last name. Except for Jimmy and me being close, everybody seemed fragmented. We wouldn't have been close if it bothered me that he was a wimp, a doofus and a warthog. I knew we were all in trouble. Daddy was running on Mama all the time because she had five kids to take care of and he wanted to party. We were her babies and we came first and she said so. He hated her for loving us. Maybe he liked the boys, but he hated the females. Said so. Feelings returned, fart face.

Then, to make things worse, Mama made me take ballet lessons. Me? I liked the tap thing and the ballroom dance, but the ballet part made me puke. I figured if I pushed one of the pointy headed little girls off her pointed little toes, I'd get out of there. It worked.

HURRICANE HAZEL

Our engines were jumped when Hurricane Hazel slapped the absolute shit out of us on October 14, 1954. The monster storm hit at the worst time a storm could come in. High tide during a full moon. It slammed into us in the fall season when the tides are unusually high to begin with. All the properties on the beach were sorta downtrodden, so they were very susceptible to being blown all the way to Morehead if somebody sneezed. We were getting a big blow. By the way, when we say a blow, we mean a storm, not a snort.

Just before Hazel arrived to wake up the dead and everybody, Mama started a beauty shop that was attached to a skating rink she feebly managed. During the day, she and a young friend of her's named Joanie, did hair and at night she took us to the rink to skate until she got off. Joanie was both sweet and pretty. She was probably the only sweet person I knew. I liked her. The shop and rink was located over the water, facing the Intracoastal Waterway that flowed between Morehead and the beach. Jimmy and I had a little routine we did do for the crowd. Remember the space boots I told you about. This shows you I wasn't doing much growing because they got a second life as my skating boots. But the crowd liked it. I couldn't do my routine without my "space" boots. In the middle of the floor was a glass partition where you could lean over rails to look into the water. Mama had spotlights on it. It was real classy if you liked crabs and oysters. Lord help us.

    I was seven years old. We got the word that Hurricane Hazel was headed right at us. Next to nothing on the beach or anything near water had been built to withstand the kind of force we heard Hazel had in her bag. If Hazel wanted to, she could reach out and whap! It was history. But, I had a positive attitude. Like everything at the beach, it would be an adventure. Between the whirlwinds created by Daddy running out on Mama and Hurricane Hazel, it was quite a year.

    You gotta understand, my idea of a good time was a hurricane. Lose your mind stuff. All that carrying on and the sheer God-awful power of it all. Here you had nature either just biding its time like its got for-damn-ever or it went completely out of control and decided to have a damn fine time tossing people, cars and people's houses around. A hurricane was not like a tornado and you sure as hell didn't want to be caught standing around in a tornado. It just seemed a hurricane could decide to last forever. I won't downplay the destruction of a tornado. Forgive me, you guys who have had to withstand that. No offense meant. I had never been in one. But, try this you people belly-aching about wind. I could show you some wind. When you had the wind, the rain and the Atlantic Ocean all raising hell at the same time, it got your attention. And, at seven, it seemed to take a lifetime to finally get here. We could practically grow up, get old and die while a hurricane sat off the coast, waiting to beat the crap out of us.

I had lived long enough to see several hurricanes, but I hadn't seen anything like this one, folks. I never knew anything like this existed. I couldn't wait for it to get here and do its dance. I mean, you could tell before this baby got here that it was going to be a hell-raiser. One hundred and forty five mile an hour winds coming across water. Damn almighty. You are crazy if you don't try it. With Hazel, you could see her coming from way-y-y out there. Mean, ugly clouds on the far horizon. Oh shit stuff, you know. There were a lot of people up and down the east coast of the U.S. who remembered Hazel. Bitch from hell, she was.

Daddy, Jimmy and I used to maim ourselves to get on the beach when we knew a hurricane was coming. Everybody else was getting off. Hurricane watching was really great because you knew a damn week in advance that ass kicker was on it's way and the anticipation of when it would hit, coupled with, will it knock the absolute shit out of you, and how much damage would it do to what, threw me into sensory overload. You wanted it to just get here. Get this damage ball rolling. Then, you'd tell yourself someone could get hurt and you really didn't want that. A massive confusion of the highest and best kind.

Everybody would be headed off the island, and we'd be headed not to the beach, but right to the water. Nuts. The island was surrounded by water that was rising and you didn't know how high it was going to get or how fast it was going to get there. Nor how fast it was going to be moving. You wanted to be right in the middle of it and know absolutely nothing about it. Dumb to the core. Only way to fly. Come get me, you bag of wind.

We'd hustle for the boardwalk. The dumb ass powers that be built a cement wall there to keep the ocean back. Right. Wonder how much they spent on that brain burst? I was a kid and knew that was stupid. Still do, and they're still putting them up. Some used sandbags and spent decades arguing about it's effectiveness. Darling, if that hurricane wanted sandbags for dinner, it was going to eat them. And the houses they were trying to save. Sandbags vs. Atlantic Ocean. Pick me up when I'm done laughing. Major bad decision. Jetties, too. All jetties did was re-direct the water from where God told it to go. Some might see that this could cause problems down the line. Some might think, "Oh, what would twenty feet of jetty into the entire Atlantic Ocean solve?" How much money do we have to waste. Some people got it. Some, but not the aforementioned powers that be.

The boardwalk wall in 1954 was about three hundred yards back from the high tide line; about seven feet high, about eight inches thick, or maybe more. I'm guessing. The good people who ran Carteret County had provided stairs in between the wall here and there so you could walk down to the beach. Guess they didn't mind giving the ocean a tunnel so it could wander on through the openings and smack you sideways. Why have the damn boardwalk if you were going to provide the Atlantic Ocean a way to meander on in like it was coming down a church aisle looking forward to getting married? Christ Amighty! Anyhow, we'd sit on top of the wall and watch the hurricane approach over the horizon. It was magnificent. Things would start to build. The air got thicker. Salt would be flying in your face. The sky would go from blue to gray and the clouds would be dark and thick. Smell it coming? The waves would get bigger and bigger, the wind would get stronger and stronger until you couldn't hardly stand yourself. You wanted to pee yourself just for fun. Finally, in addition to the unbelievable howling of the wind, those waves would be ten to fifteen feet high and almost break right at your feet. You knew they would be coming right over that wall soon and it was time to run like Jesus Christ was chasing you.

We'd sprint for the parking lot giggling and jumping, trying to guess if we would get killed before we got back to Morehead. Somehow, that seemed to be more fun that getting back to Morehead. Once we got into the car, it was just a matter of time. We'd squirm all over the car, begging Daddy to let us out. Let us out!! She's here. Daddy! She's here! Our eyes would bug out, watching it build in strength. The wind, the waves. Good Lord Almighty, this was a boggle. I'd pay good money to have a hurricane every week. But ,I was a kid, you know. Forgive me for stupid thoughts. We had bad winds ablowing, guys. Not even hurricane strength yet. Usually, by now, it would be raining like a son of a bitch. A calling card to let you know it was coming. Yes!

When the tides finally hit the parking lot, we took off again. This time we drove like a bat out of hell for the bridge connecting the beach to Morehead. The island was only about a half mile wide so whatever was going on the ocean side was going on the sound side, with the exception of the height of the waves. But the water and waves had risen around us. It was still an island and we were stupid to still be on it, but we wanted to be where the action was. We would milk it for everything it was worth for as long as we could get away with it. We'd get to the bridge and park, waiting for the time to take off across it. It seemed Daddy would time it to the last minute. This sucker was not a high rise, guys. We had boats run into it all the time because it was so low. It still had the drawbridge on it. But stupid us, we'd watch the storm continue to build until the water started to get really high under the bridge. When the water was only about two feet from swamping the bridge, just before they lifted the drawbridge and trapped us on the island, we'd scoot for the mainland. The only way to experience a hurricane was to hang around in it as long as it let you. Mass havoc. Great stuff.

    Bouncing around in the car toward what we finally hoped was safety, we ended up at a friend's house right across the street from the rink and beauty shop. We wanted to see what the hurricane looked like over the water on the sound side. Being outside during Hazel was a monumentally stupid idea. There was a cacophony of noise all around. If you hadn't peed yourself yet, you were a better man than me. I tell you something, there was a mess of sight and sound. More so than any hurricane I had experienced in my tiny life. We flew to the top floor so we could see everything possible. Well, we saw everything all right. The winds were unbelievable with the howling. The trees were bending over like they were being polite and bowing to you. Branches and limbs took flight from the trees and headed right for you. You'd forget there was a house between you and you'd duck. It gave you the shivers because it kept going on and you kept ducking and giggling because you were so damn scared. It was not like TV where you could cut it off when it got to be too much. This was on the hurricane's terms. It would let you know when you could quit ducking. Suddenly, the wind must have hit the roof of the beauty shop and rink just right because it picked the roof off the rink and slung it at us. I mean, right at us. Whap! And it didn't come at us slow. I ducked for the thousandth time. Pure reaction. It landed, most of it anyway, right on top of the house we were in. Sounded like the roof was caving in on us. We ran downstairs, arms swinging, hollering and screaming and adrenalined to damn death. We were scared to absolute pieces and excited enough to die right there. Wonderful stuff. Believe me, at a time like that, you don't fake anything. Jimmy peed in his pants and I was laughing and crying so hard I was afraid I would fart right in front of Mama. Don't think I was not having an awesome time. After we realized that the roof of the house we were in was not going to cave in, we ran back upstairs and gathered around the windows again. When we did, we got a sight we would have never expected. Apparently, God told Hazel to have at it. Hazel had a hissy fit. Right in front of me.

    What a sight. Mama's skates, about a hundred of them, were flying all over the place like hummingbirds on crack. In a hurricane, the wind would be blowing every way it can think of. There was breaking glass, tree branches and skates going in all directions. Not to mention, the water had come right over the road and was in the yard. Woo-Ha. Gimme more, gimme more. We heard later that skates came right into living rooms and bedrooms and whatever of houses. We just got the roof. They didn't kill anybody that I know of, but the skates must have sure as hell surprised a lot of people. As a kid and a certified tomboy, I wasn't real concerned about the beauty shop, but I was pissed as I watched the rink go under water. When the wall connecting the beauty shop collapsed, it was a goner, too. This was going to be a mess to clean up and I had a feeling I knew who would be on the clean up crew. Short and tiny me.

    The brains of the family, Teeny, went downstairs. Mr Potato Head opened the front door to go out and inspect the damage before Hazel decided she was through screwing with us. She whipped a shingle at him doing a hundred and forty miles an hour. Went right over his head and stuck in the wall. Just like his knife had. If it had come in lower, it would have decapitated a very swelled head. Would have been terrible. Probably.

    I lost my space boots that day. It was kind of like losing your virginity. To me, anyway. You knew you'd never get it back. Mama lost the rink and the shop and was ready to drop kick Daddy. She had "HAD IT!" Whoa. She threw Daddy out like he could have done something to stop all the destruction. All the fighting had a tiredness to it. I don't know if it was all the stress or if Hazel wore us out. The time had come. 'Bout damn time, guys.

THE UNRAVELING

    While we were unraveling, I thought about times we had at the Eagles Nest. Good ones, in spite of it all. Mama made us take the picture on the pony like we were a normal family. Down South, all the grown ups made the kids do it. The only reason they got away with it was the pony. I wonder what the grown ups would have said if I told them to get their butt on a tired, worn out pony. Our pictures were taken with Crystal and me on one shot, MaryBeth with an amazingly grumpy face on another. Jimmy and Teeny on the last shot. Girls and boys, gotta keep them separate, you know. So nobody forgets who really counted. I got pissed off and set fire to Jimmy and Teeny's shot. Hell with them. I was asking for trouble, as usual, because this was way back when I was even short-er. Anyhow, we were all tan, healthy and had snow white hair on the pony pictures. Good looking bunch, if I do say so myself.

It was about this time, when I tried to remember stuff, I got the heebie-jeebies. I did remember a lot, but I let a lot run together, too. I rambled. The chrono order was out of order. This was what happened... unorderly. I didn't think you'd mind the jumble, you'd still get the point. I think the fumbling and the tumbling started about 1957. We got a stench we didn't expect.

Remember I mentioned Joanie? Mama's friend at the beauty shop? It just so happened she was Daddy's friend, too. In a stench sense. I didn't understand a whole lot back then. I was a kid. I didn't understand the flow of evil events that circled around you when you cut a guy off. This was a man who ran on you even if you didn't cut him off, so I really didn't see how that helped things. I believed in taking a stand, but there's no point to it if someone knocked you off it every damn time. It seemed to me like Daddy would have gone out and gathered up more stenches, just for spite. I have wondered if Mama really thought that through. Maybe she was just tired of it all and rushed it towards disaster. Then again, she might have thought she was the only one he really wanted, the rest didn't count. If she thought that, she was wrong. Way wrong.

I might have been around a tomboyish eight or a world weary nine years old. The kitchen was starting to get on my last nerve and I had the bannister rail down pat so the only thing left was to let the fire ants chew their way through until they met in the middle. One day, Mama came out real quietly to get me from the yard. We got in the car and rode around for awhile. She was in a odd mood. I couldn't tell what she was thinking. Not melancholy or anything, more like she had something weighing her down. We loved to ride, so we drove around for awhile then she headed to Beaufort. For a little kid, I was somewhat savvy.

Nobody meandered to Beaufort from Morehead. That was like going to hell when you didn't have to. Morehead people hated Beaufort people and vice versa. Each town thought they were better than the other. Personally, I liked Beaufort. It was pretty and I liked the waterfront. But, you would have thought they were a million miles from each other. Actually you just crossed two bridges ...one at the port, and one just after Radio Island, where Carteret Towing Company was located. That was where Daddy worked. It was like Morehead and Beaufort hated each other so much that one bridge separating them just wasn't enough. When we crossed the second bridge, I knew Mama was on a mission and had somewhere particular to go. She wasn't talking. She went to the first stoplight in Beaufort and took a left. This female knew where she was going. I didn't know what it was but I knew I was stuck in the middle of it. Not good. Bad Karma. Yikes.

    She went to the stop sign and took a right. Into a motel parking lot. God awful sleazy place. Smelled, too. This was a place where rats hung out. The parking lot was torn up from years of neglect. The motel had end units that had almost fallen down. The place could have used a good paint job, too. In other words, it was run down and ugly. Looked like the roof would cave in if the wind was blowing. Hell, it looked like it would cave in if you just put a big fan on it. It was the kind of place you would think of as a whorehouse, but I wasn't sure even a whore would go there. I knew what a whorehouse looked like, and come to think of it, I even knew what a few whores looked like. We had a lot of them around and they weren't all on the beach, although they seemed to breed well in the heat there. Mama and I sat in the car for a few minutes. She told me there were things in life that get out of control. Mama said there are things that have to be and there are things that didn't have to be. She said you always had a choice. One of the things that you didn't have to have was guaranteed misery. One misery could be better than another, so choose. I knew things were getting ready to happen and she wanted me to know it was coming. She pointed at something behind me. I turned around in my seat, and I saw Daddy's Cadillac and Joanie's car parked outside one of the rooms. It looked like they were together, if you know what I mean. I sensed there was no way this was going to be party time, but I was glad she brought me. Mama and me, that's the way it was. No matter what shit may fly. Crap was definitely coming.

Once we were out of the car, she took my hand. We walked up to the room in front of their cars. Mama scooted right in the door. She didn't knock or anything and generally she was a very polite person. Had a mean streak, but was polite as a rule. Made us kids act right, too. Well, the door wasn't locked, but they were. Together that is. There on the bed was Daddy and Joanie...nekkid as they say. As a jaybird, like that's the only naked bird. I froze right up. I couldn't believe my Mama actually wanted me to look at two naked people. These two, anyway. The last thing I would ever want to look at, I tell you now, was Daddy naked. Big Yuk. Joanie didn't look too bad since she was only twenty four. I decided I'd better not say that out loud with Mama in the room. I thought I should just ride with this one and keep my mouth shut. Play it like I was back in the womb. I often did that. I figured this would end up as the carrying on of a lifetime. I thought Hurricane Anna was going to let loose, but she didn't. Everybody just looked at everybody. Except for Joanie starting to whimper, it was quiet as a church.

As the silence seemed to crawl along, I wasn't about to say a word. Joanie got quietly hysterical when she saw me, but it bothered her more than it did me. I finally figured out what was going on here. Apparently, Joanie had not cut him off. Mama and Daddy were quiet..scary kind of quiet. They just looked at each other. Neither one had anything left in them to say. I knew this was what people meant when they said someone was caught running, cause it seemed to me that Daddy shouldn't be in bed naked with somebody that was your Mama's friend. Him with five kids and all. See how smart I was? That was what they meant. That was running. I found out that day what it was and I have never forgotten it. Mama didn't call Jackie a stench, she called her a whore. Said it soft. She looked at her for a long time to let that message settle in good. I didn't know if that was better or worse than a stench. That's when I found out they weren't really stenches. They were whores and Joanie was one. For a minute, I was pissed that nobody had bothered to explain to me before that Joanie was one. Maybe it was my age. Who knew? However, I didn't think it was too hard to understand how hurtful that had to be for Mama. No matter what anybody had said or what anybody had done, running was just not right. Fart face.

That ended that. As they say. Mama knew the world was going to frown on her. She was fried crispy. She was the little woman and she was supposed to take it. Well, she had taken it and taken it and taken it. No more. Not for her. I don't know, maybe he'd never done it to someone she knew before. Maybe he'd never done it to someone she liked before. Maybe he'd never done it and been caught with his hand "in the cookie jar." Lots of never before's could be used here. Maybe she'd never caught him actually in bed with someone before. But, she had now. All the little "maybe's" were neatly put away. She took me with her because she needed someone with her or she would have probably killed them both. I gave her strength. She gave me an understanding of her pain and why what was going to happen, had to happen. No matter what.

She tossed his clothes, along with his ass, out. Bye, bye, Daddio. Sad to see you go. Not. Oops, then we were tossed out of the Eagles Nest. I still passed by it. What a waste. That house deserved a whacko family like our's to keep it breathing. Probably some normal family lived there. I wondered if that floor still had parts of my head attached to it. The people who lived there probably thought my brain matter was part of the design. Sometimes it would be kind of dilapidated, the next time it would be freshly painted and proud looking. I wondered who lived there each time I passed and wondered if they still had the ghost, and gave it a name like I did. Hell, Wilson had been a part of the family. I wasn't about to stop and tell the people living there about him, though. Their Daddy might have a gun. Wonder how many times that damn ghost had been shot? I figured our ghost probably gave the house up and went where ever he was meant to go because he thought people were too stupid to hang around with anymore. Maybe he got tired of going to the bathroom. Wouldn't surprise me a bit. If he could have come back to life, after experiencing us, there was a good chance, he wouldn't have wanted to. All those memories. Some people would say it wasn't the happiest of times, but to me it was well worth remembering. We had lived through it, anyway. I miss you, Wilson. If you weren't dead, I would hope you were doing well.

GOING TO HELL IN A HURRY

Mama still had her feisty, kiss my ass self, but now she got to sprinkle more Mama dust around us if we deserved it. I saw it now and again after we got rid of Daddy, but it wasn't daily anymore. Well, we didn't get rid of him. That would have been too special. Did I mention we gave him to Jackie?

Once Mama found that out, we went to hell immediately. We learned a whole new vocabulary for the word "immediately." Going down hill at super sonic speed. Except for me, the whole family, Granny, Granddaddy, Aunt Elly, Uncle John, Aunt MaryJo.. Even Aunt Brenda who had it even worse than Mama with Uncle John's carrying on, all got mad at her. She was supposed to take it. Had they met this female? Clearly, they didn't know her at all. You'd think they'd never even listened to her caterwaul if they believed that. She caught him, guys. Naked. With Jackie. Weren't these people taught that this crap was not acceptable behavior? Mama used that term a lot and it sure fit. How could they not see that? It was also our first look into the hell hole we were getting ready to crawl into. Nothing like a preview to set you up. I didn't figure it could get any worse. Shows you what a kid I was. The adults didn't help, though. They provided the shovel for us to dig our hole deeper.

Let me lay out the adult response to Mama drop kicking Daddy's ass out of her life. Granny: Mama wasn't welcome at her house anymore. She wasn't even recognized. Like she disappeared. You could have thrown me down a well and I wouldn't have cared if I ever saw Granny again. She looked like Daddy and Uncle John. Mean, nasty ass face. She could have cared less if she ever saw us again. Granny used to have to get someone to haul Granddaddy's fat butt from at his girlfriend's house. The girlfriend would Granny and tell her Granddaddy was drunk so come get him. Granny would call Daddy and Mama, when they were together, ask them to pick Grandaddy up from his girlfriend's. They would go to her house, carry his two ton, drunk ass out of there, take him home and put him to bed, for Christ's sake. Then Granny would make him soup, shut the bedroom door and service the fat sum'bitch. We'd all be sitting in the living room pretending to watch TV, but we knew what was going on. Its too bad Mama didn't smack her when she had the chance. I'd have liked to. How much energy can you expend disliking a female like that? A lot. However, all I had to do was suck it up for Sundays, the day I had to go to Granny's. She had a washer dryer room out with the garage. I went there. Did I give a damn for her or her opinion? Nadda. Gimme a nasty noise.

Back to the subject. Mama had thrown out their son. The God child. Publicly. Not their first born son, but their son, nonetheless. Consequently, he must be god-like and Mama was too foolish to know it. Oh yeah, he was special. Manure in clothes. Granny despised Mama because she had guts and did something the old hag never could. Which was kick a man's dick in the dirt.

Granddaddy: He thought Mama had lost her mind to throw out his son. Let me tell you what a great mind this old fart had. Granddaddy called me "bottle ass". Guffawed when he hollered it. In public. When we left church, we all headed for the Rexall Drug Store. It had a grill, booths, tables and a counter. They made great hot dogs and hamburgers. It would fill up with screaming kids as fast as we could run there after Sunday school. The old cronies moved a little slower. Granddaddy and his crew always took up a booth in the rear. Of course, they didn't go to church. They just made you go. You wondered what they were drinking because they acted so weird. Once the kids started crowding into the grill area of the drug store, Granddaddy would start bellowing from that fat stomach of his, "Where's bottle-ass? Where's my bottle-ass?" Like I was going respond to that request and show everybody he meant me. He did this loudly so every damn body could hear. He would keep bellowing until I went over and got on his damn lap, just to shut him up. If I got off, he would start hollering "bottle ass" again. Jerk. For an understanding of the previous comment, re-read the damn paragraph.

Uncle John and Aunt Brenda: They became our surrogate mother and father. Good thing, too. We didn't have damn anything to eat unless you liked a roach sandwich. They had six kids of their own that were around the same age we were so we became real close to their kids. There were eleven of us running the streets with people knowing our whole family history. They had the same problem we had with the running. Difference was Uncle John brought his women to his Sunday lunch table. To me, sometimes it seemed he was worse than Daddy. He would sit at the table and unzip his pants. I think Aunt Brenda was quietly impressed with Mama, but she didn't have the whatever it took gene. Said she wouldn't do that to her kids. Didn't mind what she was doing to her kids while they had to sit there and watch their Daddy with his girlfriends. He'd be all over town with them, too. There was one named Terry that went to school with us.

Gross. I liked Aunt Brenda but I sure as hell didn't get it. How can you not like someone who made peanut butter sandwiches, cut them into wedges, and then put some more peanut butter on the top slice so when you ate it, it stuck to the top of your mouth for days? Just the way you liked it? But the rest, go figure.

Aunt Elly; The raging, fat mountain of vicious venom. Hated Daddy, hated Mama, hated us, hated her own kids, hated life. Hated everything about everything. Got the picture? And she hated everybody in a very LOUD way. Ten tons of pure, spilling, all over you, acid. Capable of spreading meanness fifty miles in any direction. Daddy was not welcome in her restaurant after that. Like he cared. Prior to Mama leaving him, she only reserved that insult for black people. Not the ones she worked to death for pennies. Daddy got off light. It was those of us that had to put up with her hate, as big as the Rockies, that had survive her tirades. She interfered with the next twelve solid, uninterrupted years of my life. Put my ass to work at ten years old. She made Mama's life worse than any hell Mama had imagined with Daddy. Mama thought it would be all over when she threw Daddy in the trash can, but Aunt Elly took his place. Big time. She helped drive her to drink. Hell, probably gave her the keys to get there.

Aunt MaryJo: Excuse me, kiss my whatever. Who cared what she thought? Didn't care then, don't care now. She was an ass. An ugly ass. Looked like Granny. She also looked like the Wicked Witch of the West, so that tells you what Granny looked like. If I already said it, so what? You can consider this emphasis. I didn't think Granddaddy was even around when Granny was spawning these mean, devil kids. She must have reached right down and slept with the devil to reach her level of success.

What amazed me was these people actually thought I would love them after the way they threw Mama in the trash can. They gave me their reasons over and over. People, this was my Mama. What don't you understand? They thought they were allowed their opinion. No, they weren't.

Sometime after we were ungraciously thrown out by everybody, we entered the era of the being deprived. Food deprived. Clothes deprived. Toothpaste deprived. You get it. Below poverty stricken. Raging poverty stricken. Let me repeat that...RAGING POOR...that translates into hot dogs with mustard and onions without the hot dog, on bread not rolls. We dined on chicken sandwiches with lettuce and mayonnaise with no chicken. Oh, and no table. Beds without covers and furnaces without heat. Baths with no hot water. Feet without shoes. Got the picture? Good times. Not.

I'LL GIVE YA' A BUCK FOR A HOME

We bounced around for awhile, living from place to place. Nothing you could call a home. I mourned for the Eagles Nest, but it was not to be. Another family was living there, for sure. I wanted Wilson back. I wanted him to kill Daddy so we could collect the insurance. That's not really true because I am sure he didn't have any, but I read it somewhere and it sounded like it was a fit. Everything bad happened that could. I'm sure if there was a God, He had moved on. Anyhow, we finally touched down at a house on Bridges Street in Morehead. We tried to make a home of it, but it was hard. It only had two bedrooms, and there were six of us. Jimmy and Teeny slept in one room and all four females slept in the other. Everybody but me was getting into the terrible teens, wanting their own space. Not going to happen. Little house, little living room, little kitchen, little life. Daddy owned it.

Legal agreements can be interesting. I always wanted to be a lawyer after what happened. Mama had five kids, ranging from nine to fifteen years old. Daddy had to give her two hundred dollars a month for the kids. She wouldn't take alimony. Five dollars per child per week for food, clothes and school. Per month. That left nothing to spend on liquor, to which she had become unbecomingly attracted, and the finer things in life, like propane for the heat or electricity. We had to walk fourteen blocks to school. No big deal. Didn't snow much, just cold. Would have helped if we had clothes to keep us warm. However, on the bright side, I told myself it kept us from getting fat and there were some great places to find trouble uptown. Once you were uptown, you might the hell as well stay there because you didn't want to be walking back and forth. So, we stayed uptown most days after school at Aunt Brenda's. She lived on the soundside of the shoreline. If you can't be on the ocean, its the next best thing, with drawbacks. We would head out into the water to see how badly we could cut our feet, just for something to do. Maybe get an infection. Anything to relieve the boredom. She was always willing to feed us and care for the feet. She had a wonderful heart. Stamina, too. Just no gene balls. To her credit, there were eleven of us crawling all over her house. We would wander around the neighborhood like lost souls. Anything to keep from having to walk all the way home.

Anyhow, Mama got two hundred dollars a month from the Evil Presence. But the same guy, Daddy, charged two hundred dollars a month rent. You remember I said Daddy owned the house. It wasn't good enough for him to call it a wash. Once a month one of us, not me by God, would have to take Mama over to Carteret Towing to get her check so she could mail it back to him. If she wouldn't go, one of the kids would. I was old enough to know how to throw something big at him if he tried to make me beg. I promised her he would not want to be within striking distance of my teeth. I'd bite him until I ripped an arm or leg off had she tried to make me do it. Maybe his face or wait..what about his dick? Yuck of all yucks. I would have stood on the tracks in downtown Morehead with a sign saying "Teen is a whore monger with five starving children" until someone arrested me. I wasn't going to beg. He made Mama and the other four wait, beg, justify, and listen to him whine about what a bitch Mama was. How she ruined things. Whatever. I have always found it very difficult to ask someone for anything since. Things stick with you. Tight.

Our very best friends were the roaches. Good Lord Almighty, the roaches. Of all the things that I had encountered, the roaches stood out in my mind as something I truly did not want to experience again. We would open a cabinet and it would be like the whole house would be over-run in seconds. Flags flying, guns waving. If the Confederate Army had the number of soldiers that we had roaches, we would have won the damn war, hands down. If you cut a light on, you would need to stand there for at least thirty seconds with your eyes closed to give them time to free up the kitchen counter. You know, you eat off the kitchen counter. Bread, cereal, everything. They'd already taken them over. We knew we had hit rock bottom. Mama hadn't yet, but we had. Uncle Russ, Aunt Elly's husband, told me a story about roaches that I never forgot. One was living in his ear. I asked did he name it? Did it have kids? Baby roaches in your ear. That's ugly. Don't tell a kid this kind of stuff. It can make them catatonic.

Still seeking small blessings, I got a baby chick one Easter. I have indicated I thought I was smart, but I didn't say about everything. The rest of the kids, still thinking I was the baby favorite, got me the chick. I got it out one day so we could play on the kitchen floor. I needed to get something out of the cabinets. Being short, I had to crawl up onto the counter to get what I wanted. I crawled. I fell. I squashed. My poor baby chick. Everything from inside squished out of more holes than I knew she had. Not ever having dealt with death before, I didn't recognize it, but I knew she was in trouble. I was still pretty young here, so give me a break. I knew ducks could swim so I filled the tub, and after only a moment's struggle, which was difficult for the both of us, she sank. MaryBeth came in and took her away. I think it either drowned or it died of squishiness. Nobody would get me another one. I never got over it.

There was also the incident with the soda bottle. I mentioned we were poor. Real poor. I never say it just once. No hot water kind of poor. About once a week, Mama would fill the tub with hot water and we would do a rotation system to control who got to get in there first to enjoy the hot water. After the first one, four were bathing in dirty water because we were dirty kids. None of our roads were paved except the main roads. Football and basketball were not played on the main roads, just the gravel ones. Or the dirt ones. Whatever was handy. One particularly dirty night, I had made it to the top of the rotation. Hot water. Yes!! My favorite thing was to fill a glass soda bottle with hot water. I would pour it over my head. I couldn't be bothered with having to bend halfway over to stick my head in the tub to wash my hair. This time, I filled the soda bottle, lifted it above my head in ecstacy and promptly dropped it. Being heavy, it broke. I scooted out of the tub without maiming myself. Being absolutely sure I would get in trouble with the rest of the kids because the water was still on the hot side, I failed to mention the glass on the bottom of the tub to Crystal who got in the water behind me. She cut her feet, her legs and her butt big time. If she hadn't cut her backside so badly, I think Mama would have beat her for the very first time. Blood was everywhere. Mama thought she had killed herself. I didn't tell Crystal what I had done until I was forty five years old. She wasn't even mad. That's what you love about Crystal. Easy going female.

Mama still made us to go to Granny's on Sunday after church in spite of her Granny's bitchiness. I knew it was to see that we got fed, but damn. I wasn't that hungry. I knew Granny could care less if we all died but she had to put on a show for the community. Mama was Methodist, Daddy was Baptist. We'd go to one, then go to the other the following Sunday. I understood religion but I forgot who believed what when. I didn't quite get whether there were angels or an afterlife. Or, who taught it. I knew you shouldn't be a deacon if you ran on your wife. Finally, I quit worrying about being Baptist or Methodist or learning any other religion because there were some real jerks sitting on those pews. I decided to be religion poor. I panicked when someone said they were Catholic.

Daddy tried to force me to join the church so Mama couldn't make me join her's. I didn't want to join either. The Baptist Church had this wonderful preacher named Corbin Cooper. I have to admit, he was a great guy. He was someone you could talk to, human to human. Daddy, being a deacon, told Preacher Cooper that I was going to join the church one Sunday night. Not my choice, you know. I wasn't standing up at the end of the sermon. This was his idea. Then he waited until nighttime so he could stack the audience with his rotten relatives. Sorry, but if they aren't there for the right reasons, they might the hell as well be an audience. Mr Cooper didn't want to do it because he knew I was against it and because Daddy was making me. Mr Cooper was going to have to lower me into the water and baptize me because Daddy said so. I didn't want it to happen. That pout came out big time.

Mr Cooper tried to talk to me that evening, but I was being, oh! who would have thought? Obstinate. He explained that he was going to lower me, but he would have a good hold on me so not to worry. I told him we couldn't do it because I wore glasses. He said he would take my glasses. I told him no because I couldn't see without glasses. See where this is going? I am all dressed up in a white robe with, as far as I am concerned, no place to go. But, I like Preacher Cooper so, fine, I went out there, fuming. He was looking me straight in the eye, anticipating trouble. I tried. I promise I tried. But, then I looked out and saw Daddy. The minute I did, I looked at Preacher Cooper and I saw that "Oh shit" look coming over his face. I picked my feet straight up and dropped down like a house had fallen. Water splashed up ten feet. Preacher Cooper went down with me because he had hold of me. Yes, I felt bad about that. But, not bad enough. Once I got under water, I splashed around like I was about to die, just for giggles. Look, I knew the really religious would be upset, but I could still say I was just a kid. Preacher Cooper finally found his feet, stood up, grabbed me by the neck of the robe and hauled me out of the water like I was a eighty pound tuna. Dripping from head to toe, I looked up at the beautiful rendering of Jesus with water dripping from his head to toe. I felt really guilty until I sneaked a look at Preacher Cooper and saw that twinkle in his eye. You could tell he knew something shouldn't happen unless it was supposed to. And this wasn't supposed to. We walked off towards the back trying not to laugh out loud, but it was hard. Once we got in the back, we fell apart. He was great. Mr Cooper had a lot of kid in him. I could tell he didn't like Daddy either.

  Going to church was the worst thing you could make me do. Adding to the ungodliness of my deacon Daddy, was a key club on the beach that was up to no good and they ran women right through the pews like they were angels. I think they were laughing at the other people in the church. I also hated having to sit on Granddaddy's lap when he dared show up. I think he was afraid God would smite him, so he didn't go often. He would shift me around on his lap until he got this beautiful smile on his face. I used to fight him, but he was in ecstacy and I didn't know why. I wouldn't stop until I finally fought my way to the floor. Granny would watch every time and did nothing to stop him. Pervert.

  Life was a bowl of pits, no cherries. Prophetic, that. Teeny stayed just like he had always been, moody and tense. Sometimes he was a professor and sometimes a clown. Must have had a dose of manic in him. He knew he was king of the hill, though. He was allowed to shoot everybody, for Christ's sake, and got away with it. No wonder he thought he was so special. Teeny picked up that male Southern arrogance thing real young. I remember he used to lay on his bed on weekends, real lazy like. He got up real early in the morning and played taps. Every morning, every day. I got out of bed all mournful. Good Lord, that's a sad sound. Especially if it was played well and he played that cornet well, I'll give him that. Sometimes he'd holler for one of us to come rub his back or go get him ice cream five blocks away. I'd always pick the back. I wasn't going anywhere for him. One of us would have to go get him an ice cream cone from the Dairy Queen. Heaven forbid it might melt before it got to the king. Jerk. But, we had to do it. He got big fast and if we didn't do it, it would be loose teeth time. Neither Mama nor Daddy ever hit me, but Teeny cranked me often. After knowing him, Daddy and Jimmy, its a wonder I ever liked men at all.

Bridges Street had its bright times. Not many, though. I think I had some fun there. These were the worst of the days of Aunt Elly. Everybody talked bad about everything. It seemed the nastier the repartee became the better everybody liked it. I would try to get in Aunt Elly's face about coming down on Mama, but she couldn't see me for the massive breasts. Mama had become an ass too, from time to time. Sad, but true. Damn funny one, though. Most of the time, I was momicking Jimmy, but I am sure I was spreading joy throughout the house and the other kids thought of me with love. Don't you believe it. Let me lay out the way we were handling our little divorce "sitiation." Parents don't get a divorce. You all get a divorce and although I didn't like being divorced, but I would have kicked him out, too. Higher, harder. Like a football flying through the goal posts.

Perfecting my role as a tomboy, most of my friends were boys. My best friend was Dean Arnold Steed. Kids always had two first names. His older brother was called Struggle. Awesome Name. I wished somebody called me that. Dean Arnold and I became mascots for the class that Dean Arnold's sister was in. We were still only about eleven years old. I was still a bright, shiny blond, petite thing. He was husky. Already a football player type. Mama spent all her time telling me to act like a lady. I was a full fledged honor graduate tomboy. Not just an everyday one..one of the best. I didn't like the way girls acted. I didn't want to worry about my hair. My hair was fine as long as it stayed on top of my head. The only color I wanted on my knees would have to resemole dirt or it wouldn't do. Other than that, I didn't give a damn about it. I'm digressing again, but for a reason. Dean Arnold and I were going to be sitting in little chairs in little white graduation gowns. The high school graduates would be lined up behind us. We would be sitting, just the two of us, forward of the them more towards the seating in the auditorium. Mama insisted that I make Dean Arnold hold my hand. Not a tomboy kind of thing to do. She thought it would be cute. What Mama wanted, Mama got. No strings. NO questions.

We got up there and things were progressing fairly well until we both got tired. This thing went on forever. I think I aged another year before it ended. Dean Arnold wasn't wild about holding my hand, and I would rather have taken a bite out of his. I mentioned none of his friends were there, so what did he care? Just do it. It was a Mama thing. I didn't realize know they were going to snap a million pictures of us. He finally dug in and yanked his hand back. I reached over and smacked him on the shoulder, grabbed his hand, and put a death grip on it. Went into full core Mama mode. Try to stop me now. He pulled his hand back, and almost yanked me out of my chair. I got in his face, screaming at him to give me that damn hand back. I had orders from the Mama lady. He chose to tuck it under his graduation gown. Lit a fire in me, I'm telling you. Needless to say that did it. I ejected myself from my seat, reached over and cold cocked him. I knocked him right out of his chair. Did a 360 from start to finish on him. As I came around, spitting angry, I saw Mama sitting on that first row with hellfire in her eyes. I sat down, red-faced from fury and stuck my tongue out at her. Damned if I was going to hold his hand another second. I'd rather take her on. I knew she wouldn't hit me, but she could always let me feel I was not too good for her to put me in the broiler and eat me for supper. I was the smartest child she had most of the time. Let me disagree with her and it was like I had lost my brains in the kitchen sink.

This and other pointless activities became our way of life. As we got older, we found it increasingly difficult to find fun things to do other than try to kill each other. It was so boring there was a time we were reduced to counting license plates. That was a sad, disgusting good time. It was truly pitiful. I knew we were not the only people who ever did this, but for those uninitiated it went like this. You saw a North Carolina plate, that's one. An Ohio plate, that's one. Another NC plate, that's two. A New Jersey plate, that's one. Another NC plate, that's three. An Ohio plate, that's two. You get the idea. You kept that going for as many plates as there were on cars that drove by the house. I never thought I was good in math, but I could add, for Christ's sake. Four different plates with four different states and Jimmy had lost count and I was outta there, looking for something else to do.

I loved sports. Easy for a tomboy. High school football and basketball was the highlight of my early teenage years. NOBODY was better than me, but I was a girl, damn it. The weekend games were free to the students, therefore I could go. Thank heavens. Morehead was very, very good in both sports. One time we were against Beaufort who had won ninety-nine basketball games in a row. We tore them a new one, by God. It was transcendental. Football was awesome. There was something about a high school football game. I bet if you went to one today, it would feel just like it felt when you were in high school. You would suddenly be a teenager for a while. Beat Beaufort at football, too. It didn't get any better than that. At one football game, we had just scored a touchdown. While we were jumping up and down, screaming like idiots, a girl of a different race came across the field and started beating my head against the goal posts. With what little brains she left me, I thought she was mad because we won. After she had me down and out, I screamed "What in the hell is the matter with you, girl?" She told me I was making eyes at her boyfriend the whole game. I told her, with my one good eyeball, I couldn't even see her boyfriend. Good grief. I seemed to be getting beat up all the time. I only won if I was fighting Jimmy, the wimperoo. Good enough for me.

    I did have one above the charts fun activity. There was the time when my idea of a good time was throwing knives at Jimmy's feet. Can you believe this guy? I would get him against the side of the house with his legs spread. Then I'd back up fifteen feet or so and try to throw the knife between his feet but as close to one of them as I could without hitting one. This explains who was in control of this relationship. You couldn't have gotten me to do that, ever. Every now and then I would get too close to his feet. Most of the time, I was mad at him for something else and I'd just haul off and try to slice off a toe. Mama told me I was using the game as an outlet for my anger. Whatever. No matter what anybody said, he would still stand there if I told him to. One time I missed a good throw. Well, I didn't really miss it, it hit it. Oops! I made dead on contact. I will say no more. I am not quite that violent anymore. Who am I going to take on, now? Nobody as stupid as Jimmy is around.

    We also played street football. The hard kind. You ate gravel and rocks on those falls. You had gravel in your ears, hair and eyeballs. Brush burns everywhere. It was a good time to be had by all. When picking teams, I always got picked somewhere in the middle because they knew I knew my job.. take Jimmy out. I was good at it. Jimmy was always the last picked. I always got picked for basketball before him, too. Jimmy was about five feet ten inches. Still, I did it and did it fast and hard. Blood flying. Jimmy crying. I sent him home crying to Mama every time. She'd kiss and hug him and feel real sorry for him. But, he hated a wimp, too. She'd look at me like maybe I had grown a dick because he was such a wipe out. Good times, gotta admit it.

While on Bridges Street, we also played Name That Tune. I think we had seven records. I knew what the name of the song was by the third beat. God awful boring. I read Grimm's Fairy Tales for fun. When I wasn't beating up on Jimmy, most of the time I'd be reading. I read everything I could get my hands on. Thank God for libraries. Gotta do something. Says it all.

One of my favorite summer places was Camp Morehead. It was a sailing club for little rich boys, at least to us, called Camp Morehead. Boys, only. Yee-haa. Bill Purcell ran it and he was a huge, football linebacker kind of guy. He would have boys sign up every year for one or two weeks of sailboat training, parties and wandering around Carteret County, which some people found interesting. These kids aged from seven years old to about eighteen. Usually by the time a guy was a eighteen, he was a trainer. All the girls in town couldn't wait for the first batch of Camp Morehead guys to show every year. We would look for a blue bus with Camp Morehead written on it, full of good looking guys of all ages. I would point my young self right in that direction, because I was a regular. I was a knuckleballer. I could get on the knuckleball table and put grown men on their knees, barfing. The Lord is good.

A knuckleball table was a wooden table lower in the front than in the back by about six inches. It was rounded in the back because that's where the wooden balls picked up speed as they came around. The table was about six feet long. It also had a wooden median that ran from top to bottom except for about four inches at the top where the balls came around the curve. The front came to just below my diaphragm. There it simply ended, so if you missed a hard wooden ball coming towards you at sixty miles an hour, it would tear a hole right through you. Kee-pow. Then, they'd break your toes when they fell. Only fools played with bare feet. Of course, if they showed up barefoot, I sure as hell wasn't going to warn them. It was too much fun watching them jump up and down. Hard wooden mallets, like bowling pins, served as the object with which to hit the balls and eight wooden balls about five inches around were what could play with. You played with two balls or up to eight balls. The better you were at it, the more balls you played. I was a high ball hitter.

When you were "up", you served. That meant you chose how many balls you wanted to play, lined them up side by side, and hit them all before they fell backwards onto your toes. I was good so I would line up all eight balls, hit them real fast and the opponent had to stop all eight balls that came flying around that back area where they picked up speed. I mean big time speed. When they hit you in the stomach after that increase in speed, it hurt like hell. It always killed me when I missed one. Or more. If you wanted to, you could hit six balls, then for a surprise gift, cut the last two. You cut the ball when you sliced it on one edge and it popped over the median so close to the edge of your opponent's side that he had to be outstanding to stop it from hitting him and putting him out of the game. While your opponent was trying like hell to stop six coming at him at what seemed like six hundred miles an hour, the other two cleared the median and dropped on his toes. He was toast. They called it knuckleball because you ripped your knuckles to shreds doing the fancy stuff and trying to stop the balls. If one of those flying balls hit your knuckles, your hand would instantly cramp and you couldn't move it. But, if you were good, when one was coming at you real fast, you could cut it when it got to you, and it would land on the other side spinning like a top. If they hit it, with the others flying in, there was no telling in which direction it would go. Even better, with me, they didn't know which direction it would come at them from. Great fun was had by all. Except the losers.

They also had dances at the end of the summer so they could play that sad song, "See you in September." I hate that song to this day. Mostly, because the summer was over. Another reason was the boys were all going home. I hated the end of summer. Mama always made me wear a dress. The same dress. Every year. It had crinolines and I am not a crinoline kind of guy. It had large roses a gray color all around with an off-white background. I am talking about large roses. Huge. People said they were bigger than me. Gray? Who ever saw a gray rose? Nobody was going to ask a big gray rose to dance with them. It used to be white, but I wouldn't clean it anymore in hopes I could throw the damn thing away. It suddenly disappeared one day. We had no idea what happened to it. Wink, wink.

TEEN TIMES

When the summer ended, we would be stuck in the house at Bridges Street, and darling, it could get cold. The house had a furnace that sat right in the middle of the floor. Most of the time the only thing in it was spiders. We had an attic but it didn't have a ghost, so what good was it? The pull cord for the attic was so far over my head that I couldn't get up there without a ladder so it was not going to be a playroom, for sure. Everybody was getting taller, but me. Aunt Elly would pull the car right up to the front door when she wanted to tear into Mama, so gardening was out of the question. The only thing to do was use your imagination or sic the dogs on someone for fun.

The family dynamics had matured a little. Right. I think we were all settling in to what we were going to be like eventually. Shiver. We never got too old for Mama to lay us out. I don't think I failed to mention Mama had a wicked sense of humor and a biting wit. She could insult you so bad it would make you want to crawl away and die. She was one of those people whose humor was unbelievably sarcastic. She smirked. I got that from her. I was very proud of that. It was better than breasts. Teeny, it might surprise you, after my glowing speeches about him, was the most droll and boring human being who ever had feet. A statue was funnier than Teeny. Livelier, too. MaryBeth had discovered boys and the boys she chose were in for the ride of their lives for the next twenty years. I used to say she was running for the slut-of-the-month club and winning hands down. I didn't know if that was true, but it had a good ring to it. Crystal was still sweet. She didn't seem to belong to us because she didn't want to fight. Come to think of it, Jimmy didn't either. But, that's because he was scared. Jimmy was still nine months older than me. Still. I had discovered that when I wasn't being a monster, I was an observer. I also discovered that everybody thought I was smarter than I thought I was. I must have had them fooled. They all said I read a lot, but I listened more than they realized. One of my most notable discoveries was Jimmy was not outgrowing the need to be a wimp. Therefore I spent all my time beating the hell out of him one way or another. I talk about it a lot because it makes me feel warm and fuzzy just thinking about it.

I found it didn't take much imagination to decide to hate bourbon. Mama had taken a unfortunate liking to it. She liked it a lot. The smell sucks and the feel sucks when you have to sleep with it. Mama took the bottle to bed with her and it was guaranteed to tilt and spill all over me. I have met and kissed bourbon. Didn't get to drink it, just kiss it. Cause it was all over the bed and Mama's mouth. Damn female would insist on kissing me good night. Some nights it seemed Mama and I swam in it. I hate bourbon and scotch to this day. Its a wonder I didn't become an alcoholic right along with her from the fumes. Is there such a thing as a second hand alcoholic? I did sleep on the couch from time to time because Mama cried a lot. A whole damn lot. Usually only after she had gotten drunk and gone to bed. Other times she was funny as hell. My poor Mama. Old Lock and Load Anna disappeared except for every now and then she would surface like waves on the ocean. You would ride it for all it was worth until she went under again. Like most drunks, she would drive you up the wall, then when she was sober she would wonder why you didn't give her the respect she deserved. She was both sad and wonderful. Life with her was a constant rise and fall. You learned from your parents. One thing I learned was to ride things out. It could always be worse tomorrow. Oddly enough, that is positive thinking from the child of an alcoholic.

We had nothing to do but grow up. Yawn. Everybody's personalities kept forming for what everybody said would be the rest of their lives. I wondered how long this damn process took. I didn't know if people changed or if they got tired of the way they'd always been. It could be a downer. Teeny took his boring to new levels, interested only in making us rub his back and whining about how much money Daddy had. He was talking more and more about wanting to live with Daddy, because of the money. I'd holler "Go, Teeny, Go." You know, like a cheerleader. Daddy only had it because he wasn't taking care of his kids, dork. MaryBeth used to have to babysit me because Mama had to work all the time to buy liquor. Marybeth would take me with her on dates and make me lie on the floor in the back seat of the car while she made out. I'm much more attuned to certain sounds now like groans. I loathe groans. MaryBeth would be in the backseat with her guy, and sometimes a girlfriend of her's would be in the front seat with her guy. I never, ever, ever want to sound like those girls sounded. I was scarred for my whole groaning life. Crystal was sent off to Aunt Elly's to become the babysitter for thirty or so young'uns that belonged to Aunt Elly's six daughters and one son. A fate worse than death to me. Except having to live with Daddy. Everyone of those kids was a shit. Jimmy ultimately discovered he had a dick and stayed a hound dog for the rest of his life. It was the only part of his body he exercised. It still shrank from fear when I got around it, though.

In spite of everything, Mama always made Christmas special. Every year Mama would give us a bike and a pair of skates. One bike, one pair of skates. The thinking was that in five years, assuming an excellent maintenance program, we would each own a bike and a pair of skates. Not a bad investment plan. In the meantime, it was share city. I really never thought of myself as spoiled but I got damn tired of trying to fit the skates with that key every time I wanted to skate. I had tiny feet, Teeny had huge feet. So, I'd hide it. I'd smile and say,"No, haven't seen it." Mama had five accomplished liars because it was our responsibility to tell the bill collectors that she wasn't home. Nobody could tell when I lied. I thought if I was their special angel, nobody would care if I lied. Bullhocky. If they really wanted to skate, God gave them the right to beat the location out of me.

We sang Christmas carols. Major yuck. We had to go out and scare the neighbors every year. I think everybody enjoyed it but me. I couldn't sing then, can't sing now. I tried out for music and the music director told me I could play the triangle. Is that an insult or what? He said I was tone deaf. I disagree. I hear tones just fine. I just can't reproduce them with my mouth. And, I can hear how bad it is just fine, too. I'm tune deficient. I wanted to be an apple in "Mr Sandman" when I was a kid but they wouldn't let me. Gave me a triangle. Scarred for life.

I had my favorite cemetery. Did I tell you about harassing kids in the cemetery, the switch blade and my cool black leather motorcycle jacket with stars on the shoulders? Heaven in a handbasket. Epaulets, no less. I had more stars on my jacket than Jimmy did. That made me Boss. I would have been Boss anyway, but this saved what little pride the boy had. He went along with whatever I wanted to do. I wanted to terrorize kids and I had the ability to do it. One of those rare gifts I had.

One block off Bridges Street was a cemetery about three blocks long and three blocks wide. It was ancient and very spooky. The neat thing about it was it's monstrous, frightening old oak tree, with a massive spread of trunk roots. It sat right beside the road with the gnarled branches and roots reaching all the way to the other side of the narrow lane. Way back then, all the back roads were really just lanes of sand or gravel. A lot of kids from our area had to walk past this tree to get to and from school so they were used to coming down this road. Even in the dark. So, we'd put black shoe polish on our faces, then we'd wait until it was real dark, around midnight or something and some kid would always come walking by. Never missed a night. I'd wait until they got right under this big, heavy branch that hung out over the road and then I'd moan as loud as I could. While I was moaning, if they were little, I'd jump on them. Once I got hold of them, I'd hang off their necks. I'd start hollering and screeching to beat the band. I would be jumping up and down, waving my arms and making an awful racket. This was only when they looked bigger than me, but not much bigger. Big kids could have stomped me into the ground. Now, this was a pastime even Mama wouldn't have taught me and she was pretty open about having fun. The kids would absolutely freak out. They thought it was a dead person hanging off them. I know some of them pissed their pants or worse. Loved it. I would pull the switchblade so they could see the white, pearl handled grip and that long nine inch blade. They'd see that and the black leather jacket and go batshit. It was too dark to tell I was female. They didn't know what had happened to them. I'd chase them down the road until I couldn't run anymore for laughing. They never once looked back to see what was really behind them. I realize now it was wrong to do this to little kids, who were truly terrified, but I didn't know that at the time. I have to admit, they were my favorite. Hell, they freaked. It was a cemetery and that made it so much scarier. They should have known ghosts don't run around in black leather jackets with switchblades. They wear uniforms. I should know.

    We also attended holy roller church revivals in makeshift tents. I did sincerely love a revival. We'd crawl up under one of the sides of the tent and watch these people reach new spiritual levels. They'd be caterwauling as bad as Mama ever did, beating their chests, hollering for the Lord to come get them, tears of rapture running down their faces. Rapture, I think it was called. They ruined the really great music once they got the spirit in them. You wondered if they were really doing and feeling the gospel or if they were putting on a show for Him. Whatever.

Didn't question a rare good time. It was rocking and rolling in there like you've never seen before. It was always black people. You would get caught between two really big women and the breasts and stomachs could tear your skin right off. They would get together for this kind of religious outing and you would definitely want to be there. They didn't care if you were a white kid. I didn't think most of them even saw us, they were so whacked out. No telling what they were serving, but the congregation was always wound up. We'd get all wound up with them. Dancing in the aisles, screaming and beating our chests. Like Indians but with a soul beat. Bet most kids didn't get to do that kind of thing. Since we had a Mama in either never-never land or working, it was a take care of yourself situation. You did the best you could to entertain yourself. When you were a kid, it meant you were allowed to get into whatever trouble you could handle. I could handle whatever was out there. No fear. No brains. At least I hadn't been arrested. Yet. Although I was getting older, it never seemed like it.

    There was a store like what we now call a convenience store right across the street from the house. We spent a lot of our time running back and forth from the house to the store if only for something to do. Play in traffic, you know. It was a little grocery store with things in barrels and all. You could always find something that you had never noticed before and/or find gross things that had been around before I had been born. I didn't say it was a clean place, just fun. My favorite thing was to get two oranges and a soda before I left for school. I always managed to have guys come from wherever they lived to go to Aspenberg's, get me the oranges and a soda, then walk me to school. One of those guys was a real good friend of mine named Bernie Moore. I found out a lot later he got hit by a car on Arendell Street. A drunk driver killed him when he was nineteen years. I hope his parents know what a great kid and friend he was. I can still see him in my head. You know people can talk to you without really being there. You're not nuts. You can still see them, hear their voice. They are talking to you. You can argue with them and they can't win. What could ever be better than that?

    It was about this time that I fell in love with a dog for the very first time. I found out there were living, breathing things in life that can love you only cause you exist. Other than Mama, this was an alien concept to me and I jumped right on it. There was a tiny, pure white Pomeranian that lived halfway between my house and school. When I walked by every day, she would run out and we would roll around on the ground, playing. OK by me. I felt no need to show up at school clean. She followed me all the way to school, went home, then came back to get me. I could depend on her sitting there waiting for me to come out the door. On the days I had to go to Aunt Brenda's, she would walk with me until I had to turn on Fourteenth Street, then she'd go on home. Smart animal. Loved me to no end and it was mutual. One day, her owner decided to move to Florida and it just killed me to think I would lose her. She and I had been pals for a year when I found out she might have to go. Her owner changed her mind. Not about going to Florida, but she decided to let me have her. I called her Muff because she was a ball of white fluff with a doughnut tail. Little bitty face, little bitty tongue. Loving. Only animal lovers even know what I am talking about. Dedicated, that's what she was. Dedicated. This dog was the first being I had ever encountered that felt no need whatsoever to argue back. She smiled at me, no matter what. She understood total devotion and she taught it to me. She was my joy.

One day I was playing in the yard with Muff and I had apparently done something to piss Jimmy off. No telling what. He went across the street to the store in a huff. Once he got done whatever he went over for, he came back to the street separating us. Muff was with me. While he was standing at the street, getting ready to cross back over, he waited until the traffic on Bridges Street got a little closer and then he decided to call Muff to cross the road to come to him. All the time knowing traffic was coming. He called her at just the right time. She was hit by a car. Crushed. When I ran over to her there was nothing left of her but blood. I never got over it. I will never get over it. I think that was the first day real sorrow set in for me. I never understood why Jimmy would do it. I don't want to. I didn't understand it since he loved her, too. I know he didn't mean for her to die, but he meant for her to get hurt to get back at me. He did get hysterical. I mean, we both watched it, for heaven's sake. That was my first experience with real, deep down anger and hurt. From that point on, when I played football or basketball with Jimmy, I was out to inflict major damage. He knew it and was scared to death of me. I'd smack him upside the head anytime I felt like it. Couldn't put it off on me. Mean, selfish, spiteful little monster shit. If I hadn't hated baseball, I would have had a bat and I would have used it on him like he used a car on poor Muff. My treatment of him up until then was a party. He paid. Big time. I don't think I ever looked at him again without thinking of her. But, thinking positively, I had learned to love animals without restraint. With people, I had deep, deep pockets of restraint, you know. Of course I loved Jimmy. I was just a hurt kid. And mad.

    I had lots of other dogs during our crappy life at Bridges Street, but not one like Muff. One was a beautiful German Shepherd named Butterball. We had to give her away because she was mean to children of another color. Then, we got another one named Skybo. Big sucker. They both had black tongues and Mama said it meant they could pick up the smell of colored people. He tried to bite little black boys and girls on the way to school every day, and got some of them, too. He was way too big for me to control. I couldn't stop him. I was not of a mind set to think dogs biting little blacks kids was okay. It was funny the first time. You kinda laugh and panic at the same time, but after that I realized he did mean to hurt them and I couldn't have that. Mama didn't teach me to hate anybody. He did come in handy one day.

    Most of the time Mama worked ten to two and five to twelve every day and night. Whoever was supposed to watch me would leave me home alone. I was scared, people. This was the South for Christ's sake. We had crazy people here. Lots of them. Things happened down here they never even thought of up North. Southerners are creative and they could be by God determined. Shit happened and it could hurt. One night, I was sitting in the living room with only Skybo for company. I was leaning up against the furnace trying to keep warm when he started to growl. Skybo was laying on top of the furnace when I saw the fur on the back of his neck rise. I was still looking when he bared his teeth. When I saw his teeth bared, the hair stood up on the back of my neck. I knew from that growl that whatever was out there was black because that was what he did just before he jumped little black kids. It was too late for black or white kids to be out and no black people came to my house but Maude and Squarehead, two friends of the family. The taxi cab guy came every now and then, but he only delivered liquor. He didn't really drive a cab. Skybo knew them well, so I knew it wasn't one of those guys. Amazing how much time you have to think when panic is in place. Slows time down to a crawl. Only time in your life you're logical is just before an attack. Have you ever noticed that? Then you have time to just lay it all out. Plenty of time. Go figure.

Time seemed to be doing it's crawling thing until whoever it was approached the front door and rattled the doorknob. My heart exited my body. Then, I ducked. Skybo came off that furnace in mid air, flew across the room like he had grown wings, and hit the front door. He landed at the top of the door, claws digging into the wood as he slid down. He was barking and snarling to beat the band. God awful racket. Scared the absolute shit out of me. I couldn't hear that fella tear outta there for all the noise, but I watched him through the window. Man knew how to move when God put the spirit in him. I hoped he'd tell all his friends about Skybo so they wouldn't come here with something mean and nasty on their minds. He must have.

As expected, we had to gave Skybo away. Even though Mama was pleased he protected me, she was scared of him and didn't like the biting black people thing. We gave him to the MP's. For those uneducated of you out there, that is the military police. They actually wanted Skybo to kill people. He'd do it, too.

But, no dog like Muff came along. I missed him terribly and mourned him every day. I would break out crying in class or where ever I was when I thought of him. I learned to cry like an adult. All out.

BACK TO THE BEACH

During this never ending stretch of time at Bridges Street, I discovered another reason to love the beach and the ocean. I realized I was stuck in Morehead in the winter and free for anything in the summer. The beach became my place to blossom like you'd planted me. The memories of my summers will last a lifetime. I have never been that crazy about the ocean itself, having been at the bottom of it way too many times. Listen here, once you have been picked up right off your feet, rolled around like someone crammed you in the dryer and forgot you. Then you were suddenly slammed to the ground. Next, you'd get picked up again, bounced around two or three times until you didn't know what was up and what was down and, damn it all, be slammed down again until you could hear your brain rattling around. All this time, there was the little detail about not beaing able to BREATHE. You eventually grow tired of it as a sport. I have had enough sand in my eyes, teeth and ears to last me forever. I think surfers need lobotomies. Or they already had one. You were able to put up with the sand spurs, perfectly named, as long as you could wander around the dunes knowing the entire Atlantic Ocean was somewhere on the other side. As long the water was not actually in my ears, I loved it. You could hear it getting louder the closer you got. You could hear the raging without needing to see it. It was an amazing sight when it was you were finally able to stand in front of it. Like, "Come get me if you can." then you'd let it chase you back to the shore. I couldn't wait to get to the beach each year. We were blessed because we got to experience it year after year. All our life if we so decided. It was the greatest place in the world to grow up; bar none. It was a perfect time to grow up. Mama would shove us out the door at six a.m. and pretty much tell us to git. She didn't want to see our faces until she got home from work that night. It was great. I could get into anything. There were no restrictions put on me. None. Well, I knew I shouldn't get arrested.

There was a family called the Gardners who lived on the beach instead of in Morehead. That made them special because, after Hurricane Hazel, not that many people had the guts to live there. They lived in a real unique horseshoe looking house across from where the police station was. The house drew a lot of attention because it looked like someone put it up a piece at a time. I mean a piece at a time, not a room at a time. It went in every direction and then ended up like a horseshoe. Like us, they didn't have heat either. The house was real run-down but Emily, Lee, Ann, John and their parents, although as poor as we were, treated me like one of the family. Mrs. Gardner was real dark from the sun and I thought she looked exotic, except for the rot in her teeth and that missing one right in front. She had solid black hair and had a touch of Indian in her. She rode around all day on a bicycle and people thought she was a nut. She wasn't, though. They left her alone and that's what she wanted. I spent entire summers there.

Emily and I would get up early in the morning to go down to one of the finger piers. They didn't call them finer piers for nothing. They were long, pointed and very thin. You could only walk one at a time. If you tried to walk with someone beside you, one of you was going in the water. That thin. We'd get up every morning with our trusty buckets of shrimp or chicken parts and head out to catch crabs. We would drop a nail with some chicken pieces hung from it, a crab would snatch it and we would haul it up, drop it in a bucket, beat it against the sides until it fell off the nail, and do it again. One thing about this type of crabbing was to remember you did not ever let a crab get between you and land unless you were able to jump high and accurate. There was not a lot of pier to land on. If you weren't careful, there would be no where to go. Don't be faint of heart either. You'd die of a heart attack, for sure. Crabs would rush right at you and tear a piece off. They would hold on until they ripped it off and then come back for more flesh and when they have shredded what skin they wanted, no matter how big you were, they would sit there and glare at you. Eyeballs rolling around like they dared you to make a move. Then, they rushed at you again. Most people were scared of stories of ghosts in the woods. Give me the woods. Give me the ghosts. Keep the damn crabs. It gave me the willies listening to them scrape around the bottom of the bucket. They'd be climbing on top of each other to get out. I couldn't get anything done for staring at the bucket, just knowing one of them was going to crawl out of it. My pounding heart said it was on it's way to attack me. They would climb out if you weren't looking and run right for you. Apparently, human flesh was more fun than dead chicken meat. That was the whole point in crabbing like this. Once you got them on that line, they weren't about to let go until you dropped them on the pier or in the bucket. I thought Godzilla was a joke, but a crab could stop my heart. Christ, I hate the thought of a loose, wild ass crab to this day.

  If you have ever had a pissed off crab rushing you and it was between you and dry land, believe me your heart is either going to go faster or stop altogether. A few cowards would jump off the pier but the problem with that is the hundreds of crabs they landed on. You either did an end run around that crab, tried to jump over it or you gritted your teeth and hoped you had help to get him off the pier. Like a loaded shotgun. Screaming did absolutely no good. The reward for this kind of entertainment was money, of course. We'd catch a bushel of crabs each, walk up to the causeway, stand beside the road and sell each bushel for two dollars. You could do damn near anything on the beach back then for two dollars. Eat, swim, eat hot dogs and play music all day. You tell me where you could get that for two dollars.

One summer day, all the siblings walked over to the beach with me. I fell asleep on a pier. For some reason, maybe to teach me to swim or perhaps to drown me, Teeny threw me off. He did the same thing to Jimmy. Guess the excitement of us rubbing his back or getting the damn ice cream for him had worn off. Could be he did it because he was mean, nasty and evil. Where he tossed me in was a place over on the causeway where boats came in to tie up. If not knowing how to swim wasn't bad enough, how would you like the taste of gas and oil, not to mention other garbage? I didn't know how to swim and I didn't waste my time trying to do things I didn't know how to do, so I improvised. I knew you could go up or down without having to swim. I paddled right for the bottom of the water, grabbed hold of the various and sundry stuff down there and decided to pull myself all the way to the other side before coming up. The side away from Teeny. I knew there was no point coming up on the same side where Teeny was; he'd just throw me in again. Anyhow, I got pretty good at pulling myself back and forth across the bottom. The other kids couldn't figure out how I got there and back, but they knew they couldn't see me do it. They probably thought I was dog paddling but I was too full of myself than to do something so disgusting as dog paddle. Big girls didn't dog paddle. Or pee in the water. The only scary thing was when the boats showed up over my head, because they weren't that far above me. They threw out dead fish, for heaven's sake. And other slimy things. I learned something interesting though. Nothing smelled worse under water than the water itself.

Mama came over with us one day and foolish me, I had not told her I had re-invented swimming. Acting like a clown, I flung myself, not knowing how to dive, off the pier. You should see how I did it. Every limb went a different direction. It was really funny. I went straight down and didn't come back up. I went across under water. Well, when I came up on the other side, more than all hell was breaking loose. Mama thought I'd drowned and was throwing as big a fit as I'd ever seen. I hollered to let her know I was ok because she was looking straight down while I was straight across. If she had wings, she would have flown across the water. I think it would have been the first time she would have beat me. I stayed over there awhile waiting for her to calm down. Before I jumped back in, I told her what I was going to do. I jumped in, pulled myself across and came back up. After blistering my face with her ferocity, she taught me to swim. Then she went at Teeny with something in addition to ferocity and gave him a few blisters. Served him right. Jerk-off.

Eventually, I learned I could walk to the beach across the water on low tide. All by myself. The only part I had to pull myself across was right where the drawbridge was; only about twenty feet. Had to time it though, because there were boats flying through there, not the least concerned about a kid stupid enough to be swimming where boats were supposed to be, not kids.

After I learned to swim and dive, my favorite place was called the cove. It was a little inlet that cut into the sound side of the island. They had a low diving board, a high one, a juke box, soda and hot dogs. You tell me what was better than that when you were ten or so with two bucks. To me, crabbing was a marketing tool. This was what the crabbing paid for. Since I now knew how, I would swim all day long. When I would finally almost pass out on the towel, I played the jukebox. We still had what we called beach music, but it was not to be confused with the Southern California stuff. This was the warm, black soul music like I remembered from the Idle Hour. The only time the music sucked was when they catered to the Marines and put stuff on like "Hanky Panky" and crap like that. You could dance there if you could find somebody who did more than shake their bootie. Listening to "Wooly Bully" would make me gag. The Continental was the favorite dance at the time. I could do it because I could dance to anything, but I have never been interested in dancing with other girls. To me, there's a two word phrase for dancing with other girls, and it is ugly. The Locomotion was all the Marines could do because they had never even seen the shag before, much had a chance to learn it. Mama told me if someone asked you to dance, you politely said yes. Those boys were protecting our country. Her philosophy was if they asked you to dance, they were paying you a compliment and you were to accept it. Graciously. But, you only had to accept once. Be nice unless they grab you and try to haul you under the boardwalk. Then you were to try to kill them.

Legend had it that you could dive off the high board at the cove, go all the way down and find a dead body there. Somebody had supposedly drowned and was still down there. Now that I am at least fifteen minutes older, I understand that dead bodies decompose, but I was scared witless of running into that dead body. I would go as far down as I could, tried to judge when I was about at the bottom, turned and swam like hell for the surface. I came up looking unconcerned and sophisticated, turned around and did it again. Finally, someone challenged me to grab some of the bottom to prove I went all the way down. I had gotten away with fooling them for years. Being challenged always motivated me so I dove in, went to the bottom, grabbed some sludge and went up. It was really creepy way down there. It got black so you lost the sun completely, and it got unexpectedly cold. Being me, I said just do it, don't worry about it. That's the Mama in me. Sometimes it took motivation to get it out of me. It was better than the slam dunk on the ocean waves in my book. When it got really dark down there, you could get disoriented. I really thrived on being scared. Ran right for it every time.

    I was also running around with my cousin, Sissy, and all the other kids churned out by my Aunt Brenda and Uncle John. They lived right on the water too, but on the sound side. The biggest difference between the ocean beach and the sound beach is the shells. The ones you would step on when you tried to get out in the water. The broken scallop shells, the broken clam shells, the broken oysters, the broken glass, whatever. And, the crabs. The ones who took a battle stance and, not knowing it, you stepped on them so they went psychotic on you. They were under water so you couldn't see them. Once they clamped hold of your foot, you went berserk. Then reinforcements would gather to bring you down. Only thing you could do was run and shake your foot at the same time hoping velocity would get it off. Ew! You couldn't go out in the water without sneakers on because your feet would get sliced open. Not cut, sliced open. They wouldn't stop bleeding until the sun went down and your day was shot. Gauze and alcohol, gauze and alcohol. No wonder Aunt Brenda didn't have time to keep tabs on what Uncle John was doing. She was minding eleven raucous kids. He was minding the teenagers. Girls, that is. We were still going there on Sunday for Southern fried chicken. Done crispy. To die for. Everybody down South made the best fried chicken. Northerners never got it right. Nobody with any pride puts chicken in the oven and expects it to come out fried. Stupid. Aunt Brenda would sometimes make me my favorite peanut butter sandwiches. She still cut them the way I liked them and added a little more peanut butter on the top of the top piece. When you ate it, the peanut butter made direct contact with the top of your mouth. It was heaven. You got peanut butter top and bottom. I still make peanut butter sandwiches that way. Tradition.

OH M' GOD, IT'S BIG ELLY

During the winter, I had to go out to Aunt Elly's restaurant on a regular basis against my will. And I had a big will. With Mama working so hard, sometimes we would have to go to Aunt Elly's to even see her. When you headed off from school to go to Aunt Elly's, you felt like you were going to be an old teenager before you ever got there. I should check it sometime for mileage, because it was mileage, not blocks. You were always scared somebody was going to drive by and pick you up. Never did, though. Maybe it was because I was so short. There isn't a damn thing I can do about being short. Just how damn hard is it for you people to look down? Its ok with you when you have to look up. Why do people think tall people are special? What's with that? I was short then, short now, short forever. That's my motto and I'm going to stick with it.

When Aunt Elly's husband, Russ, was alive, he had a sawmill right beside their house and restaurant. When Jimmy and I would have to go to Aunt Elly's, we'd always head for the sawmill. It had a tall sloping high chute that was way up high and curved around on its way down. We'd crawl up there and chute down into the sawdust. We really made a mess of ourselves. We loved it. There was no easy way to get sawdust out of your hair. Even if you wanted to. You could wash for an hour and it dug right in there. For those of us in this world who never wanted to feel completely clean anyway, you can't beat sawdust. It got in your eyes, ears, mouth and every orifice it was able to reach. And it stayed there. Nothing could beat the chute. It would slam you from one side to the other in an attempt to beat your dumb ass half to death on the way down, and whoosh, in you'd go to the sawdust pile. The pile could stand as high as ten or eleven feet sometimes. Once you hit it, you'd disappear into it and have to try to climb your way up. It gave when you moved, so you couldn't get a foothold. You'd slosh around like a drunk acting like you were trying to get out of the sawdust pile, giggling all the time. If Mama was hollering for us to come help out, we'd be carrying on like drunken sailors on purpose to pretend we couldn't get out.

She called the ambulance on us one night and with one thought of my having to go to the hospital, I shot out of there like a missile. She just grinned. I knew she wasn't about to come in and get us and she couldn't call the ambulance every time. They'd catch on eventually. It was a raucous good time while it lasted.

In addition to the sawmill, Uncle Russ had a small hutch slaughterhouse for the bar-be-cue. I hated what he did there but the smell was past awesome. I only went in there a couple of times. It was truly not my thing. I tried to avoid blood and death if I could. Dead, cut up animals deserved a funeral. They didn't deserve to be hanging, bleeding from a spike. Gross. I didn't want even to think about it.

Uncle Russ was a sweetheart. He had warm, soft, beautiful blue eyes with a twinkle in them and a mischievous smile. A rugged looking, skinny guy, he never had much to say unless it was tell the screaming females to shut up. He sat in the back of the restaurant most of the time in a rocking chair with his pipe. Not bothering anybody. He would listen to all the unbelievable carrying on. Only every now and then would he stand up and tell everybody to shut up, and he'd take control. Aunt Elly controlled everybody else, but he controlled her. He's the one who told me the story about the little kid who had a roach crawl in his ear and decide to live there. It still grosses me out.

I had several roles out at the restaurant. Working came natural to me. I didn't whine and fuss like Jimmy, I just did what I was told. Hell, if I had to be there, I wanted something to do. I also wanted Mama to be proud of me. I knew if I didn't work, it would give Aunt Elly one more thing to blast Mama for. At first, I was a bus boy. Not a great choice since the tray was bigger than me but I was a hard worker and I tried. We had those swinging doors between the tables and the kitchen. I can't believe someone ever thought that was a good idea. Sure wasn't for me since the glass pane was way over my head and no one could see me coming. Once you ran into somebody, you'd get into a little dance with them. Bodies bending up and down catching plates and glasses in mid air. Not attractive, either. You'd do an end around trying to keep from breaking the plates and sending used food in all directions. It was a mess to clean up.

One evening I was cleaning a table beside a very distinguished, good looking older man. He had beautiful white hair, much better than Daddy's, and gorgeous blue eyes that had a warm smile in them. He winked at me. He looked like he had lots and lots of money. As I was bussing the table next to him, he called me over and asked me if I saw a particular lady who was sitting at another table across the room. She was sitting with two other women who were also beautiful, even though elderly. She exuded a warm, sweet glow that only Southern women have. That serene, never been smacked around look. He asked me if I would go up to her to ask if she would have dinner with him. Hell, yes. I sidled up to her, pointed him out and asked if she would have dinner with him the next night, which was Friday. She looked over at him, smiled sweetly and with a honeyed voice told me she would love to. I ran back to his table and told him she said yes. I was ecstatic. Jumping up and down. I knew they would be a beautiful couple and I felt like I was a part of history or something. After a couple more runs, I was able to exchange enough information for him to be able pick her up the next night.

To my surprise, they came back to the restaurant for the famous first date. I came out through the swinging doors and there they were. After they ate, something not easy with me jumping for joy as they ate, or my refusing to leave them the hell alone, he called me over to the table, told me to go out to his car, open the trunk and get what was in there. Being a good girl, I tromped out to the car, opened the trunk. My mouth dropped open. I gently brought out a beautiful fishing rod and reel. I held it for a few minutes, pretending it was mine. Then I went back in to give it to him. He told me it was mine for asking the lady to have dinner with him. He told me he was in love and would be the rest of his life. I was swooning. It was so-o-o romantic. She was laughing at him. Hellacious tip.

I went back to thank him before they left and noticed she was clearly laughing at me. They looked happy, calm and sophisticated, but they were laughing at me so I took a little umbrage. A fishing pole does not buy my pride. Pouting, he got me to the table. He gently took my arm and introduced me to the lady. She was his wife. His name was Gregory Poole. He told me when I grew up to come to Raleigh and look him up. He would get me a job. Years later I did just that, but I met his son instead. The Mr. Poole of my childhood and his wife had died. I told his son the story as we sat in his Dad's office and we both cried. He said it was just like them. Then he got me a job like his father had promised to. Great family.

Another other chore for me was cracking open pecans for the homemade pies. Aunt Elly could cook. No doubt about that. She was a cooking fool. My job was to come up with complete one-half pieces. She wouldn't use pieces in her pies, just whole halves. You're nuts if you don't like the taste of pecans and you are even nuttier if you put me to the chore of cracking them. I got to eat the ones I broke. Ate well. Not many pies cranked out when I was around.

I also cleaned shrimp. I never felt the need to clean out that little black "vein" that runs along their back. But, I didn't tell anybody. I couldn't believe it was a vein. It took me thirty years before I would even eat shrimp. I had funny eating habits anyway. I only ate hot dogs. Four a day. I was fa teenager and had never tasted a hamburger, spaghetti or pizza. I had never eaten a french fry. If I didn't eat those things, you can rest assured I wasn't going to throw a slimy shelled shrimp with its feces in a noticeable location down my gullet. Gross.

As a result of working at Aunt Elly's, my right arm was significantly stronger than my left. This was because I was put in charge of making french fries. We had that gadget where you would put a peeled, washed potato (peeling was also my job) into it and pull a lever. It would slice right through the potato and voila, you would have raw french fries. I crave raw potatoes. Like the pecans, a whole freaking bunch didn't get past me. For years.

A major downside of the whole Aunt Elly connection was Aunt Elly, her big ass self. At the risk of being redundant, but with the need to be accurate, she sucked. She was a mean, vicious, nasty Southern woman. Mouth from hell. She couldn't just talk, she had to bellow. When she bellowed, there's no word in the English language for the ugliness that emerged from that hole in her face. She hated Mama, her own sister. I think she hated her because Mama was always the little, bitty pretty one. That's the name of a song we used to dance to and it was true of Mama. Aunt Elly, on the other hand, was huge, ugly and mean. But, I'll give her this, she was consistent. She was always mean as a rabid dog. Did I mention that Mama had, unfortunately, become a non-functioning alcoholic? If I had to listen to Elly like Mama did, I'd become something, I promise you. Since Mama worked for Aunt Elly, it gave her sister the right to say anything and act any way she wanted because she had Mama in her crosshairs. Being family gives you those rights. If Mama didn't show up for work, which was often, Aunt Elly would drive right up onto the lawn, up to the front door, bellow her way into the house and say every nasty thing she had in her repertoire. I was afraid to lock the door, because I figured she'd tear it down. Sometimes I think she practiced so she could get humiliating Mama down just right. She beat Mama down so low she couldn't get back up. I don't know how in hell Aunt Elly thought Mama could stand the barrage coming at her and yet, get up, get dressed and be perky after she was done with her. She'd throw Mama's clothes at her, scream for her to get up. Yeah. I bet Mama couldn't wait to. I think Elly enjoyed it. It gave her a chance to get out all the hatred she had for own rotten young 'uns and put it on Mama's head. I learned something from all that. Don't argue with a drunk. They ain't listening. They don't hear you. They could care less what you think. Elly never learned that. She kept it up for years.

After years of listening to all these women bitching, I learned to pretty much hate women. I had already known I didn't want to be one before I encountered these lovely monsters masquerading as females. I never wanted to grow into anything like them. I would rather stay a kid until I fell off the tomboy wagon. I didn't want to act like these women acted, ever. I hated it when they kissed me with those mouths from hell. Trying to scream my way through that female logjam every night was exhausting.

In spite of it, Mama could crank out four hundred seafood dinners a night. She ran those deep fat fryers like they were an orchestra. She knew exactly what oyster went with what scallop. She would stand there and be literally covered in grease. Get her near a little grease and she would inhale it right up her nose like it was a drug. She always had a cigarette in her mouth because she needed her hands for cooking. When she talked to you, the cigarette would be crammed over to one side of her mouth like she was a gangster. It would jump up and down when she spoke and there would be a big, blue cloud around her face and her eyes would be squinting. If you wanted to talk to her, you had to walk into that cloud with her. I loved the smell of someone else smoking a cigarette, but I hated the taste of it in my own mouth. When I see her in my mind at Elly's, that's my first thought..the blue cloud and the jumping cigarette. You couldn't be quite sure what she looked like unless you got up early in the morning and snuck a look at her while she was still in bed. The minute she got up, in went the cigarette and the blue haze dance had begun for the day. I'm convinced she had grease and cigarette smoke going up her nose for eighteen years. If she got legitimately sick and couldn't work, her own sister wouldn't pay her. I hated that place. Nothing good about it except hot dogs. At least Mama had somebody there to push back the wolves. Me. I'd snarl and growl at them. Like I learned from Sky-bo.

Everybody who worked there was a miserable human being. Aunt Elly had six daughters. One of her daughters, Louise, was nice and had class. The rest had no redeeming qualities. But Louise was smart enough to stay away. Three of them were Tina, Tawnya and Monique. Sounded like Aunt Elly was in labor when she named them. The rest of the crew was great. There was a big, black woman named Elsie that I adored. She looked ten feet tall. She was a warm, wonderful, huggy kind of lady. She always had her arms around you. There were Letha May, the cooks and dishwashers. They were all fun loving and kind to me. The bitches were Aunt Elly and her offsprings. The steak cook was named Frank. He was married to the Monique Monster, the oldest, most powerful witchy woman. Huge woman. She was so damn mean I never saw where the attraction could be. Frank was built like a linebacker so I guess he could handle her. If I wanted a steak, which I got once a week, I'd have to let him pick me up and hold my whole body over the charcoal grill until I was crisp. Loved my food crisp. He was huggy, too. Everybody else was female and family. Problem with family businesses was people didn't care how they talked to you. Because you were family, they didn't think they owe you any respect.

They treated me ok given they were bitches and couldn't seem to help it, but it I despised the way they treated Mama. You mess with my Mama and I will hate you for life. They thought they were better than us because we were more poor than some of the black people who worked there. They looked down on Mama because she was a drunk. True. Some days she just couldn't crawl out from under that bourbon. Apparently, bourbon not only stinks, it must be heavy. She couldn't get up. This phase with Aunt Elly dominating our life lasted until I was about sixteen and shot myself out of there like I was in the business end of a serious barrel. Put my tiny size 5 foot down. No more. Now I could drive a car. Who would put up with that shit when they could be racing down the street?

BOURBON AND ME

In spite of the drunkenness, I loved my Mama. Deeply. Even drunk she was the funniest person I ever met. I have never had the memory for ditties. As I was getting farther into my teens, working at Aunt Elly's, my most dominate memory of Mama is her warmth, generosity and humor. She'd get mad at me about something and I would get on my knees so she'd think I was going to pray but I would chant a little ditty. As I've mentioned, it was not my fault that I was religion-challenged. They did it to me. That's my story and I'm sticking to it. Mama would always come home eleven or twelve o'clock at night with something to eat. One meal for however many people were there. Most of the time, it was our only meal of the day, people. She always brought enough side dishes for my friends and they always knew they were welcome and would have a good time. We all knew we were going to sit around the kitchen table, roaches and all, and listen to Mama tell her ditties. She was never vulgar, but she made sure you knew what word was missing. She would drag it out. She always skipped right over the bad words like they didn't exist. Her ditties could go on forever and rhyme. She would get drunker and they would get funnier. I never figured out if this was memory work or if she was making it up as she went along, but she was powerfully funny. She had a smart mouth and a kiss-my-ass look on her face and her upper lip would have a little curl. She'd look at us one by one and make everyone feel included. She'd hug us and kiss us, tell us she loved us, then she would throw her hip out of joint and we would run, screaming out of the room, all grossed out. She loved it. So did we.

Through the drudgery time at Bridges Street and Aunt Elly's, I was valiantly working my way through my teens while trying hard not to kill myself. Or get arrested. Or get pregnant. That was the hard one, pregnant. I think I inherited my parents sex drive. His, plus her's on top of it. I really, really liked making out. I didn't like guys touching me all that much..just kissing. I could kiss for hours. It is amazing what a teenage boy will put up with if he thinks he is going to get a little. We'd kiss until we both had fever blisters. Mama used to say fever blisters came from having too much shit in your blood, but the only time I got them was after a marathon kissing event. I think I set my lips on fire and that was their reaction. Erupt. Hey, ok with me, I didn't have to put up with a baby the rest of my life. Give me erupted lips anytime. I didn't even have a boyfriend, nor did I date. I had guys I ran around with. Nothing serious for me, boy. The teen years were good and bad. Like most kid's during the formative years, I was one mixed up young 'un. But I struggled on.

AND THEY'RE OFF

While all the fun and games at Aunt Elly's was going on, the home front was under attack. Where'd they all go? Teeny had packed up his crap, his cornet and his smart ass self and left. Thank God and little acorns, there was a heaven. After years of strife and discord with us, Daddy offered him a car and a room at the house on Country Club Road with him and Jackie. Living with Daddy was always Teeny's first choice, because he was the first male child. Daddy didn't know yet how incredibly boring Teeny could be, since he hadn't spent five minutes with him since the divorce. However, he was going to find out. Of course, Daddy didn't want Teeny until he was at least sixteen, a more socially acceptable age. Daddy didn't want to have to bring us up. He only wanted us after the teenage kinks had been worked out. Teeny was the first to go, but not the last. Mama started to drink more and the funny side of her started to disappear except for the out of the blue wildly funny moments. She loved us. Drunk or sober, we were what she lived for. The only thing the rest of them saw was the drinking. I could see right through that to the sacrifices she made when she had us. Five of us in six years. So poor she couldn't feed or clothe us. The jerks and the jerkettes seemed to forget the hardship she went through. Teeny left when he had just turned seventeen, I think. That made Marybeth sixteen, Crystal fourteen, Jimmy thirteen and me, thirteen.

MaryBeth still craved attention from the guys and was gaga over them. I mean GAGA, guys. She was a sexy little thing, too. She was petite but she had Mama's body and breasts. I don't know where she got them, but MaryBeth also had what we called cat's eyes. Her eyes weren't brown, they had a gold cast to them that you see only in cats. With her body and eyes, she could be sexy without trying. I used to say she hit the beach lying down. Personally, I wanted to keep my feet under me. She's always said that she was a good girl, but there were rumors. I started most of them, but they were true stories to me and rumors to everybody else. She'd sneak out the windows late at night and nobody pretended she was sleep walking. Hell, there were nights I left the window open for her so she could get out. If she wanted out, believe me, you wanted her out. It also prevented a thousand useless fights with Mama. Mama was a cat, but she was a lady. MaryBeth didn't have that problem. She probably forgot how to use the damn front door. She'd talk about being a good girl. She'd rewrite her personal history. I was on the floor, dumbwat. Mama and MaryBeth would screech at each other like fighting tigers. Mama was trying to keep her straight. I guess MaryBeth didn't want to be controlled. Ya' reckon?

Crystal was still at Aunt Elly's. I was afraid she'd be baby sitting until she died. Looked like it. We figured she should be happy, though. We couldn't figure out why she was so mournful. To us, she had food and clothes and that meant something to kids who didn't. I have to admit, sometimes it looked like ten different people dressed her in the morning, but she had clothes. I figured all that crazy dressing just showed how many clothes she had. I couldn't figure out why people thought there was something wrong with the way she dressed. She was wearing what she had, just like we did. We didn't look any better. None of us had learned to be fashion followers, believe me. Clothes were not something the rest of us had in abundance. Especially shoes. I couldn't wear cast off shoes because my feet were so small. I went shoeless a lot. Even to school. Let somebody say something to me. I'd get right in their face. I was good at it, even though my having to look up took some of the fire out of it, I have to admit.

Jimmy was gone but in another way. The boy I knew had gone completely over the top about girls. He went into a brainless, sexual rut. I'm not talking about a normal, teenage boy nuts. He became a rutting animal. For some reason beyond me, he could actually get some. And he wanted a lot of some. He could get some any time he wanted. Perpetual erection syndrome. It was really kind of unbelievable. If you asked someone if they remembered Jimmy, that's what they remembered. The girl addiction he had and their addiction to him. He was extremely good looking, I must agree. He ended up with the beautiful skin from Mama plus the almost coal black hair with blue tints and the most beautiful blue eyes I ever saw. His eyes were big, too. You weren't going to miss them. Mesmerizing.

Jimmy was very much the charming Southern male with gracious manners and a sweet temperament. For God's sake, he was tall. The sum'bitch was over six feet tall. Daddy never got past five feet eight. Whose was he, for heaven's sake? Where did he and Teeny get this size thing, damn it? But, above all, he knew when to pull out the sweet. No macho in Jimmy anywhere except between his legs. Apparently, those little bitty balls I once knew had grown enough to please the girls. We'd be dancing at the Pavilion and he would leave me to go out with one girl, she'd fall in love and he'd git her down. An hour later, he'd head out with another. And, they all knew it. God, I hated it. I felt he was trying to be like Daddy, but I finally realized he wasn't trying to be like Daddy, he was like Daddy when it came to the erection thing. I wished I'd cut it off when I was throwing knives at him.

I was still the baby and always would be. I was also still a tomboy and never hit a boy crazy stage, except for the kissing. I had taken up real skating out of sheer desperation to get away from Aunt Elly's and my whole rutting, sexual family. They had built a skating rink near the restaurant and saved my life. It gave me a great opportunity to walk most of the way without having to go all the way to the damn restaurant. Nobody cared if I showed up or not. I was high on the nobody special list. I worked hard and found myself very good at skating. I won a lot of speed racing, my favorite. I surprised myself by getting very good at free style and dance. I loved the jumps and spins. The instructors were incredibly encouraging but everything they wanted me to enter cost money. Still trying to hold onto some slight piece of my brother, I tried to get Jimmy into free-style couple skating, but after he dropped me on my head a few times, I forgot about that. I already had brain mass getting out every day on it's own. I didn't need gaping holes to help it along.

Other than Teeny leaving and Mama continuing to sink in stages, things seemed pretty much the same. Inevitably, I found myself in an unfulfilled sexual frenzy. I just didn't want to do anything about it. Mama drank and Aunt Elly bellowed, and the tension between MaryBeth and Mama increased exponentially. I think MaryBeth should have listened to Mama, but they couldn't seem to talk, just scream. She wanted to do what she wanted, when she wanted. That was date and run men. She was already considered the family wild child. There was something sexually wrong with this family. MaryBeth had a wonderful heart and stood up for Mama, but at night she was liable to not come back. Maybe she didn't know the way. She tried every other lie.

Teeny would stop by every now and then to tell us how lucky he was. I'd rather eat dirt and die than live with Daddy so he didn't make much of an impression on me. One day, he told me he had fond memories of when I would rub his back. He asked me if I remembered those days when I rubbed his back, we had a few sexual feelings for each other, but decided not to pursue them. I told him I didn't like him then; didn't like him now. Then, I tried to kick him in the nuts. What was he thinking? I had sexual feelings for him? Pervert. I doubt it.

As expected, Daddy popped up again. Please, couldn't somebody shot this guy? I didn't know what he offered MaryBeth to get her or why in hell he wanted her, but she went. I remember it was a powerfully sad time for Mama. I didn't know if MaryBeth would have left had she known how bad it tore Mama up. I admit Mama seemed to take everything out on MaryBeth, but she was deeply loved by Mama, and she knew it. MaryBeth couldn't see the running was causing all the tension between them. Mama would not accept that she might have begat a whore. Maybe MaryBeth wasn't one but she wasn't home enough for us to be sure. I believed that. If she could have made herself settle, Mama would have treated her as good as she did me because it was her way. However, if you gave her a little resistance, she would tear into you. We all knew that. Cranky, she was. Why MaryBeth had to step right in her face every time was beyond me? Then she'd act like she didn't expect it when Hurricane Anna came her way. Yes, Mama slapped her. Nothing like MaryBeth says. No matter what she said, it wasn't as bad as she made it out to be. She always forgot I was there. I remembered.

Exit MaryBeth as she headed off to Daddy's. Teeny's room was available because he was at Duke studying architecture. Maybe he needed to make another damn knife like the one he threw at Wilson. Now, Mama only had Jimmy and me. I knew Jimmy was going to go first chance he got. He wanted clothes, cars, money. Lord knows, my loving sisterness wouldn't hold him. I couldn't believe Mama couldn't see it. I ached for her. Daddy was going to get to Mama where it hurt..her kids. He knew all teenage boys wanted a car and he knew Jimmy wasn't going to get it living with us. He didn't give a damn about us. He had a heart incapable of love. I was as floored as Mama to find he cared so little, though. These people weren't just leaving Mama, they were leaving me with her madness. They had all told me they loved me and everyone of them walked out on me, too. As an excuse to make themselves look better, once they knew they had an out, they'd build up all these emotions, and became hateful to her. It was all her fault they would say. She should have stayed with Daddy and not fought back. We never saw MaryBeth and Teeny after they left.

Well, finally during the final drunken throes of a previously fine human being, Jimmy got fed up and used it as his excuse to leave right in the middle of it. A fine, upstanding young man with manners deserted a very sick mother and desperate little sister. Well, I would still dance with him, but other than that, I didn't want anything to do with him. I would dance with anybody, so it wasn't a compliment. If I didn't like to dance so much and if it wasn't pretty much the only joy in my life, I would have gone ahead and brained him.

They were gone. As for it being all her fault.. my ass. I thought they left because they were so damn selfish. They walked out on a wonderful woman in pain. I was only a kid but I knew that was how alcoholism worked Bye bye family. "Hello loneliness. I think I'm gonna cry-y."

THE SLIDE INTO HELL

It was like seeing the death of an icon. This bigger than life mother I had always adored was trying her best to kill herself, no doubt about it. They talk about a long slide into alcoholism. I guess if you counted up all the years she drank and the fact that she drank more and more you could call it that. I saw it as a race down the mountainside on a sled. She threw herself into drinking. Bourbon. You'd think if you were going to kill yourself drinking, you would at least want to enjoy the taste. Not with this stuff.

Who ever came up with that crap? There oughta be a law. If the Wild Turkey people don't like it, let them try to convince a Court of Law that it tastes good. If something is that destructive, not to mention tastes that bad and smells that bad, one of the damn governmental agencies ought to step in and throw the stuff in the toilet. God knows, I did. There's a governmental agency to interfere with everything else you can think of; smoking, child abuse, same sex marriage...but it's ok if you drink yourself to death as long as you don't get behind the wheel of a car. Go ahead, make orphans of your kids and make them damn miserable while you go about it. No food, no hot water, no shoes. That's legal. So is Wild Turkey, whose owners are siphoning your mother's dying life into their bank accounts. You can't run moonshine in North Carolina, but it's ok for the State of North Carolina to distribute and profit from selling the liquor and wine that make alcoholics of mothers, for Christ's sake. I hear the mantra now, she had a choice. No. She didn't.

I'm the one who can't keep her damn head up. This is the only picture we have of all five together. Thank heavens

Crystal and me. Nice, happy faces

MaryBeth
Check out that face, people.

Jimmy, Studly, Do Right. Told you he was a hunk

Comatose people don't make choices. They just keep doing what they are doing while everybody else waits for them to hit rock bottom. They don't step in to help. They just stand back and say its because she has to hit rock bottom, like its an excuse for not stepping in. She just has to. Why? Why does she have to? Nobody lifted a finger while she was on her way to the bottom except to scream at her and take away her dignity. They'd rather wait until she slammed into the bottom, face first, like she dropped off a cliff. Out would come the smirks. Oh, they knew it would happen, they said. Of course, it would happen, nobody tried to stop her. Makes me wish I had more hands to slap them with.

    Believe it or not, sometime around here we had a crisis in the family. Just thought I'd make you stop and think about that. Now, we had a crisis, unbelievable. Like it hadn't always been a crisis. A walking, talking, family crisis. Shoulda given it a name. A bed. A bath. Mama bounced off bottom like a basketball.

    Let's just say we all were amazingly crazy, just to keep it clean. If there was any bottom left to the hill, we went down it. I could not be enough for her. She missed her babies. She sank. When they describe the descent into alcoholism, someone watched it who had a fine grasp of the English language and who, oddly enough, must have been a fisherman. She sank, simple as that. She wasn't coming up. No matter what. Until she decided to and because of Jimmy, she didn't want to. I hated him. What was I going to do? I could still get her laughing and get her telling me and my friends her ditties, but when everybody left, she just cried and cried. It broke my heart. I still had to sleep with her. Half the time she couldn't work and Aunt Elly wouldn't pay her. She wouldn't let go of me. It was like she had me by the neck. She clung to me in fear I was planning to go out the door. No matter what I said, she thought I would go. What were we going to do? Could somebody give me a way to haul her back into the boat instead of bleating about her sinking? Well, I got what I wanted. Not in the way I wanted it, for damn sure. Hell, if I had known I was going to pay the price, too, I would have just drunk it with her.

SEX ENTERS THE PICTURE

I was in my sixteenth year. It seemed to have taken ages. When I was thirteen, sex wasn't an issue I was interested in until Mama had sat me down and told me about it. She said I was going to love it. It was great. I would want to do it all the time. How many times do mothers tell their female children that, do you think? I didn't want to get knocked up. I knew that at two. She dropped the bomb. I could do it any time I wanted. Now we're talking, boy-o. However, after the first time, I had to call her. I asked her what the hell she wanted me to call her for? She got that yoga-looking face and said, just call her. What was I going to say? "Mama, I just got laid. Its a done deal." I thought this was a little warped. I have a reason for dropping this on you. You'll begin to understand my existence. She didn't think I would call. She was wrong.

Anyhow, it put me off having intercourse. Kissing and feeling up a little, yeah, but not the real thing. As a result, most of the guys were still my buddies, not boyfriends. All the guys knew it was not going to happen. I do think there was more than one bet that one of the guys could pull it off because the kissing didn't diminish. Other than that, it was a non issue. While I was sixteen, it was a little harder, literally, and I got a little more pissed. I tried to talk to her again, but she did the yoga face thing. I was NOT going to make that call. What would I say? What would I say?

I met a guy in high school that I really liked. He was pretty much my first crush. He was from Newport, one of the scruffy, dangerous types. He knew what he wanted and it was me. I told him he could stuff it anywhere he wanted but he wasn't going to stuff it in me and I didn't want to talk about it. Apparently, he went about stuffing it until he reached Letty Guthrie who told her friends his girlfriend was pregnant. I was his girlfriend. She was pregnant. Most of the kids at school didn't know about her. Its complicated.

I started running around with one of his buddies, Ralph. That was his nickname, not his description. Not a beautiful sight to see, but Ralph was one of the good guys. The problem was, he pursued me a lot more than I pursued him. An example was one of the nights the wind was howling and the rain was pounding. It would bend you over backwards if you tried to walk in it. I was in my hot 1960 Ford Fastback with a bored out 409 engine. It was a piece of junk, but fast. My reward for all those years at Aunt Elly's. A couple of girlfriends and I were driving around and we were riding the "circle." This was where teenagers went from drive-in to drive-in to see who was around and who was with whom. Not doing anything wrong. You know, jumping in and out of each other cars, that's all. There were the girls that thought the backseat was only good for making out. All in all, it was the girls going out with girls, ending up with guys kind of thing. Mostly good kids having fun.

Ralph, for some reason, started rutting like a caveman. Deciding he wanted to **be** with me, he started following us wherever we went. He kept screaming at me through the rain and the wind like that would motivate me to be with him. Duh. Ranting on about how we had a date and I had stood him up. Hell, I wasn't even dating him, just running around with him. He finally got on my last nerve so I took that bad ass Ford and flew out of that drive-in as fast as I felt like going. Off through the rain. I decided that boy could use a good dirt bath to settle his arrogance down somewhat. You gotta know, he drove a car that looked just like mine, but it wasn't a fastback. It didn't have my engine. I tore down Highway 70 until I got to Newport, took a hard left and cranked it down Nine Foot Road. It was pure mud. I knew what to do with a car and mud when a guy has gotten on your last nerve.

Ralph was trying to keep up with me but couldn't so when I got way down Nine Foot Road, I slowed a little. I wanted to give him a chance to get in place. Ralph pulled up behind me. He blinked his lights so I pulled over like a good girl. He jumped out into the rain and mud, but I wouldn't lower the window. The girls in the car were having the time of their lives. They knew I didn't take this macho man shit attitude lightly. Then he started pounding on the window. My window, people. Kissa my assa. I acted like I was pure-t sorry. You know, lifting up my hand and make gestures like "What did I do to upset you, sweetheart of mine?" I listened to him rant a minute and decided to put the game in play. I told him to go on back to his car and I would be there in a minute and we would talk. After he turned around, he got as far as the back of my car when I hollered his name, waited until he turned around, then hit the brake, hit the accelerator, eased off on the brake and buried him in mud. Car and all. The second I called his name, he got the mud full face. That ended that. Hot damn. Hate that. In the charming South, that's known as a dirt bath. Sometimes we buried whole crowds of kids and everybody does it for fun. Most of the time, it was enjoyed by all. Sometimes not so much.

    I got six of my friends in my car one Saturday afternoon and we high tailed it down a road in Newport that was a straight stretch from Highway 24 to Highway 70; about nine miles. As soon as I got on it, I kicked that tricked out Ford and was barely touching pavement within seconds. We were flat damn out. In the car, we were all happily hooting and hollering when, all of a sudden, out of a left side road way up in front of us, an old Ford model pick up truck pulled out onto the road I was on. In front of me. I was suddenly behind him, coming up on him at what seemed like a hundred miles an hour. Way up there. I looked at the speedometer, saw I was going more than a hundred miles an hour and shuddered. I looked back up and he was a whole lot closer and I was closing in on him so damn fast I couldn't spit. All of a sudden all the hooting and hollering became kids screaming in my damn ears while I was trying to think. Oh shit time. There was so much noise in the car, I couldn't think. There had to be a way. Oh yeah, great. A car is coming at us so I can't pass him and we are still closing on that damn truck so fast I can't even focus. Ok, guys. Only one thing to do. I took that steering wheel and whipped it hard to the right. I went off the road at eighty miles an hour. Seconds later, I passed that pick up, passing him between his pickup and the signs on the left side of the damn road. I kept going, trying to avoid the signs, until I got it down to sixty and, at forty I, unfortunately, whipped it back onto the highway. When I did, we spun around four times We ended up headed back toward the pickup. When I passed him, never having stopped, I was still doing fifty miles an hour. I finally got the damn car stopped. Pulled over. Everybody crawled out. Bobby Ainsworth came to the driver's side and gently pulled me out. I thought I was fine, actually. It wasn't until I tried to get out that I realized my knees had turned to water.

CRISIS AFTER CRISIS

I wanted to go to a junior senior prom. Me? A tomboy, still. I had never been to one before but I wanted to dance and I wanted to dance with some of my classmates. A lot of them weren't allowed at that cesspool of sin known as the beach. Problem was I didn't have any shoes. Nor did I have a bathing suit for the house party the next day. I had to give up the suit because the money went for bourbon. The bathing suit I wanted only cost five bucks at Cato's and Mama had promised me she would pick it up before she went to work at five. I went without shoes. I didn't care. I always danced without shoes, anyway. The people I went to high school with were great. Nobody treated me like I was trash even if I felt like it sometimes. I had a lot of friends and they knew how things were. They may have talked about me behind my back, but they were great to my face. Really great. I always remembered that. I ran in the house after the prom, hoping she had gotten me the bathing suit, when I walked into something even I had not thought of. Usually I could see all sides of most issues. I prided myself on that. Duh.

Remember when I said she bounced off the bottom. Mama was lying on her side, wet and incredibly filthy. She was whacked. It wasn't until I rolled her over, covered in bourbon, that I realized she had cut her wrists. Did a piss poor job of it, too, if you want to know the truth. I sat there on the bed, knowing where the money for the bathing suit went. If you were going to spend the money for my bathing suit for some more damn bourbon, could you at least not let it be the bottle that drove you to try to kill yourself? Is that too much to ask? I knew she wasn't going to die because it wasn't that bad. There was a lot of blood but not a very big cut. I was torn between being scared, mad or slapping her so hard she would see stars. She saw them anyway, so what was the point? We ended up doing the norm...we held each other and bawled. Oh well. I had already figured out that I was going to hit rock bottom with her, but I never figured for this. My patience was ragged. It wasn't all about her. It was about us. We were in it together, but I realized I had no say in the process. She was going to take me down with her. She didn't love me enough to fight for me or even with me. I would have fought for her. Hell, I did fight for her. With Daddy, Aunt Elly, Granny and everybody. I was the only one who stood up for her. She had chosen to take every ounce of my ability to keep going out of my hands. Daddy was going to get me. My God. Oh, my God.

Jimmy had left for college and Daddy had that damn empty bedroom from hell. He'd already put the word out he was going to get me by proving Mama was an unfit mother. Which she clearly was. In his eyes, it was how he made himself look good to the community. He took in those poor, miserable kids from their drunken mother and gave them a better life. Gag me.

After we quit crying, I told her I had smelled all the bourbon I wanted to in this lifetime. I was done. If she was that miserable..if she was that unhappy and had no hope..if she was ready to leave me and never see me again, she needed to do a better job of it. I gave her back the razor blade. Que sera, sera. Whatever will be, will be. I decided what I would be was be-gone. I left. I jumped in the car and batshitted out of there. I went straight to a pay phone to call Crystal. I had to depend on her to be able to do the right thing, whatever that was. I told her what happened and then jumped back in the car and pointed the front end of that sucker towards South Carolina. I started to drive like Satan was chasing me. I didn't know where I was going, but I knew damn well I wasn't going North. I would do anything to keep Daddy from getting me. Somebody find me a nice bridge abutment. Worked for me. To me, he would ruin my life, not Mama. Unless I got lost fast, Daddy was going to get me. I was too young to do a damn thing about it. Major crap. I did know one thing. If Daddy got me, he would pay. Big time. It would not be an experience he enjoyed. Not in this lifetime.

DO I HAVE TO DO THIS, GOD?

I was still going like a bat out of hell when they caught me. I put in five hours of world class pedal stomping. Did I mention what a speed freak I was? Oh, ye-a-a-ah. Once we got a car, I worked to make sure we always had gas. I knew how to use it. Oops, five hours into it, a Statie was on my tail. I gave that highway patrolman the run of his life. We were on the highway, my favorite place. These were the days of the 409, ass kicking muscle cars. He had to put on his afterburners to bring me down. Unfortunately, he had them with him. Slapped me on the back when he got me out of the car and told me that was the most fun he'd had since driving school. He didn't charge me with anything. Then he called Daddy, who was waiting to hear. He hauled my great driving ass off to the police station to wait for Daddy to come get me. And wonder how Mama was. Did she kill herself or did Crystal get there in time? How long before I would find out? Did I even want to grow up more? Boy, it would do real damage to his reputation if I blew my brains out in his living room. It was a thought. Hadn't there been enough? Couldn't I stop now? Questions were flying through my mind. I couldn't concentrate. Maybe if I picked a fight with one of the patrolmen, they'd shoot me. Better than living with Daddy. It was not good, I tell you. The patrol guys were being great and trying to feed me, but I just cussed and bawled. The guys hated it. Men hate it when little women cry. I couldn't believe, after everything that had happened, that Mama let Daddy have me. I was the one who wouldn't have left her. She must have thought it was just a matter of time before I abandoned her. That's what Teeny, MaryBeth and Jimmy did. Unfortunately, to Crystal's way of thinking Mama gave her away. It was never that. Mama couldn't afford to feed her.

Not matter what, the way Mama saw it, the other three had abandoned her. I never would have. No matter what she did. Why didn't she know that? How could she have abandoned me? Thoughts just ran back and forth in my head. Before you knew it, there he was. Evil incarnate. What was he going to do to me? I decided to quit crying and become me. I got mad. Real, raging mad. I can handle anything when I am mad. I could make this man's life hell for a very long time. I decided right then and there to stay mad forever. He couldn't hurt me. He didn't have the power. I was going to make damn sure he knew it. I hold the Olympic medal for holding a grudge. Let him come near me and I would jump on him like a damn banshee and take part of his neck out. Try me. I worked myself up into a damn fine fit when I saw him. The patrolmen were stunned. I did good job of scaring them, too. I think I have been mad ever since.

We slid into his car for what I hoped would be five hours of blessed silence. It wasn't ten minutes later, he told me that I would not graduate with my class. He was going to send me off to a place in Raleigh to have my baby. I was back in la-la land. Thank heaven. I thought I had lost my mind. Now I was sure. What baby? Whose? What fun did I miss?

Since I didn't know what the hell he was talking about, I decided not to join in the monologue. Apparently my dearest of brothers, Jimmy, heard I was pregnant by the guy who got Letty pregnant. But, not me. Daddy wanted me to enjoy the anguish, his word, of ballooning up in front of my friends until I was five months along. Then he was going to send me away, just before graduation, to one of those "homes" for "bad" girls to have their baby in secrecy. He wanted to wait until I started to show so I could experience the embarrassment I was putting him through. Oh joy! At least I got to put him through something. Too bad it couldn't be a wringer. What's that thing they put your head through and then slice it off? Oh, a guillotine. Maybe I could put him through that thing. I kept my mouth shut. The whole ride home. I started to live inside myself. You can do that, you know.

I was not pregnant. I was the only one of these jokers who knew it. I might have told Daddy had he asked, but I doubt it. Let him have his fun. As a matter of fact, I'd not had enough real juice in life yet to get pregnant. Not getting pregnant had been a goal of mine since childhood when Mama first explained sex to me. She made it clear if I got pregnant, I would be stuck in Carteret County the rest of my life. Probably slinging fish or having five kids while my husband ran on me. I wanted to be shot out of there like I was in a cannon first chance I got. I heard from somewhere that I had a cherry and by God, I planned to hang onto that thing until I was ready to get rid of it. Whatever it was.

When we got back to Carteret County, Daddy took me to this god awful orange bedroom. You would never believe how orange, people. Either Joanie or Daddy had been expecting me and had gone to the trouble of decorating (?) the bedroom. I would rather live in a hovel than four walls of orange, with a orange comforter and orange sheets. Somebody find me a torch, please. This man did not know me at all. That's what Joanie and Daddy said they thought I would like. Yep, Joanie, Mama's old friend from the hairdressing days. This was gonna be difficult.

One big happy family. In spite of what I thought of the decor, you couldn't get me out of that orange room with a crane. I learned to become solitary to the max. I became a reader of the finest magnitude. Jane Austen, Edith Wharton, O Henry. Things like "Little Women." Why not? I was one. I read with a vengeance. I read everything I could get my hands on. The only good eye, the right one, flew back and forth like a typewriter platen. I felt like a cyclops. Only the starving need for food got me out of that bedroom. If you whistled for me to let me know dinner was ready, I might have come out or might not have. I might as well read as much as I could at home because I knew Daddy would not pay for me to go to college. Jimmy, yes. Me, no. I am a female. English was what was going to get me to college. That and a program they had in North Carolina to help the disabled. I was legally blind in both eyes. That little defect and all that reading was the answer to my prayers. I was a disabled person, but I could get to college. How great was that?

Oh, they still thought I was pregnant. I guess. I hadn't bothered to tell them I wasn't. I didn't give a rat's ass what they thought. That orange bedroom could have caused a miscarriage. I've hated orange since. Eventually, Jimmy and Daddy figured it out. Nobody mentioned it again. I am sure Daddy could have chewed nails since he spread it all over town. I never gained weight, I lost weight. I sent them a father's day card around the time I was supposed to drop the little sucker into the world. I was scarred for life by this crap. Jimmy probably sweated condoms for days thinking he'd gotten another girl knocked up. Notice I said "another girl." Daddy was fixed so I am sure he didn't worry.

Damn it all, I missed Mama. The bad and the good. I missed all of it. Daddy made sure I knew she was in a home for alcoholics in Maryland. I didn't care where she was as long as she was alive. That way, I could at least hope I would see her again. Make her proud of me some day. I felt good that Crystal got to her in time. Here, I knew where I stood. Outside the family. Jimmy was at East Carolina with his buddy, Ernie. Other than the fact that Daddy insisted we eat at the dinner table, and Jackie made good tea, I was left alone. I didn't talk. We ate together only on nights he didn't have meetings. Yeah right. Meetings. Was Joanie naive or what? I finally realized she actually believed him. What was she thinking? It was hard to like her at first and it took a long time. She truly regretted what had happened to Mama and us, but she never discussed it with Daddy around. And, damn it all, she made the best damn tea I ever tasted. That's how she got through my defenses. Tea, for Christ's sake.

Most of the time, it was Joanie, my books and me. I would still go out. As always, I was still dancing. All the time. It was an outlet and I loved it. I would go and dance every song all night with a hundred different guys. We didn't even know each other's names and didn't care. We just wanted to dance. It was allowed for girls to just walk up and grab a guy who danced the way they wanted to. Some girls didn't like it, but that was their problem, not mine. I'm gone after the song. I am not after any girl's guy, believe me. This beach can manufacture some amazing bitches. And they are in your face bitches. Some would walk right up to me, not knowing me, and ask if I knew my Daddy was a legend. A legend, my aching ass.

HELL HATH NO BOTTOM

Then things went even further to hell. Can you believe it? Daddy decided I couldn't go to the beach (right!). This guy pretended he was concerned with sin. He would let me go to the Teenage Age Club. A clean place where I got thrown out for doing the Twist. The lady who ran it was way too much like Aunt Ella. I knew she was trying to keep it clean, but I was never a bad girl. She said I did it nasty. I did not. I did it just like Chubby did. But, I would go every chance I got even when she would evil eye me. Then I'd grab a ride to the beach and dance til midnight, grab a ride back to the Club and then grab a ride home. During this time, Jimmy and Ernie would come home on weekends and Jimmy would talk about how much he was getting at college. And it wasn't education. But we would dance, a lot. He would always do something to make me mad and I would get in his face right there in front of God and everybody. I had a "do not get on my nerves" sign practically posted on my nose. I literally dared him to piss me off twenty four hours a day. He was scared to death of me and he had good reason. My love for my childhood brother was long gone. One, for being the father of my baby. That's what I would tell him he was because the lie came from him. Jerk. Because buried under all those women he screwed were the five little Jimmies running around with blue eyes. One was a redhead. I would see him from time to time in Beaufort.

Daddy would let Jimmy take me to the beach if he would stay with me. Of course, he would take me to the beach, leave me and go off somewhere with some new cow. At two and three in the morning, I would still be sitting outside the pavilion on the steps all alone except for the drunk high school kids, the drunk Marines and the drunk college kids. Fun ended when the doors shut and he would forget about me. If it wasn't for Ernie, half the time Jimmy would have just gone on home and left me sitting there to get raped. Wade was a cop on the beach. He made sure no one bothered me. He'd check on me every fifteen minutes or so and shake his head that my own damn brother would abandon me. I didn't care. Its not like I expected anything more from him.

These were hard, fighting times. I would always be on my toes, hoping for a fight. People would fight at the beach with whatever they could get their hands on. Fighting dirty was second only to dancing. It wasn't unusual for people to pick up a pool stick with five hundred people cheering them on. Then came the melees. Good Lord Almighty, I do love a melee. Great times. Its like a party. The more the merrier. As long as my ass is out of the way of the swinging, I have always loved a good fight. You never knew what was going to happen from one minute to the next. I could handle myself. Hell, there would be a melee sooner or later. Hell, most of the swinging was way over my head. I always morphed into somebody like Aunt Elly if some guy gave me a hard time. Squat and snarl. Squat and snarl. Worked for me.

One unforgettable night, I was getting ready for the TeenAge Club while Daddy and Joanie were having a fight. I was chewing my gums, just waiting for it to end. It had gone on forever, but Joanie was taking a stand. Maybe a stupid one, but a stand, nonetheless. I couldn't hear anything but the sound and didn't want to. Once you have heard as many of these fights as I have, you lose interest in the context. Well, out the Master from Hell came. We jumped in his Caddy to head for the Club. He told me he was moving out. Oh, great. I'd only been there four months. He was going to live with his folie bergere girlfriend. I had seen her in church with him a couple of times. Red hair out to here kind of sleazy female. First pew. Jesus. What a piece of shit he was. Did I know her name? No. Did I give a shit what her name was? No.

So, ok. I got to live with Joanie all by myself. Great. Daddy moved out. I'd miss him, the piece of shit. Jimmy was gone most of the time since he couldn't put on his big dick show with Daddy not there. Daddy was gone all the time except when he wanted to come home for a "good time." He knew Joanie would give him some hoping he would come back. Fine. Lord knows I was going to miss him. My ass. What I was going to miss was a chance to kill him. Bummer.

A really cool thing happened right around this point in my life. Life did that for me. Threw me little joy buds. MaryBeth had gone around the bend. Daddy had paid her to get married, but it didn't work out. I didn't mean that was cool, just what happened after that. She had run from her husband and kids and went right around the mental bend. She had gone back to being a flower child, her favorite thing, and all the benefits therein. She got in trouble and after three years, despite her wailing, they paroled her to Daddy. She'd seen a psychiatrist who told them not to do it, but they did it anyway. It was a mess getting ready to happen. Was no one listening? Did anyone ever? I figured Marybeth told them one of her stories, and I'm sure they truly enjoyed it. She had gotten so bad she was telling people Daddy molested her. Darling, Daddy didn't have to molest women. Even I admitted that. End result was they stuck a wild mare with a walking, talking bastard. Hell was sure to fly. The good times were sure to return. Yee-ha.

What I truly liked about MaryBeth was she was different. She didn't just cause trouble. She carried it around with her like a suitcase. She'd come up with shit nobody else would ever think of. She'd come up with a story and then dive right into it like it was water. Splash around, you know? She never realized it was the gift of story-telling. To her, it was merely a lie. She could have run with it, had she known. One of my favorites was the time she came flying into the driveway in Daddy's Caddy. Right away, you knew there was going to be trouble because there was no way in hell that man would let her have his pride and joy. Joanie wasn't home when MaryBeth came banging on the door, screaming and freaking out. I opened the door and she came tearing into the house, carrying on about Daddy being after her. Who would have ever thought that Daddy would actually want his Caddy back, for Heaven's sake? Did she think he would give it to her? Mr Generosity? She soaked up trouble like she was a mop. That's my girl. I took her upstairs to the living room and told her to hide behind the ugly surround sofa they had. I'd handle it. Let him try to get past me. This was chance to screw with his head a little. I lived for these moments. Gimme, God. Please, please.

Here came Daddy, all pissed off, with gravel being spit all over the place as he slid coming into the driveway and when he braked. He was driving folie bergere's car. You knew he was pissed. Yee-ha. Good times are about to be had by all. Me, for sure. He rushed the door not expecting me to stop him or expecting to push me aside and take over, as was his way, but I had already gotten my hands on that shotgun of his. He hadn't kept it loaded, but I did. I was not afraid of burglars or rapists, I wanted to have an opportunity to pop his ass one if I ever got the chance. I wasn't going to lose that by stopping and asking him to be my target until I got the gun loaded. No sirree..I want to move right into it if I could. So, to get his attention, I pointed the gun in his face. Only so he could see it, you know. I pointed out he lost the house in the divorce (nudge, nudge). He was fit to be tied and I was the girl to do it. When I didn't back down, he finally backed off, still hollering, demanding to know where she was. I told him she took off across the golf course. We lived on the sixteenth green. Off he went in his precious little tennis whites, fat butt and skinny legs flapping in the breeze, looking for his long lost girl child. Not to mention the keys to his car. Which she still had on her. Sure enough, his faithful house bitch charged me next. Sorry, I didn't want to mislead you. I was talking about his folie bergere female; expecting to come in and look for MaryBeth. I had that gun by my side and suggested, rudely, that she might want to wait in the car. Or-a else-a. She had no business on Jackie's property and if she got on my nerves, I would make damn sure the gun went off accidently. She might loose some of that ugly hair. I could also have her arrested. It probably wouldn't have been for the first time, but it would have been my first time and that was good enough for me. She stomped back to her car, grumbling about bad manners. Bad manners. She was one to talk. She was out there screwing another woman's husband and she thought I had bad manners. Daddy came limping back to the house. Red faced and sweating. You could tell he was not quite sure if I was a liar, but since everybody else in the family was, there was a good chance I was. But he was really not in a position to do much about it since he was ready to die from heat stroke, and I still had the shotgun, so he went back to his car all red faced and pissed, grumbling under his breath. Too bad it wasn't his last one.

After they left, I got MaryBeth from behind the couch. I had to ask her, other than steal his car, what else had she done to make him mad? I figured it might be more than one thing because she wasn't the type to limit her possibilities. She said she didn't know what he was so mad about. Other than his Caddy, she only took his underwear. Underwear? What in hell did she want with his damn underwear? She was kind enough to explain. Daddy was the same size as her boyfriend. She actually wanted her boyfriend's dick in the same underpants Daddy's dick had been in. Gross. I loved it. It was so expressive of the deep bowl of crap I was born in. Thanks for the memories, guys.

I was only seventeen, believe it or not. One year older than most of my class because of the October birthday thing that was one more ignorant law in North Carolina. Jimmy was still in college, believe it or not. His girlfriend was from Rocky Mount and I was her best friend. I had been to Rocky Mount with her a couple of times and found out her Dad was bad as mine. In all ways. One thing I did was beg Jimmy not to knock her up. I begged often. I told him if he got Jessie pregnant, I would shove his balls into his intestines and he would have to have sex through his navel the rest of his life. I don't know if that's anatomically possible, but he wasn't that smart so I wasn't worried about him figuring it out.

I was stuck dating a guy named Mason, one of my least favorite dates, who was a highway patrolman. I still had the law thing in the back of my mind, but I knew I could never make it to law school. It was 1966. You didn't go to law school when you had no hope for a future. Mason was an ass. He spent all his time trying to catch me speeding. And not succeeding magnificently, I might add. He was tall, spindly and the only guy I could go out with without an argument from Daddy. But, the guy could kiss like a movie star. Only redeeming quality. I think he thought Mason might take me away, but no chance of that.

After we had been dating about six months, I went over to the John Yancey, a motel where Mason lived. We were supposed to get together to go to the beach. By then, I had my little yellow Volkswagen convertible, a gift from Joanie for being the only one in the family who didn't leave town when she finally took Daddy to court. When I pulled up, lo and behold, there was he was.. with two women, one on each arm. He had his back to the parking lot so he didn't know I saw him. These women were two low rents. They did everybody on the beach. They were in skimpy bathing suits on the balcony with him. Breasts everywhere, as were his hands. He would kiss and squeeze one slut and then do the same to the other. I'm sure it was male heaven but he had told me he wasn't seeing anybody else. If I had known he had kissed lips that only God knew where they'd been, I wouldn't have gone near him.

I lost it. I let loose a holler for all time. Big one. One big "Hey, you. Mason. Turn around. Your ex-girlfriend's here." Royally pissed. I tried to limit the times in my life when I indulged in the Female Hissy Fit, but believe me, if one came on me there were no holds barred. I was deep into it in a second. I wasn't even out of the car yet when I started screaming like a banshee. However, I was coming out of it, around it, and over it. I have discovered I crouch when in a hissy fit and my lips pull back from my teeth and I snarl. Pretty picture, huh? Anybody see any evidence of insanity here? If so, sorry. I just cannot stand guys like this. If I got stuck with one and found out about it, I was no longer required to be a lady. These are my rules. Mason jumped two feet off the ground and you would have thought his arms fell off, they came off the girls' shoulders so fast. He spun around, panicked and herded the girls into the motel room like they were cattle, as they kinda were with their udders bouncing like that. I ran upstairs to the room. A lady would have left, but hey? What fun is that? When I got to the door, he had locked it and that made me even madder. I hate it when big boys are scared of little girls. I pounded on the door, kicked it and screamed if he didn't open it, I would take that Volkswagen right through the motel and run his ass down. He must have figured I might do it. He opened the door, but he had shut the girls up in the bathroom, then locked the door so I couldn't get to them. You could hear them crying. Poor cows. Once he let me in the room, I spat on someone for the first time in my life and, by God, it felt good. He got off easy. I pushed him down on the bed and snarled that's where he wanted to be so he should get his skinny ass there. I got his gun off the dresser, which scared the hell out of him. I took it with me and threw it in the water when I went over the bridge. I slung it with all my might. I don't know what he told his commander and didn't care. Fart face.

    I finally graduated from high school. Damn, about time. I attended my graduation with no shoes on and the tallest guy in our class escorted me. Again, the best thing about my class was no one appeared to look down on me. Not noticeably anyway. Then I proceeded to get the hell out of Carteret County as fast as I could. Unpregnant, too. I started summer school at East Carolina in Greenville, the same college Jimmy went to. He was now a Theta Chi. It was a Registered Drunk Frat and each and every one of the guys was gaga gorgeous. Every damn one. I thought I had died and gone to heaven when Jimmy got me a date with one until the guy threw up on me around eight o'clock that night. I walked two miles back to the dorm. Jimmy couldn't take me because he was drunk and had already wrecked his car once. I couldn't find Ernie and didn't really want to. I liked Ernie and wasn't in the mood to find out something I shouldn't. I still had respect for Ernie and didn't want to lose it. I had respect for so damn few people. I think that was the last time I even saw Jimmy at school. Yet, I was still friends with his girlfriend from Rocky Mount, who was going to Peace College in Raleigh. I was lonely but I was out of Morehead. I figured I could get through college in three years max.

    Mason kept trying to get me back. Why, I don't know. I'd make a date with him so he'd have to drive the two hours to Greenville and not be there when he got there. He had pissed me off with the udder thing. I could stay pissed off better than anybody I knew. I believed in grudges and get backs. Ask anybody.

    Of course, I was still shagging. I eventually ended up with a whole set of dancing buddies and some friends from the dorm. The girls from the dorm and I would often go to the Coach and Four, a great little club downtown. We were too young to drink, but old enough to dance. To get there, we'd have to cut behind the library which was on a steep hill. Cars had to struggle to get up the incline and then have to park to face going down or they'd roll right off the hill trying to maneuver the car the right way. We'd have to run down the hill because it was too steep to walk down. We decided to back up and then run down as fast as we could, sincerely hoping a car wasn't coming. A great fright. Just great. When we came back, we would back away from the incline and act like we were trains, running forward and then back again getting up momentum. Looking like idiots, but who cared? We were college kids. Our arms would be churning like wheels on a train because now we had to run up down the hill, then run up fast. One of the girls we called Janice Blillis. we made everybody's name start with a "B". Silly nonsense. She was tall, slender, funny as hell and way sexy. I loved her to death. She was a hoot.

Coming back from the Coach one day, we started our trains going. Arms pumping around, running back and forth when off went Janice like a rocket in heat. She ran down the straight up the hill and OOPS..right up the back end of a Volkswagen that was backing up. Her skirt had flown over her head and everything sexy about her was right there in plain sight for all to see. Especially if a guy was sitting in that Volkswagen when she sprawled over his back window. Yep, sure was. He got out of the car to see if the rest of her looked as good as the view from the rear view mirror. Butt up, she did. Well, her fine Southern ass did the deed. He fell in lust. Janice was history in five minutes flat.

ANYBODY LOSE A WEIGHT LIFTER?

One night a bunch of us got together to dance. We went to a large club I had never been to. Once you got in, you went down about five steps. To the left was this long bar that took up one whole side of the building. It was huge. Behind it stood three of the best looking men I had ever seen. They were all weight lifters. You could kinda tell. Good Lord, just give me one. I looked at one of the girls I was with and said, " I don't care which one, but one of them is going to be mine. Soon." And I meant it.

I always preferred to pick my men. I was dancing at the time with Tommy Jefferson from Burlington. What a super guy. He was so sweet and thoughtful. He danced very much like a ballroom dancer. You were always going around and under. It was beautiful to watch and do. Unfortunately, I had no interest in falling for him. I needed somebody witty who could put me in my place if I needed it, and Tommy was way too nice for that. I eyeballed those weight lifters and flirted with them all night. I got all my Mama flirt mojo going. By the end of the night I knew where they hung out on campus, and I planned to be there the next day. They were all seniors but if they thought they were getting rid of pesky, little ol' me they were wrong. Dante won me. Apparently, they discussed who was going to take me out with Dante the most aggressive. I was ok with it. He was not a dancer, but you sure could look at him all night. Dante knew how to have fun and bring everybody into it with him. He was a hoot. I adored him.

    I was suddenly running with an older, more sophisticated crowd. These guys had been around and they knew women. A lot of them. They had their own house and each guy had his responsibilities. Each had their own cars, jobs and were grown up in a way I was not used to. Even though Dante was the one I was dating, Ted always flirted with me and I had a hard time taking my eyes off him. He dated the most beautiful women. You could see they were all over him, but he wouldn't stick. All the girls in my dorm thought I had died and gone to heaven and I was damn sure I had. I still went out with my friends, and Dante dated other girls, but he seemed to enjoy my company and kept asking me out. He knew he wasn't going to get any but he was great about asking me out. I really liked him but I wasn't in love. It was a good thing, too, because he was graduating in January. I had been dating him about six months when he left. I was truly surprised when he asked me to go with him. I didn't have a clue. I figured he wanted to take a buddy with him when he left. Of course, I said no. I figured it was all over with the guys when Dante graduated.

    I went home for the January break. Before I left, Ted smiled and kissed me on the cheek. He looked into my eyes for a long time. It was easy to look back. It broke my heart. I felt like it was for the last time. I really liked Ted. A lot. The goodbye with Dante had been sad, not shattering. I knew shatter when I saw it. But, I was going to miss the guys.

    A couple of weeks into the break, the phone rang. Joanie answered it, looked at me and said it was a man, for me. That was weird itself. To my huge surprise, it was Ted. He told me he needed to tell me he was in love with me. He didn't want to wait until I got back to school to say so. He wasn't willing to let me come back to college and take the chance of my finding someone else without my knowing how much he wanted to be with me. He told me he almost came to blows with Dante when Dante told him he was going to ask me to go home with him. He told Dante how he felt and asked him could they stay friends? He knew Dante would be coming back from time to time for parties and reunions. Dante told Ted I turned him down flat and if Ted wanted to be with me, there would be no hard feelings. They both knew my feelings for Dante didn't run deep. The sweetheart told Ted that he and I would make a great couple. I was floored. I could not believe these two hunks actually discussed me in those terms. Me!

I was honest with Ted and told him I could never get serious about Dante. He was playful, not romantic. Ted was very romantic and manly and I was so attracted to him. But, he was always with beautiful women. I never thought I could compete with them. Ted said he brought them home hoping Dante would get attracted to one and leave me alone. Ted and I made a date to meet at the dorm on the day I came back. He said he couldn't wait. For the rest of the break I was on cloud nine. I couldn't believe I was going to get two out of three. Good Grief. Me? I and really wasn't interested in number three...too negative.

These were great guys. That's how I meant the two out of three comment. Each had wonderful qualities. For once, I wasn't being flippant. However, I had a feeling deep inside me that Ted was going to be something special. He was a something special kind of guy. Ted had been willing to show his feelings, not macho like Dante. He was gorgeous, sweet and very sexy. He had a body to die for, forming a "V" from his waist to his shoulders. He had a very strong back and I have always been attracted to that. Go figure. Ted was blessed with very, very soft green eyes with a laughing twinkle in them. A gentle smile, soft, light brown hair and just the right size for me. He was one of those rare guys who knew everything he was doing and where he was going in life. No mistakes. If he wanted me, and I had been told he wanted me, there was no reason to hide. I was a goner. Nobody had ever asked my permission to love me before. The man knew me. He knew me, and still loved me. I fell in love for the first time in my life. I was twenty and I was in heat. Finally.

I got back about two in the afternoon. Ted was at my dorm within fifteen minutes. He was wearing a heavy coat because it was so cold. We drove to the football field where some guys were scrimmaging and parked where we could watch. After cutting the heat up, he turned in the seat, looked at me and took my hand. He pulled me gently across the seat and wrapped me in the coat with him. The warmth from his body made my eyes roll back in my head. Not something I was used to. Not a word was said. I had never been so content. I turned around in the seat so I could look at him. He had the softest, most beautiful smile and it was there for me to see. He was content as well. Those gentle eyes told me everything. He looked down at me and said, "Finally." That was it. I was his. It was the most natural thing in the world. No turmoil, no fussing, no screaming. No questions. He accepted me the way I was and still wanted me. This time it was different. Just Ted and I. Something deep inside me settled. Sitting there, feeling safe and warm, I thought of that song by Etta James, "At Last." She sings, "At last, my love has come along...and life is like a song." That's how it felt.

We had a wonderful time together. We couldn't take our hands off each other, but in a good way. If we were in the same room, we were touching each other. Needless to say, everybody made fun of us. When Dante came for the first time, it was clear he was happy for us. My twenty first birthday was looming and I was figured it was time to tell everybody about the phone call to Mama. So, we had a party. I had decided to have a "Losing My Virginity Party". Ted didn't argue..

HIGHEST AND BEST USE OF A VOLKSWAGEN

First, I called Mama, who was doing well in a home for alcoholics in Baltimore. She'd been there over three years and was finally acting like the old Mama I loved. She was happily working in a cafeteria in the hospital. Mama was always about food; the woman could really cook. She wasn't making much money and didn't want to come home because of the bad memories. I didn't care that she wasn't here. She was alive and we had reconnected. With me and Mama, nothing else mattered.

I told her I knew what she had been doing when we had the conversation when I was a 13 year old tomboy. The one when she told me to go ahead, have sex and then call her. It seemed light years away. She was trying to use that phone call to deter me until I either fell in love or was old enough to accept what I was doing. She desperately wanted me to go to college and knew I never would if that mess got started. I'd told her when I was eighteen that when I got twenty one, if I hadn't had sex by then, I didn't care if I had to drag a drunk off the street, I was going to get laid. I knew I wouldn't. She knew I wouldn't. I never dreamed at thirteen that it would take so long, but it really wasn't difficult since I stayed a tomboy for most of it. My tomboy parts shed like leaves once I was with Ted. The time was right.

We had one hell of a party. A Carol was going to lose her-virginity-party. We sang it out loud. A bunch of us who ran together went to a restaurant first, where I lost my only contact in my spaghetti. I didn't wear two since one eye didn't work anyway. What the hell. At least when I had sex, I'd be able to say I couldn't see what I was doing. I drank my first Michelob. Three, in fact. Then we went dancing. Ted didn't dance, but he liked to watch me because I loved it so. He said he fell in love with me that first night at the club when I was flirting with all of them. He just wasn't forward enough so Dante snatched me up right under his nose. He decided to wait for me. God love him. I wasn't really dancing all that well because I didn't have my contact and couldn't see. All in all, it was like an engagement party. We had a tremendously good time, then we all went back to the house so I could get laid. So weird. Everybody cheered us on when we finally went into the bedroom. We fell on the bed, laughing. There was no embarrassment, no fumbling or timidity. The loving just came naturally. Everybody's first time should be like that.

I called Mama at three o'clock in the morning. I had to talk one of the clinic people into going to get her. The person with whom I spoke had to be a big, black woman. I could hear her booming belly laugh when I explained why I called. Served Mama right. When she got on the phone, I said simply, "I just got laid." She waited a second and finally she said, "How was it?" I couldn't believe it. That's what the girls in the dorm were going to ask. I couldn't believe she wrapped eight years of hunching into eight words. One word per year. I was speechless. Mama said, quietly, that she wanted to be the first person I talked to if it was bad, like if I was raped or forced. Or, if I made a bad choice. If it was right, she wanted to be the first person to know I was with the right man. I was. I told Mama, "It was worth it the wait." There was this long silence where we again felt that connection we always had. Then we cried. She was wonderful. I knew I could love Ted even better because I learned how to love her in spite of everything.

I'd made it to twenty one the night of my first loving. Unfortunately, time didn't stop right there. Why did things have to be so hard? How did so many people go through life without realizing that people like me exist? A disaster magnet. Everything was a struggle. People had normal lives with normal families.

Things fell right into place for them. They didn't realize there were people out there born to have to struggle for everything. Your's truly had certainly been chosen to fight the good fight. Good things didn't last. You could count on it.

BRACE FOR BATTLE

If you remember, I mentioned my best friend, Jessie, was dating my brother, Jimmy. There was no way in hell this could be construed as a good thing. In reality, it was a very cataclysmic bad thing. She and I went on and on about it every week because all he was interested in was running other women. I'd never understood why women would want a man like him. Too much Mama in me, I guess. As much as I was in Jessie's face about it, I was in Jimmy's. Why go with a girl who's a hundred and twenty miles away when you had all the loose women you could want right here? He obviously wanted to have his girlfriend and the running, too. Like Daddy. Well, that's how it looked to me, but what did I know?

One night..one very unforgettable night, my phone rang about three in the morning. I knew something was wrong. It was Jessie. She was pregnant. I asked how pregnant? Don't correct me. We talked like that here. She was seven months pregnant. She had been hiding it by not eating, and she was a skinny thing to begin with. Jimmy was definitely not dating her for her chest size. She had not gained any weight the times I had seen her, but I hadn't seen her for the last couple of months. With her in Raleigh and me in Greenville, it was getting harder and harder for us to get together. Any time we tried, something would come up. I hated to say it, but we were moving away from each other. Not away from the friendship, but away from the closeness we had when we only had each other. I had Ted. He was worth everything to me. Ted was not a running around kind of guy so I didn't have her problems. Now, kids were having sex at thirteen years old. I was still in the cherry tree at thirteen. I didn't know what a cherry was a thirteen. Ted had become more important to me than Jessie, but I needed to support her if she needed me. I'd never been less than loyal to someone who put up with my crap and was still my friend.

I asked her what she wanted to do. It wasn't a surprise when she said she wanted to marry Jimmy. I hung up and called Jimmy. He already knew she was pregnant, of course, but wasn't about to tell me. He was still afraid of me at twenty two. After the call from Jessie, he had a right to be. I laid him out. I can be pretty much like Mama when I get mad. Don't test me. You'd lose. Of all things, he said he wanted to marry her. I knew right then that this was about presenting Daddy with a grandchild. A stamp of approval Jimmy's manhood. I thought Daddy would shoot him, but what did I know? I could only hope.

As always, the planning was up to me. Jimmy was helpless and Jessie was sick because she wasn't eating. If she ate, she stuck her finger down her throat to throw up. I'd never heard of that. I couldn't believe it when she said she hadn't even been to a doctor. I was very worried so I decided to move fast and get her back to Morehead where I could get my eyes on her.

I found out they could go to Little River, South Carolina to get married. In North Carolina, you had to have the approval of the parents. Jessie was only seventeen and I knew her Dad would throw her out when he found out. No doubt. I was pretty sure that was one reason she hadn't told anybody. I went out and got the rings. I set the time for Jimmy to pick Jessie up at Peace College to head for Little River. It was real important to me that Daddy not find out because, grandkid or not, Daddy didn't want Jimmy married unless it was to somebody important. Jessie was as much a nobody as any of Daddy's kids, and Jimmy knew it. If he actually did get married, without Daddy knowing it, he'd better bring along a papoose. Preferably a boy. He'd better have proof when Daddy went after him. Given that, at least, Daddy would not throw them out. He'd make their life hell and play that two hundred a month game he got such a kick out of, but he would not throw them out. There were two reasons; one, Jimmy was a male child and two, Daddy wanted to keep sitting on that first pew. Even high society in Carteret County (what a chuckle that brings out of me) frowned on disposing of a male grandchild. Even if he turned out an idiot with an uncontrollable dick defect.

Off Jimmy went, ring in hand with me glaring at him. My fingers were crossed. My toes were crossed. Hell, my eyes were crossed. Mixed messages bounced around in me. I really didn't want him married to Jessie, but I wanted her to be happy.. If she thought Jimmy could do that for her, fine.. Most of all, I hoped Daddy wouldn't find out before it was a done deal. What planet was I on? Jimmy got to Raleigh and before he even picked her up, he called Daddy. What a unbelievable gut-wipe that guy was. If I'd have gotten to him, he wouldn't have had a dick left.

After talking to Daddy, Jimmy picked her up and took her to Rocky Mount to get her things. To her Dad, for Christ's sake. Told him everything. Good move, fart face junior. Out she went. Clothes and all. She was thrown out with Jimmy watching and sick to boot. I was beside myself. I always liked that term because it draws such a weird mental picture. I had so much anger in me that it defied description. He was lucky I couldn't get my hands on him. In three hours, though, his ass was going to be mine. I was going to Morehead. Somebody was going to have to deal with me.

I had to say Ted thought this was all very interesting. He did not pass judgement on my behavior and was behind me all the way. He didn't particularly like dickheads, either. Apparently one had taken away his first love, so he was prejudiced against them.

I headed home in my little yellow Volkswagen convertible. Three hours passed and there they were. I couldn't believe what I saw when I took that first look at Jessie. It looked like she had died, but her body was too weak to figure it out. I couldn't believe Jimmy didn't see it, but intelligence was never his strong suit. I totally forgot about Jimmy and put Jessie in my bed. I'm sure the orange didn't help her nausea. Whatever. I asked her who her doctor was and why had he let her get in this condition? She still didn't have a doctor. She had never been checked. Jimmy had not been up to see her in two months and she'd been terribly depressed. She had gained just enough weight that I could tell she was pregnant. But not by much. I made her eat, then let her sleep because she was so exhausted. I stomped downstairs to ruin Jimmy's day. He was gone. I waited. I figured I would get my chance to tear his throat out if I was just patient. I had read a lot of books with my cyclops eye and knew many interesting ways to ruin someone's good mood. The good news was I did not care if anybody knew it was me. A new twist in planning a crime. The cops would love it. However, it is important to understand I was not in a hissy fit. Yet.

He never came back. I mean it...he never came back. Can you believe it? Three weeks later, he had still not come back. I had taken Jessie to a doctor and he told us gruesome news. The lack of food and care had prevented the baby from thriving. It caused the baby to perish. In her, and it might kill her if she didn't take care of herself. She wouldn't. Her spirit was completely dead. Jessie was too weak to even care. Her Dad had thrown her out and Jimmy deserted her. The doctor gave her medicine but it was useless because she wouldn't take it. It was a terrible, terrible thing to have to watch. My rage grew to mammoth proportions. I no longer cared how I was going to kill him. But, not yet. I wanted him to come see her. She wanted it so badly. Well, getting him back was my next job. No matter what. I had to talk to Jimmy.

I jumped into my little yellow Volkswagen with a black convertible top and headed to the beach. Daddy and Julie, the folie bergere slut, were living on a houseboat I heard had a bed shaped like a heart, for pity's sake. How many normal people have to picture that in their minds when they think of their father? However, I figured I might find boneless, spineless there. I pulled up behind Jimmy's Buick. Julie's Pontiac and Daddy's Cadillac were around the side. I got out and knocked on the door. A simple procedure that produced no results. I could hear people in there, but nobody would answer the door. I screamed, "I am five feet tall, people! What are you afraid of?" Pissed me off. Well, this went on for about twenty minutes until I finally got the shits of it. Now, I was mad. 'Bout time. I jumped back into my car and headed back to the house. I had a plan, and they were not going to like it. I was. Daddy's good old shotgun. That would work. Worked before.

I went back to the house, took the shotgun down from the perch above the den door, and picked up the phone. I called the highway patrol dispatch, and told them who I was. I then proceeded to say they needed to call Mason to tell him I had a gun and was headed to Daddy's. The rest of Daddy's day didn't look bright. Then, I hung up. I knew Mason would bust his highway patrol ass to get to Daddy's, and he would bring plenty of reinforcements if he thought I was mad. He knew a gun, Daddy and me were not a combination for fun and games. Somebody could get hurt. I could only hope.

I had no intentions of telling Ted what I was doing. I didn't want him to know what a freakoid I was from time to time. I really had no intentions of hurting anybody. How many psychotics can say that? With a straight face, anyhow. Insanity, where? Did you see it? Whatever. I definitely intended to get somebody's attention. Fast and hard, if necessary. One of those people was going to talk to me or I just might lose control and run that Volkswagen right through that houseboat; heart shaped bed and all. The Hissy Fit was on me. Yee-ha.

I pulled up behind Jimmy's car again. I looked at it for a moment and decided, "What the hell?" I angled my car right behind it. Crept up behind it nice and slow. The creep was the part that fit my car to that Buick's ass-end and allowed me to slow–ly push it into the water. Hell, it was too good to pass up. What are they going to do? Arrest me? Tell the courts that all these grown ups were too scared to come out and face Daddy's dwarf baby child? They didn't even know I had a shotgun. By the way, I didn't realize that cars bubble when they go down. Cool. The last thing I saw was Jimmy's paperwork from East Carolina floating around in the back window. It ended up with the tail sticking out of the water. Cars look kinda stupid that way. Especially Buicks.

Ho-ha. Got somebody's attention with the car dip. I could have pushed the Buick onto the front deck of the houseboat and sank it if I had wanted to. The next thing I saw was somebody peeking out the window. I could hear the muffled disbelief. Hell, the houseboat was rocking. There were at least three mad people in there, but they couldn't touch the mad person who, slowly, reached into the car and got the shotgun out. Believe me, I did it slow. I wanted them to enjoy the view. I wanted to give them time to lose their jaws, maybe their bowels. Poetic, don't you think? I lovingly put it against the side of the car. Where they could see it.

Again, I didn't plan to hurt anybody. But, so often plans go awry. Hopefully. In spite of my wishes, my hopes were dashed. Mason came flying into the parking lot with that patrol car like a man on a mission Blue lights flashing, tires screeching and two other patrolmen tearing butt behind him. Mason was coming on strong because he knew what my hissy fits looked like. He hit the brakes and damn near skidded right into that shotgun. Then he tore his six foot, skinny ass frame out of the car. The first thing he asked me was had I done anything to cause the be-ass-hind end of Jimmy's car to be sticking out of the water. I told him I had pushed it into the water with my trusty VW. Was that against the law? Where was it written that you can't push family's car into the water if you want to? Hell, why not? Had nothing else to do while I WAITED FOR THEM to answer the door. Just playing around, you know. Just a joke? Snicker, snicker. Oh? Is it possible? He didn't understand our particular family? Well! Did he possibly think Jimmy had the guts to take me on? Or Daddy, for that matter? If they did, they would have the time of their life, because I would tear their damn throats out. After all, they should have answered the door the first time I knocked. Nicely. I was going for the "they asked for it" defense. Didn't care if it didn't work.

Mason watched me expand like Mama used to. I don't know how, but we grew when you wanted us to stay small, you know? I made sure Mason knew damn well I was going to get somebody's attention. Some damn body was coming out of that houseboat so I could talk to them about what was going on with Jessie or I was going through that houseboat. Jimmy had to come back. Soon. She might die in my bed. She refused to go to the hospital. He had to come back and get her to a hospital. I told Mason they might not realize I was there. Smirk. Maybe they didn't hear me blowing the horn. Everybody else did, because they were watching. Maybe they didn't hear me pound on the door. Maybe they didn't see me push the Buick into the water. Admittedly, pushing the car into the water made little to no noise. Maybe they didn't know I had a shotgun. Maybe I was too short. Who knew? Who gave a shit? Perhaps they were just stupid and needed lessons on how to open the damn door. Maybe they'd see or hear Mason. Somebody's coming out. One way or another. My jaw set. Bring it on. Did I still love Jimmy, yes. Was I mad? Oh yeah.

This was all crap. I told him about Jessie. I watched that face harden as I was telling him. Ass that he had been, I thanked the Lord in his Heaven. I had an ally. And, he carried a gun he could use if he wanted to. An honest to God law enforcement officer on my side. Yee-ha!

He went to the door and pounded on it himself. The big, strong men in my family sent out Julie to be their representative. How quaint. Good. I would like to take a little piece off her amazingly big butt. Perhaps she thought she could handle little ol' me. Not in this lifetime. I would get in her face and tear her nose off if she thought I needed a good talking to. Nothing she could say could save her. I was hissying big time. Mason was tap dancing trying to get this settled. He knew a hissy fit wasn't something he wanted to be in the middle of. Down South, we call it a hissy fit because that's sorta like the noise we make when we suck air through our teeth when we are trying to get enough air in our lungs for the expansion. He told Miss Julie, being polite, one of them needed to talk to me because he had seen one of my hissy fits first hand. I had scared the hell out of him. He didn't think she wanted to see one from a housebat. She could see my face already. Probably not a pretty sight. She started bawling about the Buick and all that crap until Mason got tired of listening to her. That was just redirect stuff and he knew it. She thought she could wear him out and we'd never get to the real problem. Which was Jimmy. He finally looked at her and said, "I'm taking the guys and we're leaving. I suggest one of the people, who call themselves men, come out and talk to this little lady. Otherwise, the other two cars might just get wet. And, if you stand there, watch it and do nothing to stop it? I don't know that I would arrest her You hear me?" I ate it up. Mason had apparently grown some balls. If it wasn't for Ted, I might date the guy again. Ew. Udders. I will always equate Mason with udders. Other than that, some things were definitely swinging my way. There was a possibility I could get a chance to take a swing at somebody. Damn, I wish I had liked baseball. A bat would be really convenient right about then. But, hell, you can use a shotgun for more than shooting. And get away with it. And believe me, I could definitely do that. Showtime.

She went back in grumbling. She kept looking back at me like she wasn't quite sure if I was really dangerous. I was definitely weirded out and liked it. Hell, I felt dangerous. Not much time passed and out came Julie, then Daddy, then Jimmy. And, along came Jane, as they say. One of the women Jimmy ran with from time to time. She was pregnant.

If I had not already lost whatever belief in these jerks I had, it was gone then. I can't even explain how I felt. I felt like I was in a cloud. Things sounded muffled. My head felt like it was under a tremendous amount of pressure. Nobody had to say anything. He had married her. They had on the rings I'd bought for him and Jessie. These people weren't human. All Jimmy could do was mumble he had married her like I couldn't see that for myself. No wonder he didn't want to come out. He was so weak a human being as to tell me Daddy gave him ten thousand dollars to marry her instead of Jessie because she was the daughter of an Army Colonel. He actually said that with Jane standing there listening to him. She heard him say it. She was so stupid she didn't know he insulted her to her face. It's what Daddy wanted. Didn't I get that? It was about Daddy. Nothing was going to get in the way of what Daddy wanted. The ill person in my bed wasn't. They didn't care. They didn't get it. All the fight in me was gone. I felt empty.

When I got home, Jessie wasn't no longer coherent She never knew Jimmy didn't come to see her. She had gone from bad to real bad while I was out trying to teach some morals to my brother. I got her to the hospital but she died two weeks later. Her Daddy didn't even come to see her. Mama sided with Jimmy. Her male child. The son who acted like the man she fought the hard fight against. It made me want to throw up. Excuse me. I meant it did make me throw up. She knew Jessie. Where was the woman I had loved. I went back to East Carolina and vowed never to speak to any of them again. I said I could hold a grudge. I prided myself on knowing right from wrong. That was wrong. I didn't need these people in my life. I didn't mind losing Jimmy, Daddy or anybody. That included Mama. She made her choice. She turned her back on me. It wouldn't happen but once. I turned my back on them all. Big time.

YA' THINK?

I headed back to East Carolina in a funk. Not the laughing happy ol' me. But, I was resilient. I had things to look forward to. I had Ted and a somewhat normal life. I was going to college. I turned my mind back to the things you need to think about if you want a future. Things like, you would think when you go to college that your professors would be smarter than you are. Or, pretend to be. I think they looked in Podunk USA to recruit these guys. Let me tell you about the two most memorable professors I ran into.

I took Psychology. Why wouldn't I? I was interested in finding out why the people in my family were such jerks. Why didn't they act like other people? Then again, maybe they did? Was there evidence of insanity? Was it a gene ball bouncing around in my brain? Could I kill it? Why did I lose it like I did? Was I like them? Would I ruin Ted's life like we had ruined each other's lives in my family? Did we all come from some weird African tribe a hundred years ago? The Manson family, maybe? Was there one single person in my family I thought had some merit? Yes, Crystal. But the question was..whose was she? She couldn't have come from Mama and Daddy. No way.

I did well in Psychology. The first year they teach you. It seemed the second year you taught them. I had spilled my guts. I told that guy everything. Life, Jessie, the shotgun, pushing the car into the water, everything. I can be very direct, so it was easy for me to unload. You probably hadn't noticed. I told him about growing up, the violence. I had to admit, even to him, that I thought the whole kitchen thing was a lot of fun. Still do. That's my story and I'm sticking to it. As his reaction, he tells me I have to take some tests. I might not be good in Psychology. I might be warped. Tests? Me? What could he be thinking? Hell, I knew I was warped. I didn't think I was the issue. You can't tell me there aren't a lot of warped Psychology teachers out there. Just look at the rest of my class. Thumb-suckers, for Christ's sake. What did these professors want? Tests, that's what they wanted. I tried to convince this guy that the sheer fact that I was from Carteret

County made me incurable. It wasn't my fault. But, he didn't want to hear it. So, we headed out for games like having Fun With Rorschach. I tell you, if they didn't see what I saw, they were the problem. To me, it was clear as a bell. That was a fruit eating elephant, swatting flies with his snout, sitting on a toilet. What did these people want? They were supposed to tell me, not the other way around. If they were going to make me do their job, they might be surprised to find out that I intended to screw with their brains. I couldn't help it. It was in my genes. It had to come from somewhere.

We finally made it to where my Professor told me what he thought of me. Psychologically, of course. He thought I was certifiable. Nutty. How rude was that? I knew that. There were things I was supposed to learn myself, but after two years, I didn't get to figure myself out. He was going to do it for me. How sweet.. I was a dangerous, waiting to be cracked open, nut. Great. Here I was, for the first time in my life actually trying to be a normal person, and he thought he could see right through it. It was a facade I was putting on to hide the more frightening me, of course. I had told him that for Christ's sake. I kept waiting for clues, like was I schizo or bi-polar or something, but he just rattled on. Talked about my family practically word for word from what I'd said for years. Then, he popped up with the kicker. Did I know that I was capable of killing my father? Well, hell yes, nincompoop. That took two years to figure out? Did people pay good money for this stuff? No wonder they needed a couch. After listening to these guys, anybody would feel faint. Or want to commit suicide, for sure. I decided I didn't want to think like these guys. It was hard enough thinking my way. Was it wrong to have a damn backbone, people? Fight back? If not, I might as well run out to the highway to lay my ass down so an eighteen wheeler could run over me.

I slunk back to the dorm, feeling terribly misunderstood. There, I was stuck rooming with a very nice, proper girl. Problem was, she was here from another planet, and she was waiting for David. She didn't think she was from another plant, she really was. She knew it's name and where it was. She'd kindly point it out to you if you were interested. She was here only to wait for David. He was coming for her. When he reached her, they would return home. She garbled another language. A whole freaking language, this girl had. Every night she would sit on the window sill and speak to him. Wherever the hell he was. In another language. Normally, I didn't mind but somebody had just told me I had problems. She got A's in Psychology. Go figure. I wished David would come the hell and get her because sometimes I couldn't get any sleep at night. She sang to him. In another language. She sounded like a bird on hash. Sort of like a warbling nightmare. Help me, Lord. I think she took the emerging 60's movement way too close to heart. I often wondered what the sweet smell in the room was. At times I slept so peacefully there. Odd.

Slipping right into my psychological meltdown and my chirping roommate was an eventful encounter with Dr Paul, my Interpretive Literature professor. Wonderful guy. A hoot, really. One of my favorite subjects was Interpretive Literature. As a rule, I enjoyed his interpretations combined with his accent. Some were hilarious. I got some of my best grades in his class and I participated more in my English classes than any other. English was important because it was imperative that I kept my English grades up because of my scholarship. One screw up and I was outta there. He and I usually got along. Most of the time you would find me sitting on the front row, frothing at the mouth striving to say something intelligent. Anything. Trying to find somebody who was willing to interact with me without being an ass. A lot of literature people can be pretty damn huffy, you know.

Unfortunately, on the same day I took that course, I also had history. I had been studying unusually hard for the history exam. Hard. I was having a difficult time because this was the kind of "who did what to whom" memory work I had always hated. But, I desperately needed to pass it. Remember I was a good girl. Truly. I didn't drink, do drugs or run any men. I was with Ted, who was a good influence. Again, I was trying to be normal. That wasn't a struggle for most people. I didn't know why life made it so hard for me to just get by. I couldn't seem to get that damn Down East mouth monster to let me go.

I couldn't stay awake to study for history. I finally asked the window sitter if she'd get me something to help me stay awake. Hell, I meant like No-Doz. She got me four Darvocets. I didn't know what they were so I took all of them about four a.m. to stay awake. I zoned. I didn't know what a zone and I was too zoned out to know if I liked it. I didn't know who I was or care. My roomie called Ted to come check me out, but I wandered onto the campus before he got there. I stumbled into the history class and couldn't answer one single question on the test. Couldn't see any, actually. And, whoa! I didn't give a damn. Then I meandered DRUGGED OUT to Int Lit. I was so zoned, I took the history exam with me when I left. They frown on that at college. That's when the real trouble began. Oh shit time.

Normally, that is, when I was normal, I sat in the front area as mentioned. Not always on the front row, but somewhere near the front. I was so short, nobody could see me if I didn't. I could be back there waving my arms and I didn't know if they could even see my damn, also short, arms. Didn't seem like it. So, I sat up front. Anyhow, on this particular day, I felt really crappy, I think. I had just blown the history exam and I was required to keep my grades up because of the Vocational Rehabilitation Scholarship, too. I loved saying that. It sounded so much more important than because I couldn't see squat. It was easier to achieve that sitting up front. But this day, I think I crawled on both knees to the rear. I felt really, really gross. I wasn't sure if I had an inside to my mouth. It seemed I couldn't control my lips. They went places I couldn't stop them from going. In every direction. Like they do when you bounce them up down and your finger. But, my finger was not involved. You could have stood me up, cut me in half with a chain saw and I wouldn't have felt any worse. A leave me alone and let me die kind of feeling bad.

Dr Paul went into the poem about the father being the son of the child. I was familiar with the work. I knew the meaning. Incest. Just kidding. Lord, I'm glad I didn't say that. Normally. I didn't want to talk to anybody. On that day, I wasn't aware I could talk. My tonsils were sick. They took up my whole throat. My hand didn't go up nor was I in the front. Apparently, these two things were reason enough for Dr Paul to attack. I have no idea what I must have looked like, but I knew I was boneless, skinless. I thought my skin was moving when I wasn't. The monster, Dr Paul, sauntered towards the back until he got to where my head was lying to the floor. He sneered at me. Fine. Ok. I could take a sneer since I couldn't focus. Then he said, with no provocation on my part, "If you spent more time studying and less time being a slut for all the weight-lifters, you could answer my questions."

Slow Walking, Slow Talking Hissy fit. Sing it out, people! Sing it out loud. I got my leg things under me first. Then my tentacles. I managed to push myself up, sloppily. Then I swung. I am separating these sentences because they were actually separate events. Slow motion had hold of me. Like a robot responding to a command. The internal command told me he wasn't going to walk to me like that. Oops. Talk to me like that. He was an enemy and must be dealt with. Well, my fist didn't land, my whole tentacle landed. I was not interested in wasting good suffering time on an aim. He flew off his feet. Flew. Winged it, people. He went ass over teakettle and toppled two whole rows of desks. The man went down like he'd been howitzered. (Word?) I couldn't speak anything but gibberish. I could hear all the racket but it was like I was deep in a pit. He had taken one of my sorority sisters down with him. Under him. She broke her arm. I didn't break her arm, he did. When he fell. It wasn't my fault he couldn't keep his feet under him. That was my story and I was going to stick to it. If I could remember it.

    Pissy Paul got up in a rage. I wasn't in a rage, I was just sort of wobbling there. I hoped I wasn't drooling, but I wasn't sure. He grabbed me by the arm and dragged me out of class. I must have looked like the Straw Man in the Wizard of Oz. I was leaning backward, then rolling forward, hollering my fallen sister's name. In my gurgling, I was trying to tell her how sorry I was that he was not sorry he hurt her. She was getting help from the other students. I think. My friends weren't particularly happy with good old Dr Paul. They knew I wasn't like that. If he hadn't gotten out of the room as fast as he did, with me practically slung over his shoulder, I think they would have charged him. And he knew it.

    While he was dragging me down the hall, I was trying to find two legs to borrow. He hauled me off to the Dean of English's office. Big Oh Shit! This could put serious holes in my grade point average. I slung my skinless self at her, blubbering, "What did I do? What did I do? Make him stop, he's hurting me." He wasn't, but what else could I do? I knew I had my hands up, trying to get them to act like I was praying, but they were just swinging in the breeze. With no noticeable joint movement and lip control, I was probably not putting on my best performance, but even my best got me in trouble most of the time, so what the hell. She shoved me onto her desk while I was mumbling something meaningless about the child being the father of somebody. Or something. She gave me the evil eye, I think, but there seemed to be a slight chuckle in them. Maybe she agreed with what he was bellowing about, but I must have appeared quite comical so she was finding it hard to be serious. I hope. When he finished disparaging my reputation, I tried to defend myself. I tried to tell her what he said to me, but the bubbling noises were not comprehensible. Oh horrors, I sounded like what Mama sounded like on bourbon, with her brogue. I was trying to talk with a mouth that was out of order, like a toilet. Couldn't do it. Quit trying. Quit thinking.

Unfortunately, I had another bad experience with this lady. Non-violent, I must say. I was in my very first English class at East Carolina when this lady, the Dean of English, came into the class and asked us to stand, state our name and our major. When they got to me, I stood up, the little Carteret County born cracker with a horrendous brogue to say, "I am Carol. I'm from Morehead City, North Carolina and I'm majoring in English." I sounded like an uneducated Irishman combined with a drunk Eliza Doolittle before the transformation. If I had put rags in my mouth, it wouldn't have made it worse. She couldn't understand a word I said. Nobody had ever cared what I said anyway. Why would she care? What did anybody care what it sounded like? I was used to not being understood because most of the time, I couldn't understand anything my Mama said and she taught me to talk. The Professor lady cut her eye at me and said, quite clearly, "Not until you learn to speak it." Ow! I probably didn't sound any better two years later slumped over her desk.

She finally wound her way through the morass, called a few other people for advise and threw me out of school. What an attitude! Even I could tell I didn't deserve that. Did I? I wasn't sure, but it didn't sound good. Being thrown out of something couldn't be good. I stumbled back to the dorm, threw up all over my room and roomie and begged somebody to go ahead and kill me. I was headed back to Carteret County, I thought. I think I thought that. It seemed that I would. Somebody finally made an intelligent decision. I still don't know who. For sure, it wasn't me. I think somebody found Ted. He finally called for an ambulance and they hauled my spineless ass off to the infirmary. I think I was making a lot of noise. Hell, I probably was caterwauling. How cool.

I was in the infirmary for three days. They pumped me out and they pumped me in. If they wanted me to suffer, they got their wish. When I dried out, I realized the position I had put myself in. What to do? I got in touch with the Honor Society of the entire Greek community. That's college speak. I used to have the black ball for my sorority. I was the one who hauled drunken girls getting laid in the bushes into the house. I wasn't a slut. Not me, boy. I had to fight. I was a former member of the Honor Society. Former because I had been chucked when this all happened. They found out what Dr Paul said to me and were horrified. Hell, I was horrified. It was the first time I heard it, too, in a way. We had a full Greek Committee meeting with the Dean of English and her cronies. Everybody stood up and defended my actions, given the condition I was in and what was said to me. Even the sister whose arm I had inadvertently allowed Dr Paul to break felt no blame should be placed on me. They explained I was unaware I was had taken Darvocet and was not known to abuse drugs. And, the history exam was back where it belonged. The Dean of English listened politely, restored me to the school, suspended Dr Paul for one week without pay and said to me, "I remember you. I have never heard such garbage coming out of one person's mouth. You're lucky. I almost threw you out of school then. Then I saw you were here under a Vocational Rehabilitation Scholarship." I started to whoop, but felt I should keep my mouth shut. For once.

WHAT YA GONNA DO?

Life with Ted was always wonderful. For the most part. We gradually moved into a relationship that was warm, soft and cozy. Except, I was a lot younger than he was and that itch to dance had to be scratched. He was from Suffolk, Va. If you look at a map, that was no where near here. He didn't dance and had no intention of learning. He thought he would look stupid with his build but I think it was really because he didn't have a spark of rhythm in his body, and he knew it. So, increasingly, he wanted me to go home with him instead of to the beach to dance. The main reason he pushed this was he wanted me to get close to his Mom, but he didn't understand. She was not about to get close to me. Around her, I felt like a cat that had been taken in that no one wanted. You'd have thought my face was a wart. Ted would go off hunting with his Dad and I would be left home with Mom so we could bond. She would put opera on the stereo and start to clean dressed like she was going out for dinner. She would brook zero interference or conversation from me. I did what I always do. I took a good book, went into the bedroom, shut the door and didn't come out. Hid. Cycloped. I could hear her passing the door from time to time and imagined her rolling her eyes when she imagined the very idea that I thought I was good enough for her son.

She would cook French meals and then steer the conversation around to see if I could speak French or know the names of the various meals. A very successful attempt to make me look stupid or feel it. Even though I had taken four years of French in high school, together with two years of Latin, I remembered none of it. I wanted to ask her could she say "hot dog?" That was the language we spoke down South. She didn't consider herself from the South. Her ancestors fought for the North. Yawn. The whole Civil War argument made me sleepy. Not the war itself, but trying to fight it with words was stupid.

Ted knew she was doing this but it didn't bother him. The good man loved me like I was and said so when I let my insecurities out. She had it in for me. He knew it. She wanted him to get back with his old girlfriend, but she had run out on him when he was in college and he wasn't interested. Mom thought he should to give her another chance before he "settled down with me." These conversations went on right in front of me. It irked Ted but he said that was just how his Mom was. I decided I had to live with it. Good grief, look how my Mama was.

I started going to Suffolk, or "Sufferk," less and less and it began to affect our relationship. Ted was a man, not a boy and he had a man's needs. He wanted to get married, but I was scared. I was frightened to marry anybody with a mother like that. I knew I would be carrying her around on my shoulders the rest of my damn life. His mother was horrified when she heard stories about my family. It was all to be decided when Ted graduated.

He graduated that January. After graduation, we drove up to Sufferk for another weekend of me hidden in the bedroom. This time, his Dad had a surprise for him. A drop dead gorgeous 1966 Corvette convertible as a graduation gift. I came out of that bedroom like I had been shot out of a rocket launcher. It was a hot navy blue, mint condition car. Off we went, having the time of our lives. We even went to the drive in movies in it for hot, wonderful smooching. It seemed appropriate for the car to be what kicked off the much needed healing of our relationship. If you want to make either of us happy, put us in a damn fine car like that. After the excellent make out session at the drive in, we became engaged. The next day we went picked a ring, and set the marriage date for July 4th. Two weeks later, unexpectedly, he was drafted. Two months later, he was dead.

Ted had gone through basic training, then sent to Vietnam like so many others of that era. Two days after he arrived in Vietnam, he stepped on a land mine. His mother was awful to me. She told me Ted came back in a box in pieces. I was told that he arrived before the notification came and she was devastated. That was understandable. However, I was not welcome at the funeral services because I had first refused to marry him. This attitude, even though she would have cut her throat if I had, threw me. She wouldn't acknowledge the ring or the wedding date. His dad and I were close, so we talked. Ted's ex-girlfriend went to the funeral, but he couldn't get her to agree to let me come. I didn't want a scene. I sent his dad the ring because it no longer had meaning for me. If I looked at it, I knew I would always think of him dead. Without it, I don't. He was a wonderful person and it should have never happened like that. Never. As anyone who was over the age of sixteen in the 60's time can tell you, way too many people heard a similar story about a loved one.

I fell so far into despair I could not begin to describe it. It just couldn't be true. I knew it would affect the rest of my life. I knew I would never be the same. It was like I was dying, but couldn't get it over with. Ever get married? I doubted it. In my heart. That was reserved for Ted.

LOST IN RALEIGH

My abilities to concentrate and function were lost with Ted. I had to struggle to finish school. I had dropped so far down, I didn't know if I would ever come up again. I had to force myself to study in spite of the constant tear bursts that came out of nowhere. I made myself go to summer school because I couldn't bear the thought of inactivity. That's when Ted would come so clearly to mind. I couldn't make myself "perk up" like my friends wanted me to. There was no reason to dance. I had no get up and go in me. There was no social life and no particular interest in anything. Ted's friends didn't know what to say to me. When I saw them they would look at me and say nothing half the time. Giving up, I picked up my ass and my little yellow Volkswagen, and moved to Raleigh. I've always liked to move. Its like sweeping unhappy thoughts into the "as soon as you get out of town, it is now your past" bucket.

I stayed pretty much in a funk until I went to work for a legal firm and wiggled around in there for awhile. My particular boss decided to teach me how to treat his clients with respect. Not that I didn't. He just wanted to dig it into my psyche to never be forgotten. So, he had me arrested. Right at my desk. They picked me up, escorted me out of the building, with me wailing at the top of my lungs. That brought me out of my daze. I couldn't believe Mr Bailey would let them do that. Surely, he would meet me at the jail and get me out? They wouldn't tell me what I had done, so I was even more frightened. They fingerprinted me, did a weapons search and took me to booking. No strip search, though. That might have been more fun than I could bear. When they had done all that, they took me to a cell, for Christ's sake. I had a roomie who looked like she had gone around the world and back on the back of a gorilla, with no showers in between. After they let me sit there for four hours, Mr Bailey showed up. He explained to me what he had done and why. I thought he really had a sensitive heart towards his clients to do something like that, but not a whole lot of respect for his secretaries, so I quit. Pissed me off. I won't even go into how scared I was. You don't want to know. The pain of losing Ted lessened but wasn't gone. But, you knew I was going to go on. I knew no other way. I came from Anna.

    It took a year after Ted died for me to start dancing again. I always thought of him and Mama when I went out dancing, but I would still not speak to her. The only thing that can drag me back from the abyss is dancing. I can only get away from it for so long before I start to yearn. I was at the Embers Club one night and noticed this guy who made it real obvious he was watching me. He had huge, beautiful brown eyes, was tall, dressed handsomely and was very good looking. He was hard to miss. He also made no qualms about his interest. The man truly looked smitten. He was with a group of guys on what looked like a boy's night out. I was disappointed that he never approached me before I went home. I was curious what he was like because he had that wholesome, good guy look about him. In my life, I had seen so many guys dancing that I would have loved to meet, but when the night ended, they were gone and I would never see them again. But, there was Ted.

    That wasn't true in Johnny's case. That was his name. I know that because the next week, there he was. This time he was alone and my qualms about Ted had gone from my head to rest in my heart. He walked up to me and asked if I was in love with anybody. Caught off guard, I mumbled at first. Then, my mojo back, I slanted my head, grinned and said "No, why?." He said "Good. By the end of tonight, I sure hope you're in love with me." I can quote that because most girls are not lucky enough to ever hear a guy say that. Don't doubt it, he meant it. I had a little reserve because I didn't want to find out he was just some well trained college boy or something. And, there was always the pain from Ted. I have to say, Johnny was the real thing. Clean cut, naturally nice and popular with everybody who knew him.

    He told me he had a buddy who owned an awesome cabin in the woods. We went up there one night during heavy snow and I was introduced to my very first wood fireplace. It was massive and I was transfixed. With about four other couples, we sat around the fire and cooked hot dogs. Heaven. I have loved the look and smell of a wood fireplace ever since. He introduced me to a lot of things and he was one of my favorite fun people of all time. Unfortunately, he was not successful in getting me to fall in love with him. There was always Ted. But, I was in a very good state of like. My trust radar just would not stop going off. Was he a turn on? Oh yeah. He had one of those fast as hell Dodges.

I also met his sister. Kathleen was absolutely lovely. She was one of those girls who glowed from good health and happiness. Tall, like Johnny, she was lithe and when she moved, she glided across the floor. Very intelligent, she always seemed much more mature than her age. She was only seventeen the night she went out with us. Someone introduced her to a man I would never have wanted her to know. He was married, had children and was also known for being a hound. I despised him. Although Kathleen and I got along really well she would not listen. It wasn't long before she came to me and told me she was pregnant. I knew the day would come and I dreaded it. What is with women who do that? Jessie flashed through my head. Were they expecting a miracle? Did they think God was going to look down at what they were doing and say, "Oh, its ok, its her." Of course, like most, she couldn't handle it. She wasn't brought up to even visualize the calamity she was facing. She came to the conclusion she couldn't have it. Her mother had raised her and Johnny alone, their dad having died in the war. Only a few weeks later she asked me if I'd help her have an abortion. I said absolutely not. I thought and think abortions are abominations. I didn't know if abortions were right or wrong, but they are wrong for me. Relax, Rowe followers. I also think you have the right to your opinion. But, that's mine. I felt Johnny and her mom had the right to know. She was underage. The only abortions available in the early 70's weren't done in nice, sanitary clinics. It was illegal. They were done in backrooms. Sometimes garages. It was true a lot of girls bled to death or worse. I was scared to death for her. I knew neither Johnny nor her mother would ever forgive me for not telling them. I also knew they would have supported her through anything. They were like that. Johnny, however, would have gone to prison, because he would have killed the hound.

Another couple of weeks passed before Kathleen called me again. This time she told me she had found someone to do it.

She was desperate. Naturally, the guy had fled. Most did. She wanted to know if I'd help her pay for it? I said no again, but it was because I didn't have five hundred dollars to give her. I offered to take he,r but I told her I would not go in with her. I couldn't do that. I froze just thinking about it.

Off we went. As agreed, I didn't know where we were going. After awhile she had me pull into the driveway of a house. A house, not a doctor's office. I had a really bad feeling about it. I was so scared for her. Lord, what if something bad happened? After she went in, I tried to read but couldn't concentrate. About an hour later, she came out, moving very slowly. I jumped out, opened the door for her and helped her in. I could not imagine what they had done to her. I was terrified for her when I saw how pale she was. I loved her like a sister. I was angry with myself for even being a part of this. I got back in the driver's seat where we sat silently for a few minutes. I had decided not to ask her any questions. She looked at me, then lifted a little glass container with a lid on it. It was full of blood and clearly had something in it. Ew! She asked me where should she put it? They had told her to take it home and discard it later. What in the hell were they talking about? I didn't even want to contemplate what it was. I decided not to question her. I took it from her shaking hand, put it between me and the console, put the car in gear and drove off. I held her hand all the way to her house, but I was so damn conscious of that container, I could have cried. I was convinced it was a fetus, but I had to admit I didn't know. I did ask her if they got the afterbirth. Hell, I didn't even know what the afterbirth was. She told me she thought that was what was in the jar. How absolutely gross. They told her how to determine whether there was more afterbirth in her. I didn't want to know. Her mom wasn't home when we got there, as planned. I practically carried her to her room and laid her down. I asked her what else could I do? She asked me just to sit with her for awhile, so I did. When I got back to the car, I got out on the highway and threw that container as high and far as I could.

Shortly after that, I broke up with Johnny. I could not rid myself of guilt. What if he found out I helped his little sister have an abortion? Had he known I had anything to do with what she had done, he would have killed me. Kathleen, I heard, went right back to the hound when she got better. I wondered if people's brains get scrambled as a result of a chemical reaction when they fall in love. I couldn't handle that. I can't explain my own behavior half the time. I'm damned if I can explain someone else's.

ANGELS AND HELL'S ANGELS

    I moved into in a re-modeled home made up like dorms. There were two bedrooms on each floor, on each side of the house. One on the left side and one on the right. Two girls slept on separate bed/couches per bedroom. In the middle were the kitchen and bathroom which were shared by all four people. If your roommate moved out and you didn't find a replacement in thirty days, the landlord had the right to move someone in. I squandered way too much time not looking. One day, someone knocked on the door in the middle of the day. I was going to end up with another roomie. Ok, fine. She needed to understand I was quiet. I thought about Ted all the time. People, she was a show stopper, I'll tell you. I answered the door and found myself speechless. Ain't that different? There stood what looked like the dirtiest female I have ever seen in my life. She was in black jeans, t-shirt and jacket with long, black hair and she had a mouth that hung open most of the time. When she laughed, it was through her nose and made a peculiar sound I never heard before. Surely the landlord had never met this vagrant looking person. I didn't realize she was normal for the times, not me. She stood there looking at me; giving me time to roll my tongue back into my mouth. When I didn't do so fast enough, she pushed me aside and came in. She only had a traveler's bag. An almost empty traveler's bag. It crossed my mind that it might contain nothing but dirt so she could smear her face from time to time if she was feeling too clean for the rest of us to gawk at. I tell you what, people. We have some damn fine dirt here in North Carolina and if you wanted to find any, this was the female to look for. Her name was Christy. Well, hell, you can bet your surfboard another phase of my life had just walked in.

    We played the getting to know you games for awhile and then we got into the nitty gritty stuff. I ended up telling her about Ted and how depressed I was. I told her about Kathleen and how guilty I felt for participating. Oddly enough, this vagrant agreed with me about abortion. I found out why later. I was about to ask her to please take a damn bath. She might actually like it when, suddenly, Christy started to talk. She told me she lost her little sister who was hit by a car while she was supposed to be watching her. She lost her mom the year before who died by choking on her alcoholic vomit. To keep it going, she lost her Dad three years before when he died in a fire, caused by his own cigarette, in a motel in Seattle. She had a brother who was a genius at John Hopkins, but they didn't speak; mostly because of the little sister. She had just given birth to twins and had to put them up for adoption. She was only 17. She made me feel like a can full of crap. I felt it was terribly unkind of someone who was clearly trying to make a good impression to lift that t-shirt before I had a chance to run out of the building, screaming. I didn't know twins could do that to a fifteen year old stomach. I must say it was refreshing to meet someone who had as bad a childhood as I'd had. Goes to show and all.

When I took her places people actually stopped what they were doing and stared at us. It was funny. Preppy people stared at her. Hippies stared at me. Let's jump right into fashion sense. I hadn't mentioned I cleaned up rather well after climbing out of that last tree. Having grown up liking the boys, I prettied up like a Christmas tree. I wore all white. I wore them a very long time because one, I never grew any taller; two, I made sure they were of good quality and style. I was still in my white phase when Black Christy came into my life. Everything on me had to be white including my hair. I never liked my hair after Joanie experimented with trying to get a brown head blond. She achieved orange and walked away. I bleached my hair white and got one of those almost white falls that you wrapped around your head and stuck bobby pins into your brain crevices for support. I had been wearing that one damn fall since high school. Even through the years with Ted. It was screaming for me to get another one. I was so attached (pun) to it, wore it to bed so I wouldn't have to look at my own head. The only piece of hair that was mine was in the front, peeking out from under the fall. I thought it gave me height. In a way it did. People usually had to look down to talk to me, but if they wanted to, they could look down less and talk to my hair. Whatever. Anyhow, what you had here closely resembled the image of an angel. At the very least, a Barbie doll. I admit it. I was in my twenties and didn't even own a pair of jeans. I think I was downright precious. People said so. People love petite blonds. Can't control themselves.

Christy, on the other hand, wore all black. I found out she was not dirty. It was just all the black and a lack of interest in combing her hair or fashion. Hell, she washed more than I did. Dirty looking black, torn t-shirt. Dirty looking black, torn jeans. Dirty looking black hair. Although she had married, she told me she decided to wear all black after she had to put her sons up for adoption. She named them Adrian Ashley and Christopher Andrew Birkett. She fit the times more than I did. We were in the hippie era that I didn't see it coming. I didn't even know it was out there. What a pair we were. She'd never had alcohol, just drugs. Mescaline, Seconal, marijuana, etc. I never had drugs except for the fun time when I got tossed out of college, like I was a salad. I only drank beer, vodka and a memorable one night stand with white-lightning. We had major differences in our choice of music. I liked beach music. Specifically the song "Anna." She liked hard rock, specifically "In-A-Gadda-Da-Vita." I didn't know if I spelled that right and after hearing it twenty four hours a day, I didn't give a damn. Naturally, it was our obligation as friends to accept each other as we were, so we did. We were ebony and ivory, so to speak. Best friend I ever had.

Every now and then, I would go back to Greenville for this party or that, and Christy would want to go. It was a two hour drive from Raleigh. Of we would go in my little yellow Volkswagen. The deal was she did not bring drugs into the house or the car and I would reciprocate with no alcohol. I failed to specify not bringing them along in her brain. One Sunday I picked her up at the local grill and we were headed back to Raleigh from Greenville. We were tooling along down this long, long two lane back road. My VW baby started wobbling. I had a flat. I was pretty used to it because the car got a flat every time it left the house. But, money was tight and I had failed to get a spare. I realized Christy was high. She was almost high enough to pick us up, car and all, and fly us back to Raleigh. I pulled over to the side and fumed. Oh shit..aren't there times you wish you didn't have a rear view mirror? Coming up behind me was a Statie. Patrol, that is. In boon-dock North Carolina. The tide was definitely going out on my luck.

I told Christy to stay in the car, and not open her mouth. You know, like you would tell a dog. Stay. When did Christy ever listen to me? Except for her head lolling on her shoulders and her tongue hanging out, you almost couldn't tell she was high. Though, if he looked at her, he might think she was dead. However, we were in luck. The angel in charge was in full dress petite blond battle gear. I looked hot. I mean good hot, not weather hot. A tiny smiley face, wind up doll, I was.

I jumped out of the car and met him halfway to tell him about the flat. I knew I was going to find it hard to find a spare because it was Sunday. Hell, I might not have enough to pay for it and that meant I might have to speak to Christy with him standing there. Horrors. After he examined the tire, and threw a questioning glance or two at Christy, he recommended we jump in his car and try to find the tire at the closest town. He knew a guy who owned a tire store. Maybe he could get him to open up and let me have one cheap. After his next glance at Christy, who had slid down in her seat until she was almost on the floor, I grabbed his arm. I told him I was going to leave Christy so nothing would happen to my car. Somebody might want the car, but one look at her would, for sure, scare them off. Then, I ran back to tell her to stay in the car and behave. These were the days when men did not automatically rape women like now or I wouldn't have left her. I figured once a guy saw her, he'd move on anyway. Apparently, the Statie agreed because off we went.

I chattered like a magpie I was so nervous. I was in my best Southern Belle mode, my tiny hands flying around as I chattered. Thankfully, his friend stepped up to the plate and within an hour we were headed back to my little yellow Volkswagen with the black convertible top. When we got back to the car, the first thing we both noticed was there was no Christy in the car. Or within sight. He jumped out to fix the tire while I jumped out and went Christy hunting. I found her almost a half mile from where we were. She was in the ditch. Why not? The upholstery was not her problem. I could just hose it down after we separated the dirt from the cottonmouths. She was singing In-A-Gadda-Da-Vita as loud as she could. That was the only way I found her. I knew it was Christy because the place was abandoned and nobody could sing through her nose, high, like Christy. Worse sound you ever heard. I got her back into the car, hauling her like she was a bag of cement. I waited until he finished so I could quickly give him a kiss on the cheek, hoping he wouldn't look at her. I've got to give the guy credit. He didn't want a good look at her. He'd seen all he wanted. He knew I was sober, so he told me I should just take her drunk ass on home. Thank heavens, he didn't realize it was not alcohol, it was Seconal. Dodged a bullet there, people.

Christy and I had a lot of fun together in spite of the differences. She had a picture of herself taken by a friend of her's.

She was standing behind a chain link fence. I swear, it looked like she was in jail the way she was holding onto it. The look in her eyes said everything about how she had suffered through life. Completely compelling. There were moments when she could take my breath away. I came to love her like a sister. Better.

We got thrown out, of course, once we couldn't pay the rent. I decided the hell with him. I would go with her. We found a great place but one drawback was we shared the same bed, but not the same sexual appetites. It was a really big bed, guys. I have to admit that. Me? I am straight as a stick and didn't particularly care for the wild ass biker guys Christy liked. She liked hippy guys and girls. The higher the better. We had a platform bed that I needed a step ladder to get on. Once up there, it reached from one side of the room to the other. One, big ass bed. Black walls and strobe lights were more to her taste than mine, but what the hell..walk on the wild side. I found I couldn't dance around in the house, because of my total inability to even think for the noise. Moreover, what was unfair about it all was, I didn't bring guys home, because of the Inna-Godda-Da-Vita. I tried sleeping in the living room. Unfortunately, that was where the damn stereo was. A couple of times, I tried moving all the way to the wall I slept beside and realized the bed didn't even bounce on my side when she was having sex. I prefer people not have sex in the same bed I'm occupying. In all fairness, she didn't even know I was there. But, I would rather listen to Inna-Godda than Christy having an orgasm. She made noise something like a horse but I won't say what they had to do to the horse to make it sound like that. Then, there was the night I got up to go to the bathroom and walked into her naked boyfriend. This was not the glue that would hold the relationship together. Being really great friends and not wanting to separate, we set new rules. No anything. The friendship held tight. We compromised every time things came up. I was no angel, either.

Most of the time we had different interests, but we went out together some. On her eighteenth birthday, I decided to get her drunk and teach her to shag. She wasn't going to be able to do it sober, for sure. There were also the problems of her bowed legs and mis-proportioned butt. The bowed legs were because when she got high, she couldn't stand up straight. The butt looked like that because of the jeans she wore. Off we went to buy something we knew nothing about. We bought two bottles of Pina Colada Mix. We both thought it had alcohol in it, but it was just the mix. We brought it to the Knave. Due to Fred Fletcher, the owner's, infinite kindness, he added the vodka without mentioning it or charging us. We got smashed. Shit stomping smashed. The sight of Christy trying to shag will be with me forever. As a nightmare. When the evening finally ended, we remembered the Knave was on the second floor, so we had to hold each other up as we shuffled down the stairs. We had never gotten drunk like this before. Thank heavens, my chariot, the little yellow Volkswagen, was parked right out front.

    I had a trick I had come up with to test my ability to drive. Since I could dance even if I were drinking, sometimes when the night was over, I was quite surprised to realize I could dance, but I couldn't drive. Then again, sometimes when I danced really hard, I couldn't tell if I was drunk or tired. Life was full of either or's. So, I had tests. For this one, there were parking meters right out front of the Knave. If I could stand beside the meter, and throw my leg all the way over the top of it, without touching the meter, or falling down, I could drive. If I hit the meter, I got a ride home. I seldom got drunk because you can't dance and hold a drink at the same time and I was mostly on the dance floor. Ever mindful that the cops in North Carolina are tough, I didn't want any blinking blue light surprises. I had recurring nightmares about Mason finally getting his chance to arrest me.

    I pitched more than threw the leg over. If somebody was watching me, it probably looked like some white girl, with white hair, slinging angel hair pasta over the meter. No problem. Over it went. Then, Lord Help us, Christy decided she wanted to try. She was wasted and she was a lot more bottom heavy than I was, so I wasn't sure it was a good idea. Good ol' bowed legs Christy. Drunk, bowed legs Christy. The leg went up..bam. She slammed her ankle against the meter. Take my word for it, it had to hurt like hell. The leg went up again..bam. Never one to give up, she tried again. Oops, she missed the meter altogether and down she went. With legs and that black hair a flyin', it looked like a million black bats after one cricket. I thought it was hysterical, so I was yucking it up when I realized there was no sound coming from the cricket. Oh shit. I sort of nudged her with my foot but I received no response. I got down on my hands and knees, because she was not answering me, and sort of pushed at her with my fingers. Like you do when you think something's dead. When I turned her head and got eyeball to eyeball to her, she started to giggle. It abruptly stopped when I grabbed her arm. She hollered. I jumped. I'm smart so I figured she broke or sprained something. Crap. I crawled back up the stairs. It was no easy feat, I tell you. I grabbed the bartender, asked him to drive and off we went to Rex Hospital. I was really worried. I think.

That lasted only as long as it took for them to put her on the thing to take her for x-rays. Her hair hung down and she was slobbering and drooling. Suddenly, she started to snort. When she hit her horse laugh level, I broke up. Couldn't they hear her? She really did sound like a horse. They threw my ass out of the hospital. No sense of humor. Did I mention it had start to rain? Did I mention the bartender had my damn keys? I was standing out in the rain, drunk and drenched. Hell, I didn't know what to do and had limited choices. Standing in front of me was a big, beautiful oak tree. It resembled the tree in the cemetery of my youth. I crawled under it and went immediately to sleep. I wasn't so drunk that I didn't know I was soaked with no where to go. It was a good thing Mama didn't see me like this.

I thought the next morning was the worst. Oh no. Besides being hung over, I was soaked, under the tree and my little yellow Volkswagen was gone. They had left me. Was there no respect? In order to get home, I'd have to pass where I worked so I wandered through people's backyards, hoping no one would call the police. It worked out ok until I got home. No car. When I knocked on the door, guess who opened it? Mama. Yeah, its oh shit, its Mama time. She had left Maryland to see how I was doing. Christy didn't know where the hell I was. What did she care? She was dry, for Christ's sake. Even with a cast, she took off for groceries. I was not exactly good looking angel material. Mama being Mama only asked one question, as always. "Where have you been?" Chin up, I replied like she'd asked me if they sold cocaine on street corners, "I fell asleep under a tree at Rex Hospital." I didn't say another word. She stared at me with that cocked head she could do so well. That mean look she had perfected, focused on my face. Never said another word about it. We hadn't made up yet, you remember.

Christy had broken her elbow, and it was going to take a long time to heal. She couldn't work so I jumped in to pay her bills for a couple of months. It wasn't too much and she would have done it for me. Best buds do that.

ROCKINGHAM ROCKS

I'd been dating this great guy named Pete. He was a lot of fun and could dance really well. One of the things I liked most about him was he talked really fast. I mean real fast and for some reason, there was something attractive about it to me. I think I had been dating Pete about two months, constantly, when he asked me to go on a trip to the Rockingham racetrack with him. This was a big deal for several reasons. One was he had never once asked or implied he wanted to have sex with me. I figured he might be gay, but he was so masculine. This trip might put the easiness of the relationship at risk. In other words, I might find myself screwed. I guess Pete was about five-seven at most. Short, but masculine just the same. Two, this was going to be an overnight trip. Three, we were going with Tommy Tucker and his girlfriend, Frieda. Weirdest couple known to man. Tommy was a mountain of a guy. A Paul Bunyan size fella with no noticeable brains, and a face that only a mountain mother could love. If she tried really hard. Frieda was a whack job. I didn't even think she could see straight she did so many drugs. I can't really tell you what she looked like, but she had that cross-eyed thing going big time. I am known for striving for privacy and they planned to sleep in the car. All four of us. That kind of thing was just not my style. If I hadn't enjoyed Pete's company so much, I would have never done it. It reminded me of the times I spent on the floor while MaryBeth rocked and rolled in the backseat of our car. I dreaded hearing those noises coming from Tommy and Frieda. Gross.

The Rockingham race track was redneck USA. Now, people don't come out of your pants. I didn't mean that in an ugly way, its just plain redneck. Period. All big logging trucks and big, nasty looking men drinking beer. Off we went on a five hour drive only to end up in redneck country. Do you honestly think I would have come had I known that? Christy was supposed to come, but she planned to ride a Harley there. Her plans got messed up and here I was. Short in the land of the tall. There are only a few times I didn't want to be five feet tall and this was one of them. Rednecks take to me for some reason. One I had known called me his Barbie doll. How insulting is that? I promise you, Barbie would have been insulted as I was. I found myself knee deep in loggers and truck drivers. I don't mind their vocations, but they damn well did not look friendly. More like lecherous. All of them were X-X-X-X-LARGE.

While we were milling around, looking stupid, they let us drive right into the pit, which was full of logging trucks. Somebody had a friend somewhere because getting to the pits was unusual. On the trucks, all the logs were gone. We were to climb to the top of a platform laid out so we could watch the race. The problem was all the trucks had what looked like forty to fifty guys up there. No noticeable women anywhere. I wanted to get in the front so I could see. If not, I would see nothing but butts and backs. I don't even want to talk about what I would upchuck if one of these monoliths turned around putting my face inches from their crotches. Tommy Tucker and Frieda ran around trying to find out which truck we were supposed to climb onto. They came back with two little fold out chairs. We found a truck and climbed the ladder to the top. It was really, really high up. Like scary high up. Good view, though. We parked my butt near the front with the drunken rednecks gathered in the back. The official car started the pace.

Right off the bat, there was one grunch who kept running his hands through my hair. From the bottom up. My hair was now my real hair, totally blond and almost to my waist. When he did that, it was like pulling my hair out of the damn roots. Enough already. Could this jerk think that felt good? I begged Pete to ask him to stop. So, Pete turned around and very fast, said, "Get your hands out of her damn hair." You know, not nice and not polite. The grunch kept it up because he wasn't afraid of anybody a fourth his size. If it hadn't hurt, I wouldn't have said anything else. But, it did, and I was grumpy because this place wasn't where I wanted to be any day of my life. Well, I made the mistake of asking Pete to say something again. So, very fast, he said, "Get your hands out of her damn hair." Then we had trouble. Pete pushed him. When he pushed him, it seemed like every guy on the truck got bigger and bigger. They puffed up their bodies and lowered their heads and damn near roared. Must have been some kind of alpha male strut or something. I was in awe of all the testosterone spilling from these monoliths. Well, the pushing elevated along with the cussing and beer throwing. I was not having a good time, people. I wanted to get down. I got my wish. The inevitable took place. Pete and this guy were doing that stupid dance where one guy pushed on the other guy's chest, moved him about six inches and then the other guy does it back. Over I went. Off the truck. Chair and all.

You know, it was often not immediately funny when something like that happened. It might never get funny. Everything slowed down. I distinctly remember thinking, "This was gonna hurt." I seemed quite sure of it. I also had time to think how stupid I must have looked with my long hair blowing up and looking like a flag, waving in the breeze, while I dropped about thirty plus feet. The good news was I didn't hit anything on the way down until I got almost to the bottom. Almost. You remember those rear view mirrors that are mounted on the side of cars that stick way, way out? There was a blue Caddy right below me with one of those suckers. I caught it with the back of my neck. It flipped me up in the air and I hit the ground with my nose first and then my two eyeballs. The eyeballs were so offended by that they rolled up into what felt like the back of my head. The ground saved my nose because instead of breaking, the dirt just went up my nose all the way to my brain. And in spite of all these fail-safe methods of helping you not die, I passed out when the rest of my head met terra very firma. Half conscious, or half dead, I could still hear the go for blood fight going on top of the truck. People were flying everywhere as they got knocked off the sides. These Bunyans were landing on me, for heaven's sake. I may have survived the fall, but I was going to get squashed to death. Oh no, like my Easter chick, all my insides were going to come out my orifices. Gross. I couldn't talk or I would have asked somebody to please tell them to not put me in a tub. For all the bodies on top of me, I could barely hear someone screaming I was hurt. I couldn't tell if it was male or female. I heard it, but you gotta understand, I could not see who it was because of the packed vision problems I was having. I thought I was buried right there on the spot. Having been pounded into the ground, I knew how a nail felt.

I knew, for sure, how hard I landed. I became aware that Pete picked me up and was carrying me. He must have been running because I was bouncing but I wasn't running. The infirmary was on the other side of the track, so they had to stop the race when he came running across it with cars whizzing past him. They didn't even slow him down. I heard later there was a full blown riot going on with weapons being drawn and all. I came to and then I passed out again. I am sure I was sorry to be unconscious. I would have like the dirt removed so I could see it. I tried again. Uh oh, the contact was either gone or it had carved a home in my brain because it was non-focus city. Can somebody tell these people I can't breathe? Soon.

Pete got me to the infirmary and they started working on me. First, I think they hooked me to a machine and blew me back up. No tub, thank God. They kept asking me if I could tell how many fingers they had up. I tried to tell them I couldn't tell them that on a good day, but all that came out was a muffled sound. At first, I didn't realize it was coming from me. At some point, I must have come to again because I remember trying to tell them I had a contact lost in my one working eye, but my words were all slurry and I felt funny. Sorta like that day in college. From far away, I heard Pete tell them about the contact just before I passed out again. Oh, and by the way, would somebody tell them I couldn't breathe? Maybe that's why I sounded like Christy when she had sex. My nose was stopped up by a quarter acre of pit dirt. Somebody had to be unfortunate enough to be given the "look up her nose" job. Oh! So was my mouth. At least I knew why I couldn't talk. They cut away some of my pants and looked at my legs funny. And, how about my legs? The ones that had hit the ground at ninety miles an hour. The ones that were the landing surface for the Redneck missiles that fell on me from thirty plus feet. I figured they deserved to be pissed. They weren't moving, but they were already blue.

I came to once more still in the infirmary. My nose was clear and they had my contact in a little box. My eyes were back where they belonged, but it didn't matter because I couldn't see since they were almost swollen shut. I was still having trouble communicating. I seem to keep running into this slobbering, gibberish thing. What was it with this mouth of mine? Totally undependable in a crisis. Could it be that as soon as my nose got out of the way, my mouth hit the turf and crammed what dirt wasn't in my nose into my mouth? Maybe it was the drugs they gave me. I heard them tell Pete they going to get me back to the car and lay me out in the back seat. Pete was to get me to Rex Hospital as soon as we got back to Raleigh. They had to stop the race again for us to get through. While they were packing my dizzy ass in the car, they stopped the race again to let the police vans in for all the arresting going on. Pete had to find Tommy and Frieda. They were still on top of the truck. They knew I had been hurt but damn, they were here to see the race. They didn't give a damn about me. I didn't know that Pete had three bruised or cracked ribs when he was running and carrying me, since I was senseless at the time. Lots of good guy in that gesture, don't you think? Pete joined me on the back seat and we were both spread out trying to be comfortable. I hurt everywhere so I didn't mind passing out again at all. Made my day. They stopped the race again to let us out of there and I am sure they stopped it over and over as they tried to control the melee. Damn it all. I love a melee.

W headed back to Raleigh. Tommy and Frieda were pissed. They drove a couple of hours and stopped somewhere to dance. Pete and I were laid out in the back seat in pain while they partied. Nice guys. At 2:00 am, they came back and we headed on to my apartment.

We got home about four thirty in the morning and horrors, the door was locked and Christy wasn't back. I'm sure she didn't realize that angel flying off the truck was me. I'd lost my pocketbook in the damn riot and didn't have a key to the door. Hell, at that point, I didn't know if I had any legs. From the back seat, I told Tommy to kick it in. I didn't care. I just wanted off that backseat. The big man roared, took that leg that look like a tree trunk back, and let go with a mighty kick. Door split right down the middle. Pete carried me again. With three busted ribs. He carried me through the front door where we encountered the "oh, shit" again. There stood Mama. Damn. Maybe she got up when the door splintered. Maybe she was on the way to be bathroom, I don't know. One thing about Mama, she always knew when I was hurt. She said she had a feeling something was wrong so she got in her car and came up. A three hour drive. Christy was there. Apparently, she'd seen me fall, but kept it to herself.

I was dangling off Pete's arms, like icicles on a Christmas tree. My hair a mess, head rolling, both legs wrapped completely in bandages. Unfortunately, I had come to. Unable to help herself, Mama asked her one question. "What the hell happened to you?" As quick as he could, Pete laid me out and boogied. I had no defense. Hell with it. I looked Mama in the eye, as best I could with my contact in Pete's pocket, and said, "I fell off a truck." Surprisingly, I didn't feel good. I stared at her even though she was somewhat out of focus and dared her to say a damn word. She limited her response to "oh." I couldn't walk for six months. Christy paid my bills this time. She was a special friend. I had more bills than she did. That was the end of that. Sorta.

A couple of months passed during which Pete checked on me all the time. He would stop by and bring me things if I needed them. Really great fella. Suddenly one day he called to say he needed my help. He sounded like he'd been crying. He told me he was married. His parents and his wife's parents were sitting in the stands when he came running across the racetracks holding my limp body. Yikes! His wife was pissed. Who'd a thought? I asked him when the hell was he married? We dated every night for two months. He told me he and his wife had a deal. He could go out and dance and party if he wanted, because she didn't want to. She was more the earth mother type. But, he could not have sex with anyone. Apparently, this had been going on for some time. I told him I didn't understand why he was in trouble, because we hadn't done anything. Pete said she didn't believe him this time because she knew what could happen in the backseat of a car. I was unconscious the only time I was in the backseat with Pete. I asked him what I could do to help. After all, he had kept his promise to her and had tried to make up for my getting hurt. He told me he wanted her to meet me. He wanted me to tell her he hadn't done anything. He thought she would believe me because I had a rather in-your-face, direct way of speaking. Not to mention I was pitiful. No problem. I told him to bring her over.

The next morning Pete, his wife and a case of beer came by. In minutes all was forgiven. She stayed with me often. Christy was working two jobs to help pay all the bills but I needed somebody to help me get up and walk around. She became my second best friend. But, I never dated Pete again. She wasn't willing to go that far. Great couple.

When these fun and games were over, and my legs healed instead of wobbling under me, I decided Raleigh wasn't for me anymore. I wanted to move to Charleston. I loved Christy but I was In-A-Gadda-DaVita'd to death. Jimmy had lived just outside of Charleston with Jane, but was getting ready to move. MaryBeth had been living there, but had also moved. It could be all mine. Too far for Mama to show up unexpectedly. Who knew that the next time I saw Mama, I would be begging her to come get me?

I traded in my little yellow Volkswagen with the black convertible top. I was losing a friend. However, I got my first 240Z and I was back in the land of hot angels. My legs weren't blue anymore and I was raring for a new life. I looked the best I had in years because I lost so much weight being ill. I would miss Christy terribly, but she had a Harley now so she could ride down. She was in love with some hippy guy, anyway. She was cool with it. I would sincerely miss Christy Birkett. Hair and all.

LIFE IN THE SOUTHLAND

As usual when I didn't have a clue how the hell to put up with myself, I packed up and moved to Charleston. I got there right before the New Year. I moved into an apartment complex for singles only. I had my new 1972 red 240-Z. Damn, I loved that car. They didn't make them red, but orange, go figure. Hating orange with a passion, I ordered it red, so they had to paint it for me. I still have a picture of me with my hair up, like I wore it for about eight years. Often, it was my own hair. I had on a white turtleneck with an awesome tan as I sat in my car. It was a great picture. One of the few of me I ever liked. Hair, eyeballs, teeth and hot car. All you could see. I started working at a golf course where I showed up a work every day in hot pants. Man, I was into myself. I also started hanging at a racy nightclub called Sam's. They weren't into prostitution or anything like that, that I knew of, but they dealt blackjack behind a curtain and a couple other naughty no-no's. Everybody knew they were doing it. One of the dealers walked out one night, so I started dealing to help them out. Soon, I quit my day job. I had been recruited.

    The head of Vice in South Carolina was a guy named Vinnie, so you knew he must be crooked. He used to visit Sam's every Saturday night. He'd come behind the curtain to pick up his pay-off. He'd do this right in front of God and everybody. Every now and then, he would bring a really cool guy named Steven with him. I would have liked to go out with Steven, but I knew he was married. You could tell he wanted to go out with me as well. He'd come in, take my hand and never let go of it until he had to go. He was good looking, well dressed, educated and when he looked at me, his eyes sizzled. My mouth watered.

    He finally got me alone one night to tell me he was the County Vice guy. The County and the FBI wanted to put together a sting to get Vinnie. They wanted to get him on a federal offense, but they needed someone to testify when it was all over. Nobody paid me, but I agreed to be their informant. I thought this was really cool. I loved this law shit. I made notes about when he came to get his money, like the date and times. This went on for two years. I didn't plan on living that life forever, though. Every now and then, I would wonder how long it was going to go on. I ended up becoming a night person, drinking until 4am. Not my goal in life. I slept all day and missed the sunlight. I found it hard to even take the time to read a good book, one of my favorite things. This was life on the fast track. It was not how I wanted to live. If I had plans for upward mobility, my tires were flat.

One night, Steven finally came to me and said they were about ready to wrap it up. I told him I wanted out. They decided they were going to put together a party at the Holiday Inn. Then he gave me the scary news. Vinnie wanted me to be his date. What you talking 'bout? I would be the only non-whore at the party. I was being asked to go to a party full of stenches! I felt like I should invite Daddy, Jimmy and Uncle John. Granddaddy was dead, thank God, or I would have to ask him. They probably knew these girls, anyway. Mama would have killed me if Vinnie didn't. I knew the only reason he picked me was because I was shorter than him. This was when I found out that half the girlfriends I had were stenches. Damn. It's what you don't know in life that sticks you in the butt. The important thing was all the biggies would be there, and they wanted to catch them all. I told Steven this scared the hell out of me. He told me not to worry, they would be there to protect me. He would be right near my side, except for when Vinnie and I went into the hotel room. I came right off the ground. What the hell was he talking about? I wasn't going into no room with no Vinnie in this lifetime. He tried to settle me down, and told me after we went into the room, somebody was going to come and give him a pay-off, a big one, and they needed me to witness it. They had the room wired and had cameras but wires and cameras can't testify. It was important. Unfortunately, I thought that comment made perfect sense so I agreed only if he promised me I would be safe. Right. He told me when we went into the room, he would be right at the door. If anything happened, he would be in that room in seconds even if he had to kick the door in. I knew he meant it, but what if..you know? I wanted a gun, but Steven said absolutely not. Vinnie could end up taking it from me. If he did anything I didn't like, I was to let loose a holler and they'd tear the door down. I looked him in the eye and I believed he would do just that. There was no way he was going to let anybody hurt me. I felt like the President. How dumb was that?

So, against my will, I went to this party with a bunch of stenches and salivating men. What fun. What the hell had I done? There were about twenty women and an equal number of guys. I hadn't even gotten to my second drink, which I desperately needed, when Vinnie took my elbow and walked me to the elevator. Good God Almighty. Oh no-o-o-o. Instead of being drunk, I was panicked. I had hoped I would at least be drunk and not aware of what was going on. I was completely freaked. Vinnie knew me well enough to know I was not a whore so I guess he just thought I was all in a lather about him being such an important man and all. Sure. We went into the room and I was freaking, people. Every time he got near me, I slithered away. If he hadn't been on the phone with somebody, he might have noticed. Shortly after we got into the room, somebody knocked on the door. Vinnie answered it and they talked in whispers for about fifteen minutes. Whoever it was handed Vinnie a case and left. Then, he sat down on the bed and patted the empty space beside him. I asked him what he wanted me to do. I'm sorry. I know it was an incredibly stupid thing to say. I was mortified they were taping it. But, he told me. It was truly gross. Ew. I hollered. That was our cue. Steven was there in seconds. He kicked that door in and he and three FBI guys stormed the room. They made as much noise as Mama used to. They arrested me too, but it was to make Vinnie think I was in trouble, too. They let me go when we got outside.

When it was all over, Steven told me Vinnie had no idea I was involved. He knew they let me go, but figured it was because I was a useless human being of no importance. I wanted him arrested for what he said to me, but no deal. They said they had a ton of evidence to charge him with, and he was going to jail for fifteen years. I, on the other hand, was told to leave town. I hadn't planned on that, but it seemed like a good idea. I managed to move, but not out of Charleston and I went about it the wrong way. Can you be any dumber in one lifetime?

Life at Sam's was over, so I was trying to find somewhere else to hang. I needed a new job and new friends. I found a really cool bar near the Citadel where you could throw peanuts on the floor. A loosey-goosey place. Clean, no girls of low repute. But, who knew for sure? It was close to the New Year and a friend of mine asked me to blind-date with her and her guy. I didn't have anything else to do because a part of my life as I knew it had just ended. I needed a jump start. I wasn't ready to leave Charleston, so if I could put another life together, I'd stay.

I opened the door for my date and I hope to this day, I did not actually begin to drool. But then, what was that wet stuff on my jaw? He was gorgeous and when he spoke he had that soft, gentle Southern drawl. Charlie's suit was cut to fit him perfectly, with a small tea rose in his lapel. He had a warm smile on his face and was movie star handsome. He was tall, lean and well built. I could have eaten him alive. The attraction was instantaneous for both of us. The night passed by like I was in a dream. We were in heat all night and no matter what was going on, we were real conscious that something good would happen at the end of the night. Oh, my God. We took to each other immediately. I have to admit, it was more lust than love, but what the hey? First thing you know, I was moving in with him. I had never moved in with a guy before but I was hooked. I didn't want to be away from him for a minute and he felt the same way. Had I known a thing or two about him, I wouldn't have done it. I would have run like hell. Oh well. But, boy, did I learn my lesson.

Charlie and I got a our jollies going to pool halls to get up with other couples to bet on pool. I was pretty good for a girl and Charlie was excellent so we won most of the time. This was when I ran fist first into his jealousy problem. After a while he seemed to get jealous every time we went out, especially if he was drinking. The drunker he got, the worse he got. It was so tense that he would make me sit in the car and wait for him until he was ready to go. He said I was flirting. Hell, I was afraid to even look up. This was the easy phase. It proceeded casually to get worse. About six months after I started living with him, he hit me for the first time. In public. We had a good friend that ran with us and it stunned him and hurt me. As time went on, it escalated. Finally, our friend wouldn't go out with us anymore. Neither would anybody else. I didn't have anybody to help me. Everybody knew about it. I learned that people, as a rule, don't help. They act like it is your problem and your problem only. They convinced me.

There were nights he would beat me before we even made it to the house. He would drive home and throw me out onto the lawn, where I would stay. All night. Because I was unconscious, you see. Forget about the choice of staying home to avoid the problem. Then he would accuse me of having an affair behind his back. It was so painful all the time I was afraid to go out with him and afraid to be in the house with him, but I lived with him. He would get violent if I said no about going anywhere at all because he thought I had someone coming over. It was always someone coming over. The same mantra over and over again. He hated to go to work because I had someone coming over. To prevent me going anywhere much less leave, he would take the distributor cap off my car on his way to work. He wouldn't let me work because every time I got a job, he would think I was going to get up with somebody and he would beat me every day until I quit. Remember my history. It was not like me to run around. After the girl banged my head upside the goal posts, I barely glanced at guys. I had no idea why he felt this way. I tell you, I was scared to death. I was also scared to leave.

I remember one day in particular. As it got close to five o'clock, I knew he would come in the door raising hell and I would get slammed. I chose to go hide in the closet. Hide in the closet. Think about that. Me. Good old Kick Ass Carol was on the floor of the closet so scared I was shaking. Something was seriously wrong here. This was the day I knew I didn't love him enough to live that way. I had to go. One way or another. It might hurt, but I was getting out of there. To this day, it pisses me off when women who have never been beaten by a man make stupid comments like "she could have left." It's not that easy, fart face, when your money, your job, your transportation, your communication and your very dignity have been stripped from you by fear. On top of that, maybe I was wrong, but Mama was getting up in years, had re-married and was happy. More than anything, I didn't want her to know. I looked terrible. Way too much of my hair was gone. He had a hair thing when he beat me. Pulled it out by the roots. She'd have been shocked. Then, she would kill me if he didn't.

I should mention, to be fair, he did wonderful things in between the slaughter. One soft and warm Charleston evening, Charlie took me to the finest restaurant in town for my birthday. He loved the Mills Hyatt House, having been introduced to it's splendor by your's truly. Its one of the oldest and most beautiful of all the restaurants in Charleston. It had that old world atmosphere. You felt that Scarlet would walk into the room any minute. They even played parlor music while you dined. You thought the waiters might be more educated than you were. Here, he could pretend we were a normal couple. He could, not me. We were placed in a little corner with three other tables so close to us, we had to whisper, which was kind of cool. It made it more intimate. I had spent the entire day trying to find some courage to wear or buy. Unfortunately, I put on the wrong size or something. Enter the mouth from hell. Namely, mine. It was in fine form that night. After a gourmet meal feast and a bottle of excellent wine, he asked me what I would like for my birthday. He knew I hated someone to feed me as a birthday present. Good grief, I have to eat. What poor excuse of a present is that? I fired back my answer, after too much wine and without thinking. I baldly stated, "How 'bout my own apartment?" He came across that table so fast I couldn't even react. He slugged me. Right in front of God and everybody. He hit me so hard, I tumbled backwards and took down the waiter behind me. I went out like a lightbulb shot by a high powered rifle.

I came to in the car on the way home. He was driving erratically down the highway; driving worse when It started again. He was slapping me, punching me and trying to drive at the same time. I was desperately trying to be the smallest target on earth; crammed against the passenger door that was unfortunately closed. If I tried to open it, I would take a full-face smack. I cringed. I was afraid he was going to kill me. It was obvious he wanted to, because of the octave he used while screaming those very words. He'd already punched me two or three times in the car before I could even try to think my way out of it. I couldn't believe what a loser I was, but he had isolated me from even the ability to think for myself. We came to a stoplight and I decided I was going to get my body out of that car before we got home or he would kill me. When the light turned green, I grabbed the door handle and tried to hurdle myself out of it as fast as I could. I prayed a policeman would find me instead of a rapist, but it was worth the chance. Hell, a rapist would take one look at how badly I'd been beaten and throw me back like a unwanted lobster. Charlie had anticipated my move and reached over to clutch me by the damn hair of my head. When I hurdled, he clutched. Both at the same time. He yanked about four inches of hair, scalp, blood and all away from my head. Ask me if it hurt.

Suddenly, he jerked the wheel of the car over to the curb, next to a phone booth. He handed me some money, the hair and bloody follicles he had pulled out of the back of my head. With lips that were hardly moving, he insisted I call my mother. I was in a state of shock but alert enough to hear him tell me to stay in the damn booth. He would stay in the damn car until she got there. I did and he did. I laid on the floor of the phone booth and watched him cry. I knew he hated himself, but we knew it wasn't going to stop. He would eventually kill me. Now he accepted it.

Mama was five hours away. I called her around 11:00 pm. Sure enough, she and Mac came rolling up to the phone booth about four in the morning. But, she came. I know Mac, Mama's new husband, wanted to kill Charlie, and he was big enough to do it, but they loaded me up in the car and we took off. They took me to the Ramada next to the river and did their best to clean me up. They took pictures of me before they finally let me take a much needed, restful bath. I hated that Mama had to see me like that. The back of my head was raw and it looked as bad as it felt. The next day Mac went to get my stuff. Charlie was waiting for him. Mac said he was sitting quietly in a chair, looking completely spent. Mama's husband told Charlie if he didn't let him take my belongings, they were going to charge him with assault. He said Charlie never said a word. He was still covered in my blood when Mac got there. How embarrassing. I might have been better off taking my chances with Vinnie. It seemed that everybody who supposedly was drawn to me wanted to tear pieces off me. Once Mac got what I would need, they took me home. I hated coming back to Morehead a beaten mess, but I healed. I was with Mama, and I was safe. It took forever for the hair to grow back. It grew back thinner than the left side as a friendly reminder.

I found out much later that Charlie had been married to his childhood sweetheart. He was working at the Navy Depot in Charleston while she was back in Morrisville, where they grew up. She got pregnant and Charlie was all excited about being a Daddy. The day she had the baby, he got to the hospital as fast as he could drive. That visit changed Charlie for life. It would certainly change how he felt about women. The baby had red hair. He didn't know of anybody with red hair in his family, but he didn't think it was a big deal. Until the sheriff walked in. The red-headed one. I cannot imagine the pain Charlie must have felt as it dawned on him. They divorced. She married the sheriff. Although he was in the physical act of pummeling me, he must have been caught up in the mental image of her being unfaithful and his pain over that Plus his whole home town knowing before he did. Even his parents knew and didn't tell him. He must to have felt like a fool, and he had been a very controlled, proud man. I was the next lady to step into his line of fire. Lucky me.

After I re-established myself financially and mentally, I went back to Charleston and found an apartment clear across town. I'm sorry, but you fall in love with the Charleston ambience. Since it is very big, you can live on one side or the other and never meet people you once knew. There were a lot of singles only complexes in my area so I made friends quickly. You could wander from complex to complex and meet people and no one thought anything of it. Given the friendliness of everyone, the Charlie episode was fading quickly. I am either resilient or I forget negative things easily. When I move on, everything goes, including bad memories. I took a job in a law office. I had worked on the Mandy Rivera campaign so I had an in with the attorneys. I worked in Mrs Rivera's office for awhile doing wills but that was incredibly boring. In my heart, I longed to work with a trail attorney. Litigation was where my soul was. Given a different set of circumstances, I might have made it to being a lawyer, but I ended up with a degree in English. With no money, it wasn't going to happen and time was passing me by. Mrs Rivera knew I wasn't happy, so she searched around for me until she found me another job. Not just litigation, but a firm that did everything. Maybe I could at least be a damn paralegal before somebody strangled me or cut my damn head off. I was very leery of pain these days. Hey, what did I know? I came from the land of the amazingly stupid.

    I called Mama the next day and told her I had a new job. She naturally asked with what firm. I said it just like I answered the phone at work, but I attempted to make it sound like the title of a song. "Steenburger, Lekov, Spietz and Bernstein." I had said it so much on the phones, I could whip it out like it was a sword. "Steenburger, Lekov, Spietz and Bernstein, may I be of assistance?" With Mama, there was this long silence on the other end of the phone. You know, that pregnant pause thing. This was an example of why I loved this woman. You never knew what you were walking into when you entered the Anna mine field. She chuckled and said, "Its nice to know you've hooked up with a nice Irish crew." And she added the Irish accent when she said it. I should have suspected she was setting me up, but what did I know? No one had never taught me about any religions except Baptist and Methodist. I was out of college, for Christ's sake and still didn't know what she was getting at. Religiously speaking, I was walking around like one of the three blind mice. It was bound to get me in deep doo eventually. It would have been nice if she had told me at least something. "Like look into it, Carol. Ask around, Carol. You're an idiot, Carol." But no. Mama decided when she wanted me to make a fool of myself and when she didn't. She must have thought I was old enough for her to take a damn break from teaching. Had I but known? I often wondered if she got her belly laughs out of how ignorant I could be.

    At the firm, I quickly progressed to the point where I was in charge of the secretaries and receptionist and told who what to do when. I had this tall, pretty receptionist who went out one day at lunch, and when she came back, she had a smudge on her forehead that had not been there before. It was obviously not a mole or something I had missed before, I ignored it for awhile, then wandered over and whispered in her ear, "You need to go wash your face. We have a meeting coming up and you have a smudge on your forehead." You know, she was at the reception desk and all. She told me it was Ash Wednesday. Like that meant something to me. Then she started laughing at me. Then she told everybody else and they started laughing at me. I wasn't laughing. I wasn't mad, but I still didn't know what Ash Wednesday was. Excuse me, is every damn body supposed to know what Ash Wednesday is? Well, I know people smudge their face but I sure as hell don't know why. I don't know why ladies from India wear that red dot on their forehead. Does that make me stupid? Apparently so. One of them could have just quit laughing and told me. But no. That wasn't the worst of it. That was just the beginning of my religious nightmare.

    I usually took dictation from Bernard Spietz. He liked to use me because I could spell well and often could often decipher some of the Latin words due to taking Latin in the seventh and eighth grades. One magic Charleston morning, he asked me to come into his office and not to forget my pad. I settled down and we got going. I did my own form of shorthand through several letters, when he suddenly asked me to take the minutes of the B'nai B'rith. Remember my mouth. Remember trouble. I looked up at him and said "The B'nai B'what?" And I emphasized it when I said it. You know, thinking I was a clown. My cheeks puffed out when I said the "b" parts like little balloons. Unfortunately, Mr Spietz did not have a good sense of humor, ever. Ever. The man went berserk. I mean berserk. Scary stuff. He lunged at my face and was screeching at me from one inch away. He was so mad, his face was red and he was practically frothing while he was hollering at me. I didn't know what the hell I had done. I really liked him and enjoyed working with him and I could hear enough to know he was firing me. But he wanted to lay a damn fine cussing on me before I left. His face got redder and his neck vein was bulging. I just sat there and didn't say anything, just sobbing, miserable at whatever had happened. I noticed all this because he was right still in my face. He was so mad he was spitting on me and I think had he known it, he would have done it anyway. He wanted me to say something in particular, but I didn't know what. I felt like I was on the witness stand and I had a glove that fit, you know? Mr Steenburger was the first of the other lawyers to make it to the office. He couldn't do much to stop it except try to get Mr Spietz to stop spitting on me. At the risk of sounding gross, I was pretty much awash in it, if you know what I mean. I think he felt bad because Spietz was furious and I was in hysterics due to his damn spitting and screeching at me. I was cringing in the chair trying to disappear while Mr Spietz was looming over me, blocking my way out of the chair. Eventually, all the lawyers were crammed into the doorway. They couldn't get in the room because Mr Steenburger was blocking the door to keep every damn body from coming in. All the girls were lined up behind the lawyers trying to get a look. Mr Steenburger finally got him to calm down enough to talk instead of scream and asked what had "the poor girl" done. That made him mad all over again. Mr Spietz practically spit on Mr Steenburger when he told him what I had said. He said it the way I said it, too. And he was still pissed. Mr Steenburg looked at me like I was a maggot. But, since I was still blubbering and stuttering, I guess he began to feel sorry for me. He asked, very nicely, why I would say such a insulting thing to Mr Speitz? I told him I didn't mean to insult him. I didn't know what I had done.

    That set them all back on their heels. They all stood back and looked at me like I was from Mars. They are lawyers, they aren't dumb. The dumb one is the one trapped in her chair. Mr Steenburger asked me, "Didn't I know I know the B'nai B'rith was their part of their religion and their temple?" I told him I didn't know anybody went to temples anymore. Not to mention I didn't know there were any temples anymore. He then asked me, "Didn't I know they were Jews?" I told him no. How would I know that? Why would I? What's a Jew? I didn't know what a Jew was. I didn't. I had heard it before but I didn't know if it was a race of people, a religion or both. I also didn't know what the B'nai B'rith was or how to damn spell it. Everybody got to looking at each other with that look on their faces that implied I just might be a certifiable moron. Even Mr Spietz. Suddenly even his ass was speechless, thank God. It appeared the spitting barrage had run its course. They stood looking at each other and then they started laughing. At me. Oh great, first they were screaming at me, now they were laughing at me. Mr Spietz asked me, "Didn't I know by the Menorahs in the windows?" How could I possibly know why they were there if I didn't know they were Menorahs? But I swallowed that response. Maybe that was an insult, too. My answer was, I thought it meant they were lawyers. They were candles, weren't they? There were candles in every lawyer's window for four blocks around the courthouse in downtown Charleston? They got a real chuckle out of that one. Made their day. As many times as a Jew has been insulted through the years, it must have been refreshing to be insulted by somebody too ignorant to know she has done it. They probably got together in one of their meetings to decide, "Have you been insulted when the person doesn't know they have insulted you?" Like the "can you hear the tree fall in the forest" moronic comment.

When I got out of there, unfired, I might add, I took my much maligned, spit upon face home and never went back. I didn't know what a Jew was and I didn't know what a Catholic was. I was twenty four years old. I went home, called Mama and cussed her out. Not funny, female. She, of course, thought it was hilarious. Nor for one second did she care that I walked away from my job. Now, I would never get another job in downtown Charleston because you know damn well the guys in my firm will tell every lawyer in town, for Christ's sake! I am sure Mac and Mama got a real giggle out of it when she told him. Maybe she incorporated it into one of her ditties. Pissed me off.

I was home one day soon after this altogether hilarious incident when I heard someone pull into the parking space outside. I glanced out the window and sure enough, it was Charlie. The guy who beat me. I had no idea how he found me. I freaked. I turned and ran out the back door, panicked. I was truly, truly scared. I ran into a guy I didn't know who was washing his car at the complex behind mine. Gently taking my arms, which had been waving around erratically, he asked me the problem and in seconds I was slobbering all over him. I was shaking like a leaf, as they say. He led me into his apartment to get us out of the street where Charlie might find us. His name was Denny. He lived there with four other guys, and they were all Navy boys. He was going to be getting out in three months and going back home to Lancaster, Pa. He was wonderful. He settled me down and told me I was safe. He and the guys would look after me and I would have nothing to worry about anymore. He took me up to his bedroom, washed my face and told me to lie down. He was going to look for Charlie. Denny wasn't near as big as Charlie. He was about five nine, but he had a body that worked out constantly, you could tell. Awesome cheek bones. Light, laughing blue eyes. Very good-looking, he had a sculptured face with a clean cut moustache. I don't usually like moustaches, but on him it fit. Lips, he had great lips. Ready to kiss kind of lips and soft brown hair like Ted's had been. Denny emphasized he was going to make sure one of them was with me all the time if I wanted it. I wanted it. Actually, I wanted it to be him. After that, I made sure I was around all the time. He dated a girl named Sally, but I could tell they weren't in love, they were just a couple who like to do the same things. What the hey. I figured I could like to do the same things. Maybe then he would like to be with me. Shazamm! What a great idea. It worked, too. It helped that Sally chose to move back home. Thank God and little acorns. We were together all the time because his Navy life was winding down.

Denny was more than just a wonderful guy. He was thoughtful, kind and very attentive to my needs. My favorite thing. I settled into a comfortable life with my new friends. One thing they liked I was mostly unfamiliar with. It was called marijuana. I was twenty five years old, and had never done two things: marijuana and pizza. These two faults came to a crashing halt one Saturday afternoon. The guys and I were hanging around the apartment watching football, eating popcorn and drinking beer. This was the good life. One of the guys pulled out a joint and started passing it around. I passed it up. Not interested. Some of the guys got the munchies and wanted a pizza. The pizza place was only about a mile way, but nobody wanted to go because they were high. I thought "What the hell, I'll go." They had been sitting there smoking for about an hour. These were the days of absolute paranoia so they had all the curtains pulled. I gathered up the money and opened the front door to head out. When that sun hit me, I thought I was going to die. The sheer brightness of it brought me to my knees. I didn't know they made a sun that bright. I felt like I had been smote, whatever that was. I got on my hands and knees and crawled back into the apartment. They broke up. It just makes my day to be the source of other's entertainment. Its what I was born for. They realized I was as high as they were and I hadn't done anything except breathe in their used marijuana. Somebody else offered to go get the pizza because I was totally incapable of dealing with the sun. I consumed that pizza. Nothing had ever tasted so good. I also got on that couch and refused to move for two hours. Probably couldn't. I don't know how people can enjoy that kind of lost mind feeling. I tend to make enough mistakes without handing out my mind for a puff on a joint. Scary feeling. I couldn't believe how many people I knew did "Mary Jane." A desire beyond me.

My next venture into fun and giggle land happened later the day the joint was passed around. The adventure everybody would want to be a part of started in my kitchen. I was still high when I staggered home and being me, I didn't want to sit still anymore. I decided to unload some more boxes from when I had moved. I had some kitchen stuff to unload so I hoisted a box onto the kitchen counter. Still a little high, stuff went here and there at random. When I got to the bottom of the box, there was only one thing left, so I grabbed it. Understand I was not in my right mind. What I had in my hand was one of those large roach-like creatures they like to call palmetto bugs down South. They only call them that because they hate to admit they have roaches. And they say you don't have them because you're dirty, they come up the pipes. My ass. I have never seen a palmetto bug in the sink. I have to admit, I have never found one around food either, but what the hell. That don't mean squat. Who cares why they're there, for Christ's sake? They have nine hundred legs so they're roaches. They're ugly, brown and look like big roaches. They crunch when you kill them, too. Just like roaches. So there.

Looking back down at what I had in my hand, high, was a big, fat, well fed palmetto bug. I came three feet off the ground and I am only five feet tall. I jumped as high as my tiny little breasts. And I let go of it. You can bet your ass, I let go of it. It fell back into the box. I took off running for the bathroom in the bedroom and slammed the door behind me. Do you think I really thought it was going to chase me? I don't know what I thought, but I was not going to be in the same room with it and it was not about to out-run me. So, there I was in the bathroom, shivering with fright. It probably took me ten minutes to stop shaking and another ten to figure out I had lost my mind. What was I doing? Hiding from it? Hide and seek with a roach, for heaven's sake? Major crap. I wasn't that high. This wasn't going to happen. However, my alternative was to go back into the kitchen and confront the roach, who was clearly in control. This was definitely not a great grits day. I was higher than allowed by law, sweating like a pig and indecisive about a roach. Could life get any better?

I slowly opened the door and peeked out. Oh shit! What if it had followed me and was now under the bed? Remember the roach in the ear legend. Little baby roaches running around in your inner ear canal, living off your ear wax. Ew. I always scrubbed my ears til they burned. That's the worse thing that could ever happen, short of Charlie finding me alone. I crept back into the kitchen, hoping it would follow me back if it was in the bedroom. Visualize this nonsense, please. I hope to this day that I was still high or there was no excuse for this stupidity. Hell, he was no where to be found. But. Big but. I had not looked in the box yet. Lord, God, I did not want to lean over and look into that box. Crap.

What the hell, I leaned over and looked into the box. If you've never been five feet tall, it would be hard for you to grasp the concept of the counter being almost as high as my breasts so the top of the box was to my nose. There was no room for error. Oh shit, again. He was still in there. I took off.

As I was sitting on the toilet, I tried to determine what my strategy was going to be. Was I high or what? I was adamant I would not be bested by this roach and I refused to call for help. That would be even stupider than what I was doing. It came to me that I was as repulsed by this roach as I was by Charlie, so I named it. If I humanized it, perhaps I would not feel so stupid. Didn't work, still felt stupid but, you never knew, I might start having a good time soon. I got up from the toilet, got into my car, went to the local store and bought some roach spray. That was embarrassing, too. Drove back to the house like I was Rambo, ran into the kitchen armed and ready to kill. There he was. I sprayed the whole damn can in the box. I'm lucky I didn't die on the spot from inhaling all those chemicals. Off to the bathroom I sprinted. Didn't even take a book because I needed to concentrate. I waited about forty five minutes, long enough for it to die, and slowly tip-toed back into the kitchen. Gotta be quiet. If Charlie was asleep, I didn't want to wake him. He was relaxing on the lip of the box. He had those things on his head moving around like he was zoning in on me. Gross. I almost had a heart attack. Off I went again.

I had to admit I was getting a little tired of myself. Don't think for a minute this was my first evidence of insanity. It had reared it's ugly head before. Maybe somebody ought to stop by and spray a Carol Killer on me. I wondered if I could use the excuse I was high. Then, by Jove, I remembered I had a back door. Yeah! It opened into the kitchen. Voila! I sprinted back into the kitchen. I wanted to be quick so Charlie would not have time to react. I grabbed that box and flung it out the door. I didn't care if he didn't go far, it was outside. After a few minutes, I sneaked up on the box and looked down. No Charlie. He had to be in the apartment. I had been watching the box and knew he didn't come out after I threw it. Damn. I decided to use the brains God gave me. I ran in, grabbed my keys and left. I got drunk. What else are you going to do? I always wondered where he was when I was home. Needless to say, it was not my favorite abode of all times.

Shortly after the roach incident, Denny called me and asked me to come over. I went over thinking everything was ok. Neither of us had worked our way into the "I love you" realm and I was steadfastly avoided it. Boy, did I get bad news. Denny was leaving. His Dad was ill and he had to go home to Lancaster. He was leaving that day and wanted to say goodbye. I knew he liked me a lot, but his Dad was more important, obviously.

It snowed there, people. A lot. Not to mention Lancaster was like another continent to me. Life crashed again. I had been so happy with Denny because he was such a regular guy. He was everybody's favorite buddy. When the guys got home, he told them. We were all depressed as hell. He told me he had talked to the other guys and they were going to keep looking after me. He promised me that somebody would be with me every night to protect me from Charlie. They had made a pact. There had already been a couple of nasty confrontations, but the guys stood their ground and Charlie didn't mess with me if one of them was around. I guess the old "nothing lasts forever" had caught up with me. Nothing you can do about it. He left. I felt abandoned, even though I knew it wasn't like that. My reasoning knew he had to go. The rest of me was in mourning.

I have a relatively good philosophy about how to deal with something that makes me unhappy. Unless its a guy slapping me around, I can ignore it. Forget about it. Do something else. Walk somebody else's dog. Whatever. I am good at it, too. Now they call it compartmentalizing. Bullhocky. You forget about it and think about something else. Period. I call it redirect. Try to move on.

A couple of weeks after Denny left, I had to go out on my own because the guys were doing a guy thing. I felt like I was intruding on their time once Denny left. I went to a club I enjoyed that should have been a safe choice, turned around and there he was. Charlie, the guy, not the roach. What did this damn guy do? Barhop every night until he found me? He grabbed my arm and started screaming in my face about me always being his girl. All the people around us assumed we were a couple having a fight and stayed back. Just about the time he started to haul me outside, one of the guys showed up. That ended that, but it started something so new, so unexpected, that it changed my life forever. I wouldn't be who I am today had Denny's buddy not shown.

My rescuer was Sammy. He was Denny's best friend and I must admit, one of my favorite people of all time. He got me out of there, shaking like a leaf, and took me back to the apartment. It was two o'clock in the morning but he called Denny anyway. They talked so long I fell asleep on the couch. I was afraid to go home and sleeping on the couch was not an unusual event. Sammy put a blanket over me and let me sleep, but when I woke up, he had news. Denny had talked to his parents and they invited me to come to Lancaster and live with them. Denny was living at home with his parents, six brothers and an eight year old sister. All in one house. I could sleep with the sister. I said yes. I decided to leave my apartment, furniture and all. While I was packing, I wondered how the eight year old sister felt about this.

Before I left, I gave a girlfriend who wanted to move into my apartment, the ok, but told her I might be back. Who knew what was going to happen? Well, I should have known what was going to happen. Within days she stole everything. My furniture. All of it. She moved, got an unlisted number and disappeared. I had nothing to go back to.

In Charleston, I had been working with an engineering company in the personnel department. I asked for a transfer if they had an opening in Lancaster. Life is good. I had good references from Charleston because I had flown through the promotions and had done very well so they made me Asst. Personnel Director in only six months. They told me they had an opening in Lebanon, Pa, which was just outside Lancaster. I took it. What they didn't tell me was what I would be doing. They just hinted it would be in the Personnel Department. I left two days later at one o'clock in the morning. God help me, I was headed North to the people who had undoubtedly killed my ancestors. My Mama was going to cut my head off when she found out. Hell, she deserved it, for the lawyer thing.

My only directions were to get on highway 95 and head North, then get off on the Harrisburg, Pa. exit. I had no idea it was a ten hour drive so I ended up drained of life. Getting off as instructed, once I found a phone, I was to call. They would come get me. Are these nice people, or what? We didn't have cell phones in those days, so if I got lost, I could end up in Arizona. Don't forget the cracker in me. This was a major deal. I had never been on a road trip like this one by myself. I was scared to death, but I didn't look back. Charlie was never going to leave me alone. I had everything I could take crammed into a 240Z. Obviously, I couldn't take a lot because I was moving into an eight year old's bedroom, not to mention you can't get a whole lot into a 240Z. Oh, by the way, it sure as hell is not the choice car for snow. Duh.

Denny had told me to get off Hwy 95 at a particular exit. Lo and behold, I actually found it and got off like a big girl. I found a phone booth at an all night truck stop and called him as directed. I sat my weary butt down at one of the tables in the "restaurant" and waited. About forty five minutes later, he and his parents found me. Denny and I followed them into what looked like a pleasant little town about fifteen miles from Lancaster.

On the way to the house the night I arrived, Denny told me he didn't love me, but he couldn't leave me in Charleston and his parents agreed. Oh, my God. What was I doing here? I had hoped love was in the cards. Now, everyone knew he had brought me up because I was battered, not the love of his life. I had left all my things, my job, my friends, the Confederate flag, everything. I became embarrassed and stayed that way for the seven years I slept with his sister.

I have to admit I didn't count on liking these people as much as I did. These were exceptional parents. They welcomed me with open arms, just like I had always been there. His parents hugged me like I was a long, lost daughter. As far as they were concerned, I had been away and returned home. They never mentioned why I was there. I didn't know. I had never known what it was like in a normal family. The good news was this one wasn't completely normal either. Little sister and all. It was never quiet. All the boys were teenagers and older. The mother ran the house like it was a country club on a schedule.

They had a bar in the basement, and between the parents and all their kids, there was a party all the time. The problem for me was I didn't feel like I belonged there. Here, I knew only them. I was surrounded by them and the partying night and day. Me, who craved solitude. I was never alone, never. I was sleeping in a room with a child. From breakfast to bed, the house was full of people. I was also deeply grateful to them for caring about me enough to open their home to me just on Denny's say so. Unfortunately, I reacted as usual. I withdrew into myself. There could be a party going on, card playing offers, etc. but I would sit in a corner reading a book and never look up. The most I ever did with them was play cards. Denny's family was a lot of fun, but I never let myself enjoy it. I should have. They never gave up, nor did they push trying to get me to join in the festivities. I would stay in my little corner. I wasn't unfriendly, I was lost. I would never acknowledge their generosity except to say thank you with my head down. It was very unfair to them. I regret it to this day.

Living with them was like living with the guys again. Except these guys didn't go to bars, they went to the Elks Club where they bowled. When Denny suggested I learn so I could go with him, I thought he'd lost his mind. I wasn't going to bowl with anybody, I was a shagger. I had dignity. Its amazing how unfair I can be. I amaze myself sometimes.

TAKE THE CORPORATE LIFE AND STICK IT

After two weeks of settling in with Denny's family, I went to work. I found out what my job was the second I sat down. I was to lay off 1600 steelworkers. Catch that? Me? A five foot tall, Southern blonde with a Down East brogue was going to lay off 1600 pissed off men. They had a reason to be pissed. Really, really pissed. They and their families had been moved from their home towns, offered better jobs, sold houses, bought houses, took kids in and out of schools for a better life. It lasted six months and then the Engineering company lost the bid on the contract for which all the guys had been hired and, just like that, decided they had to go. There was a Personnel Director who had been there thirty years but they didn't want to use him because they thought it was bad P.R. Laying off 1600 steelworkers was bad P.R., numb nuts. Using a short, Southern blond to do it was incredibly bad P.R. You could always tell when you were in the corporate world by the ridiculous decisions they made.

This situation quickly translated itself into normal daily activities like death threats. Like right away. They never came to the house with threats, or burned it down for that matter, because they liked Denny's family. They were unrelenting with the slashed tires, though. They slashed them at work and at home. Shredded them. It got so I couldn't drive to work and drive home on the same day. It was a long walk home, I tell you. It's not like I had a lot of friends at the office. People with leprosy got more respect than I did. They didn't mind letting you know who was doing it, either. They told me it was the big guy. They were all big guys. In addition to having to put up with this crap, I ended up having to do labor negotiations with steelworkers, electrical workers, truck unions, every damn body. I had people in my face every day and had absolutely no training or confidence to get me through. I'd rather take up bowling, for Christ's sake.

Ed, the Personnel Director, only did the hiring and firing and he did that badly. I found out one day that we had been paying one of the draftsmen twice the normal pay scale for two years. There's no way he didn't know. It wasn't until I suggested a survey of surrounding pay scales that it came up. When I told Ed about it, expecting some sign of professional behavior, he went over to the draft department, grabbed the guy by the arm, pulled him into the personnel department, threw him in a conference room and then made him sign a piece of paper that Ed wrote out by hand, agreeing he would pay it all back in a year. With interest. Stupidly, Ed also made a copy of the paper, gave it to him, and then fired him. Unfortunately, you can't do that type of thing anymore. You eat it. You can rant and rave, but not to the person, only to underlings. You can put someone back to the correct pay limit, but the pay you have given him is gone forever. When I tried to get the Vice President of Labor Relations involved, he passed. I ended up having to go to Stanache, the President. He sent me to the guy's house to plead with him not to sue us, and for me to get him to tear up the paper, then re-hire him. Mission accomplished.

After that, the Vice President of Human Resources, took me under his wing and, over time, gave me what knowledge I needed to get by, but he was swatting these people off like flies as I was. I was given only eighteen months to accomplish my "objective" and I made up my mind I was going to make it. Piss on 'em. That's aimed at the corporate guys, not the lay-offees.

Your heart breaks for these people. The steel industry was dying. Our division made electrostatic precipitators. We were not actually a steel factory so other than making the precipitators, we didn't have jobs for these people. I got to know a lot of them and their families. I decided to get into it from their point of view, as well as that of the company. I brought them all in as a group and we talked about problems and possible solutions. I made it a point to understand each individual situation so when I had any solution, I knew which family would be best for it. I made sure they understood how awful I thought it was that they were in this conflict. It softened the blows somewhat.

Didn't help my tires, though. Not for a long time. It was obvious there was someone I did not convince. I know some of the guys tried to make whoever was doing it stop, but he wouldn't. I also made up my mind that I would try to find them jobs as hard as I would work to make my objective. Maybe I'd hit on him. Ergo, solve my problem. Out-sourcing was not really well known and it certainly wasn't known to me, so I had to approach it like a crab. Slow, but steady progress was made. Once the word got around that I had placed some of the guys, I could feel the spirit of cooperation begin to flow through my veins.

It was hard, and I knew rough times. I was very low in spirit as well as in confidence. I was a fish out of water. Every now and then, things would not go as planned or promised. Naturally, there were always those hot heads who wouldn't work with me. Oh, and it snows in Pennsylvania. What a concept! I would work and by the time five o'clock rolled around, the snow would be over my head, for heaven's sake. I grew up with oceans and fish and boats, not chains on my tires. Think about it. Chains on a 240Z. I don't think so. I was also not used to being shut up in the house because I couldn't get out for the snow packed against the damn doors. For your information, snow is beautiful but slush is not. I tried to drive to work one day but the drifts were five feet tall. Recognize the number. That snow was past my nose. The highway patrol in Pennsylvania let you get on the highway, drive fifteen miles from home, then told you to go back rather than put "Stay home, fools. You can't make it." on the radio. They only cleared one lane of traffic and everybody who backed up behind you was on it. You couldn't turn around. They had to start turning around from the back end. Think about it. And they were known to be stubborn in Pennsylvania. I think some of them would sit there until the drifts melted out of sheer stubbornness. I hated it.

Ask me how many times I had to fight the damn civil war. I always lost because I was there and had nowhere to go with that whole freaking issue. In the South, we were taught it was an economic war while, at the same time, in the North they were taught it was a war caused by incredibly stupid Southerners who were knee deep in incest who wouldn't give up slavery. I hate the movie "Deliverance." A no-win situation. That movie did absolutely nothing for bettering relations between the North and the South, believe me. People up there think that's how the whole damn South is. How ignorant is that? For the most part, Denny didn't know I had to do battle every damn day, so he couldn't figure out why I didn't just want to settle down, party and bowl. But where ever I was, all I had to do was open my mouth and let that Southern sound come out of it and I might as well put on a gray uniform and sling a musket over my shoulder. The battle was on. Needless to say, I got vehement from time to time and made some real enemies. I pointed out that we Southerners are a proud people and if you think you are just going to step on us and expect us to take it, you'd better rent another head. Your's was going to be gone in a second. Either that, or step aside. We didn't lose the war because we wouldn't fight. We fought until we had absolutely nothing left to fight with, not nothing left to fight for. The black people believe this monstrosity, too, but I can't blame them. There were enough of the plantation owner types to make it so, but not everybody who fought, much less died, was a plantation owner or people who owned slaves. Think about it. A whole culture fought, not just the rich and greedy. We believed what we were doing and we believe it today. I would come back at people arguing the war and make my views well known. I am proud to say there were times I didn't act like dainty, brainless Miss Scarlet. I would get right in their face. Damn it. I love the South and the damn war is over. Didn't these jerks know it? They won. What's their problem? Still looking for blood or what? I'd say, "Fine, get me a knife. I"ll cut myself for you. I rather get a damn book and get you out of my face. Take the bayonets home with you when you leave."

Life continued its weird way at the Engineering company. I had been made Personnel Director over Ed, but did the same job I did before. I worry about job promotions where the job doesn't change. Scares me. And women's lib was rearing its very loud head. I didn't care about Women's lib, mainly because I was too busy, the corporate heads were listening. I never pushed my way around because I was a woman, I just worked hard. I only wanted something if I earned it. Like Mama taught me. However, it had never actually crossed my mind that I might have some brains. I thought it was all my hard work that got me promos. Mr Buerk, the VP of Labor Relations mentioned that one day. He brought me into his office and said, "Why is it you don't realize how smart you are? Why don't you think you can do the job you have to do and accept how well you are doing it?" What do you say to something like that when you absolutely do not think you are either smart or confident? I could take a three hundred pound steelworker to his knees with a good Southern insult, but thought that was luck. It did make me think and I walked a little taller after that. I didn't remember anybody even implying that before. I was flying through these promotions. Actually, I always had. I hoped it wasn't all because of the lib thing.

I found one guy who still respected women. We were having a high level conference at the Ramada in Lebanon. All the other Presidents and VP's had flown in from around the country, including some way-up-there guys from Menlo Park, Ca. I got the schedules out and the room set up. I was going only in order to be there if Mr Stanache needed me to go back to the office for anything, although I ranked as high as some of them.

We had just arrived at the Ramada with Frank Weems, one of the higher ups, when Mr. Stanache decided we needed a typewriter and paper in case memos needed to be prepared. I explained I had my pad and would be taking notes, but I did not bring a typewriter assuming I could do it later. Mr Stanache rudely ordered me back to the office for the typewriter. Because our office had those big and heavy Correcting Selectric II's from IBM, I had to get help getting it into the car. When I got back to the meeting, I struggled to get it out. My arms were so short, I couldn't get them around it. I finally got a good grip on it and was doing fairly well until I got to the stairs. Mr Stanache and Mr Weems were standing in the hallway and glanced my way. When Mr Stanache did nothing but open the door, Mr Weems looked at him, stunned. He snarled at Mr Stanache, "This young lady works for you. Get that damn typewriter out of her arms and carry it yourself! And make sure you are the one who carries it back. I do not want to ever see anything so disgraceful again. Your office will have a full manager meeting on how to treat women. Little lady, if you see or hear anything at the office from now on you think I should know, call me. And get another female down here to take notes. You are going to attend the meeting like you are supposed to." I was both thrilled and scared at the same time. However, no negative feedback came my way.

Mr Stanache, somewhat chastened, decided to send me to New York City to take a seminar on assertiveness. After working with the 1600 steelworkers in a very bad situation, I couldn't believe he didn't think I could be assertive. However, you can't get any more scared than I was then. Everybody knew that anybody who went to New York died. Nobody came out alive. Those people were crazy and they talked funny. I must say, I did not appreciate Mr Stanache calling the concierge at the Americana to tell her not to let me out the front doors. He knew this little Southern cracker would be a walking dinner for some nut. I would get killed. But, he should have trusted me. I damn well was not going out those doors, no matter what. They'd be blessed if they didn't have to drag me out of the room to attend the seminar. Seven days of pure nightmare. I thought they would break into my room and rape and pillage me. I did room service every night. However, I have to admit I bought a five hundred dollar dress in the shop in the hotel. Can you imagine that? In the seventies..five hundred dollars for a dress. That made me an official New Yorker in my mind, not to mention a success. That was not a Southern thing to do in Carteret County. I bet there weren't ten women in the county who would buy a five hundred dollar dress. Instant sophistication. I wore it around the room. I never, ever wore it in public. I didn't have to. I had it. That's all it took. Between Mr Buerk backing me up every day, New York and a five hundred dollar dress, I had to be spot on. Little black dress, hot damn! I decided to start dressing even better than I did, be confident and whip ass. I never looked back.

The assertiveness class was better than awesome. It taught you how to bring everything down to a common level. No high highs or low lows in your attitude. Just go straight down the line. No reactions, just solutions. No problems, just solutions. Since I was already solution oriented this was great for me. They taught us not to spend five minutes placing blame for a problem but to expend all your energy on fixing it. Who did it made no impact. If you were dealing with me and wanted to whine, go to the end of the line. If you wanted my help with a solution, step up. I could do this stuff if you were ten feet tall. Get in my face, go home. I got so good at this, the company put fifty women under my supervision since they were obviously the hardest to control. That went over real big with these women. Some of them had worked there fifteen or more years and they were all taller than I was. If size was a qualification, I was lacking it. However, I was smart and I knew my stuff. I laid a little bit of that assertiveness stuff on their butts and they shut up. I had a little meeting with the problem ones and told them I knew they all had more years on the job than I did. And they knew more than I did. I regretted that I had been promoted over them but, I could fire them, and until they could do that to me, step in line. You know, the line I am heading up. If not, step out of line and you know the way to the door. I didn't offer a back door. Head out the front and pass everybody in the company on your way to the parking lot. Perked them right up. Southern style. We don't have to snap a whip in the South, we laid pure sense and an insult on you all at the same time. I had earned some power and wasn't ashamed to throw it around. Yee-ha.

I had a redhead that wanted to be the office troublemaker. I loved these idiots who wouldn't listen. They gave me a reason to get up in the morning. I told her the next meeting she was going to have was with her doctor if she didn't shut her mouth. She asked me was I threatening her. I told her no, I was stating a fact, because her husband would probably beat the hell out of her if I fired her. So, unless she wanted her husband to get in trouble and lose his job too, she'd step up to the plate. All I wanted was for her to do her job and stop making trouble. It was as easy as that. I wasn't looking for a friend, just a hard worker. Period. She saw my point. Those were hard times and there were hard men with no patience for the wife losing her job if he hadn't lost his, yet. Losing her job was her choice. Anybody got a problem with that logic? I did have some smarts. My confidence soared and so did my abilities. Of course, people still had to look down to me. The confidence wobbled from time to time.

Mr Stanache brought in some psychologists to determine if everybody was in the job best for them. I was the only non-Vice President that attended the staff meetings and was invited to take the psycho-tests. These were a snap. Hell, I used to give these tests when I was studying Psychology in college. I already knew most of the answers but I convinced myself to simply take the test the way I should. Who'd a thought? There's the elephant on a toilet, again. Christ. They mailed them back a month later and nobody was supposed to read them but the boss. Since they sent them directly to me, I did. Hell, I was Personnel Director, these would go in my files.

In their summary, they told Stanache I was his most effective staffer and he would be lax if he didn't make me Vice President of Human Relations. I also had a recommendation from Mr Weems. But, people, that was Don's job. I was horrified. He had been my mentor and had taught me so much. I resealed my evaluation and gave all of them to Stanache for his review. I was sorry I had read it. But what the hell, Stanache had never done anything he was told anyway. I convinced myself that Weems meant for Mr Stanache to promote Don to something else, but it wasn't written anywhere. The next day, he did it. He fired Don. Don had eight kids, was Catholic and was never going to quit having kids. All his experience was steel related. I was heartbroken. I told him that I felt this was so unfair. He had taught me so much and I needed so much more but he laughed and said, "what will be, will be." Before he left, he sat down with me and spent three hours telling me things he thought would take me farther along in my career. I had a career. I never knew that. You know, the only definition I found for having a career was it meant you could kick somebody's butt. If you didn't have a career, you were the butt kickee.

One of my favorite new functions was to see that Mr Stanache had a secretary who was actually willing to come back from lunch. Good grief. They didn't even wave good-bye, they just never came back. In all honesty, I couldn't blame them. I knew why. He had a tendency to one; think he was somebody and two; think because he was somebody, you'd be dying to sleep with him. Eventually, the inevitable happened. One of his many secretaries went out for lunch and didn't come back. I was the first girl he saw when he walked down the hall. I got my own glassed-in office, right beside his. I had been promoted from Vice President of Human Relations to his secretary. You notice I put that in no caps. Its because this job meant nothing to me. Now, the company had no V P of Labor Relations or Personnel Director so Ed was back in play. I think Mr Weems would have killed him if he knew. At least, I had managed to either lay off some or find almost all of the steelworkers I worked with other jobs. I had managed to work with the unions and get flexibility on both sides of the table so there could be open discussions. I knew I would miss my job terribly, but it wasn't the same after Don left. I knew my tires were safe, but I didn't know my sexuality was going to be under the gun.

Mr Stanache knew that Denny and I had drifted apart. It was a small town and everybody knew everything about everybody. After seven years, we finally moved out of his parents home and got our own apartment but we were going separate ways. Denny was still my favorite person and my hero and would always be. I would damn well not bowl, no matter what. Sorry, bowlers. Its just how I feel. It was great to not have to sleep with his sister but our sex life was so bad that it might as well have not even existed. We even talked about it like it had died or something. Neither of us wanted to. We had become great friends, not great lovers. Something was wrong.

Every now and then, in spite of my best efforts to avoid it, I would be called into Mr Stanache's office. He always started his where or how or when. It went this way. "Where would a guy like me find a girl like you if he wanted to be discreet.?" He didn't want to be discreet as bad as he wanted to get laid. And yes, he was a married man and I didn't like him anymore than I had my Daddy. I never forgot how to hold a grudge. The first time, my answer went like this. "There's this great little bar in town where some of the paralegals go. You know about paralegals, don't you?" I didn't know squat about paralegals, but a seed is a seed is a seed. He thought I did. Off he goes. Mama calls this method re-direct. It's when you re-direct someone's plan elsewhere. Namely, off me.

At least a week went by before he called me in again. These little chats were the only reason he ever called me into his office. I knew it was trouble when he would tell me to bring my book, like I took his damn dictation. The second time, it went like this. "Where does a guy like me take a girl like you if he wanted to be discreet?" No imagination. Same meaning. Different answer. "There's a bar in Hershey right across from the Hershey Hospital. You know about nurses, don't you?" Good show. Re-direct.

Another couple of weeks went by and here we went again. And, yes, by now I was getting pretty tired of it. I had been thinking about leaving and opening my own employment agency because I didn't feel like batting him down every week or two. He wasn't going to promote me because I was the only damn one who came back from lunch. This time it went like this: "How would a guy like me ask a girl like you to go out if you wanted to be discreet?" Now we were at the stage where he was getting real personal and re-direct was essential. My answer was easy and prompt. "Mr Stanache, there's a girl in Accounting who thinks you are a dream, I can set it up for you if you'd like. She's a friend of mine." Now I was pimping for the shit. Ok, another couple of weeks go by and here we go again. Will this never end? He asked, "Where would a guy like me take a girl like you at the end of an evening if he wanted to be discreet?" He was emphasizing the "end of an evening" like a motel wasn't good enough for him. Maybe he needed music to get it up. Exasperated with this foolishness, I said, "For Christ's sake, Mr Stanache, you are the President of a the precipitator division. Let me get a company apartment. You can say its for visiting dignitaries or clients. Everybody else has one." Hell, I didn't know if everybody else had one or not, nor did I care. Immediately, I was sent off to find an apartment and furnish it. The way I wanted. Perhaps the girl in Accounting was waiting. Who knew? The good news was I was in control of the keys. Cool.

Right after I got the apartment, life took another twist. I went into serious heat for the first time. Or, I lost my cool. I lost my head. I lost my sanity. All at the same time. Really. Hell, I was struck dumb. Remember I said earlier I wondered if people's brains got scrambled when they were in heat. Mine were cooked well done in a less than a minute flat.

I was sitting in my little glass world one morning, near the end of the hall, hoping someone with a real mind would wander by to talk to me. Anybody. Well, anybody but Mr Stanache. I knew why all those girls left now. Since nobody liked him, being at the end of the hall was like being stranded on a desert island. Nobody in their right mind came all the way to the end of the damn hall. Stanache's office was at the very end, then me, then Larry who was V P of the precipitator stuff. One morning, down the hall came the best looking man I had ever seen. I looked up just as he entered Larry's office. There was nothing but glass between Larry and I, so I got a good look. I think I had an orgasm. In fact, I am fairly sure I had an orgasm. If my mouth didn't fall open I'll eat the first hat I see. You talk about tall, dark and handsome. I never knew what that meant until then. It means just what it says. He had all three. He had mesmerizing eyes. I could tell from where I sat that this eyes were deep green and you could tell just from looking at him that he had a gorgeous, easy smile, beautiful teeth and a relaxed way about him. He looked better than any movie star I had ever seen. He was well dressed and the whole package fit the high class, well fitted black suit he was wearing. If I had still been Personnel Director I would have hired him just to look at. For two and a half hours Larry interviewed him and I got hotter and hotter and hotter. I didn't care how hot I got, I was not taking my eyes off him. Where's a camera when you want one? Hell, where's a bed when you want one? I thought about calling Larry on the intercom and asking him to tell the guy I had keys to a company apartment. When Larry looked at me, I would shake them at him and leer. I restlessly waited for the interview to end so I could find out when I could get a chance to throw myself at him. Literally. I would change my fingers to suckers if it helped me get him close. Every now and then he would look around at me and smile. It didn't take long before I could tell he didn't want to take his eyes off me, either. He was trying to keep the heat from showing in his eyes when he looked at me. Me, I didn't have that problem. Larry was chuckling because he had picked up on it. Sweet little fart. But, he was cooperative, I will give him that.

    As soon as the interview was over, he brought him into my room and introduced him to me. Michael Gray. God was good. He had put a man that damn good looking right in front of my face to look at. Perhaps God, in His glory, had him made just for me. I couldn't say a word. All he could do was nod. He couldn't speak, he only gaped. I had never made anybody gape before. Larry was having the snickering time of his life. They left to visit the precipitator equipment, but Larry said they would be back, to hold onto Michael's coat for him. I was stuck to my seat like glue. He was coming back and I wasn't going anywhere until he did. Not even to the bathroom. If they didn't come back until nine that night, my ass would be glued to that chair. When he came back, he was kind enough to walk right into my office without my having to kick the glass down to get to him. He said he was glad to meet me and hoped Larry would give him a chance. He told me to tell Larry good things about him. Do you think for one second Larry had a thing to say about it? He didn't even want to think about what would happen to him if Michael Gray did not appear on my payroll sheets promptly. Good things, my ass. I'd give Larry anything he wanted. Hell, I was willing to give Larry a shot at me. Know what I mean? He wouldn't even think about not hiring him. Not when I was done with him. I couldn't believe I was actually thinking about going "too far" to get Larry to hire him, but I restrained myself. After Michael left, Larry propped himself against my door, and said, "Well, how bad do you want him?" My answer was, "Almost, but not quite." He looked pretty let down about that. Then I added, "But, you never know." Perked him right up.

      He chuckled and walked off, knowing I wouldn't go that far. He came back with a smirk on his face. He came to tell me they were going to the Ramada Inn after work for a drink since it was already the end of the day. Just thought I would like to know. Hell, yes, Modeen Gunch. I quickly called a girl I worked with and told her to meet me at the Ramada. I told her I wanted to get there fifteen minutes after they did. That way, they'd be seated and I could ensure I would sit beside him. Then I would have an opportunity to squeeze my fine ass beside his fine ass. Capture his attention. And whatever else he was willing to have captured..that was my goal. And I hit it.

      We volleyed back and forth with little chit chat and then, bam. He was married. Damn. How could he not have been? It didn't stop my infatuation, though. In spite of all those years of despising people like that, suddenly I was one. But, it was unstoppable. When the night was over, I offered to take him home, which was in Hershey, about thirty miles away. We sat in that car and talked until one o'clock in the morning. Although I didn't do anything I shouldn't, I was horrified at the way I was acting but I was already lost. So was he. He told me his wife hated him and didn't care what he did. But, he loved his two boys and would never leave them. His wife only liked him for the social side of things, and they hadn't had sex in years. We are talking people in their thirties, but then I remembered Denny and I were the same age. I told him I wanted to meet his wife. We knew something would happen if we were around each other a lot and I knew I couldn't keep doing this. Maybe if I didn't like her, we might proceed. At the time he was kissing me like he couldn't stop. Oh, I think I was kissing back. You bet your ass I was kissing him back. Once I got home, I didn't like myself very much. I immediately sat Denny down and told him what I had done. He was great. He knew it was over, but we shared expenses and he said it was ok with him, but he didn't want me going out with a married man. Me either. It was sad, but what was said needed to come out. I didn't know, of course, that he had been seeing a girl he met at soccer.

I'll give him credit, Michael went about it. He set it up with his wife that Larry and I would meet them at a pizza place across the street from the Hershey Hospital. You know, the one I sent Mr Stanache to. I kind hoped we'd see him there with a girl, but it was not to be. I disliked Michael's wife instantly. She was one of those "You're not even good enough for my time" kind of snobs. She waved her hands around in that droopy way the snotty have. Ruined the taste of the pizza. I immediately felt sorry for Michael. He looked at me like "See? Told you so." If it had been about her, Michael would not have gotten the job because Larry couldn't stand her. It showed. At one point in the conversation, she regaled us with her college education that was "a complete waste", because she married Michael and had her first accident. That was her kid she was talking about. She went on about being so smart in college. Number one in her class. I finally told her to quit waving her Phi Beta key at me, I had done pretty well myself. When we were done, she invited us to their place for a drink. I was very conflicted about the whole thing. I didn't know if I wanted this to go any farther until I looked at him and was lost all over again.

Naturally when we got to the house, she started the showing me around thing. I truly hate that. I really don't want to be wandering around someone's house having to mouth platitudes when I might really hate the decor. Anyway, we finally reached the upstairs and you know the only thing upstairs are bedrooms. We came to the children's room first, but they were asleep. Michael was already in there, kissing them on the forehead. Not even approaching her children, she took me to "her" bedroom. They had this huge king size bed that took up the entire room. And the bed was all mussed up. She hadn't even made the bed that day and she didn't work. I couldn't stand to leave my house without the bed made I started having little fantasies about what went on with that bed when she, obviously, with her Phi Beta Key and all, picked up on that. She looked me right in the eye and smirked, "It's not what you think. He's a thrasher, that's all. Nothing juicy." Nothing juicy? Gross. She actually told me, a complete stranger, she was not interested in Michael at all. He bored her. Pissed me off. I looked her right in the eye..well, almost..she was taller than me, and told her if she didn't want him, I did. I would dearly love a chance to have him even try to bore me. I would, if she didn't mind, borrow him for awhile. I got downright pugnacious about it. I dared her to try to one-up me. She wasn't even inclined to say no. She said, and I quote, "Take him. I don't want him and he knows it." Bitch. But that was a fine, damn offer, I must say. I did just that.

For two years, we couldn't keep our hands off each other. Two exquisite years. Memories you could not get from movies. Memories so wonderful you don't even want to talk about it. I will say this, the company apartment was very useful. We loved the same music. We never cut the TV on. We talked and loved. I'll keep some of my memories to myself, thank you very much. He was one of those awesome people I'll never forget, no matter what. He was kind, gentle and wanted to be with me all the time. Made it worthwhile, too. My Lord, he was a retired Air Force pilot who flew from time to time. Did he look awesome in that uniform or what? With that hat on his head? He looked like Wilson had come to life. I never, the whole time I knew him, could take my eyes off him. He made me completely happy.

Unfortunately, he got more and more dissatisfied at home and wanted out. He knew what being happy was now. Everything was up front. We did things with the kids. They had to know we were in love.It was obvious. It was obvious their mother knew and didn't care. He called me one night after he had checked into a sleazy motel outside of town. Not somewhere Michael and I would go, believe me. He had a bunch of clothes with him. He had left. I had a long, painful talk with him and reminded him of his boys. I knew his wanting to get away from her was above and beyond any affair with me. I insisted this would not be placed on my head. Then, he stopped my clock. He said she was threatening to name me in the divorce. She didn't want him back. She wanted a divorce so she could move on. I didn't care about what she wanted. I cared about those two boys. I told Michael he needed to stop and think about how he would feel without those children in his life. This was a vindictive woman, as so many are. She would make sure he didn't get access to them. I told him to tell her no when she asked for a divorce. Not to discuss it unless the visitations rights could be agreed upon. He went back home the next morning. No, I didn't stay or have sex with him. He was at a major crossroad in his life and he needed to be alone. If only he had been divorced when I met him, who knows what the future could have he d?

Life went on, but I was still stuck in that hallway with Mr Stanache, the lech of all leches. By now, everybody knew about Michael and me. Mr Stanache called me into his office one day, acted very serious and told me I should expect for one or both of us to have to quit. I asked him why because I wanted to make him say it. Let him say it was for sexual conduct. Just let that foolishness come out of his mouth when he knew what I knew about him. I had records from the apartment. I told him I was ready to serve notice because I had achieved as much of my objective as I could, stuck being his secretary. If he preferred, I simply wouldr't come back from lunch. In six weeks. That would be familiar to him. He asked me if I knew what he wanted in a replacement. I said sure. He wanted a tall blonde with tits. The next day at she walked into my office for an interview. I told her I had a job for her, for sure. I didn't even interview her, just threw her butt into his office. That girl was a willing prey and Mr Stanache was a predator. Worked for me. I left a six week notice in his box. When I left that same day at six o'clock she was still in there. When came in the next morning, she was in my chair. I demanded, and got, eight weeks termination pay. It would carry me for awhile. I had good experiences and great references. After all, I had a copy of my own file together with the Psych report. I knew I would be ok. I wasn't quite ready, financially, for my own employment agency, but my little fund was growing. I would miss Michael desperately. At least, while I worked there, we would run into each other and laugh and carry on like we always did. That wouldn't happen now. It was truly over. I was heartbroken. I thought I must have loved him because I never thought of Ted when I was with him.

There was so much change going on, it was frightening. Denny and I decided to go separate ways. He wanted to move to Florida and I didn't want to go. He had always wanted to be a beach bum, though. I lucked out. I found this cool one bedroom efficiency with a Murphy bed. Is that a great concept or what? I settled down to looking for a new job and a new life. Little did I know what prompted Denny's decision to leave.

HOW DID CARTERET COUNTY GET HERE?

I had my great Murphy bed and then wham, Mama called. Same old crap. Mama wanted me to let MaryBeth come up. "Mama! Please, please, please, please, whatever you want, but not that." She wanted me to make peace with her. You have no idea how bad I hated this making peace theory. I was not the enemy, folks. I just stood off from the rest, that's all. Making peace or even conversation was definitely not something I wanted to do. MaryBeth and I walked on different sides of the morality line. Mama can talk me to death until she gets what she wants so I gave in. MaryBeth and her dog, Honey, a golden retriever came rolling into town with a guy she had bummed a ride with who was going on to Delaware. Honey was a doll baby but MaryBeth was just an older version of the same girl. Fast. The first thing she wanted to do was go out. Sound familiar? I took her to the club at the Ramada, the only place in town where I didn't know anybody. We really didn't have a lot to talk about because pretty much everything we had in common was a downer for one of us. She wandered off and let herself get picked up. Who'd a thought? I started dancing, and, no, they don't shag in Pennsylvania. While I was talking to the bartender, she sneaked out with a guy I couldn't stand. I wouldn't have let him in my damn apartment for any reason. I thought I had just lost sight of her, but no. Then, I told myself she had gone out to the car with him or something. I waited until 2:00am, closing time, but couldn't find her. It finally dawned on me; she had taken the keys to my apartment and car. She also took all my money. I had to wait for the bartender, who was a friend of mine, to close up so I could get a ride home.

I got to my place around 3:00 in the morning and had to pound on the door. The guy I disliked so intensely finally opened the door with next to no clothes on. MaryBeth had pulled my Murphy bed down and, of course, they had sex. To top it of, between the two of them, they drank a whole bottle of Couvousier. He told me she had thrown up so much, her throat had started to bleed. The dog had gone nuts because she didn't know what was wrong with MaryBeth, and tore my place apart. The guy had passed out on the couch, grossed out by the blood all over my sheets. Only my pounding got him up. I am sure my neighbors appreciated it. I threw him out with just his pants on. As soon as his ass was out the door, I grabbed MaryBeth, stood her up, and threw her out that same door. Stark naked. Worked for me. Hey, she decided to take them all off, not me. I locked the door, made up the bed with new sheets and went to sleep. Hell with her. She knew I wouldn't let her back in so she didn't even knock. She got what she asked for coming to my place to act like that. I kept Honey. I liked her. I got up the next morning and went to work. I should have known it wasn't going to be that easy. Never is.

When I got home from work, the phone was ringing. It was Mama. She asked me to please tell her I didn't do what MaryBeth said I did. It pissed me off. Does nobody's behavior but mine ring Mama's chimes? Did she not see me as the good kid here? What the hell is the matter with these people? I told her she was damn right I threw her out naked and if I had it to do over, I would have thrown her out the first time she stepped in the door. And still kept the damn dog. If she wanted her clothes on, her ass should have kept them on. Mama, screaming at me, told me some man had picked MaryBeth up on the side of the road at 3:30 in the morning, stark naked and bleeding, and took her to the hospital. My response was, good grief, it wasn't that bad. Not for MaryBeth. She spent half her time naked in front of strangers anyway. Had she mentioned why she was naked and bleeding? I sure didn't cause it. What was the problem? By now, Mama was shouting in some previously unheard of brogue. I had to listen hard to figure out she was saying I was to get my ass over to the hospital, with some clothes, and get her. Pronto. I told Mama I would go get her when Mama got her ass to Lancaster and made me. Of course, I went to get her after about twenty minutes of blistering, foul, nasty language coming from Mama. Damn. What's the big deal? Look at what everybody else in my family does daily.

I was pissed. MaryBeth knew she wasn't welcome at my abode for another minute so she asked me to take her to Delaware where she could get up with the same guy who brought her to Lancaster. You can bet your underwear it wasn't a woman. I packed her up, threw her and Honey in the car and off we went. I had to go on a two hour trip there and two hour trip back to get rid of this rutting female. When we finally found the right college dorm in Delaware, she told me to wait in the car a minute, and keep Honey. Two hours later, we were still sitting in the damn car. MaryBeth had no clue how close I was to doing some serious cussing. However, I was not about to go in there, yet. If it hadn't been for the rule that I couldn't have a dog at the apartment complex where I lived, I would have taken Honey, threw her clothes on the curb and left. Finally, some guy walked up heading towards where she went. I asked him to please remind her we were sitting there and just about ready to leave her. He went in and came out a few minutes later. He said they were in the bedroom and he wasn't about to go in there. I didn't blame him. However, I loaded his arms up with her clothes, gave him Honey and left. Fini this crap. Peace made? What do you think?

    Naturally, six months later Mama demanded I make my peace with Jimmy. It had been almost two decades since I had pulled away from that houseboat with Jane and him standing there with the wedding rings on. As a matter of fact, it had been that long since I had talked to him, Daddy or Teeny. MaryBeth, too, except for this past disaster. Fine. Ok. Damn. Got it? Jimmy arrived like nothing ever happened. Where the hell did his face go? I didn't recognize him and didn't want to. He looked awful. Like Popeye with black hair and blue eyes. I wouldn't have recognized him at all except for the eyes. He had a full face beard and looked like he had been burned to death by the sun. He had deep wrinkles my face hadn't even begun to think of. Never one to just shut up, he thought I wanted to be brought up to date on his life, like I gave a damn. He'd put Jane, or Cleopatra to me, in a mental home. I figured he had finally driven her nuts with his running on her. I didn't care if he had thrown her in the trash. His pride and joy was his daughter, Paige, about whom he was obviously crazy. He had a picture of her and I have to admit, she was lovely. Paige was about fifteen with almost pure black hair and Jimmy's beautiful blue eyes. She had a sweet look about her. God knows who she got that from. I didn't know anybody in my family I would characterize as sweet. Crystal would be as close as you could get. Paige looked like a ballerina, with her hair pulled back and her sweet face front and center. I had to admit she looked a lot like Jimmy did as a child.

    Lo and Behold, he wanted to go out. This time, I kept my keys but left the door open so he could go on in with whomever he decided to screw that night of our Lord. And he did. Of course, he did. Next day, I sent him packing. From now on, nobody was going on my Murphy bed except who I chose. I'll say it again, what the hell is the matter with these people? Is it a gene disease or something? Was I born without it? If so, thank God. As far as Jimmy went, its over. One more down the drain. I didn't throw him out like MaryBeth. I told him to go home. Git. Period. He wasn't welcome if he was going to act like a horny dog in my house. I told him we were two different people and it was my house. Therefore, it was my say. Of course, he had to leave because he didn't know how not to be a horny damn dog. Forget making peace. You can't make peace if its only the job of one side.

Soon after that, I got my next phone call from Mama, cussing me out. I must admit I took it with equanimity, Denny came back for a visit and asked me again to move to Florida with him. He also told me there was something I needed to know. Whap, upside the head time. The reason he had moved to Florida was because he got the girl at the soccer field pregnant. They had gotten married and had twins. He had the twins but they divorced almost immediately afterward because she met another man. I loved Denny as much as you can care for someone, but I knew he was not the love of my life. I couldn't make up my mind if it was Ted or Michael, but it wasn't Denny. I said no, but I knew I would continue to miss him. I probably would have been happy with him, but after Michael, I knew what real sex was like and he and I could not achieve it. He was a great person and had been a great friend to me. Just before he left, he unexpectedly got me a precious little schnauzer puppy. I named him Tuborg. I loved big dogs, but this puppy was so sturdy and confident, I fell in love. I didn't care about the no pet rule. I had forgotten what it was like to have to train a puppy. I found out, though.

I had gotten a district manager job with Avon. They hired a man named Richard and little 'ol me. We were told we were test cases because Avon had never hired anyone at that level who had never sold Avon. My regional manager, Helen, made it quite clear to us that she disagreed with this test concept and was not exactly on our bandwagon waving flags for us. I knew it would be a long term disaster but I could earn some great short term money.

Avon was a great company. Part of the hiring rules were you had to have a garage, because they gave you a company car and travel vouchers. If you think the garage was for the car, you're wrong. It was for all the crap they sent you every Friday. Tons of it. They gave me so much Avon that even with one hundred and fifty women reporting to me, I couldn't make a dent in it while trying to give it all away. I gave Avon away like I was Santa Claus. It just kept piling up like a giant dragon made of boxes. I knew this wouldn't last long. Especially because of how I got paid.

They put you in a district that has fallen apart and producing little to no income. They pay you on percentage of increase in business. You take it on, you do well, you make money the first year. The second year, you are competing against yourself the previous year. They make money but you don't. Works for them. Doesn't for me. I knew it would be short term but I could make excellent money if I hustled. More than I had realized. I didn't have a car payment. I didn't have to pay insurance on the car. Best of all, they paid part of my rent.

One day, I made the foolish decision to take Tuborg on the road with me. I was only going to be doing some mapping so I wasn't going to have to get out of the car except for gas. You know how dogs can eat upholstery. I didn't want that to happen to my brand new four door, for easy box movement, Pontiac Grand Prix. I got out on the open highway and within ten minutes Tuborg took a diarrhea dump right on the front seat. A diarrhea dump. Bad. Awful. Even worse, he was walking through it trying to get away. Horrors. Then he jumped up on me, with it all over his feet and face. I could have strangled him. I didn't have a paper towel or anything and no exit close by to stop for help. It was oozing down the seat, between the seats and the back, onto the carpet. Smelled awful. What the hell had I fed this poor puppy? I was screaming my head off and he was pacing back and forth frantically, wondering what the hell this female was hollering about. Since he didn't speak English, we had some trouble communicating. I was so mad, I could feel brain matter oozing out of my ears in concert with the diarrhea flow. In my heart, I really wasn't mad at him, I knew he couldn't help it. I was mad at myself for a: bringing him and b: feeding him whatever I did. I finally found an exit and, thank the Lord, a friendly station owner who gave me a whole roll of paper towels and let me use his sink to clean the seat as best I could. In case you are wondering, yes, the smell lingered for days..days. No matter what I did. Oh well, it wasn't really my car.

Winter had begun again and in Pennsylvania, that meant snow. I decided to take a picture of Tuborg to send Denny to show him how cute he was. Denny had been gone about two months and I really missed him. I picked Tuborg up and walked to the back of the complex. I thought I would drop him down on the snow, run a little way, turn around and snap a picture. Great idea, right? I dropped him, I ran, I turned around and he was gone. Gone. No sign of him. I ran back to where I had dropped him and there he was..buried over his head. The only things I could see were his eyes and nose as he gazed up at me like "What?" I decided to try again. I was going to gently set him on top of the snow, run a little way, turn and shoot. So, I tried that. When I turned, I lost my footing and went down, camera clicking. When I hit the ground, he instantly jumped onto my chest and the camera clicked. All I got that time was a monstrous black nose with whiskers and teeny tiny black eyeballs because his face was about an inch from the camera. A monstrously cute photo, people. I kept a copy of that one and sent it to Denny. He knows I can't take pictures. Can't take 'em, won't pose for 'em, that's my motto.

  Steadfastly trying to be a good owner, Tuborg and I began the training to get him to go outside. An adventure both cool and tearing your hair out stuff. The biggest obstacle for me was I lived in an apartment that had a long hallway from the door to the living room. From the rest of the apartment I couldn't see the hallway at all. So, being the smart little pup he was, he would go to the door, wait for me, and if I didn't show up in time, he'd go right there. When I would go looking for him, I would find him there with his head down on his feet, ears drooping and shoulders conveying complete sorrow. Without lifting his head, he would look at me with those heart melting eyes. I could hear my heart crack into small pieces. He was trying so hard to please and was so smart. The problem had to be me. Therefore, I used the brains I had left, not to mention my location, and went out to buy a cow bell. They were everywhere..this was Amish country. They didn't have small cow bells so I had to get a huge one. I hung it from the door, but I didn't get a rope long enough to reach down to him. Intentionally. When I arrived home, I hung my rope and bell and then picked him up by his two front paws, bounced him twice on his back legs and then swung one paw at the bell. Ting-a-ling. I bounced him again. Ting-a-ling I did it a third time. Then I took him out. About ten o'clock that same night, I was in bed when I heard ting-a-ling..short pause..ting-a-ling. I got up and there he was. I took him out and he went. He got it the first day. God love a duck. After that, I took him everywhere. That little ting-a-ling set some sort of bond of a lifetime going. He was proud of me. Isn't that great? We were proud of each other. We beamed disgustingly at each other like we knew a secret. I even took him to breakfast on my days off. I liked him better than any boyfriend I ever had. He worshiped me, that's why. To him I was a strange and powerful creature. Hell, I probably even looked tall to him. Damned if that wasn't different. Food also appeared magically from my hands. Good enough reason to love me right there.

MEETING THE BIG 'C' HEAD ON

I got a call from Mama. Daddy was losing the battle with colon cancer. She told me he only had a few weeks to live and wanted me to come home. Naturally she wanted me to make my peace with him. Lord, I hated it when she did the "make your peace" mantra. She had made her peace with him. I'm sorry I missed that. I hadn't thrown up in a long time. What a show that must have been. I can't fight Mama so you know I made my plans and headed home. It was a good time to go because I had recently found out it is not a good idea to use a tree stump for weight in the back end of a 240z when it snowed. When I went downhill, I looked in the mirror and the tree stump was coming right at me. It slammed me up against the steering wheel and damn near killed me. I was ready to get out of snow.

On the trip, I came tearing across the Sparrow Point high rise bridge doing a hundred miles an hour and smoking dope. It was like something out of Star Trek. I did this every time I came home. Best reason to go. Always, at the bottom of the bridge there would be two highway patrolmen. Not once did they ever stop me. I would tell myself in my dopy haze that I was going so fast, they couldn't see me. I'm lucky they didn't stop me, because the haze in the car was a dead giveaway. I made it home alive, and headed straight to the hospital since it sits right on the highway on the way into town. I went to the elevator to punch the button for the fourth floor. That's what we always called the death floor. Once you got there, you probably weren't coming down. The second I got out of the elevator, I heard all this screeching and hollering. All hell breaking loose. Females were carrying on to the limits of their abilities. Damned if I didn't know I was home. Good God, I did miss this shit up in the land of normal. Not.

I turned the corner, and there they were. MaryBeth was doing her full share of the bellowing. Helping with the a capella was Daddy's former secretary of what seemed like nine hundred years. The other screamer kicking in was a stranger to me. But only in name. She looked like every woman Daddy had ever been interested in. Slutty. Tall, dark hair, breasts and lungs for belting out that hollering. They said MaryBeth had been trying to get a diamond ring off Daddy's finger while he was on his death bed. Daddy had just married the tall one, named Annie, and she had just found out that Lionel, the secretary, was the executor of the will. Lionel was trying to tell her she wasn't anymore, but Annie was mad he ever even thought of it. Needless to say, the conversations were ugly and the noise was of monumental proportions. Hell, I was used to pissed off women. Made my day. At least they weren't pissed off at me. You'd think these people would realize they were in a hospital with sick people. They may have realized it, but they sure as hell didn't care.

    I was not in the mood to renew old rivalries, familial arguments or meet wife number five, so I slipped into Daddy's room without getting involved with the bad harmonizing. There he was. Evil incarnate. The nemesis of my life. Wasn't a nemesis female? Whatever. Skinny as a rail. That "love of his life" hair was no longer pure white but yellow, and a lot of it was gone. Basically, he looked like he was going to die any second and would be glad of it. They had a morphine drip on him that I had been told kicked in every ten minutes. On top of the women's carrying on and his screeching, my guess was his ninth minute had come around. He was clearly in agony and wasn't holding back. I think his mind was gone. He didn't know who he was, much less who I was. My guess was he wouldn't have cared who I was unless I had something to ease his pain. This man wasn't long for this world, and he was going the hard way. So sad, Dad.

    As I sat there looking at him, his unfortunate circumstance brought to mind some of the memories generated by this evil man. There are too many to convey them all, but there were a couple of eye-openers. This particular weirdness also all took place while Daddy was married to Julie, the folie bergere slut.

    Even in their sixties, Daddy and Uncle John were constantly having fights because Granny would pit one against the other. One day Daddy would be running the company, the next day Uncle John would. She always picked the one who agreed with her. Daddy finally got the shits of it and quit. He formed his own company and took most of the business. A lot of that had to do with the fact that he was the only one who could read or write. This did not go well with Granny and Uncle John. It was time for strategy. At the very least, it was time for revenge.

    On Friday nights, Daddy and Julie always went to the Eldor Restaurant on the beach. The Eldor had been in existence forever and everybody loved it. The staff was friendly, the dining rooms spacious and the food was excellent. Half the time, you knew everybody who worked there, so it was real down home. The restaurant itself had mostly big pane windows on the outside walls, so everyone could see out. Inside, the some was restaurant, then there were counters for water and wine, etc. where glasses hung from racks on the ceiling. The kitchen was also mostly pane windows so you could see into it while they worked.

Uncle John schemed with the woman he was dating to meet at the Eldor the coming Friday night, knowing Daddy and Julie would be there. Uncle John didn't like Julie either, even though he had screwed her before Daddy did. Excuse me, had relations with the woman. Do you like that better? For that matter, so had my brother, Jimmy. Anyhow, the woman with John was called the Squaw, because she was one. Her assignment was to bring her ex-husband who had just gotten out of jail for nearly beating a guy to death. The plan was for John to go over to Daddy's table to pick a fight with him. When Daddy hit Uncle John, as he almost always did, the ex-husband was to come over and beat the crap out of Daddy. Good plan, huh?

Nobody knew Daddy was wearing a colostomy bag. No one in the family knew he had colon cancer. If that bag broke, it could kill him. I am sure, had John known, he would have done it anyway, but I thought you should know the whole story. Well, Uncle John went over to Daddy's table to pick the fight. In spite of his feelings, Daddy restrained himself because of the bag, although he did jump up and get in John's face, as expected. This pretty much ruined the dinner of everybody at the restaurant. Well, except those who knew these jokers. What was not expected was Julie jumping up and bitch slapping Uncle John. Without pause, damned if Uncle John didn't smack her back. When he did, all hell broke loose. Daddy and Uncle John tore that restaurant to shreds. They broke the windows overlooking the parking lot. They broke all the glasses on the counters and racks and they broke the windows in front of the kitchen area. They broke everything except the colostomy bag. Wade was called. Remember him from Bud Dixon's Texaco station? I do.

Unexpectedly, the squaw's ex-husband didn't get involved. The ex-con said he didn't jump in because Uncle John hit Julie. He didn't like men who beat women. Go figure.

Wade picked up Daddy and Uncle John and threw them both in jail. In their sixties, it was a little late in life to take them home to their mother. However, he did call Granny to see if she wanted to post bail and send her boys home. Grumpy Granny was in her eighties. She jumped in her big black-ass Cadillac and raced to the beach. When she got to the police station, she got in

Wade's face about throwing her boys in jail. Apparently, she showed herself to be Granny I knew because Wade got pissed and showed her his attitude about women cussing him. He threw her in there with them. All three spent the night.

It cost Daddy and Uncle John a fortune to fix all the glass at the Eldor. However, they were still welcome there. No charges were filed. I know this was true because MaryBeth was kind enough to send me the Carteret County News Times with the articles and all the in your face pictures. Dear boys, what will we do with you?

Then there is the story about the radio D.J. There were a lot of people in Morehead not overly impressed with Julie. A lot. Some didn't mind saying so. We had a radio D.J. who was one of them. After having attended a high society event at the Country Club where Daddy chose to bring Julie, a lot of people were offended. Sorry, but Daddy pretty much offended people left and right. The man didn't give a damn. He had a dick.

Having been given the chore of radio reporting on the goings on of the party, the D.J. mentioned that Daddy and Julie proceeded to get both drunk and offensive. He then commented that when someone goes to such an event, one should probably give some thought to not bringing their slut. Go boy! Yes, it was in the paper. Pictures and all.

How do you think that went down? Poorly. This is a true story. Southern style. The evidence of insanity exists. Daddy jumped into his big green Cadillac, kicked it, drove it to the D.J.'s house, drove it right up his front steps, across the porch, through the front door, right into the damn man's house and pinned the D.J. against his fireplace. Some people just have a knack for making a statement. Daddy's statement ensured that he would end up in court where I heard he lost $30,000. Rumor has it the Judge scheduled Daddy and Uncle John's events so his son could make it down from college to watch. The son of the judge, Claude Wheatly, told me his dad called him at Carolina in Durham and told him to get his ass home. He would not want to miss this. He told his son he'd never, ever see people like them again. Legends. To the law.

I was also told a story about Daddy and Uncle John showing up in Salter Path in their business suits with two females. They were, of course, not married to them. Everybody was all dressed up. Daddy opened the trunk of the Cadillac and took out four fishing poles. They went out on the finger piers and proceeded to fish. Once they had caught what they wanted, they opened the trunk again, got out the wine and the fixins'. Then laid out a table, linen napkins and all.. Having brought four chairs with them, they sat down, still dressed in their business suits and dresses. Then, the four of them had dinner.

Thinking about these stories and all I had known about him, I stood there looking at him, trying to drum up some sympathy to show that I was a real, normal person, but it wouldn't come. The anger had been in me too long, too deep and too intense. I remember thinking Satan wasn't waiting for him to die, he had come on up to get a look at him. He decided a bit of kick ass suffering might be a good idea before he got him. Daddy? This son of a bitch was going to hell and God had decided to let Satan go ahead and start the process early. I didn't mind a bit.

I turned around, walked out, got into the elevator and went back to the Land of Oz, which was what Lancaster was to me. Every mile on the road I passed during that ten hour drive was a mile of yellow brick road. I wanted to get my ass home before some of their crap rubbed off on me. I called Mama when I got home and told her I had been to the hospital and what went on. She raised the ceiling on her house letting me have her whole mind, not just a piece of it. Hell, I was home. I was safe. She couldn't hurt me with anything but her mouth. However, she did a pretty good job of that. I guess I could have gone by to see her, but it had been fairly traumatic being thrown back into that maelstrom. I was only focused on getting away from it. I loved my Mama but she was, for sure, part of the problem. Sometimes I simply had to do a drop kick and get out of there.

Daddy wasn't dead yet, but he was history to me. I went back to my groove. Every chance I got, I would go to breakfast before work. I got a newspaper, took a seat in a beat up little restaurant that looked like a trailer car. You've seen them. They generally have the best food. At this diner, there was a table commandeered by a bunch of women. One would leave and another would sit down. Another would leave and somebody else would sit down. They just kept coming and going. These weren't farm worker type women but they weren't executives either. They dressed like middle aged and older women do. Homemakers. They spent a lot of time staring at me. I was a regular, but nobody knew who I was, where I lived, or whether I was married. The whole "Who's that female bit?" It was killing not only the females, but the men, too. I was having a little fun with it. I made sure I buried myself in my paper so they couldn't tell I knew they were watching me. The men sat at a counter that ran the whole length of the trailer. They were bolder. They would turn right around on their stools and stare at me. One good looking one came up to me one day and introduced himself. I told him my name and said hello nicely. I am unlisted so I knew it wouldn't go any farther unless one of us wanted it to. This little dance went on for two years.

One day I went into the little diner and there were no seats available. I was always on a schedule. I had about twenty minutes to get in, eat and get out in order to get to work on time. Usually the diner could get me out in plenty of time, but not that day. I stood there a second trying to decide whether to go on to work when one of the ladies walked up to me and invited me to join them at their table. They became my closest friends. They became the kind of "friend for life" type of friend. They know how to do that in Lancaster. I tell you, its an art form and its a sin that most people do not use it. It took two years before they were willing to stick that hand of friendship out. And they waited until the diner was too full to seat me. They didn't jump at it easily. They told me they had always wondered what I looked so damned confident about. That, and no woman walked into that diner alone. Except me. It wasn't done. Well, I guess they finally figured out I was playing with them because they didn't mind giving me a hard time about why I didn't come over and introduce myself. They didn't know that's hard for me to do. Always has been unless I'm drinking, then I, if I'm interested, I don't care who you are.

One day at home, unexpectedly, my phone rang again. This time it was MaryBeth. To put it bluntly, Jimmy had cancer and wasn't going to make it. I couldn't believe it. Oh no. He threw up blood one day when out hunting with some guys. Then he went been to a doctor and found out it was terminal. He also took into account his wife was seven months pregnant. Because his wife was a nurse, she would know what was going to happen and he didn't want to put her through the stress of his taking chemo. Although, it was terminal, MaryBeth didn't find out until a month later when he decided to tell everybody. She had found out because he couldn't stop throwing up blood. He and his wife, Patty, had decided to do oral chemo anyway, and it had thrown him into malnutrition. She was, only now, telling me.

I found out all sorts of things were going on. Daddy had called Jimmy about four weeks previously, not knowing Jimmy was dying of lung cancer, to ask him to come home. Daddy had not told Jimmy he was dying. This was about only a couple of weeks before I went home. Jimmy had already started the chemo and the malnutrition problem was his scariest issue. He took a stand and made them put him into an ambulance to head home. He wanted to find out what Daddy wanted. He didn't know Daddy called because he wanted Jimmy to come run the pilot business and run the towing company. Having Daddy turn his company over to him was Jimmy's lifelong dream. It meant Daddy finally accepted and trusted him as a pilot at the port. It came too late. Jimmy was living in Charleston again. Jimmy only made it to Wilmington, ninety miles from home, when the paramedic decided they had to take him back to Charleston.

This was all coming out of MaryBeth like bile. She spewed this family tragedy like all the ones I had heard before. Like it was what was being served for dinner. No inflection, just this is it.

She finally got to the point of the call. By this time, all the anger I had ever felt for Jimmy was gone. I only thought of him as the brother I had loved so desperately until my teens. Until Jessie. Until then, it had been only sibling rivalry issues. Marybeth told me I didn't need to rush. They were only going to insert a tube into his stomach so they could feed him. There should be time for me to get there. MaryBeth told me the cancer seemed to have gone into slow motion so the operation itself was a simple one that should only take forty minutes. Mama, Marybeth and Crystal were there so she didn't see any sense in me rushing down. I was a good fifteen hours away. She said I should come after the operation when he was mending. I figured it was pretty hectic there with five females telling the doctors what to do. I told my boss I was going to have to take at least a week to see Jimmy. I sat and worried, waiting for MaryBeth to call to say the operation went well. The my memories ran through my mind at warp speed. Anything that was negative, I edited out. I didn't want Jimmy to die thinking I was angry with him.

The next call was not my favorite. MaryBeth told me there was a glitch in the operation. Somehow they hit the bad lung during the operation. Jimmy had gone into respiratory arrest and he was on life support. He was in a coma. I told her I was on my way. Before I could get out of the house, she called again. He had come to. He could not talk because of the tube in his throat. Mama was there and he could communicate with her with a pad and pencil. After he and Mama had gone back and forth writing, he slipped back into the coma and died. I was still sitting in

Lancaster waiting for the outcome of the operation. Like I was told to. I should have gone anyway. When did I ever listen to MaryBeth? I will never forgive myself for that. I left for the funeral. Jimmy died at 39. Daddy died the next week.

When I got to Charleston, I found MaryBeth, Mama and Crystal in a hotel room. They all had seen him before he died. I admit I was feeling something, maybe jealousy or anger that they had made it and I hadn't. Plans were being made for the funeral. Patty cremated my brother's body forty minutes after he died. Forty minutes. Doesn't that seem awfully quick? Was she afraid he'd come back to life? How could Patty do that? You would think we were at the bottom of the well now but believe me, it had only begun.

When we got to the funeral home, we were met at the door by someone acting like a major domo. He asked were we with the Piner family from North Carolina. When Mama answered yes, he led us to the pews on the left. It was like the bride's family was on the right and we were on the left, not all together. We were ignored. There was nothing there of Jimmy. No casket. No pictures, no urn. Nothing. Being used to traditional funerals, Mama could not grasp it. There was nothing of Jimmy for Mama's one last look. She was in complete shock; shredded to the core. There were over six hundred people at the funeral. The naval officers were in full uniform. It was clear that regardless of how I had felt about Jimmy, all those years he had been in Charleston, he was very well respected. Obviously, he was very well respected by officers far older than he had been when he died.

Ernie told me there had been a time when it was necessary to turn a large ship around in the basin. No one thought it could be done. Except Jimmy. Bets were flying. The next day, he and Ernie boarded the ship, Jimmy went up to the bridge with Ernie. On the first try, he turned that ship 360 degrees and took it out of the channel. From then on, I understand he was a legend. Daddy would have been proud had he known it.

After the funeral, they led us to a reception area. The whole affair seemed like a marriage with the groom not in attendance. Again, our side of the family was ignored. This was more like a Charleston social event. Champagne flowed. I just didn't get it. With me by her side, Mama finally confronted Patty. Patty told my Mama that she had been told by her mother that the Carteret County branch of our family was trash and she hoped we would not come back to visit. Lord, how could she have gotten the truth this far South? She said this to my Mama who was the grandmother of Paige, and Jay, Jimmy's two month old son. Had I known this at the time, I would have slapped Patty's face for breaking my Mama's heart. Mama was not buried that day, but a slice of her heart died.

Since we were all in mourning, we were unprepared to find out our cousin, Manie, Uncle John's oldest girl, was dying of pancreatic cancer. Manie had been Jimmy's age when we were all growing up. I took Mama back to Morehead and headed over to see Manie. She looked normal, not sick at all, but they had given her only six weeks. She opted not to fight it but to take the time to plan her own funeral. She picked out the casket, wrote the eulogy and had pictures of herself made to mail to friends. This all happened while I was driving her around. She couldn't drive herself because she was already in a wheelchair. I did what most people do. I asked her was there anything I could do? She said yes, but it was a secret. I couldn't find out until that night. She wanted me to come by and have dinner. She whispered not to plan anything after dinner. I knew something was up, but I didn't know what.

After I got there, someone knocked on the door. It was one of my favorite people. Gene was a guy from Down East with whom I had danced a million times. He was a fast dancer just like me, a boogier. Like me, his feet hit the floor with every single beat. He would toss me all over the place, snatching me right off the floor, but I never missed that hand when it reached out to catch me. It would have hurt like hell if I had. We were so familiar with each other's dancing, I knew what he was going to do before he did it.

I didn't know why he was there. Manie told me. All those years I had been in Lancaster, he had been teaching Manie to dance. Manie. Who was the only one of the eleven of us who not only couldn't dance, but refused to learn. She would go to her room to get away from us since we were having a ball. We never understood why she wouldn't join us. Well, I found out. She told me it was because she had let us get so far ahead of her. She was ashamed. Apparently, she made up for it after we were all grown and gone.

That was all well and good, but apart from knowing he was a favorite to both of us, I still didn't know why Gene was there. He grinned, then reached down and put her wheelchair into his van. I didn't know what was going on but I decided to go along with it. I figured we were going to visit her Mom or something. My curiosity was further piqued when he crossed the bridge to the beach. He drove straight to Ray's. Ray's was one of those old beach shag clubs. It was all about dancing there. Ray Willis was one of the guys I had danced with years ago when Mama and Daddy used to take me to the Idle Hour. That had been twenty plus years ago. After all the hugging and kissing, Manie told me what was going on. All she wanted before she died was to watch me dance with Ray and Gene. She told me I had always been her favorite dancer and she had always wanted to dance like me. Gene had seen to it that she was able to for years. Now that she couldn't dance anymore, she had talked Ray into opening just for us. I told myself not to cry. Do what she wanted. So, I kicked off my shoes and she started laughing so hard she almost fell out of the wheelchair. Everybody always laughed at me when I kicked my shoes off to dance. I never wore shoes when I danced. Couldn't still. We danced our butts off. It was near eleven when we loaded her up in the wheelchair and took her home.

The next morning she gave me a copy of the picture of her she had taken for all her friends. Then I cried. We sat there until I had to go. I cried the whole trip back to Lancaster. A whole lot of things that had happened while I was in Carteret County seemed to have a finality I had never anticipated. I didn't know how I felt about that. There were a lot of fences I had not mended and time seemed to be slipping away. I finally understood about Mama wanting me to make my peace. I had always been so angry and felt so isolated. The only person isolating me was me. Even knowing that didn't change anything. Manie died two weeks later. It was not even June. Daddy, Jimmy and Manie died within six weeks of each other. All of cancer. All of different cancers. And, I was still angry; but not as much as I had been.

I went back to the Land of Oz and resumed the life I had put together. I was still reserved but a weight I had been carrying on my shoulders lifted. Two of the people who had caused so much of the anger had died. I knew the anger wasn't gone, just submerged by the pain of loss. It was hard to hold onto and I didn't to want to anymore. I hoped I didn't become boring. Heaven forbid. Give me a little of that hissy stuff every now and then.

Determined not to become boring, I hit the streets running. I was out doing the town one night when I met my husband to be. I ran into some buddy-roes at a pizza place we used to go to. You wouldn't be surprised to hear most of them were cops. I had gone snow skiing with one of the guys. Of course, I didn't know how to ski, but that didn't stop me. I told myself to use the old "I used to water ski" routine and just jumped right Into it. First things first didn't happen. He never told me how to get off the lift chair. I am sure I am not the first person that ever happened to, but I can tell you this, you feel awfully stupid. When I did get off, I fell flat on my face. Not a good start at all. He took all of two minutes to tell me how to go from side to side and then he took off down the hill. The deal was, I was to watch and then wait for-damn-ever for him to come back up on the lift. No way, Jo-se. I took off. I did pretty good but I didn't like how slow I was going. Little kids were passing me, for pity's sake. So, I opened those skis up just a little. Liking the result, I opened up even more and took off. I mean took off. Now, this was not a great idea. Naturally, I didn't know how to stop. I would have had I waited for my second lesson. My date came tearing down the hill beside me screaming something about the lodge being right in front of me, which I could clearly see for myself. Stupid place to put a lodge. If it were me, I'd stick that sucker in front of the really hard hills where the skiers know what they are doing. But no, they put it right in front of a dumb ass like me. Whatever. I know this, if I ever wanted to stop when water skiing, I fell on my ass. Worked every time. I used that method a lot that day. But, kids, by five o'clock, I was shushing down moguls. Yee-ha. Insanity in attack mode.

They had seven hills and I hit every one of them running. Scared my date silly. He had released a monster to the snow hills. I loved it. We finally left when the sun set and he got a ticket for speeding on the way home. I don't know how they can expect you to speed all damn day and then crawl forty five miles an hour in a car. When I got home, I crashed. I guess he expected some sort of sexual payment, but he didn't get it and he wasn't going to. He never went out with me again. Okay. Fine. Only time in my life I went snow skiing.

He did stay friendly. At the table that night in the pizza place, he introduced me to a very large person named Dave. He was not all that bad looking. I always liked wide-shouldered male specimens with strong backs and he was definitely that. I do hate a mustache big-time, though. We had a good time at the table but Dave wasn't much of a talker. I tried to put on my comedy routine like I do after a few drinks, but he didn't seem to have much of a sense of humor either. Maybe he was not into girls. So be it.

However, providence stepped in again. I ran into him again a few weeks later at the same pizza place. This time I was at the bar when he came in with a date. I had been there awhile and had imbibed more than usual. I was feeling flirty. I am good at it. He said hi but kept moving. That got my interest. I expected to see at least a spark of "She's not bad" in men's eyes, but I saw nothing. Got me riled up. His date went to the bathroom, so I did one of those little "come here" finger gestures. Nice and slow, make it sexy, you know. Mama fingers. He came over and looked just as disinterested as before. Hot Damn, turn the engine on, girl. I was sitting on a bar stool, which made me about chest high to him, so I simply wrapped my legs around him, brought him in real close. Then, and talking about his date, I said, "Damn, I would have thought you could do better than that, and I'm better than that." Like magic, that interest light went on. His eyes got big and he looked at me like he'd never seen me before. Which he probably hadn't. When his date walked out of the bathroom, he took her ass home. Came right back, he did. Just like a good boy. By now, he was listening to every word I said, leaning close, hoping he wouldn't miss a come-on gesture. He seemed to be a good puppy so I took him home. We made out until our lips bled, but, alas, he was going to have to wait. I wasn't one to jump right into it. He stuck it out, I tell you that. We became the very best of friends, but there was a sexual package attached. I just love a man who likes to make out. You know, one who doesn't forget how to do a stage show before going to the main event. We became a couple. A normal every day couple. I don't think I had done that since Ted died. I thought I had forgotten how.

I hadn't been home since Jimmy and Manie died, but Mama and I had been talking a lot on the phone. She was literally giddy with joy about Dave. Her little package of trouble had fallen into the normal pit. She wanted to see me. I guess she wanted to know if I looked any different. She was still with Mac, and had been for years.. She was happy and living a normal life herself. No alcohol, but she found she could get just as high on the drugs she took, so she just changed her preference. She and my cousin, Barbara would trade drugs so they could see what would happen.

Hanging onto my independence with both hands, I had been running around with a girl friend named Rondi, who was way wilder than I had ever been. Rondi had naturally gorgeous hair and was shaped like she had been an athlete. Big shoulders and big breasts. She looked better in her style of clothes than anyone I knew. She always had it going on. She talked me into going to Wildwood New Jersey with her one summer. I didn't know, but in case you don't, Wildwood becomes Canada. Everybody you meet is doing that "A-a" thing. She wanted to go out to get picked up and although I didn't mind going, I wasn't into the pick-up part. Five minutes after we got there, she was out on the floor throwing her very beautiful hair around. I hid in the corner and decided I was going to stay right there.

Nobody was getting me out of that corner. Well, nobody except that deadly good-looking guy who was looking at me. And just at me. We did the locked eyes thing. I held his to see what he would do. He held his. Hey? That's different. I decided I would play the eye games with him but his feet were going to have to do the walking or it wasn't going anywhere. I had Dave. I didn't need to pick up a guy. Neither of us would make a move, but we still had the eye-lock turned on. Finally, a girl walked up and asked him to dance. He looked at her, then looked at me. I thought, oh hell, at least she is in the mood. He put his index finger up to her in that "Wait a second" gesture, walked all the way across the dance floor, handed me his cigarettes and said he would be right back. Was that hot or what? That was the baddest of the cool pick-up lines I ever had. He was seventeen years old. I'd like to know what they grow hot guys like that in. Apparently, they can grow them in Canada because every damn one of them had world class butts. We partied all weekend.

His name was Giles Charbonneau. He was unbelievably sexy. I got to know him real well that weekend, but not that well, you know? He invited Rondi and me to Montreal and we went. When we got there, it was their Thanksgiving and the town was empty. It was beautiful. It was also my very first real vacation. Giles wasn't bad either. I decided I had to focus on the bottom line. He was seventeen. Let's just say I wasn't. I couldn't help but invite him and a friend of his to Lancaster, where he said he'd always wanted to go. We took him to the best restaurant in a town of wonderful restaurants, which was the Tally-Ho and gay. I took one look at Giles' fine ass and told him he was not going to a bathroom anywhere near that place. I'd never see him again. I don't know where the relationship might have gone had I not decided to head home to see Mama.

When I went home for my birthday in October, I noticed an angry looking spot on her nose. It looked like it had been torn open. Whatever it was appeared to be pulling her nose from the inside. Weird. It was raw and infected looking. When I asked her what it was, she said it was a mole that her doctor kept taking off. I know my eyebrows hit the top of my hairline. I told her to go back to her damn doctor and have a biopsy taken. I advised her to have it taken off again immediately and I tried to talk to her about skin cancer but she was high on prescription drugs and I could tell she didn't get it. I talked to MaryBeth and urged her to make Mama do something about it. I couldn't believe it hadn't already been done. I told her I would be back Christmas and I wanted it gone. All gone. I pleaded with Mac to take it seriously.

When I came back Christmas, half her nose had disappeared into her face. It was still very red and angry, but much worse than before. Its hard to describe but it was like there was something inside her sinuses pulling the entire left side of her nose in. I truly thought of a demon in there. It looked so not real. Noses do not look like that. Ever. For any reason. I couldn't believe she didn't understand the seriousness of it. It was like she didn't even see what was happening. Remember Mama stood over deep fat fryers with cigarettes in her hand for 18 years? Inhaling her heart out. When I talked to her, the cigarette would bounce up and down inside a blue haze of smoke. She would always have her face slightly tilted back for some reason. I stayed home and waited until January 3rd, then MaryBeth and I took her to the New Bern emergency room. I would have done anything to get her away from her doctor. Everybody knows if your loved one is near death, do not take them to the local hospital. Even the hospital is smart enough to send them to Greenville or New Bern. Duke, if necessary.

They took half her face off on January 5th. I won't ever forget it. The cancer was headed both to her eyes and brain. They took her face off from the forehead, around the eye to the tear duct, then down half the nose, around her mouth and over to the left side of her face and then back up to her ear and up to the forehead. She lost a tear duct and a lot of her hearing from the subsequent radiation. She never did any chemo. They said they "got it in time," but the alternative was much worse. It took half her face being removed to "get it in time." Remarkable. Did you know there's nothing under there? Nothing except fat, gristle and bone. It was a terrible sight. She wouldn't look at herself, much less what was under the bandages. Somebody had to clean it twice a day to prevent infection. We all jumped in to help. We knew it had to heal before they could try plastic surgery, but I knew there was not going to be any pulling the skin closer and getting a little scar here. Mama didn't grasp it. Half her face and forehead was gone. She went around with most of her face under bandages, thinking some day they would come off. The plastic surgery over the next few years never worked and was mostly excruciatingly painful for her. She wouldn't stop smoking so the edges of the new skin would die back and ruin anything they tried. Pretty little Anna ended January 5th 1983. She began to crash and burn, again. A slide began that seemed to never end.

WHO YOU CALLING A CHOICE VESSEL?

Traumatized by Mama's experience, I returned to Lancaster and resumed seeing Dave. Mama was always on my mind. I knew what she wanted. Me married to Dave. Before long, we were living together. For the most part, we were happy with each other, but my focus was not on him. I was eight years older and every now and then, I would feel like I was bringing him up. I always had a tendency to stay with my men for a long time. Dave and I had been together for seven years when lightning struck.

Lord love a duck, he began to talk about getting married. He had missed me while I was gone. I told him to go ahead. Marry anybody he wanted, but I wasn't going to. I spent most of my time ignoring him. What was he thinking? I never wanted to get married. Not since Ted died. The Dave love and the Ted love didn't compare. However, I finally agreed to get married, with clenched teeth. Dave came into the bedroom at 4:00am after working the night shift to work on me. I hated the thought of getting married. It seemed such a stifling concept, but he was relentless. So was Mama. I think I agreed mostly because Mama wanted me to get married before she died. To her, it was like a car. She wanted me to drive a "successful" car. I personally wanted a fast car; ie sports car. To be fair to Mama, I was also tired of being called a slut by his mother. That gets to you after five years of hearing it. I compared it to the IRS being after you. It was continuous. I never knew what people meant when they said they had the mother in law from hell. Now, I knew, and I wasn't even married. She was one of those whiny old farts. Pretending to be nice, but actually a barracuda carrying a loaded gun. Tight lips. Partial smile. Grumpy all the time with the face of an ugly leprechaun on speed. Believe it or not, she even resembled Granny, who still wasn't dead. She ran her household like Dave's

Dad didn't even live there. The whole package. The barracuda showed front and center. She thought people didn't see it.

Unfortunately, I did agree to get married and everything immediately went to hell. First, we argued about where we would have it. I didn't want anybody but Dave, the preacher and me. That meant no church. She wanted it at the Lutheran Church. She didn't even go to church, nor did Dave, but it was where all the "in" people went. She talked us into going to the church to meet the man she wanted to marry us. His name was Dr Seil Hamner. To me, that says it all. He looked like Sebastian Cabot and had a mustache like Hitler. His nose stayed up in the air like he didn't have to share his part of the planet with drones like us. Once he found out we lived together, he would glare at me like I might slither closer with an apple. He treated us like we were a disease that had somehow found its way to his office. He sniffed a lot. Like we smelled. Maybe I smelled like a slut. He went over some of the marriage vows which was guaranteed to get on my nerves. Don't make me do memory work and for Christ's sake, don't read to me. I hate that. Nor did I fancy arguing with a guy ten times bigger than I was. Especially one that can talk to God. I knew I couldn't. I'd tried. Not being able to stand our odor, he put me and Dave in a room alone to discuss it. I had already talked way too much about something I didn't want to do. What was it that made people want to do something so damn stupid? I didn't get it. If I didn't get it, I wonder what the hell I was doing going along with it?

I didn't know we were going to fight about the reception either. What reception? I didn't want one. The rehearsal dinner. I didn't want one. The photographer. I didn't want one. Dave was constantly on me to just go along, but my feet were digging in as hard as they could. I could have left heel marks in the carpet. If you can visualize it, you have it down pat. I was pissed. I tense right up when somebody tries to take control of me. My head goes down and my shoulders go up and I'm ready for verbal battle. My hissy was about to fit unless somebody got off my back. I decided to compromise to get some of the pressure off Dave. Why? I began to see how hard Dave's mom was stressing him. A mean, nasty female. She could have been a Southerner easy.

I finally agreed to the reception. She wanted it, she could pay for it. She was going to pay another way, too. She wanted it in York, Dave's birthplace. I wanted it in Lancaster where all our friends were. With York, both her friends would be there. We decided to wed York and have the reception in Lancaster. Our friends would go to the reception. I figured I won that round. Then she said she would not allow drinking. Hell, nobody would come. I put that size five foot down again. We agreed on wine and sodas. She'd pay. I said they could bring their own bottle if they wanted. I'd make sure orange juice and stuff would magically appear.

    Deal here was Mama was not going to pay for anything, Or it wouldn't happen. Then it got nasty. She wanted a head-table. I thought that was too conspicuous. Like we were pretending to be somebody we weren't. This wasn't a formal wedding. I wanted round tables so people could drink and talk to everybody. Its friendlier. We fought so long about the table that we missed the first wedding date. I said no round table, no marriage. Hell, that was easy. Finally, we agreed on a head-table for the family and wedding party and round tables for everybody else. To show you how stupid this was, there was only a best man in the wedding party.

    I made my own dress. I used a pretty, cream silk fabric that cost me about five dollars. I was not about to show up in white. Let her explain that to both friends. Dr Seil Hamner could stick it. I envisioned a dress in which I would look like a bag lady. Worked for me. It ended up quite pretty. I made it so the bodice was gathered at the top and I could pull it down past both shoulders. I have an ok neckline. I also gathered the waist because I had a tiny waistline. It showed how proportionate I was and we all know how damn important that is. I wore a pair of shoes I already had. I didn't care if I didn't wear any. I was in th mood to paint a pair with indoor-outdoor paint. I made sure she wouldn't see the dress ahead of time. I told Dave to just shut up when he saw it. I didn't care what my family thought. They had met me before, they shouldn't be surprised at anything I did. By now, this was all Dave's fault. She wasn't my damn mother. I was really not into this whole wedding thing. I should have listened to my instincts. All this animosity was spilling out of me like I was the girl in the "Exorcist". The worse I got, the better I liked it.

    We got to the church. Mama and my sisters had arrived. Mama's face was half under bandages and she was extremely sensitive, as you would expect. Dave's mother was horrified when she saw her. I'm sure she wouldn't have done this if she had known my mother looked like a monster. I glared at her and dared her to say a damn thing. She started this. I think she regretted taking things this far because her friends would have to see Mama. Crystal brought her two kids. MaryBeth was still herself.

Big time. I was scared to absolute death. When I got to the church, I hoped God or somebody representing him would swoop down and throw me out. I wanted Him to save me somehow. Before the service, MaryBeth broke into the room I was hiding in to slobber all over me about how happy she was for me. I really, really did not want to see anybody. Anybody. I felt explosive. My feelings were scattered all over the place like the damn rice was going to be. Stupid stuff. I hate rice at weddings because it can kill the birds. Any chance we can change it to popcorn? Maybe not. With MaryBeth there, I had an uncontrollable urge to hide Dave's underwear. God only knew what size her current boyfriend was.

According to our sanctified flower child, I had everything. I got everything. I knew everything and she didn't get, have or know anything. In other words, a major jealousy attack was in full force. Everybody in my family loved me, and I loved them. Like me, they were a little hard to deal with. It was the genes. You have no idea how my stomach churned and knotted. Down the damned aisle we went. The same aisle I had already walked down a hundred times because, according to Dr Hamner, I walked too fast. If I wanted to walk fast, by damn, I will walk fast. My stepfather, Mac, was giving me away. He was a nice guy and good to Mama. If I wanted to, he'd run right along with me. He was going to give me away. Give me away? What the hell does that mean? Does anybody really think about this whole wedding process? What a stupid concept. Damn, I hated this. Did women ever think about this morass they were getting into? Does anybody ever really need ANOTHER FAMILY.

I ran Mac down the aisle as fast as I damn well pleased. Actually a little faster than I would have, just to piss Seil Hamner off and to let him know I was still in control. Right. I dared Dr Hamner to say a word to me with my look. I was in a rage. We only had to pass six pews of people so what was the point of worrying about being proper? They wanted to get this thing over with as bad as I did. I thought maybe I could get out of there in just a couple of minutes. Then, I discovered, Dave had recruited his Lieutenant to take pictures. Steam was coming from my ears. I hated having my picture taken and he was snapping away. It was very distracting. Almost slowed me down. There were about sixty people there. I only knew about fifteen of them. I wanted to get up there to whatever that area is called, stop, turn around and tell them to all go the hell home. There would be no show today. But, I knew Mama would be pissed. No telling what she would do. It would not be pretty. She had gotten almost as bad as Dave's mother. This would happen or she would hissy on me, for sure.

Mac and I finally got where we were going. All I remember was Dr Hamner saying two things. One, I was but a choice vessel. What do you mean, a choice vessel? It sounded like I was a pot to piss in. Then he said Dave was God in his house as God was in His House. Wait a damn minute here. There was none of this vessel and God in His House crap when we met with Dr Hamner previously. Sorry Lutherans. I stopped it right there, leaned over to Dave and asked him did he hear what that man said? Had he lost his mind? I wasn't going to agree to that. I wasn't exactly shouting, but I was a lot pissed. David told me to whisper. I told him to jump up my ass. I laid in to him to speak up so I could hear him. Dave begged me to just keep going. He said it was just a figure of speech. I said they didn't put "figures of speech" in the Bible. He said he wouldn't hold me to it. I wanted it in writing. By now, everybody knew there was an "issue." I hated this crap. I gave in, but I didn't like it. I was standing there with a grumpy face and Dave's Lieutenant was still snapping away. I wanted to run, not walk, up the aisle and smack him. I was shaking. I was mad and nervous and felt like I was going to throw up. Neither Dave's mom nor Dr Hamner were close enough to hurl on, so I controlled it. Not with a smile, I tell you that. Somebody was going to pay for this nightmare. I was willing to wait for how ever long it took. Maybe Dave's mom didn't know how long I could hold a grudge.

We went back up the aisle. A lot slower this time. One, I was with Dave, and two, I was in a state of shock. When I reached the doors to the street, I was no longer who I was before. I had a different name, and I had legally agreed to things I didn't like. I had let the law into my home. Then, Dave's Lieutenant asked us to come back in and pose. Right. What chance do you think there was of that? My ass was going to Lancaster at warp speed. I wanted to either get drunk or go to sleep. Maybe this was a nightmare and I would wake up soon. Everybody could come if they wanted to, but I was getting the absolute hell out of there. Keep your damn rice to yourself. If one particle touched my face, I would take them to the moon.

We had brought our 1972 Corvette to ride back in. Our friends had put on the side windows, "1/2 his" and "1/2 hers." Funny thing. I had paid for the whole damn thing. Because I went through this stupid ceremony, I would automatically lose half of everything I had. Who in their right mind would do that? I was getting grumpier and grumpier and it was only eleven o'clock in the morning. It was definitely time to get drunk. However, I did have a little ace in the hole that was guaranteed to make me chuckle. Its time was getting nearer and nearer. As we headed back to Lancaster, I tried to focus on the fun part coming. However, I did give Dave an earful of how I had enjoyed my damn day so far. He wasn't having a great time either, I have to admit. Anyway, we made the forty minute drive trip to Lancaster in war zone silence. The closer we got to Lancaster, the more Dave got all bubbly. I wanted to crack him one. But, he was my husband now, so I just sulked. I hated this day so far and had a feeling, I was going to hate the rest of it. What was I doing, for Christ's sake? Even worse, what had I done? Given up life, liberty and the pursuit of happiness. That's what I'd done. Do Lutherans allow annulment? What are the requirements? Anybody know?

We got to the Ramada and scooted for the reception room. There was my good time to be. There was a head-table and the rest were round tables like agreed. After about twenty minutes, Dave's mother showed up. Now, I got to chuckle some. Na-na-na-na-na. The room was mostly filled before she looked for her place card. Once she found it, she looked me in the eye and said, "There is a problem. It appears you have put my back to the guests. I think we should all be facing them." I looked her right back in the eye and said, "You wanted a head table, lady, you got a head table." I had put her right in front of me. Eye to eye. As planned, she was the first to go. Dragging Dave's poor daddy in her wake. Who in their right mind would have married her? That's how you can tell this whole idea sucks.

It was always very hard for me to be the focus in a room full of people. I tended to list off to the side. Where's a good book when you need one? But, I worked the room like I had been taught. Everything went down very nicely except for two things. Dave shoved a piece of cake in my face. I had only been to two weddings and didn't know this was a tradition. Have people lost their mind? This stupidity was a tradition? Well, it sucked. Why go to all the trouble of trying to look the best you've ever looked so somebody can shove cake in your face? I had demanded chocolate cake because it was my favorite. I didn't care what "tradition" was. That looked real good falling off my face. What's that about? Dave saw the look on my face and backed off. It wasn't going to happen a second time and there was no way in hell I was going to shove cake in his face. A gun maybe. But not

-183-

cake. Then, I noticed one whole bottle of wine had been drunk by one person. That person was slinging a second bottle around and whining. Yep, MaryBeth. I got out of there and avoided everybody, including Dave. I took a cab. He happened to be having a good time. I wasn't. Let him drive his half of the damn Corvette home. I left my half there. I had four hours of peace and quiet during which I contemplated my choices of painless suicide. I was surrounded by Dave's guns, so I was having trouble focusing on the "painless" part. Then I was back to the Ramada for dinner with my fine Southern family. And mama-in-law, Grumpface.

It was obvious Dave's mother was not enjoying my family. Who'd a thought? Having ordered from the menu of a fine restaurant, Mama received a pepper steak which is different that of the North. When Mama got the steak, she took one look at it. Being a cook, she picked up her plate and headed to the kitchen. I was finally beginning to enjoy all this. Mama was going to make it herself. Dave's mother was having a hard time getting her mouth back up to where her teeth met. She had to meet Southern crackers for the first time. It was good for her. Shut her up anyway. Mac, who was also a good cook, ordered his steak well done. And he meant it. After they brought it back the second time, Mac wouldn't eat it. The chef came to the table to tell Mac he would not cook it anymore. That was fine with Mac; he picked up his plate and joined Mama in the kitchen. I thought it was great. This was a fine restaurant. Mama and Mac didn't even know what that meant and didn't care. To them, the "fine" part meant they used the good silverware. Not that they had good cooks in the kitchen. As I was chuckling about Dave's mom's white face and fearful look, I noticed that wine bottle in MaryBeth's hand. She was on the third one in about six hours. Getting jolly, she was. Mournful right behind it. Her moods were hopping back and forth between the two. She never got anything. Pity Party Patty.

Just to make things more joyful, Crystal's kids came in, dripping wet, straight from the pool. Tom started hanging off Crystal because he wanted something and she wouldn't let him have it. He started to howl. All I wanted was for somebody to bury me. Please. I should have used the gun when I had the chance. The next move was a classic. One of those things, you and everybody else never forgets. With different versions. Not to mention, different reactions. MaryBeth reached over, grabbed Tom's arm, turned him around and slapped the shit out of him. I wanted to laugh, but I thought it was inappropriate. The laughing, not the slapping. I only thought it was funny because it was so stupid, it released some of my tension like I was a balloon losing air. Then, I thought, what the hell, its my wedding so I let loose. Crystal went ballistic. I didn't laugh because I thought it was funny. I laughed because MaryBeth was the only one who was willing to slap the shit out of him when we all wanted to. However, you should never, ever hit someone else's child. A deep freeze settled over the table. Could we leave now? Oh yeah, we could leave, but they were all coming with us. That included a couple of glarers. Is that a word? You know what I mean. Would this day never end? I hoped it lasted long enough to get a divorce. An annulment? Or, just get me that gun. I figured it was all my fault for agreeing in the first place. When I did that, I agreed to bring these people together. If any slapping was to go on, I should have slapped the shit out of myself for even thinking this marriage would work. It was doomed to die. Hopefully, before the sun set.

    Off to my little A-frame we went. Sixteen of us. I was hoping they wouldn't stay long. Maybe five minutes, no more. It was a pretty little house, but it was falling down a cliff. Like I felt that day. In the basement, there was a stress fracture. A monster stress fracture. The putty looked like it was screaming for pity as the concrete was about five inches apart. We found out later the footers were only five inches below ground when they were supposed to be three feet. Every time the ground froze and thawed, the house lifted and fell. The chimney had been added after the house was constructed. It had pulled away twice. That explained why there were steel straps holding it onto the house. Aside from all that, I liked it. Where the roof pitch formed the "A" was a great place to grow marijuana, Dave's favorite thing. A cop.

    After mingling a few minutes, I noticed MaryBeth was gone. It was a small house so it didn't take long for me to find her. My bedroom door was locked. Since I didn't lock it, somebody was in there. I knocked and knocked, but she wouldn't answer it. I finally screamed, so she let me in. She was totally wasted and could barely stand up. Maudlin. Way maudlin. I listened to her whine until she got it all out. I really don't think she liked me at all, but she was hanging onto my chest, slobbering about loving me. She finally calmed a bit and asked for coffee. That was trouble because I didn't drink coffee. I wasn't sure I even had any. I left her in my bedroom to go into the kitchen where I found some instant. I boiled water, and fixed it like a real hostess. I should mention I was still in my five dollar wedding dress.

I took the coffee back to the bedroom but the door was locked again. I was balancing the coffee, trying to open the door and hollering at her all at the same time. Naturally, I spilled the coffee all over me. For some stupid reason, it pissed me off. Everybody was standing in the hallway staring at me like I had lost my mind. I guess it was because I was not hollering nicely. Obscene words were spilling from my lips. With my Mama and Dave's mother listening. Who cared? I finally completely lost my temper and did what I did best in a crisis with a locked door. I kicked it in. Believe me, it was not my first kicked in door. Everybody in the hall, except Dave, jumped a foot. He was used to it. Restrained violence was my middle name. Nobody better say a damn word to me. It was my door and if I wanted to kick it in, I would kick the damn thing in. I went into the bedroom. She was gone. Why not? Out the damn window. She had opened my bedroom window and crawled out. Probably with neighbors watching. I headed out to find her with everybody in the hall watching me crawl out the window. It was better than dealing with them. Dave's mother was one of them. I was liable to cut her head off if she said anything to me.

    I finally found her sitting by the "creek" that ran below the small cliff. She reminded me of Christy except she wasn't dirty yet not singing Inn-A-Gotta whatever. As for the creek, some could call it a ditch and get away with it. I plunked my ass down beside her. Oh no, the bargain basement dress was ruined. Like I gave a shit. I looked at her and asked her what she thought she was doing. She said she was communicating with the forest. She understood forests and they understood her. I got a death grip on her and drug her out of the ditch. I had to drag her while we crawled and stumbled our way up the hill. Her half was drunk. My half had HAD it with this day. It was over. I had all the fun I could stand. I went up the hill, ran everybody out, including Dave, and I went to bed, alone. I was traumatized. Never again.

    After about six months, we reached a settlement on the settling of the A-frame. I was doing a lot of planning for our new house. We bought eight acres and I centered the house on one four acre plot so we could sell the second plot if necessary. We didn't have any landscaping done because I wanted to do it myself. I had spent the four years it took to get rid of the A-frame, designing the house and the yard. When I took the plans to the builder, he only moved one window four inches, so this really was my custom home. It was a little salt-box, only 1400 square feet.

The house sat three hundred feet from the road and was fifteen degrees below the road. I loved it. All in all, I planted 400 plants including hemlocks, rhododendrons and azaleas. I had three rose gardens, one for fragrance, one for cutting and the last was for fun. I planted them on three sides of the house. With thirty five windows that opened, I could get the fragrance regardless of wind direction, except North. Then, there were my orchids. My first love. They were everywhere. I designed the house around the needs of the orchids. Not mine. Not Dave's. He loved them, too.

The first three years were awesome as I kept putting all the plants in the ground I could. The downside was Dave was doping more and more. I was still growing it to keep pace with him. I always made sure Dave had enough marijuana to get him through the day without whining. I want to try to describe this marriage I had gotten into. One day I headed to the top of the driveway to add more plants. If I had to head out in a wagon pulled by four horses, it would have been ok with me. I had plans. I was going to make a landscape showcase out of this place. You could just barely the property from the road up top. Just barely enough to want to stop your car and look down like you do when you go to the Smokies. I wanted to plant azaleas and impatiens on both sides of the driveway all the way up to the road. I also bought white cottage roses from California. Behind the house was a small hill that framed the house, so the gray of the house contrasted strongly with the deep green of the forestry on the hill. The roses were pure white and would vine through the woods. I had white azaleas, rhododendrons and white small forest flowers to compliment them. Behind my house, it would look like white snow sprinkled around. I saw a picture of a castle in England done like that and it was breathtaking. I hoped in two or three years, mine would be too. I had a beautiful Japanese Red Maple, I had done in a bonsai style just for the corner of the house. We had a small pond on the property and I planned a water garden there, with koi. I had big plans for this place.

One day I got a rude awakening about what a mistake this all was. I headed out with my trusty wheelbarrow full of soil, perlite, vermiculite and plants. I had been working with this soil for several days, making sure it was well drained because of the natural clay. With so much in it, the wheelbarrow weighed a ton. I was sweating like a dog. I would work an area and then have to go higher. The wheelbarrow was so awkward, I had to put the handles on my shoulders and push. Most importantly, we had a gravel driveway. It kept slipping and sliding and threatening to tip over. My husband, all 260 pounds of him, was walking up the driveway with me while I was pushing, talking to me about some nonsense or other. I finally put the wheelbarrow down, whipped my head around, and asked him would he mind taking it to the top of the road for me? All I seemed to accomplish was pushing it into a rut. That sucker looked me right in the eye and said "sorry." Told me he had to put gas in the truck. Apparently, right that minute because off he went.

Did I mention I was in the driveway? Of course, I was in the driveway. He knew I was in the driveway. He headed right for me. He got behind me and started going real slow. He had to go real slow. I WAS FRONT OF HIM. I started trying to push the cart to the side but I must not have moved fast enough because HE BLEW THE HORN AT ME. Right in my ear. Not once; but several times. I was ready to tear his face off. But, I'm a big girl. I ignored him. I kept trying to get to the side of the road. I must not have moved fast enough because he took that big ass truck and went RIGHT ACROSS MY LAWN. All the way up. One foot on the brake and another on the gas. He tore-my-yard-up. It was times like that I remembered why Mama cut Daddy off. I jumped in my Firebird and took off after him. I caught up with him at the gas station. Unlike Mama, I did not ram him, but I did ream him. That gas station got to enjoy a little hissy fit. His ass was coming back to the house and he was not only going to take the wheelbarrow up, he was going to do everything I asked to clean up my yard until I quit asking. You can bet your booty I was locked up tight for some time after that. Choice vessel, my ass.

HOW TO RUIN THE HOLIDAYS 101

The real joy in my life was, of course, his sweet mother. Yeah, right. She was like one of those Southern Magnolia steel walls, but didn't have the false charm to go with it. When she wasn't making you wish you could tear her heart out, she was pitiful. I mean that's how she would act..major pitiful. My favorite times of year were Thanksgiving and Christmas. Dave would drag me over, practically by the hair..let's say for Thanksgiving. She would be slaving in the kitchen. Dave's dad and brother would already be sitting at the table, and it would be close to the time to eat. Believe me, I never got there early. Everything would be ready, but the turkey. She needed more time to overcook it. She'd make us sit down, then demand that nobody be allowed to help her. You got the feeling the 'or else' could be a painful response to a polite gesture. I didn't like her anyway, so I wasn't offering squat. Understand, this scenario went on every single time a turkey holiday came around. We'd sit there with nothing to say to each other because if we opened our mouths, she'd be the only one answering. It had nothing to do with whether the comment was directed at her, or not. She'd answer. She would assume she was the only one in the room worth talking to. Alright, fine. Whatever.

The turkey would finally be overdone. She would place it on the table and tell us to get started; don't wait for her. She'd head right back into the kitchen, which was right beside the table. We would have to watch everything she did. We didn't say no, because we didn't know if she would have a fit. Sometimes she did, sometimes she didn't. If she didn't say anything, we would reluctantly dig in. Reluctantly, because it was always, always overdone. It would be dry and stick in your throat. The creamed corn looked like it had been creamed, like in run over by a truck. The bread was always cold as were the potatoes. She would watch us like a hawk, all hunched over and mean looking. If we didn't put enough on our plate, she'd walk over to your plate and put however much she wanted you to eat on it. A turkey Hitler for Thanksgiving. Who wouldn't enjoy that? Then she'd go back into the kitchen to stand watch. Guarding her little treasure of delicacies. The bread was hard, too. If you really want to ruin my day, make the bread hard. I'll bet she heard me say that somewhere and did it just so I would drop Dave.

The table was always silent. Like a tomb, people. Then she'd start to mumble from the kitchen with enough whine in her voice to grate your nerves. It was always about the food being cold by the time she got to eat. She'd make her plate when she made our's, so she never left any in the pots to stay warm. Consequently, her plate was always colder than it had to be. Understand, if we wanted to roll our eyes, we had to turn in our seat and look at the other person, face to face. I not only rolled my eyes, I would put on the whole pig face look. The guys would be busting a gut trying not to laugh out loud. You didn't want to get caught by her. Hell no. She was always capable of slinging that potato ladle at you. Full of potatoes. As for this whining act, it was because she slaved so hard, not because she was stupid enough to make her plate before she sat down. She'd rather bitch about it. Finally, she would get out of the kitchen. Now, the fun started or it became more of a pain in the ass, depending on how you looked at it. I always found it rather fun, but then I had a morbid sense of humor. It was show time.

She'd choke. That's right. Every time. Every meal. Every Thanksgiving, every Christmas. Without fail. She'd lean over the table and go Aaa—gggg—hhh, choke, choke. Something like that. She'd grab her throat, throw herself back in her chair like she was going to fall over. Aaa—gggg—hhh, choke, choke. I loved it. Her family, excluding me, always look worried for the first three seconds, then they'd get that look of "Oh yeah, she always does this." She'd jump out of the chair and take off for the bathroom, Aaa—gggg–hhh, choke, choking all the way. We'd look at each other. Oh well. The reason we were looking at each other was because we knew she wasn't ever coming out of that bathroom until one of us went to the door to see if she was alright. "Please be ok and come back to the table to finish". Big Zzzzzzzzzzz.

Realize. We had to have this in the right order of person begging. If we are out of order, she would go aaa–gggg–hhh,choke, choke until we figured out we were out of order and then we'd rotate until we got it right. I liked to go because I could beg and make faces at the guys at the table at the same time. They would be laughing into their sleeves to keep her from hearing them. I tried to make them laugh out loud enough for her to hear and often did, which would piss her off to no freaking end. Everything was so close together you could hear a chuckle and all the guys had really deep voices. If I could get them to laugh, sometimes they would completely lose control, get hysterical and start to giggle. They'd get into it and couldn't stop laughing. I'd get set me and it would be bend-over, hands on knees laughing going on right outside the door. Jesus. There were good times. While this was going on, there would be a deep silence coming from the bathroom. I'd be right outside the door going, "Please come back to the table." Face. When she came out, the guys would still be in hysterics. All hell would break loose she'd be so pissed. There would be thunder coming out of those eyes. Damned near smoked. She'd want to kill, especially if it was me. Then, she would go into the cold routine. Thank God. It was over. We could leave now. As soon as I saw that, I would drag Dave's ass out of there. One holiday day down. How many to go?

We also had to go through another routine every Christmas, just for fun. This was in addition to the choking, which had to take place before the giving of presents. Once we got that out of the way, we would solemnly exchange gifts. Like somebody died. I would always make sure Dave and I got her a nice present. She was his mom. I could pretend to respect her once a year. I would make sure I spent at least a hundred dollars because I knew she was tested me. If I got her a cheap gift, she would throw us out. Although that didn't bother me, it hurt Dave. It was the only time he got together with his brother and Dad, except Thanksgiving. She would always give Dave a shirt he wouldn't wear, except to her house. She would always get me something for about ten bucks. She wouldn't even wrap it. She would hand it to me, just like it was when she picked it up, receipt and all. Then, she would tell me if I didn't like it, I could take it back. I was not about to drive forty miles from Lancaster to York to exchange a ten buck present. And she knew it. She always made it something she knew I wouldn't like. Like one of those things that show you how to knit. Knit..what a concept. Ok for some people but not me, boy. I push wheelbarrows in front of Ford trucks for fun and listen to horns blow for excitement. I do not knit.

Right after one more raucous Christmas, the third year we were married, I went to bed around ten o'clock. I was completely unaware of what was to come. Dave had been on the midnight shift, so I knew he would be coming home miserable. It seemed he was miserable all the time. Avid pet lovers, we had accumulated seven dogs, a cat named Aja and a parrot. Dave's job when he got home was to let the dogs out, one at a time. If he took them out late, we could sleep later in the morning. His idea. We had a fifty feet dog run in the back and the dogs all had collars with clips on them, so this worked really well. As a rule.

For some reason, Dave came home in a worse mood than usual. He picked Ti, my wonderful chocolate lab to go first. He was beautiful. Ninety pounds of quivering joy the minute he saw you. This dog could drag me up and down the road. He was four and refused to be trained even though I took him to a professional. I had decided to love him just as he was. Instead of putting him on the run, Dave just let him go. Let him go. Dave knew on some level Ti would take off, and he did. And wouldn't come back. Then, for some unknown reason, he took Ti's two year old and let her go right behind him. What woke me was their feet hitting the cold, hard ground on January 21st, 1989, running away from the house. When I tore down the stairs, he told me what he had done. I was numb. I couldn't believe it. I ran out into the freezing weather, barefoot, and called my dogs for two hours. I could hear each way they ran, but they wouldn't come home. My heart was broken. I loved animals more than anything, other than Mama. We were surrounded on three sides by Amish farms. The other side is a major highway. It was hidden from us by the tree break, a small hill and the pond. At 2:30 that morning, I was standing in the yard when I heard a thump from far away. I looked towards the road and saw a car's red tail lights. Someone had pulled over. One or both of my dogs had been hit. I knew it.

    I looked at Dave, who was standing there, motionless. He knew what he had done. Just like Jimmy did the day he called Muff in front of a car. I told Dave to head down to the road. To take the pickup. If both of my dogs were dead, when he came back down our road, have the back end down. If, at least one was alive, put it in the cab with him and leave the back end up. Then, I waited. I could still see the red tail lights. It seemed to take forever. I seldom remember crying uninterrupted for hours ever in my life. Hell, not even when everybody thought I was pregnant, but me. I did that night. Knowing nothing, except one or both had been hit, I cried from the not knowing. It went on forever.

    I finally saw the tail lights of the car pull off. A few minutes later, Dave came down our road. When he got close enough for me to look, I saw the back end down. They were both gone. I was destroyed. I walked out of the house, and met Dave at the driveway. I was broken and furious at the same time. I would not look at my dogs. I told Dave he would bury them under the tree next to the road. It is a beautiful tree in an area where they used to like to play. The ground was frozen. I didn't care. He was not coming back into the house until they were properly buried. It was not, by damn, going to wait until morning. Tears were running down Dave's face. I knew he was devastated, too. Maybe more than devastated. One: he had done it. Two: he had to hold their dead bodies in his arms. He had to see what had been done to them. The damage, if any. Or, they could have looked like they were sleeping. Either way, they were never waking up. They were never jumping on me again. They would never again make me laugh in joy. Like they had so many times.

    The next morning he left for a trip. I didn't see him again for three weeks. I cried the whole time. I tried to forgive him. I truly made an astonishing effort to excuse whatever the hell he could have been thinking. Especially with wild and crazy Ti, and a barely trained Honey. I think I told myself that I had managed to forgive him, but perhaps not. I don't know. I know it caused a knot in my stomach that never went away. Not only when I think of them, but also when I don't. It feels like it is always there. The house settled into a home of sadness. Every time I looked at one of the other animals, I felt the loss. Dave wasn't there to even try to ease my pain. He ran. He seldom stayed home long after that.

I throw myself at something when I can't handle things. That's what I do when I'm hurt, I throw myself at something. Those that know me know what I mean. Obsess. It does wonders for the mind. You forget everything else that would be taking up space. I threw myself at my orchids this time. They were what filled my mind when the snow was on the ground. I waited for spring. It seemed to take forever. Every time I looked at that tree, I grieved anew. Spring finally arrived and I bloomed, as I always do. I am a sun person at heart and crave it. I tried to fill my thoughts with things that were not sad. Anything.

I remembered the twists in life that can be so interesting. If something is bothering me, I often think God places something else in front of me to deal with solely to give me a break. There were always unexpected tidbits to fill your empty heart in Lancaster, the Land of the Amish. Things that would pop up so quickly, you had to re-direct your thoughts to your surroundings, not your personal heartbreak. I remember the first time I laughed after my dogs died. You had little to worry about in Lancaster. For one, you had very little crime, but you had cows. Big damn cows. Smart ones, too. One day I got up to go to work and headed out to the car. Right behind my car was an enormous cow. I looked around and there were about eight other cows, eating my flowers. Since I am not much of a range hand, I ran into the house to call the State Police who did everything; fairs, funerals, everything. I got a real nice lady on the phone, but I was told since the cows were in my yard, they couldn't help me. I would have to run the cows up to the State road first. I tried not to think negative thoughts about my husband, but it sure would have been nice if Dave were home, you know. Just those five days or six days out of the year when you need him.

I took off for the Amish farm adjacent to our property. We were surrounded on three sides by these farms, so I headed for the closest. When I told them about the cows, they told me there was a part of the fence that was weak and the cows knew it. If they were smart enough to know it, why didn't I know it? I had never really thought about cows having brains. Apparently, the cows will go right for it every time. There was even a head cow.

Like the President of a company, I guess. A head cow? The Amish man was going to send his little boys to get them. These kids were smaller than I was. I headed back home and waited for the fun to start. A few minutes later, down the State road, came a wagon pulled by two horses with three kids in it. They looked like they were going fifty miles an hour. When they got to my driveway, they pulled those reins like pros. That wagon shot to the side of the road with the kids bailing out as it did. They didn't even wait for it to stop tearing down that 300 ft. driveway. I was standing next to my car and the cow that was absolutely humongous, when she looked up and saw those kids running down my driveway. Oh shit. Meet the head cow. Her head went up and she took off. Took off, people. She cleared a ditch! I didn't know cows could jump. High. She was in a dead run in a second. Cows can move faster than you think. As soon as she did, the other cows looked up and took off after her. I was jumping around, excited as hell, but trying not to die in a stampede in my own damn yard, for Christ's sake. They took that stampede right through my rose gardens. I had cow pies everywhere, too, which had me tap dancing while I was trying to stay out of the way of crazy cows. Seconds after those boys had jumped from the wagon, the boys, cows and all were history. Gone. No sign of them. I was bent over laughing. Good grief! It was better than dancing. Tears were running down my face.

However, the horses and the wagon were still there. They were also still there when I got home from work. I walked back over to the farm to let the Amish farmer know. He hadn't even missed them. He did, however, scold the little boys which I felt bad about. They were great neighbors. I had been invited to a barn raising, which is an amazing sight. The women were wonderful and always brought me little gifts. Did you know the girls and boys are allowed to "sow their wild oats?" They have to quit when they marry. That's better than the deal Mama offered me.

I found that weak spot unexpectedly. Apparently, Dave knew about it. We went walking one day down the little creek that ran on the east side of our property. Once we got to the more brushy part, I was ready to go back because I had a top on that exposed my stomach and rib area and I was getting cut up a little. Dave wanted to keep going. Trying to do that "good wife" stuff, I followed along. All of a sudden, he stopped. Not realizing it, I kept going. Right into the electrified fence. That shock hit me, burnt me and pissed me off. I turned around and slapped him harder than he has ever been and will ever be slapped again. That man took me right into that fence on purpose. When his head came back around, I hit him again. I didn't stop until he got his hands up good enough that I couldn't reach him. So, I kicked him in the nuts. Try it again, sucker. One of us was going to be limping home and it wasn't me. Pissed me off. This guy was getting on my last nerve.

ANOTHER SLIPPERY SLOPE

Although I loved Lancaster and my Amish neighbors, the damn cows got through all the damn time. And, things had gotten a little out of hand in the marriage area. People ask me why we got a divorce. He was a slug, but a nice slug. He was living proof you can love a slug. I loved him when I met him and I loved him when I left him. Sounds like a country song. The demise of the marriage took a long, long, unpleasant time and more or less it wasn't more his fault or more mine. Maybe I was unable to forgive him for the loss of my dogs, I don't know. I tried not to dwell on it. I don't think it would have ended so soon if there had just been the everyday things that get on your nerves. Our problem was a larger issue that couldn't be solved. I couldn't solve it and he wouldn't

I mentioned Dave was a cop. All man, a Mr Macho kind of guy. He had a big, barrel chest and usually got what he wanted when he puffed up. One night there was a fire in Lancaster. Dave was there. He ended up with a two year old black girl, who'd been in the fire and wasn't breathing. Those were the days of not knowing what caused AIDS so they had been told if you give mouth-to-mouth, you are on your own and its your decision. So, he did it. It didn't save her and he didn't get AIDS. Soon after, I noticed he had been more lethargic than usual. How do you determine if a slug is more lethargic? He smoked an unbelievable amount of marijuana. I couldn't grow enough, but I refused to but it. He'd hit it first thing in the morning and go all day if he was off. One morning he came down the stairs with a strange expression on his face to tell me he was having trouble with his urine. When I asked him what kind of trouble, his said it was brown. I was stunned. I sure didn't know what it was, but it sounded like something you need to fix quickly. I argued with him the required couple of hours, then drug him to the hospital. After what seemed like hours and hours, they came down and told me a: they caught his drug use and b: he had hepatitis. The bad kind, "C". It was deadly and it was a bitch to deal with. There was no real cure.

He was in the hospital for about eight weeks. He almost died while they tried to stabilize him. When he got out, the police department put him on a desk because he had gotten so heartbreakingly emaciated. His Lieutenant told him they didn't think he would ever be put on patrol or detective work again. Well, naturally, here came depression in a full dress uniform. You just don't tell a man that he'll never be that man again. It was a depression of the deepest kind. There was nothing I could do to get him back on his feet. His unhappiness about his job took over. His granddad was a cop, his dad was a cop, his uncle was a cop..you get the picture. He wasn't even Italian or Irish. We just couldn't get him back on track. I know the loss of the dogs weighed heavy on him. Now, he had to look at that tree, too. Daily.

      Trying to pick ourselves out of the doldrums, I dived headfirst into another. I took a close look at our finances. I was doing well at work. I owned two search firms and we covered the Lancaster, Philly, Harrisburg, and York regions, plus anything that word of mouth brought in. Our commission cuts were phenomenal. I paid my people very well, and they responded with production. We had a great reputation and were really going gang busters. I had been successful doing executive searches mainly for high end CEO's, so our savings looked great. Given that, we decided he should just quit the force to take a year off to try to get himself out of the blues. He was going to travel and do the things he loved best..which was kill things. He'd shoot or fish anything that moved. Off he went to Big Sky, Montana to kill elks and upstate New York for salmon fishing. Alaska, for whatever salmon they had up there. Unfortunately, this lasted three years and he broke us. I tried to stop it when we still had a hundred thousand in the bank, but he wouldn't stop. I begged him from then on. When I cashed in my last CD of $25,000, I gave him the evil eye and said, "Don't spend this," and wondered what he would buy. Within the hour, he bought our third riding lawnmower for $11,000. I'm the one who mowed the lawn. we had five cars and I only drove one. We had a Mazda pick-up, a Jeep CJ-7, a 1972 corvette, a black Trans-Am and a restored 1968 Chevy convertible. I drove the Trans-Am. He drove everything else. He made terrible money decisions. I had let it go too far. I just couldn't say no to him because of what had happened to him. Even on his trips, they might have to hospitalize him. I'd be home, worried to death, and he'd be off somewhere. The last year, he was only home four weeks. It was time for me to go into a private think tank.

I came home for seven days. I didn't tell Mama I was coming. Thanks to MaryBeth, I stayed on the oceanfront at a place called Beachwalk and contemplated the state of my marriage. I played good music, ate good food and danced around the condo. All the while, I knew I had to realize that although he was depressed, I was now more depressed than Dave. I couldn't work. I couldn't concentrate. I had worked so hard to end up back where I started. Yeah, I had two companies, but I didn't have any savings or cash anymore. Nothing liquid. After that week at the beach and seven years of marriage, I decided to end it. Dave was never going back to work as long as he was married to me because I had made it my job to make it easy on him to spend money and hard on me to make it.

I went back to Lancaster, talked with him, and asked him to leave. He knew it was coming when I left Lancaster. We didn't fight or anything. Hell, we didn't even know each other anymore. All he said, before he went out the door is, "I know what I have done." I wonder at what point he figured it out and why he didn't stop, if he could have. I had decided to make this a friendly divorce, give him what he wanted and just work my way out of it. No fussing. No arguing. He would call and we would talk. All his stuff was still at the house. I guess we were trying to figure out if we could get back together, but I really didn't think so. I just didn't want to hurt him any more than I had to. I knew he was lost but I was lost as well. I was only good for money to him. And marijuana. I had done my mourning the forty eight weeks I was alone that last year. He was a good man and it had been a good marriage until the incident with Ti and Honey and the little girl. All in all, we had the five years I was a slut and seven years as a married couple. It was 1990.

After he left, I always felt someone was watching me. We had a car port, so if you wanted to know if I was home, my car was in plain view. There was a large hill behind the house that you could drive to the top of if you went around and up the road beside the stream on the east border of the property. I would never be able to see the vehicle. However, with all the windows, you could see right into the living area. I felt like he was up there all the time. I guess he was checking to see if I was dating, but I wasn't. On the good side, I thought maybe he was keeping an eye on me. One thing was for sure. He wasn't traveling anymore. For six months, I never left the house except to work and get groceries and things like that. After nine months of separation we had done nothing to finalize the divorce. Naturally, someone had to toss out that last straw. It was a biggie.

I worked with a woman in my office who was trying to be my friend. She was a tall, skinny, blond who drove a red Camaro. She reminded me of Janice, the girl who had run up the back end of a Volkswagon when I was in college. Sheila had been working on me to go out with her and finally convinced me to go to a comedy club. I didn't find it all that funny but it was nice to be out again. It was also nice to have someone to talk to after five o'clock. After the show we stopped for a drink, but still got back to my house about ten that evening. I was surprised how dark it was coming down my lane. I realized it had been a very long time since I had been out after dark. On the way down the driveway she said she had to pee. I replied it was nice she had eight acres to pee on because I really didn't want to invite her in, kidding around. She seemed to drop it because she drove down and turned around. We were sitting in the car chatting about the routines we saw. You know, what we found funny and what we found dorky.

Out of nowhere, her door was pulled open, then slammed back hard. One arm came in from the darkness and a right arm violently slammed her back against her seat, then the same arm held her head pinned, helpless, against the seat by her neck. The left arm quickly reached around, grabbed her keys and slung them into the yard. All in one smooth and utterly frightening motion. I saw that hand come in, and saw the speed with which this all happened. It was a cop move. I knew instantly who it was. I realized he would be wearing a gun and knew in my heart he thought she was a guy. I was so mad I could have chewed nails and spit out metals heads. My mind refused to grasp that he would go this far. To attack someone! By the time he slammed her head against the seat, I was already out my door. I flung it open and crawled right over the hood of her car. I came over the top of that car in one slide and grabbed him by the shirt front all the way up to his neck. I was so furious. I couldn't control my shaking I was so furious with him. I started shoving him backwards so fast he couldn't get his balance He couldn't keep his feet on the ground long enough to get a good foothold. Finally, I had his back against the house. If I could have physically lifted him off the damn ground, I would have. When I bitch slapped him, he dropped the gun. It was in his hand! He didn't even fight back he was so surprised. I hit him again just to make sure I had his attention. I told him, growling, not to move a single damn muscle

-198-

until I got back or I would get his own gun and shoot his ass with it. I went back to the car and told her to get the hell out of there. She had seen the gun, since he had it in her face and was afraid to leave me. I knew Dave would never hurt me. The gun was for whatever guy he thought I was with, not me.

I was hissy fit pissed. What was he thinking of? I told him to get his ass in the house, get every gun he had, and get the hell off the property. I told him I was going to get a restraining order. I didn't care if it embarrassed the hell out of him or not. He had just decided to deserve anything I could throw at him. We were through. Over. Shazamm. I told him to come back the next day with as many friends as he had, get his shit out of the house and not to say another word to me about my behavior ever after what he had just done. And he did just that. He showed up the next day with his head hanging down like a beaten beagle about to howl. I had packed his stuff all night so it was nice and damn tidy when they came for it. I figured my embarrassment was what I got for being so indecisive and worrying about trying to work with him and not hurt him any more than I had to. She was going to tell everybody at the office what happened. Now I was really depressed. The next door neighbor was a cop, so I figured Dave would tell him to watch me for him. Fine. I kept my own gun, just in case. I stayed in the house and laid low for a while. I was too miserable to do anything, including work. Hell with the plants, I was caught up between being sad, pissed and broken hearted. Pissed mostly. Financially destroyed, too.

Six months later we finally got to the divorce. It worked well except for the financial arrangements the judge made me eat. Ow! Other than that, it wasn't too bad. Dave and I had used my lawyer. A man he knew well and liked. I proposed the settlement and he was ok with it. It was as fair and equitable as it could be. The problem was the judge, who had worked with Dave for ten years, threw it out and declared my orchids a business even though I had never sold one except to buy a better one. I never sold them commercially, just to friends. Even that was only rarely. He gave me thirty days to sell them. I couldn't keep even one. I had grown some of these from flasks and had waited five years for them to bloom. I had three 50 gallon aquariums with baby orchids in them. I had orchids growing up the side of my fireplace. I had orchids growing all over a lattice walk-way from the house to the car. I had orchids that you had to push aside to get into the large tub, like in the jungle. I had them everywhere. I had over 500 orchids. That was where my money went when I spent it, but it took me twelve years total to get that many. Most of them were babies when I got them so they came 10 in a bottle. I couldn't believe it. Dave was horrified. He never thought I would lose my orchids. He begged the judge to no avail. He would have never wanted this to happen, but the judge seemed to think this was another bored housewife throwing out the sick ex-cop. Not the case at all. Nobody told him about the hundreds of thousands Dave spent traveling all over the country, like a man of means. Nobody told him about Dave attacking Sheila and pulling a gun on her. He wouldn't let us speak. No, I was the bad guy. All I had done was work and play with plants. Anyhow, a university in Maryland bought them all and paid $10,000, Dave got half.

The judge gave me eighty percent of the debt and fifty percent of the assets. I also had to pay Dave alimony for two years of seven hundred a month. I wasn't able to even feel pissed. My despair was so much greater than that. I got to keep my one car and he got to keep all four of the other vehicles That included the Corvette that I paid for; then Dave had totaled it and I had to completely re-build it. Not to mention the custom paint job Dave decided it needed. That I paid for. Oh, and the boat. There was no water within fifty miles of us, but he had to have a bass boat, engines, trailer and all. I paid for that. I didn't care if he took all that and the dirt from the vacuum cleaner. Let him have it. End this thing. It was like an out-of-control vine strangling me. End it. The only thing good about this was I wouldn't have to listen to his damn Mother choke anymore. Yee-ha.

I sat in a house with five dogs, two cats and a parrot. I had to sell the businesses to pay the bills he had run up while going all over the U.S. I had never been anywhere except for work and that one trip to Montreal. He had never once invited me to go with him. Things took a hard slide downward. He would stop by every now and then. I never told him he couldn't come by, but our conversation was very stilted. He had started dating his high school sweetheart and wanted my advice. He didn't want them to end up like us. One thought I had was he could kill his Mother to eliminate one possibility.

TOO OLD, TOO UGLY AND BARREN.

While the demise of my marriage was going on, I had a friend named Gary who worked for me for while I was a head hunting success. He and his wife had been very good friends to me during my divorce. Unfortunately, now they were separating. They had a darling little girl and I had fallen completely in love with her. She was the only child I have ever been close to and I fell hard. The first word her mother taught her was "mall", the second was "more." She couldn't say Mommy or Daddy at three years old or wouldn't. But she could say "Carol." I became a babysitter for the first time in my life. Consequently, Gary and I became real close. He didn't like being alone and he would call me all hours of the night. We morphed into best buds. We went to dinner, anything to keep either of us from having to think about the ruin our marriages had become. I thought he was someone I could talk to. However, the people he really wanted to talk to were backers. Of us. He tried to talk some friends of his into backing us for another search firm. We had several dinners about it, but I was real reluctant. I knew I was being used. I was also really broke. I tried to explain I was not at my best, you know. But reality set in, the house was going into foreclosure so I had to do something.

With the help of his friends, we opened a company called "PowerSearch." I picked the name and I loved it. I designed the logo and the stationary. I got excited about everything. I liked the name, the backers, everything. It had promise. Real promise. I had all the files from my former companies so we were able to start right up. I dove into calling all my former contacts. Some of them had missed me and were kind enough to be worried about me. I truly, deeply appreciated that because I knew it was sincere. I had worked with these people a long time and we had a tight relationship until everything fell apart. They didn't know what had happened to me and were excited I was back. Oh my. The office was a dream, too. Lancaster is a beautiful city and we were right downtown on the third block of Queen Street. We were next to a beautiful old church with an ancient cemetery that had benches under lovely trees. We used to go into the cemetery and have lunch. You remember I have an affinity for cemeteries? When I would step into the cemetery with a book or lunch, it was always a wonderfully serene, quiet time. I will always remember the quiet comfort I felt in the atmosphere. Very unlike my childhood.

As time passed, I learned a great deal from Gary. For one thing, I learned to play cards all day long so we couldn't get any work done. I realized that Gary would show up at eight am sharp, but wouldn't do one lick of work all day. Unless he fell into it, nothing happened. Some of his friends even came by to play cards with us. I had gotten into this bad habit of doing whatever he suggested. Even if it meant closing the office to run to the country club to see his buddies. He had been rich at one time, and he definitely ran with a crowd more sophisticated than I had ever known. His country club friends accepted me right away because they realized Gary and I were only buddies. Maybe they had thought otherwise, but something in our air together seemed to settle them down. They were a little touchy about Gary having dated a few times because they were hoping he and Sandy would get back together. It was clear that his buddies' wives were out to restore the norm. That meant Gary and Sandy, together. As long as I was a partner, I was acceptable. Out in the clubhouse one day, in front of all his friends, he lost a football bet to me and instead of paying up, he gave me three lessons with the pro at his golf course. Although they didn't usually let people play there who weren't members, they let me. I fell in love with golf. Deeply. From that moment, I played golf everyday after work and twenty seven holes on Saturday and Sunday. I played alone, and I played fast and I became very happy with my progression. I also learned to hate to play when they made me play with certain types of women. Slow, bitching at every hole, women. Some women were great. Personally, I would rather play alone. It was only something to do for them. Not me, boy. I was going for the gold every round and I didn't like distractions. In the meantime, I slowly began to fall in love with the whole package. The country club style of living fit me to a "t." I wasn't interested in social climbing. The ground floor of the style was good enough for me.

      The tilt in the relationship between Gary and I really started one night when we were having drinks after work at the Lancaster Brewing Co, a great bar right down town. We had been to an opera when, I mentioned that I had never been anywhere, except Montreal. I told him the places Dave had been, and he was astonished that I had never been invited along. My birthday was coming up and he said he was going to do something special for me. We left on what he said was a two hour drive and we thoroughly enjoyed it ..talking and laughing. He had a great sense of humor, and we found everything funny. All during the drive, I didn't know where we were going. It was Inner Harbor, Maryland. I was so excited. We got out of the car around 7:30 that evening and he took me straight to a fine restaurant. Better than any I had been to in Lancaster. There were well-dressed, sophisticated people with jewels sparkling galore. After the host took us to our seats, Gary ordered from a wine list and went through the whole tasting routine. No Golden Corral here, boy. Nobody rushed us. When the waiter came back, Gary ordered for me. That was so cool. We had been out enough that he knew I was a meat lover so he ordered the filet. It came with the best sauce I have ever tasted. I could have oozed right out of my seat, I was so impressed. I decided right then and there, in my 40's, to learn to cook, and to have sauce on everything I did. I would develop them myself. Grand Marnier with wine in all of them. Oh my God. Yes !!! We went dancing and wandered through all the little shops. Late in the evening, we stopped at this little bistro and had a little more wine. Not too much, just enough.

We returned to a gorgeous hotel. We had already checked in, but they had taken our bags to the room, so I hadn't seen the rooms. This was the nervous part. I really wasn't sure what was expected of me because he hadn't mentioned it. When we got to the room, it was a two bedroom suite. I was so very impressed with his thoughtfulness and insight. That Friday night and the next night will be memories I will carry forever. We were truly friends and not lovers and it was exhilarating to be with a man who had no expectations except companionship. You knew that was not going to last.

It was two months later that we had sex for the first time. Let me mention here, he was the worse lover I had ever encountered then or since. It mattered not. The kindness, the gentleness and the way he seemed to just adore me was so gratifying. He would call me at home after working together all day and we would talk until the night was gone. If he wasn't right in front of me, he was calling. I thought that was how much he wanted to be with me. I was very reluctant to let him come to the house because I didn't know what was going on with Dave. I knew he was still dating his high school sweetheart because he was still calling me for advice. That was all well and good, but it didn't mean he was ready to find out a guy was sleeping over in the house we built together. That pesky cop neighbor was still there, too. Gary was still seeing his wife, too, but not often. While we were at Inner Harbor, she took everything out of the house, leaving him only a TV and chair in the living room. Clearly misunderstood our relationship at that time. I could absolutely, never, ever do that to a man and I deeply despise women who do. They give the rest of us a bad name and scar our relationships with the men they leave behind. Sandy accepted me as her friend, but that was selfish because she knew I loved Missy, her little girl. All she cared about was the baby-sitting. I would even baby-sit nights that Gary and Sandy went out. All in all, it was very friendly, but complicated. I have to say, Gary showed all the symptoms of a man deeply and happily in love. My mistake.

For some reason, Gary made a decision right out of the blue. Apparently, it had been bothering him for some time, but he had never mentioned it. Therefore, it was a bomb to me. Again, my life would take an unexpected turn. Gary told me I was "too old, too ugly and barren." Sounds like a take off from "The Good, The Bad and the Ugly," but unfortunately, there was nothing good in it. He was thirty eight, I was 45. He wanted a woman his age, divorced, who, listen to this, had a house worth about $300,000, two kids and said so for Christ's sake. He meant it. He set up parameters, and that was supposed to be it. He also wanted her to live on the west side of Lancaster, where all the ritzy people lived. It had suddenly, overnight, become his mission. I couldn't believe it. He never took one moment to think how badly that hurt me, or even asked if it affected. He was oblivious about whether I had any opinions or feelings on the matter. It was like he was tossing me over the side like chum. We were sitting in my office when he dropped that on me. How could he have not known how hard I had fallen for him? I didn't sleep with anybody! Of course, he knew. It just didn't matter. I didn't meet the specs. We had been inseparable. I knew, without doubt, that he loved me. We had breakfast, lunch and dinner together and often sex. He was getting better, but not by much. We played canasta during lunch with his friends right in the office. I played golf with them. They had accepted me completely. There were no negatives that I was aware of until he told me I was "too old, too ugly and barren." I was cool with the barren. But, old? Ugly? Nobody else I knew thought so. Several of his unmarried friends had asked me out. He bragged about me. What the hell happened? Did I suddenly end up in the wrong movie? I had been the happiest I had been in a long time when he dropped me right off the face of the earth. Bam !!! I was so shocked that I didn't know what to say, so I did what I did best. I kept my mouth shut, stood up and walked out. I got in my car, and left. He was running behind me trying to stop me, even hanging onto the car when I pulled out into the street, but I was going and there was nothing he could do to get in my way except fall under the tires. I would have run over him. I was unbelievably hurt. I was mad and I was humiliated. I knew Gary well enough to know he had told his friends of his "decision." He was like that, an open door to everybody. Except me.

I went home and barricaded myself in the house. Although he had never been there except to pick me up or drop me off, I didn't know if he would come by. I knew this. His ass wasn't coming in. The phone started to ring immediately, and I knew it was Gary. He called over and over. I knew then he wouldn't come to the house because he didn't know what my reaction would be. Smart boy. As expected, I cried. I was well aware how important Gary had become, but I didn't realize how devastated I would be if he did something like this. Not to mention so suddenly. And the "too, etc " thing was a major bummer. Couldn't he have said he wanted someone in his life that met certain criteria without insulting me to my face. I lost my confidence like I'd put it in the trash compactor. I had let myself be out there, warts and all, and it was thrown back into my face. I knew I was not going to be able to work with him. But, because I was broke, I would have to. I knew if he found "her," he would be taking her to breakfast, lunch and dinner because he was like that. He would think nothing of bringing her into the office to introduce us. Then, it would be twenty four hours a day, like it was with us. It was my first taste of what Sandy had to deal with. He made decisions about feelings with his mind, not his heart. What a kick in the ass it is to find out.

The next morning I went back to work. There was no doubt he was surprised to see me. He was so upset. He was so worried, he said. No clue. I tried to maintain a distance but it was hard because I was so drawn to him and things had been so natural between us. He was like the puppy who loved you more than the rest. You know, always jumping up, looking for your attention. That was Gary. However, he was also in full force "find the woman" swing. He was going out at night, letting friends set him up, joining clubs where a woman like that might be. He didn't mind talking about it. His version of honesty. He would look me right in the eye, and he had to know it hurt, but it seemed he wanted the openness and companionship to continue. He made it clear that with whomever he chose, she would have to accept me. I couldn't believe he could be so stupid. He never asked would I accept her. He assumed it.

This merry go round went on for about four months. I would be sitting at my desk, he'd start talking about who he'd met and I'd get up and leave. I didn't want to hear it. Just do it. He would hear me go out the door and follow me downstairs begging me not to go. He wanted me to get over it. He didn't want me hurt and I think he was truly surprised at the depth of my feelings. Obviously a problem he never experienced. If he came near me, he would explain one more time, his mantra, "too old, too ugly and barren" over and over as the reason we couldn't be together, but he wouldn't give me up. If he had just stopped saying that for Christ's sake. But no. Every time I walked in to work, out it came. Like it explained everything. He wouldn't let me work. Wouldn't leave me alone. Who do you know who would say ok to that? Name me one. When we went out, still trying to keep the work part together, we would get all worked up. He would get all sad because he knew he was losing me. We'd get all worked up emotionally. Neither of us wanted this relationship, whatever it was, to end. He saw finding this woman as getting his old life back. I never heard anything from him about feeling the need to be in love with her. Little details.

    To get away, I came home one week to see Mama. Seven days, that's all. When I got back he had found her. He didn't even go for comparison shopping. She was perfect; met his criteria perfectly. He said she wasn't good looking or well built but she had the money, age, house, kids and lived in the right neighborhood. Ok, then. He went after her with a vengeance. With the gentlemanly charm of his, she didn't stand a chance. Neither had I. After he waved her off after introducing us, he came back up to see what I thought of her. I did something I have been proud of ever since. Its an unmentionable. I left him shaking like a leaf in a tornado. Top that, jerk. He'd never had anything happen to him like that in his life and it never will again. He'd never understood sex as it could be until then. Worked for me. Scared the hell out of him. He couldn't even stand up when I walked out. I walked out with a smile on my face. I knew he couldn't stand up.

    I got my groove back. I never went back. He called on the phone to beg me not to leave him. I was gone. I wouldn't answer. He even came down the driveway and pounded on the door, begging me to let him in. It was over. However, Gary, you can stick your too old, too ugly where it best fits. Let her match that, Jack. He didn't understand I only said goodbye once to him. No seconds. Fifty ways to leave your lover? You only need one really great way. He'd never feel that electricity again, I betcha.

    MaryBeth and I had been communicating all the years since Mama's face surgery. We had finally made up as best girl pals. The old MaryBeth was gone. She took unbelievably good care of Mama, running her to Duke, which was four hours away, once a week. She stayed with her overnight, made sure she took her medicine. All of it. I couldn't have done it, I know. I truly came to respect her dedication to Mama, which, I must admit, came as a complete surprise to me. She would back those world famous doctors down and tell them exactly what they should do. They would do it. She would call to try to make me feel better about Gary but talking about it made me cry. I had never been this weak before, but I had lost everything. My mojo still was proud of what I'd done, but it didn't pay my bills. My house was ready to go into foreclosure again. I knew I couldn't work with Gary anymore. Didn't want to. I knew Gary would make it happen with this girl. I knew he would become whoever he had to be to, like he had with me. I heard two weeks later he had already moved in. He was calling MaryBeth to get to me. I guess he wanted to tell me how well it was working for him. Shove it, Gary.

Since I wasn't working, the mortgage was two months behind. The only reason they hadn't taken it already was I had it for sale. MaryBeth told Crystal and her husband, Dave, how bad things were for me. These sweethearts drove all the way from Appleton, Wisconsin to Lancaster, Pa. to try to comfort me. They asked what I needed to save my house. All in all, it was around five thousand. Dave wrote the check. No questions asked and no remarks about my needing to pay it back. They told me it was a gift. I took it, but you can bet your ass it would get paid back. It was an obligation and I don't understand people who can't see that. If somebody is offering to help you, they shouldn't have to give up their hard-earned money to a relative who can't see they deserve it back. The ASAP was going to take a long time, but I would reach that "p", don't think I wouldn't. Somehow, someway, someday. Count on it.

After getting tired of hearing me wail, MaryBeth unexpectedly pulled into my driveway pulling a little U-Haul. I only had Tuborg and Aja, my cat left. They were used to making the trip to North Carolina. Yee Ha. Road Trip. Good enough for me. Get back into that Carol body I used to know. Go home. Heal. Fine. All right. We packed up what clothes I wanted, my dog and cat and I left Lancaster behind. Forever.

After I got home, both Dave and Gary worried the hell out of MaryBeth, but not me, boy. I was done with the past. They would want to know if I was ok. Oh. Right. And if I wasn't? Anybody going to try to tell me they would bother doing something about it? It was guilt. They wanted to know would I be coming back, etc? And if I did? For what. Somebody going to come up with a whip to beat me with next time? Sure. I'll be right there. Uh huh. She would not answer their questions and I would never take their calls. Gary called for at least two years. I cannot imagine what he thought he was going to say to me. Did he really think I needed him to tell me his mantra of why it wouldn't work, like I didn't get it the first two hundred times he flung it at me? Go bye, bye, Gary. MaryBeth never asked was he still with that woman because I told her I didn't give a shit. We obviously couldn't remain friends with me so far away. What was the point? I said my goodbye when I left him. He couldn't stand up. There wasn't a working bone in his body. Yee-ha. Yet, he would not give up. Part of me wondered if he was calling because he had broken up with his new love. The other said it was to tell me how well it was all working for him. Common sense told me it wouldn't matter. His character had serious defects, don't you think?

That voice, though. There is something about a baritone that gets right into your blood, bones and soul. I downright shiver when I hear one. I'd miss that. He knew I loved it so he would ramp it up a little. I never heard it again after I walked out of that office. I had it on my answering machine, practically crying, begging me not to leave him. I tossed it away when I got home. I hope he is doing well, but somehow I don't think so. There was a shallowness to him that I had never seen when I was bright eyed and bushy tailed. He surely would not have been good for me, especially since I was "too old, etc.". He must have thought that every time he looked at me. What a terrible thing to say to someone. I have never forgotten it. Who would?

A LOST KEY

Not being someone who wants to dwell on bad karma, I went to the local shag club hoping someone would ask me to dance and even more importantly, hoping I could. Some falling down drunk named George took unwanted control of my arm and decided it was going to be his toy for the whole damn night. He kept dragging me around like he was Tarzan. Sum'bitch wouldn't let go. He was not just drunk but way drunk and at that moment, I knew I was home. Deja vu. Was I used to this crap after the Pavilion of my teenage years? I think so. After I let him manhandle me a minute, hoping he would come to his drunken senses, I decided to act like Mama. I looked him in his whisky drenched eyeballs and told him if he didn't let go of my arm, I would gnaw his damn hand off. He took a couple of seconds to think that over. I don't think he got it, but he figured out it didn't sound like sex so he let go. Good. I should be free from groping man handlers for at least a few minutes before some other grope person took over. Lord, save me. What made me think I would be happy back in Carteret County? Much to my delight, I actually danced the night away. I understood later that I was new blood to be sucked so the guys were checking me out. Some recognized me and actually told me they used to watch me at the Pavilion. That was as big a compliment as you could give me. Mostly because it was so unexpected and it was clear my dancing had given somebody pleasure so long ago. Although it had been forty years, they remembered it all this time. Guys and dolls, that's humbling.

After I got my dancing toes back under me, reality told me I had to get a job. I found one at a marina called the Crow's Nest where MaryBeth used to work. Now, this place was fun and you sure had enough time to enjoy it. I went to work for $4.25 an hour, does that suck or what? Seven days a week, from seven to seven were the hours. I ran the captain's store. However, I couldn't afford a place to live. My boss and two of his friends let me move into an oceanfront duplex, furnished it and paid the expenses. So that $4.25 an hour was worth a whole lot more than it sounds. I was afraid it would result in their putting a run on me, but they never treated me with anything less than respect.

The computer was very big and the counter so high, I couldn't see a single key. While Jake was trying to teach me, I had serious reservations about this working out. The maintenance crew came out from the back with a 8" stool. The fun started when I talked to people, being the short thing I am. When we got to the counter, I'd step on the stool. People got the biggest kick out of that. Eight inches made a big difference. I got a lot of mileage from that stool. Hell, I could take a whole lot of ribbing. Mama taught me to laugh, not bitch. I really enjoyed that job and met some really fun people. There were a bunch of guys who would come in first thing in the morning to sit, run their mouths and drink coffee. They made me one of the guys, and you know how I love that. Great bunch.

My real pleasure in being home was getting to see Mama. After work, I would head to Beaufort to spend as much time with her as I could. Since she was getting up there in age, I wasn't so interested in dancing that I went out every night, but I have to admit it was a close second to Mama. We settled back into our old routine of her making me laugh and just being corny with each other, even if only on the phone. I saw Reba on TV and realized her gestures, face making and moving with every insult was like Mama's way. They didn't look alike. The mannerisms were similar. Sometimes I wondered why I ever left, but then I remembered I was not pregnant and Mama did not kill herself, but I was supposed to be and she was supposed to. On days I couldn't see her, she'd call me at the marina and be her normal falling down laughing self. If I was talking to her on the phone, everybody would want to talk to her because she was so comical. I didn't have to defend the past alcoholism. I didn't get it when people only see one side of someone and work their damn hardest to make sure its the wrong side. I didn't get off much but I crammed as much time into seeing her as I could. She fluctuated between the fun and being tired all the time. Lord, she could sleep a lot. She was seventy three but even with the bandage on her face, she didn't have a lot of wrinkles and her hair was still almost all black. She had gained a lot of weight over the years but I think that was pretty much because she refused to leave the house unless it was to go to the doctor's so her butt got tired of holding her up and spread out.

    Aunt Elly had raging diabetes and it took her apart in pieces. I did hate to see that happen, but I never got over how she treated Mama. A woman who had treated her with contempt. She spent months at a time, leaving Mac alone, taking care of a woman whose five daughters wanted nothing to do with her. Said it all. She knew it, too. When she died, she left them everything. She didn't even leave Mama a thank you note. Ugly ant hill that she was.

    Mama was a mess. They had tried several surgeries on Mama's face but, as I mentioned, they never took. One time they cut a piece off her inside thigh to try to re-build the nose, but that was an unbelievable disaster. Because of the smoking, that didn't take either and the pain from the skin they took off the leg hurt worse than the nose. Later they did something unforgivable. They cut more skin and tried to stretch it across her forehead. The skin was stretched so thin you could see her skull. She was in agony because the skin was so stretched. Every time they did something, she felt more and more like a monster. All this from a small mole. The right side of her face looking nothing like the left.

The left looked patched together. And not with skin. Pay attention, people. Get those suckers off. NOW. Even when Mama was in a good mood, she still wasn't the only fun I had. Work could be a hoot. A lot of people were funny down this way, not only Mama. People did things Down East that nobody would even think of doing up North. We called it "gitting yourself in a sitiation." Yes, I know it's spelled wrong, but that's how we pronounced it. However, there were a few things at work that were high up on the oh shit list.

One unforgettable example was the day my boss called me on the marine radio to tell me to clear the parking lot. I don't think I had ever talked on the radio until then, but it was well worth the wait. How the hell did you clear a parking lot when half the drivers were out fishing? Duh, the cars were locked. I couldn't knock the windows out? Wouldn't that be fun if I could? I ran back and forth screaming at everybody because I knew it was an emergency but I didn't know how much time I had. I have to admit, I acted a whole lot more panicked than I really felt because, why not? Huffing and puffing, I finally called him back to tell him what little progress I had made. His answer was to get everybody the hell I could, out of the parking lot adjacent to the ramp. Forget the cars, get the people out of the parking lot. His throttle was stuck on high speed, he couldn't get his off switch to work and he was coming in. He was going to take those two Mercury engines, and a twenty one foot boat right up the ramp, into the parking lot. I abo-so-lutterly could not wait to see that. I hollered for all the guys to come running. I knew they wouldn't want to miss it either. Jake wouldn't care, he'd be a tad busy. The shop had two floor to ceiling windows that looked out towards the water. I planned to watch him come around the inlet, then sprint outside to see him wind the sucker up that ramp. You knew there would be a racket to beat the band coming from those propellers when he went airborne. When he came roaring in like a bat out of hell, I ran outside where I could see everything. As expected, he took that boat, engines screaming, right up that ramp, right into the air, planed out, then crashed in the parking lot. I couldn't believe how high or how far he went before he came down, it sounded like a plane had crashed. Yee-ha. Damn, I do love speed. I do. I do. I do. The boat came to pieces on the bottom and hull so you knew it was pretty much a throw-away. Jake walked away like it was something he did every day. Great guts, hey?

Another fine and dandy event happened because of Dan, who had a bad ass drinking problem. Jake had a soft spot for him because he was a grown man and still had to live with his mama to take care of her. Jake's mama had died right at the kitchen table when he was only fifteen, so he had the compassion that sometimes accompanies such an terrible thing. Heartbreaking. Well, that led Jake to be inclined to put up with some things I know he didn't want to. Specifically, Dan coming in either drunk or still drunk, however you wanted to look at it. Unfortunately, he was the marina foreman. We were not only a quiet little fishing village here, we had some speed boats that would kick ass. Fountain boats. Lord, almighty, they were not only pretty things, they took your breath away when they were wide open. I'd never had a ride on one, actually I hadn't been on a boat since I came home, but I would have almost unlocked my doors for a ride, if you know what I mean. Side issue, the first thing some women here asked men when they met them was "do you have a big boat?" Ugh, of the major ugh class of females.

One of the Fountain Boat owners called to have his boat brought out. This meant putting the boat on a fork-life, an amazing feat to me, taking it down to the ramp then lowering it into the water. That's hoping it didn't fall off the fork-lift, because it was a whole lot longer than the fork-lift. Dan was on duty. He picked up that big, beautiful boat, a gift from God, for sure. He took it to the edge of the ramp. I was in the captain's shop when I saw him bring it towards the ramp. I saw it start to tilt. Slowly it would tilt down in front and then slowly it would rise. I saw Jake standing on the gas dock watching. He didn't say a word because he was holding his breath. He also didn't want to spook Dan who looked like he didn't know there was a problem. It was either put it down right or lose it. These weren't cheap boats, guys.

It was great. It was like the boat just plain didn't want to fall off that damn fork-lift. They had to lift it up really high because it was so long. If it fell, it was from the maximum distance up on the lift. It was awesome enough watching it tilt over and over. I watched it slowly do one last tilt forward when over it went. Ka-boom. Oh shit, it took the fork-lift with it. Ass over tea kettle. Dan bailed out like a parachuter and its lucky he was over water by then. The lift or the boat could have hit him. Oh my God. Because it rolled sideways at the last minute, part of the boat hit the water and part hit the concrete ramp. Shred city. Damn fine wreck, that. We'd be picking up parts for a month. Feeling a little guilty over my exultation, I hung my head to look over at Jake. He was devastated. It wasn't just the loss of the boat to him. He ran a good marina and didn't need people thinking they couldn't put the big boats in the water. I had told Jake earlier that day that Dan reeked of liquor. He told me he knew and he would handle it. I don't doubt that he planned to, but that gorgeous fountain boat came out of that stack first. Damn.

Since we are talking about crashes, let me tell you another one. Jake, who considered himself an accomplished pilot, took his girlfriend to South Carolina for the weekend in his own two seater Cessna. They were coming back when his left engine quit. He called me to tell me what was happening. When I asked him what he was going to do, he said he was going to land it on the highway. He was afraid the other engine would go out if he tried to limp it to the next airport and if it did, he couldn't control the plane. His girl was great. He said she was so scared, she just sat there, holding her breath and didn't say a word. That was better than screaming in his ear which is what I would have done. I can't tell you how many times I would have hollered for Mama to come get me if she had to grow wings.

He was over a four lane highway and below him was one car that he couldn't get away from. If he sped up, it did. If he slowed down, it did. The car stayed right under him the whole time he was trying to land it. Finally, he cranked back some, the car got a little ahead of him so he decided to cross the highway and get that plane down. He came down at an angle, skidded across the road off balance, crossed the median and ran, propeller first, into a ditch on the other side of the road. He lost one of his wings when he hit, but they were ok. His voice never shook the whole time they were landing. I heard the whole crash. When I asked him wasn't he scared, because he sure didn't sound like it, he told me there was no excuse for a good pilot in a good plane, to die. I don't know if I agree with that, but if he was flying a plane I was on, I'd sure want him to think like that. Man had guts, no doubt.

I had to admit life wasn't boring down. Something was always going on somewhere worth jabbing about. I was moving up. I had a little money. I had Tuborg, Aja, my snotty cat and Mama. One unforgettable day in May, I drove to Mama's, but couldn't get in. I had forgotten Mama's keys. I never forgot keys. Well, almost never. I couldn't believe I could have forgotten her keys knowing I would need them when I got there. It was stupid and I was pretty irritated with myself. Whatever. So, I banged on the door, which was glass. No answer. I opened the glass door and banged on the wood door. No answer. I went around to the back and banged on the glass door at the back. I wasn't very happy about the lack of response, as you can imagine. I was starting to hop up and down in frustration. I figured I could break the glass door. Since it would not be visible from the front, Mac could fix it before any low-lifes knew it was gone. It was a great plan. But. Big but. I didn't want to do that. Mama and Mac didn't have a lot of money. I was starting to panic. Why wasn't she answering? I wasn't sure if something was wrong and the hair was standing up on my arms. Mama had a bad tendency these days to fall down and not be able to get up. For the record, I don't find that damn commercial funny at all. I banged on her bedroom window. No answer. I began to get queasy. I mean it was physical, not just mental. I was almost sick to my stomach. I had to bend over to slow my breathing. I was trying not to get hysterical. I was worried that this was all about me not getting into that house for a reason. I began to think I was not supposed to get into that house because my Mama was dead.

    I had seen her two days before. To my surprise and total dismay, she sat in her recliner, talked to me and cried for hours. She was inconsolable. I tried to settle her down but I knew she was re-living it all. She went through everything that had happened to us, the divorce, the hard times, the kids deserting her, alcoholism, the suicide attempt and Jimmy being dead. Whether she wanted to do it or not, I didn't know. We talked about Jimmy for hours. The Jimmy my Mama knew, not the one I had such a struggle with. She had never gotten over Jimmy's death. MaryBeth would try to tell her she had four other kids, but I knew Mama. Each one of us was loved individually. We weren't a packaged set. The loss of one was not offset by the lives of the rest. Jimmy was special to Mama. Everybody said I was always her favorite, but I believe in her heart, Jimmy was. There wasn't anything sweet about me and Jimmy had it all. I also knew I was the one she went to when she needed to talk or laugh. I was special, too. I didn't view it as a contest. She was a mother. She had the job down pat. She held me and squeezed me, looked me in the eye and told me how much she loved me like it was for the last time. Then, she told me she was tired and going to bed. I sat there for awhile, scared to leave, but she seemed to be resting normally..

    She was in terrible health on top of the depression. There wasn't anything noticeably more wrong than usual, but the deep depression had concerned me. I had discussed it with Mac. He told me Mama was both religious and spiritual. She believed things were supposed to happen for a reason and it was your destiny. Mac, MaryBeth and I had been taking her to see her doctor, and there had been no warning signs until the severe depression. I was spooked

You should know by now that I also believe in something whether you call it religion, spiritual, or karma. I was calling on it now to help me know what to do. I knew she had trouble hearing after the surgery, but I was banging pretty hard. I decided I could either break in or head back to Morehead to get Mac. I was scared that something was wrong and she might die if I took the time to get him. I didn't know what the hell to do. I decided to get Mac. He would at least calm me down. It was his way. As I pulled out onto the road, I was staring back at the house, and could not rid myself of a very bad feeling. The house looked very still. Like a house looks when its empty. When I crossed the bridge, I passed Mac. He was less than five minutes from the house, so I went on to Emerald Isle, forty minutes away. I figured rather than walk into something I don't want to walk into, I would call him when I got to my apartment. So it took awhile.

When I walked into my apartment, the phone was ringing. I froze. I didn't want to answer it. My brain could not function I was so frightened. Please, God, please. Don't tell me Mama's dead. I picked it up, didn't say hello or anything, just listened. Some nice lady asked if I was Carol. I said yes. She said I needed to come back to Beaufort. I knew Mac had seen me then. I asked her if Mama was alright. Very nicely, she said she wasn't allowed to discuss it. It slammed into me. Oh, no. Also nicely, I said, "Look. You can either not tell me about Mama, forcing me to drive the next forty minutes like a bat out of hell, crying hysterically, hoping to get there before she dies, because I know that's why you're calling. You can take the chance of killing me and everybody who gets in my way, or you can just tell me the truth and trust me to behave, because then I'll know she's gone and I will never see her again. I'll be crying, but I'll know." She paused, and I'll never forget how gentle her voice was, then said, "She's gone, baby, and there's nothing you can do to help her now, but pray." I asked her had Mama already been taken away and she said, "Yes, baby. I thought you would rather I did." How right she was.

I hung up, saw the keys on the kitchen counter that I had forgotten and knew. My Mama was dead when I got there that morning. God didn't want me to see my Mama dead so he made me forget the keys. I know that as sure as I breathe. I would have never gotten over that. How was I going to live without Mama?

The same lady was there when I got there. Again, striving for control, I asked her what happened. I also asked did it look like she had been crying. I didn't want to think my Mama died unhappy. She told me it looked like Mama got out of bed to make breakfast. She took the breakfast tray into the living room and cut on the TV. She sat back in the chair, put the tray on her lap and died. No pain. She didn't die from emphysema, which she had. She didn't die from diabetes, which she had. She didn't die from cancer, which she feared terribly. She sat back and died. No heart attack. She simply stopped breathing. Then the lady said, "No, baby, she hadn't been crying." I knew she would say that even if it were a lie because she knew in her heart that I needed to hear it. She was right. As to dying like that? Mama would have loved it. She would have celebrated it. Mama was 73. It was May 14, 1991.

She buried her demons before she died and then she let go. Did she go to heaven? Who knows. I know she was a sinner and she taught her kids to be sinners. She was good at heart and treated people with kindness and respect. She was my Mama.

I found out later that Mac was running out on her. I knew as soon as I heard that Mama had known, and it broke her heart. That was what brought that deep depression on. It was why she let go. Years had passed and she was right back where she was in the beginning. Mama knew the concept of love and spread it around her. Unfortunately, she never met a man who did. So, she gave in. She let her spirit go to whoever wanted it. It was time. The Carol I knew died with her. Deep in my soul, I felt something missing. It would never come back. I couldn't believe I would never hear her voice again. Cocky or sad. Any of it. Oh God.

I never saw her again. I refused to look at her in the casket. Mama's was one of the very few funerals I ever went to. I always had a problem with them because I embarrass myself with my crying. I can't go anymore because I can't go to a funeral now and not think of her gone. Don't think something in me didn't die. And stay dead. I may be here. I may be laughing and carrying on, but I will never be who I was again. Because knowing she was where I could call her, go see her or somehow communicate with her made life worth living. Living and laughing with Mama. Now, its just a matter of counting time. What will I do now that most of my heart and very soul is gone?

BAD CHOICES ABOUND

Eventually, being me, I rebounded from the shock and pain of losing her. Even though she was no longer there, I could function again. In a state of mourning, I was looking for anyone I could talk to about her. I re-met a guy I knew from the Pavilion days. His mom had just died so we had that grieving thing in common. You could sit and cry with him, and he would cry back. We became confidantes in sorrow. But, there were some issues that popped up when we started more on the dating route. Although he was a cutie, he was a drunk. Had been as a kid of fifteen in the Pavilion and still was. He had been around so long that everybody knew him and loved him. He was lovable, no doubt. However, he would drink all night, but not show it until one or two o'clock in the morning. I had a problem with that because of the marina job. Also, he was living with two drug addicts and a drunk. The drug addicts were female. Really dirty, slouchy, sloppy people; not that much fun to be around. They would bring the dregs of the earth into the house and I began to realize this was not the direction I wanted to go in. I didn't want this kind of crowd to be my friends. They couldn't be friends actually. Their only friends were alcohol, cocaine and marijuana. I may have gone downhill, but I hadn't forgotten the kind of person my Mama wanted me to be. Believe me, this life wasn't it. He even had a rapist, convicted, who would come by and tell me how good looking I was, with Bobby sitting there. The guy held me down on the couch one night and refused to let me up. When I hollered for Bobby who was upstairs, he didn't even come downstairs. He hollered down for him to let me up. Good grief, people. This crap happened when I was a kid. I didn't want it to happen again. But this behavior was commonplace for these people. Also, he had a guy named John living with him. John was one of the funniest people I ever met, and one of my favorite people, but a screaming drunk. This guy could bring drunk to new levels. For instance, he would stand up straight sober, but when he was drunk, he looked like he was about to fall over. Like his spine was off line.

Bobby and I were sitting in front of the TV one night after having gone out. He was drunk. I was sober, about ready to go home. We had been arguing about a grill on the wooden deck that was a piece of junk. It was all rusted out and was missing two legs. The only way it could stand was to be propped up against the stationary glass that goes with the sliding glass door. They cooked with this piece of junk. Rust in your food, for Christ's sake. He wanted to cook. I didn't want anything off that damn grill. I kept telling him somebody was going to throw open or close the sliding glass door hard. Hot coals, food and all was going to go flying. Being a full blown alcoholic, unable to envision reality, he wasn't worried about anything unless it was obvious to him. Well, John came home one night totally snockered. When he got to the outside door, you could hear him shuffling his feet, because he always did, trying to unlock the door that was already unlocked. He worked the lock two or three times, still shuffling, until I got up and let him in. He lurched in the door, pushing me into a wall with his hand in my face. He then proceeded to hit the wall in front of him, ricocheted off it and hit the other one. The poor boy was trapped in a hallway leading to the living room so he ricocheted off each wall until he launched himself into the living room. Once he stumbled his way into the living room, he found a barstool and held himself up long enough to be polite, which he always was. Then, he turned around to fumble and shuffle his way back into the kitchen to get some chicken. He worked his way out to the deck, pushing himself off walls along the way. This guy was so drunk he was almost bent over double and I knew damn well, he couldn't see. I don't know why he couldn't stand still, but his feet keep that little shuffling thing going the whole time. Maybe it was his way of staying upright. Who knows? Another thing was I didn't know why these people had no concept of what an oven is; they gotta grill.

    Bobby and I were sitting on the couch, but I was keeping my eye on John. Earlier that day I had gone outside and tested the water pressure and drug the hose closer to the deck, just in case. After burning the chicken about half an hour, he stumbled back out to the deck to check on it. You know enough now to know he slammed that door and the grill, chicken, hot coals and all went air borne. After arguing with Bobby a second about what he should do to save the house from burning down, I jumped up and ran out, cut on the hose and started hitting the coals. It was really cool. I had figured out how strong the water pressure was. I could hit a coal and it would go skittering around the deck at mach speed. If I hit it just right, I could get it airborne and run it around the deck. John came staggering out, horrified that his chicken was in danger. He got on his hands and knees, shuffling around in the coals, water and chicken trying to rescue the chicken from me. I realized I could have as much fun with the chicken, if not more so, if I started hitting the chicken. I would wait until just before he got his hands on a piece and then I'd pop it. Off it'd go at fifty miles an hour. He'd crawl after it as fast as his drunken butt could go. As soon as he got to it, I'd hit it again. By then I was having a hellaciously good time, but John wasn't. The poor guy was hands and kneeing it all over the place trying to get to a piece before I hit it again. Poor boy never reached one single piece before I popped it and it skittered off like it had legs. He finally got tired of it, leaned over on his elbow, his head almost touching the deck, teetering and exhausted and with this plaintive voice said, "Carol, please don't hit that chicken no more. I'm worn out and 'bout to starve." If he hadn't been so pitiful, I'd have kept it up, but I gave in. I quit having so much fun and went back to trying to save the deck from the hot coals.

He gathered up his soaking wet, sooty chicken pieces and put them in the broiler. Apparently, he did know what it was for. I looked at Bobby who didn't give a damn about anything and warned him John would set the damn house on fire. I wondered, did nobody acknowledge the stupid drunks in this house or was everybody too damn drunk to see it? About fifteen minutes later, black smoke was coming out of the oven, but no John. I went back to his room to tell him he really needed to rescue that poor chicken but he had passed out. I decided the hell with him. Before I could get to the kitchen, he must have heard me because he came staggering back to the kitchen, reeling, to get the chicken. Maybe he thought I would sneak a piece and eat that scorched crap. I know Bobby would. When he opened the door to the oven, black smoke just billowed out. We had to open all the doors and windows to try to get the smoke out of the house. By now I was good and pissed. This wasn't funny anymore. One of these jerks could kill me one night if I was stupid enough to sleep here. John saw how mad I was. He was standing in the kitchen, leaning on the counter because he couldn't stand up, when he looked up at me, and with the most polite expression on his face, he said, "Carol, honey, you just don't know how hard it is to be me". It was the first time I had ever heard that and it was pretty funny. Especially that night. He was right. I had no idea how to live with a fried brain. Thank you, Mama for giving me good sense and making sure I didn't fry them before you died. If you are up there, keep an eye on me, will you?

Two nights after the fun with the chicken game, Bobby and I were sitting in front of the TV, just cooling it. It was two a.m.

again. John had been in the bedroom for a long time, but he had been amazingly kee-bashed when he came in. Who'd a thought? He came out of the bedroom, reeking of alcohol and barely able to stand at all. He kept rolling over to the sides of his feet and had to grab something to hold himself up. The only reason he had to hold himself up was because he was dragging his huge, king size mattress through the living room out to the deck. He took the mattress out on the deck and started hosing it down. Now, this was strange behavior to me at two thirty in the morning and I honestly did not have a clue why he was doing it. Bobby looked at me like it was everyday behavior, and maybe it was, and said, "He peed on his mattress." Of course, why didn't I think of that? I knew people all my life who peed on their mattresses and then drug them through the living room right in front of people. Not. I'll tell you why..because I never ran with people drunk enough to pee on their mattress. Not knowingly. Especially people with whom it was normal behavior. Help me, Mama. This relationship was on shaky ground. But I had to admit it had its moments.

Our favorite daytime beach hang was the Jolly Knave. It was built by the same guy who had the one in Raleigh where Christy and I were the night she fell and got hurt. An old friend of mine, Bill Harper, had bought the one on the beach and turned it into a shag/dance club. It was right on the ocean where you could dance and drink and have a good time. The only downfall was the club itself was on the second floor. It is my understanding the walk up or down the stairs had seriously damaged some of the beach's favorite drunks. Bobby included. We all headed there one bright, sunny day to do the dancing, drinking thing. I had gotten some time off so this was a treat for me. I hadn't seen what these people do during the day. There were Sophia and Jack, Dwight, Fred and Sam, Dean, Ernie, Tank, Dwayne Wells and Ronnie Coker. All the crowd. And I can tell you what they do on a hot summer day. Dance and talk trash. Same thing they do at night. That's all people do here. Its a beach. Bobby's roommate, John, came in with another buddy who was driving his Jeep. After more than enough beers, and who knows what else, they got bored and decided to engage in their favorite pastime which was driving up and down the beach looking at all the bikini-clads. After driving as far as was fun, they were headed back to the Knave from the Sportman's Pier, another drinking hole. Our buddy was driving his Jeep and John was riding with him. On the way back, John had diarrhea on the seat of the Jeep. Sorta like what Tuborg had done years before. But, you realize, Tuborg was a small dog, not a person, so this produced much more of it. That said something about John right there. I doubt he even tried to hold it back. From then on, all the way back to the Knave, John had to stand, bent over, trying to keep his gross pants from touching him. This was probably normal, too. Needless to say, the Jeep owner got pissed, since it was all over his seat. He took John back to the parking lot at the Jolly Knave and kicked him out of his Jeep. This was only after he refused to take John home and talked John into not going into the Knave to clean off. What a major YUK that would have been. He made John waddle the two blocks to his house in front of all the beach traffic. Waddle is definitely the word. No, I didn't have a vehicle to take him home in and wouldn't have, anyway. John wasn't a dog. This crapola was by choice. Then the guy left to hose his Jeep down. Of course, everybody went down to watch John waddle off. It was pretty funny, I have to admit. As long as I wasn't close to him. He grabbed a couple of girls and rubbed himself against them for laughing at him. I stayed well away, boy. I was way reluctant to ride in it that damn Jeep after that. Just a bad taste in your mind, you know.

Things do not always turn out funny. Sometimes they are tragic. Bobby often took my car to go out drinking when I was working. I didn't know at the time that his license had been suspended. He promised he would be back at ten. I should have known. The problem was the love of my life, Tuborg, went into convulsions. He had diabetes for the past three years and up to then, we had regulated it well. I had no car and Bobby didn't have a phone. I ran down the block to a phone booth and called the Channel Marker, his Tuesday night watering hole. He said he would finish his drink and be right there. Bobby didn't show. I was in a panic. I finally called a cab to take me to Morehead. It was one o'clock in the morning. The vet told me Tuborg's systems were shutting down and I had to let him go. It absolutely killed me. This was three months after Mama died. Tuborg had been my rock. He was thirteen. The vet was kind enough to take me back to the beach and when I got there, no Bobby. He came when he wanted and he went when he wanted and he didn't even hear you try to talk to him. He'd never see anything wrong with anything that happened that night. He blocked everything if he didn't want to deal with it. Somebody bought him a drink, so he had to finish it or it was bad manners. He always said that. A block of ice settled where my heart had been. I wasn't real happy with me either.

What was happening was I was getting over what little was left of any warm and fuzzies I had for Bobby full speed ahead. Tuborg died August 15, 1991.

Since I brought up Tuborg, I should mention Dusty, Bobby's dog. She was an amazing dog, as well. Without her, losing Tuborg would have been much harder. Dusty and Tuborg had been total buddies. Dusty was only about three feet high with Tuborg about two feet so there was no major size difference. Dusty showed it when Tuborg didn't come back. She seemed to go into a period of mourning. This was a surprisingly intelligent dog in many ways. She was also a dog who would look at you with eyes that said she understood your pain. She'd let you wrap your arms around her for a good cry. Even if you didn't have your arms around her, if you were crying, she would not leave your side.

Dusty looked like a cross between a shepherd and a wolf. Bobby always said she was sired by a wolf and, although he was a liar of mammoth proportions, there was a teeny tiny chance he might be right. She was a variation of all the colors of gray. Her coat was somewhat wiry but not rough. She was devoted to Bobby and he adored her. I think they had been together about fourteen years. You could tell she was slowing down some, but Bobby refused to see it. When I was sitting on the couch late at night sometimes Bobby would get out the love of his life, his long bow. Bobby was unusually strong to be so small. He was only about five feet seven inches but he had really strong wrists and a beautiful back, probably developed while working with this and other bows he had. He would make his own long bows and arrows. The man couldn't function any other time, but he could sit down to do that and in five minutes, he would be in a full state of concentration. Beats the hell out of me. At night, he would open the sliding glass doors and launch an arrow onto the beach and Dusty would take off, search around in the darkness and retrieve it. Bobby would yell, "Incoming!" and she would flatten herself on the sand. They would do this over and over and she never failed. I tried to tell Bobby there was a slim chance, but a chance nonetheless, that people could be walking down the beach when he decided to impale them on his arrows, but he didn't care. Sprong!! Out it would go and off Dusty would go in full gallop.

While I spent an enormous amount of time looking for a redeeming side of Bobby, it sure helped for awhile that he could dance really well. We liked to go out and would always have a good time right up until he would get drunk. Eventually, in order to even get him to dance, he had to have so many drinks in him, he had to have said hello to just so many people, the temperature had to be just right and it had to be a particular song that he was in the mood for at that very moment. Get it? Then, he would get shit-faced, would want to dance and sure enough, he would fall down. Every time. He always said it was because his ears were damaged by bombing in Vietnam. I doubted it. He would want to stay all damn night and I would want to go home because I had to work the next morning. He didn't have that problem. He lost one job after another.

As expected, before long we stumbled headfirst into another "EVENT". An event is something that happens that changes the whole direction of a relationship. Tuborg dying had been such an event. A relationship can only take so many. This boy was on the back end of a line about to break. I was at work when the phone rang. It was Bobby. Without wasting time for an explanation, he told me he wouldn't see me for a week. He'd be around, but he didn't couldn't see or want me to come by or call. Call? Call who? He didn't have a phone, for Christ's sake. When I asked him why, thinking it was a normal question, he said his ex-wife would be there for a week with his son. After you count the girls and John, there was only one available bed..Bobby's. I asked him was he going to sleep on the couch, but he made it clear he didn't intend to. That would be where his son slept. I came right out and asked him was he going to be sleeping with his ex-wife, about whom he spoke horribly. His answer was, "Why not?" He apparently didn't see a problem with that and when she left, he planned to pick right up where we left off. Done. Done, done and done. I kept seeing him as a friend but the romance was no longer an issue. He thought I would get over it. To me, people like this weren't human. This was why I wanted to get away from the beach in the first place. Monsters lived here.

Eventually, I was able to move to a better place called Reefstone. It was a pretty one bedroom condo right on a little lagoon. There was an old oak tree hanging over the pond and everything had a lot of Southern charm. I wanted to get away from Bobby who had lived next door to me. Then he told me they were going to sell his place and he would have to move, too. I told him he would have to find his own place. When I got home from work, Bobby had moved his stuff in. Timely, huh? This guy wasn't real. Real was he didn't have any money. I told him his young ass would be on the couch. The bedroom was mine. We were not sleeping together. Ever. I must admit, though, since leaving Dave, I had this problem with throwing people out when they have nowhere to go. I really had to get over it, too. We shared the living room, kitchen and bathroom, but the bedroom was off-limits. I cared for his kind heart but hated his drunken ass. Little did I realize you can't sleep through someone grilling drunk at two am. Complex situation in River City.

Dusty really liked it at Reefstone because we had ducks she could chase. She didn't try to hurt any. She would run them around the yard until she wore them the hell out. It was very noticeable that Bobby was paying less and less attention to her because he got so drunk at night and then slept all day. I would devote my evenings walking around the complex with her. Nights, after Bobby left, I let her sit on the couch with me while I read a book. I noticed she was still going down hill. One night she went out but just wandered around slowly. It was very un-Dusty like behavior. I got her in the house and she immediately laid down. I tried to give her water to see if she would take it, but she wouldn't. I told Bobby he needed to pay some attention to his dog because she might be dying. I felt it but I wasn't sure. He didn't believe me and naturally, would not adjust his behavior. Bobby was never wrong.

A couple of nights later, she wouldn't get up at all. She hadn't eaten all day and her stomach seemed to be swollen. I told Bobby he needed to get her to the emergency vet but I didn't think it was going to do any good. He was honestly not willing to spend his money on a doctor for him or a vet for his dog. I would have, but I really thought it was too late. To me, it was obvious. But, I kept my eye on her. Later that night, she started panting and laid down in a corner across the room all by herself instead of being in my lap or at Bobby's feet. I got her favorite blanket and went and sat with her. I put her head in my lap and gently stroked her head and down her back. She knew I was there. I started to cry and screamed at Bobby to get over there; his dog was dying. He realized it was true but he couldn't deal with it. He wouldn't get off the couch, which was clear across the room, but he started to cry. I held her until she died. She made a very heartbreaking sound, shivered and died. I held her for hours, crying as hard as I cried for Tuborg. She was a wonderful, loving and fun dog. It was too soon. There had been too much death and too much crying and I fell apart. I held her all night. I could hear Bobby crying from across the room, but he never came over.

I wrapped her in her blanket, got Bobby's ass off that couch. We took her down to the beach and buried her in the sand near the house where Bobby had lived. It took me a long time to get over it. I was struggling and I knew it. I wanted to get away so badly. Maybe go back to Lancaster. But I didn't have the money.

WHO LET THE PSYCHOS OUT?

I got an outstanding job offer from a friend of my boss right out of the blue. This means huge compared to what I had. He owned a real estate company and the sales administrator had just quit. He and his partner broke up, he bought it and she went with the partner. He offered me $15,000. I told Jake about it. He was on vacation and asked me to stay until he got back. I told him I would stay three weeks to train his new person. Jake said he would make me manager and we would discuss it when I saw him. And he did just that. He offered me the manager slot at $5.00 an hour. Good Grief, Jake. No wonder he's rich. I liked him when I worked with him and as far as I know, I like him now. He treated me well. Damn it, I wanted to come back up from losing everything. I was a fighter and I was fighting for the life style I wanted and I couldn't get it with no time off and little pay.

Just for the record, I ran into the D.J. whom Daddy pinned against his fireplace one day at the marina. He was in a wheelchair. I was horrified. I recognized him, but I knew he didn't know me. He took one look at me and said, "You must be a Piner." Damn, I hate that. Using the manners my Mama taught me, I told him I was Anna and Teeny's baby girl. He launched into the story about the day Daddy came up his porch and into his house. He was howling and carrying on so much he drew a crowd. I didn't know if people thought I had done something to him, so I merely stood there. Embarrassed. I couldn't stop thinking about his being in a wheelchair, for Christ's sake. He finally noticed and said that Daddy didn't put him in the wheelchair, a heart attack did. Then he said, he damn near had a heart attack when Daddy came right through his living room door in that Cadillac. He said "he wouldn't have missed that experience for a million dollars. The thirty thousand was nice, though." Clearly, these people were legends whether I liked it or not. Don't ya think?

I had some issues at work that I wanted to see if I could use as bargaining chips. I had found out that John, the real estate guy, was really interested in getting me down there. He came to the marina from time to time and knew I was a hard worker. I had also been offered a job behind the counter at Star Hill Golf Course, where I played. I would get tips, a small salary, but I could play all the golf I wanted. Hoo-ha. I went back to the real estate guy and told him I would take it if he would pay for my membership at Star Hill Golf Course for $700.00 every year plus give me a bonus at the end of every summer. He accepted. Hoo-Ha! I'm moving up. Slowly, but I'm moving just the same. Sort of in Carteret County time. Dead ass slow.

Off to the new job I went. I got there and found out there were factions. You know factions, don't you? That was when parties square off against other parties for absolutely no good reason. I hate that shit. The only friendly woman in the office was leaving to go with her ousted boss. The other lady slammed the office door in my face any time she wanted. Hard. At work. I don't get that. She was very tall, which didn't help when she looked down her nose at me. She was also very good looking and had hair out to there. However, she talked with that high octave Southern voice women have when they were completely false. The phonier they are, the higher the voice. She didn't even pretend to want to like me and she clearly hated her job. On Monday mornings, when she was doing deposits, make way. I asked her what the hell had I done to her? She said it was because she was so unhappy here. Then go elsewhere, bitch, and leave the rest of us alone, I thought. The people who do it her way are not only unhappy, they make everybody around them unhappy. Another lady was the top salesperson and her nose pointed straight up so I had to look up it every time I wanted to talk to her. There were some fun guys there, thank God. I missed my captains shop.

Then, of course, tragedy struck. The lady I encouraged to leave actually did but she left on July 31st, right in the middle of the summer. Believe me, she just slammed doors on me. She was not about to train me. We rented vacation condos and houses and I didn't know how to use the computer. I was going to have to check people in, check people out, pay back deposits, pay the owners, pay the state and pay the county. I had to print out cash receipts when I couldn't enter the money in the first place. I had to print out cash disbursements when I didn't know how to pay anybody. Then I had to print out audit trails and balance with the bank every day. I didn't know what an audit trail was. Hell, I didn't even know how to find out who was leaving and who was coming.

I spent some late nights I tell you. I called the Real Estate Commission and told them what had happened. They told me they would run with me unless they got a complaint and then they might have to act. So, on that note, I took the easy way out. If somebody called me and said they hadn't gotten their money, I asked how much they were supposed to get and sent it to them. That would be one less to worry about. It took me until October to figure everything out. In the meantime, I got real moody. Pissed off kind of moody. Eight in the morning to nine at night will do that to you when you are going top speed.

    I had also been working with a lady whom will we will call Marge. I am using "lady" loosely here. We both showed up for work June 8th to serve notice. Neither knew the other was going to do it. We sneaked into one of the offices to decide who would quit first. She was in a worse situation that I in that she was having personal problems..boyfriend style. We both had that day as our final day. No notice. I figured I could do her job if I had to, but there was no way she could do mine and she sure wasn't interested in learning it. She'd watched me struggle. I knew the summer could not go on if we both quit. The season had already started, and we would be hurting innocent people. I let her serve notice and I stayed. I missed her, though. She was certifiably psycho. Normal for the weirdos I knew who inhabited this island.

    She'd been dating the guy whose family owned Shelton's. His name was Lee. I had gone to school with his wife and didn't think much of how he acted. Of course, he was one of Bobby's back slapping buddies and Lee's attitude was as long as he didn't get caught, it didn't hurt anybody. This is the kind of guy that the lady I worked with was drawn to. Slime. Her way of dealing with it was trapping him in his office on a busy Saturday night, bellowing at the top of her voice and beating the shit out of him with his own phone. And I am not talking about little, bitty cell phones here. These were the days of the big, black monster phones. As far as I am concerned, they were the last generation of phones you could really hold up to your ear and do something else at the same time. I loved them. So did she. She liked them as battle armaments. Lee was bald except for those bands that go from one ear, around the back of his head, to suddenly appear at his other ear. Nothing else. Except for the scars on the top of his amazingly stupid head. I always figured he deserved it for being so open to abuse. Yell for help or something. Don't just stand there. If you're a woman and you live with a man, it might be hard to get away. If you can walk out of your own damn office after letting someone brain you night after night, week after week, get the hell out of there. Good Lord.

They went out one night on what we called the "booze cruise." The very name is one reason I wouldn't go. The biggest drunks in town and the sleaziest women would be on that boat. Unfortunately, for my friend, a waitress that had caused a lot of the trouble between Lee and his wife, was also causing trouble for my friend. Lee was running with all three of them. It seems everybody got drunk and when they disembarked, my friend, who was much taller, saw her chance. She grabbed the waitress by the hair of her head and yanked her to the ground where she proceeded to pummel the crap out of her. There they were, rolling around in the dirt until the police finally showed up. Did I mention that there were three reasons I didn't go on the cruise? One, the name. Two, the people going. Three, it was raining buckets. These women were rolling around in mud. I know this because I could tell by their pictures on the front page of the Carteret County News Times. Reckon Lee was busted? These were the good old days. You wouldn't expect such fun to stop there, would you? Oh no, hell no. These people walked right into messes and then wallowed around in it. I gotta admit, living here is interesting.

Lee and Marge quit dating all the time. One night they really quit dating. My friend went out for the sole purpose of getting drunk. Never a good idea for her. At two in the morning, she drove over to a condo he was at. Even though Marge saw the car of that same waitress, she banged on the door. He didn't answer. That was the last time he showed any sense. When he didn't answer the door, she called him on the phone. He answered that. She started crying and asked could she come up? Even with the waitress in his bed. I ask you, is there a word for this man? He opened the door and let her in. What did she do? She headed straight for the phone and beat the crap out of him with it. The biggest problem he had was he couldn't call the police because she was using the phone. Think about it.

Her sister was even more fun that she was. Let's call her Sissy. Sissy had been married and because of her husband's womanizing, they broke up. I don't know why, but he got the house and dog. He also got one of the other waitresses at Shelton's. Hell, it could have been the same waitress for all I know. You wouldn't expect any female raised in that family to show any compassion. Who brought these girls up? Early one morning, Sissy headed over to the house where her husband is shacking up. Her husband had just left to go to work. He worked for his wife's dad, for Christ's sake. The waitress was still sleeping in. Her car in the yard. Sissy banged on the door. The dog went nuts. She banged until the waitress came to the door. There was a screen door and a front door. You need to know this to understand what happened next. The waitress opened the front door. Sissy had a key for the screen door since she had lived there. This was so much fun. They were face to face. Sissy decided to deposit some recently deposited dog doo right in the face of the waitress. In her eyes, up her nose and into her mouth. Just for the record, it was nice to know that the evidence of insanity showed up in families other than mine. This story was not gossip. I know because the waitress took Sissy to court for assault and actually told everybody in Carteret County it happened to her. God love her for her honesty. I wouldn't want anybody to know.

HAULING ASS

Things were pretty boring at the office after Marge left and her sister got quieter. However, looking for the positive, the location of this office was a gold mine. It was a two square mile development done by the relatives of Theodore Roosevelt. They kept his mantra of preserving the land when they planned the development. It was absolutely beautiful. The landscapers won a national award for the work they did, and over the years it has grown together beautifully. The property manager and the various associations did a great job of keeping it up. There were eight condo complexes; each with their own pool and there were three more everyone could use. There were several single family home areas, seven tennis courts, hiking and biking trails and a marina. It was like working in the middle of Savannah to me.

It seemed like I had worked there for decades, but I hadn't. I had worked there long enough to get a good grasp on my old assertiveness training and every now and then I liked to haul it out and dust it off. I put a sign on the wall in front of the rental office. It said, "If you do not treat the staff with respect, you will not get what you want." If someone came in with an attitude, I would make them sit right in front of it for a while. Read it over and over. By the time they came in to see me, they behaved. If not, I had them removed from the office. By the police, if necessary.

I also had problems with a girl I had hired named Donna. She had long, dark hair almost to her waist. She was very tiny, although not quite as short as I was. She also had that "kiss my ass attitude" that some good looking women favor. She could get in your face, snarling and cussing far worse than necessary in a business office. She didn't take well to supervision, either. Although she seemed to get along well with the renters and owners, when she wanted to, every now and then she seemed to feel a need to take me on. I felt it inspiring.

Donna and her boyfriend planned a trip to the Bahamas, but since she was basically living pay check to pay check, she didn't have the right clothes to take with her. Since I dressed specifically in island wear to pump up the renters, I told her she could take some of my clothes with her. The next thing I know, she picked out twenty nine outfits, plus shoes, for seven days. I knew she really wanted to quit to go back to college but her boyfriend wouldn't pay her bills, so she couldn't. I also knew she was going to take the trip as an opportunity to change his mind. I was very interested in the outcome of the little deception. She acted like I was too ignorant to figure out she was manipulating a way to quit work. I was her boss, for Christ's Sake.

Did Donna come back with an attitude? Oh yeah. She practically threw my clothes at me, dirty, like they were rags. I knew something was up. That night, every single person in my office called me to tell me that Donna planned a confrontation with me the next morning and would quit. She was going to tell her boyfriend that she and I had a fight. Supposedly, I would threaten to kick her butt or something. I would hurt her feelings so bad she had to quit. We could deal with that, right? Oh yeah, party time.

When I went in the next morning, Donna was in the rental office. I noticed everybody in the building was in the lobby so I figured they wanted to watch. Fine. I sat down on one of our tall captain's chairs and waited for the fireworks. Donna was mouthing off about something, all pissy faced. She came into the lobby and stood behind the lobby desk. I noticed she saw everybody sitting around, so she must have figured she would have an audience when she took me on. I smiled at her and said good morning. That threw her off a little but I could see she was not going to change her mind. So, with everybody frothing at the mouth and tense, waiting to see some action, I said, "Donna." Then I paused to make her look at me so I knew I had her attention. I dropped the bomb on her. I told her, "Get your stuff from the rental office, go home. Don't open your mouth. Don't come back." Then I added, just for fun, "If you say one word, I'll have you arrested and removed." That did it. She got her stuff and went out the front door and laid rubber leaving the parking lot. Everybody sat there for a moment still holding their breath. They couldn't believe not a shot was fired. I heard them exhaling like balloons dying. Nobody said a word. Finally, one of the maintenance men looked at me and said, "You've done this before, haven't you?" You betcha.

  For fun, we had two hurricanes back to back right after that. Bertha and Fran. In that order. In July of all times, Bertha tore Beacons Reach up. We'd never had a hurricane in July. Not to be outdone, Fran came right behind her with ten summers worth of rain and one hundred of the oldest oak trees in Morehead gave up and fell over. That was a mortal sin. We practically had to take a boat to get to the condo because the lagoon was so full from the Fran rain. Windows were blown out, screens were down, every walkway to the beach was gone. I had renters who had no way of getting onto the beach which can create some damn irritated renters. So, they went right across the dunes, which is illegal. It was easy to catch them, though. If they were on the beach, they had to have come across the dunes or be brought in by helicopter.

  While all the fun and games at work were going on, I found I began to like putting up with Bobby less and less. The warm and fuzzies were frozen and scratchy. I needed rest. I didn't need his drunken butt taking up my living room and having the TV on until two a.m. all the time. I was overly stressed with all the work and the lack of sleep largely because of him. I didn't appreciate the phone calls late at night asking me to pick him up at this bar or that because he didn't want to get a ticket. The man couldn't spell cab. I had become his chauffeur. My fault, I know. Do not say the word "enabler" around me like I don't know what it means. The relationship started to get ugly. My hissy fit was just around the corner and I could feel the level rising. I warned him, too. I warned him. He didn't listen. He couldn't hear, remember?

  We weren't even friends anymore. One night at B.T's, a dive we went to, I got sick of his one more drink crap and started to walk out. He grabbed me by my leather jacket, in front of everybody, and slammed me up against the wall, telling me not to tell him what to do. Understand people. I am a lady. I am a lady who does un-ladylike things when provoked. I still look like a lady when its over. That's my prayer. I stood there quietly until he regained his barstool and then I walked over and cold-cocked him. Knocked him right off his chair. Nobody said a word to me. Was I acting like a lady.? No, of course not. Any man who hits a woman should expect no less. I earned the right to hit back from Charlie. There will be no apologies.

A few weeks later, he asked me to take him to Shelton's, the hang-out for the Wednesday night crowd. I liked the place myself so I would take him around five but I was always ready to leave by 7:30. He always played the game with me that would bring the rage right out of me. He would tell me he would go when he finished his drink and then he'd signal for another drink. I had always been pretty sure that's what he did the night Tuborg died, so when he did it this night, he more than ruffled my feathers. I was spoiling for a fight. When I asked him about the next drink suddenly sitting in front of him, he said say somebody bought it for him. Like I was stupid. One night, I flipped. I was tired, I was cranky and all my chips were on my shoulder, dying to get knocked off. I looked at him, then walked out the door, leaving him behind. His male testosterone got up. He followed me out the glass door, tearing my blouse as he grabbed me and slammed me back against the door. People, I have always worn nice clothes. I hate to shop, so when I do I have the money to buy nice. You don't find size two just any damn where. When he did that, hell fire went through me. HELL FIRE, PEOPLE. The hissy fit was on. I grabbed him, slammed him against the door and started like I was firing bullets out of an Uzi. "You want to tear my blouse. You want to tear my good clothes off me. I'll show you how to get rid of clothes, bud." The blouse came off right there at the glass door. The bra flew off onto the grass about six feet from it. By now, Bobby's mouth was hanging open. Not a good idea, because I was liable to toss something in it. Before I reached the car, I'd ripped my pants off and flung them onto the parking lot. As soon as I started the car, he jumped in. Reversing, I damn near ran him over. Too bad. His window was down, so my shoes went flying past his face. While in reverse, I tore gravel backing up. Slammed it into drive and tore the same gravel up again. All my clothes were strewn from the door to the parking lot. He was freaking out, screaming, "What if you get stopped!" I hollered back, "I'll tell them you tore my clothes off and tried to rape me. So you had best pray to God I don't get stopped. Stay the hell out of my way or get the hell out of my car!" If he had said another word, I would have put him on the grill and had him for dinner.

It was a only short distance from Shelton's to the stop light at the beach. I took that right on red doing about 60. By the time I passed the police station right around the corner, I had hit eighty.

That Trans Am was screaming and rubber was being laid. Bobby was flat against his seat. Scared white. I knew the little shit wished he had never jumped in. I took that Trans as fast as it would go the five miles to Reefstone. I took the first right ninety degree curve on two wheels. Then I took the left ninety degree curve on the other two wheels. Then another immediate right. Pulling in front of the condo, I slammed on brakes, slammed the gear into place, and jumped out. I was striding to the front door, stark naked, ready to kill. As I was unlocking the door, Bobby ran up, ignorant person that he was. He looked me up and down, then foolishly said, "You ought to see yourself." I yanked the front door open, grabbed him by his shirt, and threw him in the condo. I told him if he didn't want me to give his ass to God, he would shut that mouth and keep it shut. Still naked, I walked out of the room, got dressed, packed my bags and took off for two weeks. I couldn't tell you where I went, but it was from city to city. Mostly, I just drove. I decided to change my life. Little Bobby didn't figure into it. He had just disappeared as far as I was concerned. I can hold a grudge and I was holding one on him. I think I hated somebody for the first time in my life. I wanted my Mama back. She could make me laugh and I hadn't laughed for a long time.

I went back to work the next Monday and quit. No, Bobby did not move out, but he moved around a bit more quietly around me. Tip toed was more like it. I was no longer even human to him as far as I was concerned.

By November, Bobby, Gene Gray and I had formed Sunny Shores Incorporated. I only did it because it was my chance to be the owner of something again. I wasn't getting any younger and had no retirement plan. In December 2004, our corporate papers came through. All the start up money came from Gene. He got fifty one percent, Bobby got twenty five and I got twenty four. I was the baby stockholder and the only one who knew what to do. My job was to take as much business away from John as I could. I got 17 condos right from the get go.

Off I went on another adventure, working my butt off and watching Bobby oil his bow and make arrows while I am trying to drum up business. Gene wanted his money back four months into it. All of a sudden, real estate ventures scared him. He was a great guy, but he sent me nervous faxes when he freaked and he brought a couple of people around like Fred who were thinking about buying him out. That's when he found out I had worded the Partnership Agreement in such a way that you didn't get a vote per share, but a vote per stockholder. As long as Bobby was on my side, Gene couldn't do anything. That did not sit well with him. I sure didn't blame him, but what else could I do? I didn't have anywhere else to go and I couldn't sit back and let somebody put me on the street. Bobby's butt was living in my house. He knew he was dead if he didn't side with me. As long as he lived with me, he'd best be on my side. He was broke, he didn't have a choice. Actually, he was too far gone to care.

On my down time, I'd go see my sister, MaryBeth. She was a shopaholic, and every time I went to see her she wanted to shop, which wore me out. She lived in Newport on an old dirt road in a run down trailer park. She was surrounded by some real scary people and some pretty frightening dogs chained in the front yard. One Sunday evening, we returned after satisfying her daily dose of shopping. Everything was cool until I rounded a corner and spotted a state trooper. He spotted me, too. I had a flashback for an instant of Mason, but it wasn't him. The second I passed him, he flashed his lights. By the time I got through the corner, there was another one. Apparently, they were there a lot because MaryBeth told me she had gotten three speeding tickets in one year there. They pulled me over because my registration had expired. They clearly recognized MaryBeth and must not have liked her much because she could be a pain in the ass sometimes. Lord knows, they didn't know me. They gave me a ticket anyway. There was no excuse for that. I explained there was no way I could get it taken care of because it was a Sunday. In spite of it, they demanded I leave my Trans by the side of the road and walk two miles down the dirt road in the damn dark, past the killer dogs, to MaryBeth's trailer. I had $3,000.00 cash from work in the car because I got off too late Friday to deposit it. I argued and argued but they didn't budge. I think they did it to piss MaryBeth off and I was just the means to do it. I got the money and we walked. At nine that night, MaryBeth drove me back to my car and I took it back to the beach with me. Still pissed.

The very next morning I was headed to work and rounded the corner at the Beachwalk complex, and there they were again. The police like to do roadblocks at that spot because you couldn't see them until you were on them. Well, here came the hell fire. I was so mad I felt it building on my face and it rushed through my ears like the pressure had to be released. If they thought I was about to sit back and quietly take another damn ticket, their asses were wrong. They'd better get ready to work for it. I had been trained with the best. With them close enough to be staring me right in my one eye, without coming to a full stop, I whipped that hot Trans Am around, cranked those gears, kicked it and headed for home. That car was tearing down the road. Flying. Trans Ams understand kicking it. They come to life like a horse you kick spurs into. A hot Trans front end would come right off the ground. My car was hot and it did. I could see their mouths drop open from the rear view mirror. Yee-ha! You want me, come get me, butt breath. One of the staties jumped in his car and came after me. That guy didn't have a chance in hell of catching me with the jump on him I had. I knew all the local cops knew my car so they figured out I was going to the casa. I wasn't sure they would tell the staties, though. They hated them. Reefstone was about four miles. I went down that road like I used to go down one with my old 409. I had a beautiful machine and a great road to spread my speed wings on. They didn't build that car to poke around, you know. When I got to Reefstone, I took the left with two wheels off the ground. I took the next left to the pond with the other two wheels off the ground. Finally, the right turn leading to the condo. You have to understand, your second ninety degree turn left and then an immediate ninety degree turn to the right had water just beside the lane. You really didn't want to not know what you were doing. Read that again. Yee-damn-ha. Lock me up. It was worth it.

    When I got in front of my condo, I shut her down. Damn near went through the windshield. All my pistons were firing, I'll tell you that. I cranked her off, jumped out and leaned against my car door with my arms crossed like I had been there an hour. Look guys, I just wanted to go home. If they were going to arrest me they were going to do it with this damn car parked at my condo. I could call a cab to take me to work if the statie didn't arrest me. I could tell by the screaming of tires he took that first turn on all four wheels with two of them not knowing what the other two were doing. I'm sure he damn near pissed his pants when he saw the immediate right turn. I could see him and he took the next turn the same way. The man had very little control over that car, but he made it. I bet you, he thought he was going to die or find himself very wet. When he made it around the last curve, he saw my car and had to slam on brakes to not hit my rear end. He was probably ready to strangle me. Or worse. I didn't care. My ass was going to be home when this progressed. When he jumped out of his car, he had his gun out and pointed at me. His hands were shaking so hard it looked like he was going to drop it. I wanted to offer to hold it for him until he calmed down, but I would have only done that to PISS HIM OFF MORE. He pointed that gun right at my face. Heavens. I didn't mean to upset him. Smirk, smirk. Much. He almost spit his teeth out when he asked, "Had I lost my damn mind?" I calmly said that I had not lost my mind and reminded him about the previous night when he chose to be such an jerk. I told him how he had made me park my car on the side of the road in an area full of nasty, scary people and people eating chained dogs and to two miles in the dark with pitbulls at my heels. I also I told him I had no intention of walking five miles on Highway 58 in Pine Knoll Shores to my office with $3,000 cash. If he wanted to shoot me, he could. But, he'd best have a better explanation than a female out ran him on a road chase when he reported it. Just to rattle his chain, I reminded him he really didn't want the rest of the guys to know that. Believe me, he and I both knew they already knew that. That's why he was so pissed. I hope my being so cool about it calmed him a little. How many people bothered with an explanation for leaving his ass in the dust? He had to know I could drive better than he could because there were no tire marks coming around those curves but his. I don't know what he would have done if I had gotten in his face.

Although he was still shaking, he had settled a little, but not much. I wanted to say, "Hey, Henry, or whatever your damn name is, your gun is still in my face." One good thing about being married to a cop is you learn how they think. And you learn how seldom they really fire that thing. The mouth goes off all the damn time, but not the gun. I can tell you this, if the gun went off as often as the dicks did, with women other than their wives, it would wipe out a whole town.

It seemed a lifetime before the gun finally sank below my neckline but he was still screaming about all the things he could do to me. Haul me off to jail, write me tickets for ten different things. Whatever. I kept reminding him that was fine. I could plead my case and I would tell them he did it out of revenge because I outran him. Not to mention his being stupid enough to pull a gun on an unarmed female the size of a ventriloquist's dummy. I would make sure it was in our stupid newspaper at least a week, just for fun. I will give him credit., he got the hell gone. By the time he left, he was a normal guy. Talking about the race and how cool it was. How I must have received excellent training to leave him in the dust like I did. I swear he made me blush. I liked guys like this. Who accepted a female when she stood up and did something they admired. Women seldom did that back then. Not until they were pushed to it.

Sometimes macho men could be so silly. When he left, he hadn't even charged me. He just told me not to drive the car until I had the registration updated. I waited about an hour and then drove to breakfast. The local cops ate breakfast the same place I did. I know they talked about it for a year. They loved it. Hell, I loved it. They knew I outran him or he would have charged me for a hundred different things. They always smiled at me and started whispering to each other with their heads down. Grinning. I knew what they were talking about. I was a nearly a celebrity with those guys. They didn't get to see much real speeding around here. You could only do forty five miles per hour, for heaven's sake. But they were standing right there when they saw the ass of my car disappear from sight before he ever got in his. Yee-ha!

WHO ZAPPED ME WITH ELECTRICITY?

On January 11, 2005, I had the wake up call of all wake up calls. Big time. I got up to go to work like any normal day. I washed my face and started to brush my teeth. Only started. I came right up off the floor. An electrical shock hit me on the right side of my face that seemed to vibrate voltage. The pain was excruciating. It hit and then it seemed to hum like electrical wires with salt on them. I had to sit down right there on the floor, trying to find my hand to keep me upright. I was afraid to move. I knew I didn't want to move my face, I tell you that. I couldn't imagine what the hell it could be that hurt that much. Or, what I had done to bring it on? After the vibrating and shocks took control of my face for awhile, it seemed to ease. I tell you, I did not brush my teeth again that day. I went to work but it seemed to be around all the time. Like lightning striking me over and over. My tongue on the right side seemed to have pins and needles shooting through it. Every now and then, I couldn't talk at all. I'll tell you what I did, though. I cried a lot. Hard, too. And it hurt like hell to cry but I couldn't help it. Anything that moved the muscle around the corner where my two lips met on the right side brought it back. What the hell had happened to me?

Talking was what I did for a living. My job was phone work. I took reservations, answered questions, got new listings, etc. All talking. This pain went on and would not recede. Every day. There were times when I felt that I could not handle it, but didn't know what to do. Sometimes I couldn't even swallow without the pain hitting. Out of nowhere. I knew if the pins and needles got sharper, the pain was coming, but I couldn't do anything to stop it. Sometimes I couldn't drink. Sometimes I couldn't eat. I loved hot dogs and it takes real pain to make me put a hot dog down. Especially two of them. Bobby was sympathetic but it wasn't happening to him so he didn't know how bad it was. How could he? He knew it had to be bad because I would be sitting there and suddenly I would scream and begin to cry. Normally, I didn't cry easily. I had no choice, but it only made it worse. This kept on, day after day, night after night, and seemed to escalate. I was terrified. I was losing weight because I couldn't eat or drink at all by now. Or swallow, for that matter. I didn't know how to cope or how to prevent an attack. I didn't know what to do.

We all thought it might help if I went to a dentist. Maybe it was dental, who knew? I made an appointment, and showed up like a good girl, even though I was terrified. I tried to explain to the receptionist what was happening, but they were caught up in their routine wanting to take ex-rays and all. I thought if their x-rays didn't show electrical wires, it was useless. I was scared to death for him to touch me. He sure as hell wasn't going to touch me until I could talk enough to describe it. The dentist was very nice and, in all fairness, he did listen, but routine prevailed. He hit me with novocaine, left the room for fifteen minutes, then came back. When he hit me with that drill, I came right out of the chair. I wanted to wrench that drill from him and turn it on him; show him what it felt like. The dentist's face turned whiter than mine. I know, because I was looking at him like he had just killed me. I didn't know what to do to stop the attack. It was awful. I can't describe it. He took one look at my face, with me screaming and crying and he had to leave the room again. When he came back, I was still sitting there waiting for the pain to subside. Tears were covering my face. I cannot describe what deep, deep horror I had just experienced. I was afraid to open my mouth or ever speak again. He took my hand and told me he had never experienced that in his life. My hands were shaking so hard, I couldn't hold onto him. I wanted to sympathize with him, but couldn't speak. I knew it had been a horrible shock for him. It showed. He apologized for the pain he had caused. He didn't know what it could be but he knew he couldn't help me nor could he give me any direction that might help. He had never seen anything like it and I am sure, he never wanted to again. I was heartbroken. What was I going to do? I was getting desperate because the pain was so very bad and nobody seemed to know how to help me or what it was. I had already been to my regular doctor. He was the one who sent me to the dentist. I decided to cope until I had a solution. It was time to try to stop crying. I found it easier to think it than do it.

In late February, 2005, my phone rang. It was John, my old boss at Beacons Reach. He was upset and kept saying he wasn't going to make it. I had an idea what he meant. I had always liked him and I was sorry he was stressed so I wanted to hear what he had to say. I asked what he wanted. He wanted us to buy him out. I told him I wouldn't even talk to him without seeing the trust account. He had hired a girl to replace me, and I knew she had worked there before me and had been fired. I didn't have a lot of faith in her since I didn't know her integrity. He refused. I told him to call me when he would let me check it out.

All this time, the pain was growing. The shocks were more often and more intense. Consequently, I was past terrified. I didn't know how this would end. I am not big on suicide, but sometimes there are things that are physically impossible to take. This was one of them.

I didn't hear from my old boss, John, again until late April that same year. This time he asked me to come to his house after work. Mama had taught me to look for the good in people and John had a lot of good qualities. Even knowing that, I knew I couldn't ignore what might have happened to the trust account. Before I went to his house, I drew up a document that said he couldn't sell to anyone but us before September 5th, 2005. It also said that we would not buy his company name, just the assets and for not more than $400,000. Therefore, we would not be responsible for any debts. He signed it and so did I. He told me I could look at the trust account before we went any farther. I knew he wanted us to put any money back if any were missing. He fired the girl before I got there so he had no one in the rental department and we were three weeks from Memorial Day. Yikes. Damn, not again.

I realized right away that there were major problems with the trust account. I had no idea whose fault it was and I didn't care. I just wanted it restored. I called the Real Estate Commission. They came down to help me audit it. Once we had, they said if we didn't buy it, they were closing the doors. All the renters would lose not only their money, but also their vacations. All the owners would lose the money they would have gotten for the summer rentals. Some of these owners needed the money to pay their mortgages. I got with Gene and Bobby and worked it out. We would buy his assets and office equipment for $275,000, some of which would go to restore the trust account. This way the owners and renters would never know there had been a problem. John would get out from under a terrible problem. I had to work fast, too. I had to figure out how much money went where. The only way to do it was to go all the way back to bank deposits and checks written. Definitely, the hard way. But, the only way. While this was going on, the only people who knew we were close to a major scandal was the Commission, Grady Fulcher, who was the property manager, Dr Dodge, the President for the Homeowners Association for the Breakers and us. The whole time this was going on, I was having to run our company, too. Taking this on, so late in the season, was a major undertaking.

When we got to closing, John refused to close. He wanted another $19,000. At the time, we were the only chance he had to get it. I didn't know if he really needed it or just asked to see if he could get it, but I was not in a really great mood because of the stress and the pain. I refused and everything came to a halt. We all had to sign or it wouldn't work and I wouldn't sign. Damn it all, people. I was at my limit. I knew we would have to pay that money back to Gene. Bobby and Gene got me out into the hall, alone. They told me I couldn't see the big picture. I said I did see the big picture. Because we were putting the money back, there would not be a scandal. I think I told Gene if he gave it to him, the Company would not be held responsible for paying it back. But, hell, I'm not sure. I hurt so bad I didn't care what they did as long as it didn't affect me or make it any harder than it was already. They finally agreed and John gave in. This all happened on the Friday of Memorial Day weekend. The Real Estate Commission met with me and told me I had to run Sunny Shores at the original office separate from the Beacons Reach office until the first of the year. That summer I nearly worked myself to death. I was exhausted and in constant pain. Nine to nine days, seven days a week. And I was the baby stockholder. Where's the justice?

The facial pain continued unabated. I hate to keep bringing it up but it was part of what was going on. Perhaps the stress caused it. I didn't know. So far, I had no solution for stopping it from getting worse. I would find myself on the phone trying to make reservations, and it would strike. Slam. From just above my lip on the right side and then straight up my face. I couldn't move or function when it hit until it subsided. If it did. It got so most of the time I would be unable to talk at all. When I did try, the pain was staggering. Sometimes I would be trying to talk and crying at the same time. Finally, one of the salespeople, actually the prima donna, sent me to her dentist. He did the whole x-ray bit so he could charge me and then told me he didn't know what it was either. It had been five months. I was desperate. He thought I should see a facial and oral pain specialist in Chapel Hill. He was a professor at UNC that specialized in facial pain problems that most dentists do not recognize. I made an appointment. I didn't know if I wanted to hear what he had to say, but I had no choice. Common sense told me I could not go on much longer. I had lost weight and couldn't sleep on my right side. Naturally, I would roll over onto my right in my sleep and ka-pow, it would strike.

  I got MaryBeth to go with me. I wouldn't have if I had remembered she never shuts up. People who talk all the time expect answers. The less I talked the better. I knew she was struggling to figure it out for me. She studied medicine like I used to study orchids and was actually very knowledgeable. I, unfortunately, was not in my best mood. She was relentless, continually asking me questions. I couldn't answer and I knew I was facing a three hour drive into traffic from hell. When we finally got there, we entered the lobby. Off she went to the desk like she was the one with the problem. MaryBeth can be incredibly dominating and you have to back her ass up every now and then. I didn't feel good enough to take her on, believe me. When the doctor came out to get me she got a little huffy because I wouldn't let her go back with me. I pushed her back into her seat and held her there long enough for her to understand she was not coming back with me. Period. I knew if he said something terrible, she would be worse than I could ever be. So I used the old dog trick. Made her sit. I held her down and glared at her.

  The doctor asked me about the symptoms. I mumbled about the pins and needles, the pain, the way it got worse and worse. I couldn't speak because I was having an attack as we spoke. I tried to explain how I could no longer sleep on my right side because I would sit straight up in bed if I did. Whap! It sent an electric shock right through me. He stopped me right there. I hadn't been there five minutes when he said he knew exactly what the problem was. He almost looked bored. Like this was first grade stuff to him. Hell, he didn't have it so he could appear complacent about it all. The news was not good either.

It was a condition known as trigeminal neuralgia. The trigeminal nerve begins in the brain stem, travels around that sharp part of the ear where the bone is and then splits into three areas in the face. One comes down to the lip area, another goes to the middle of the face and the last goes to just below the eye. This condition can occur on either side of the face. The pain is generated when the myelin sheathe that wraps itself around a nerve to protect it from rubbing against other areas is worn down. In my case, the sheathe had been worn down right there at that sharp bone behind the ear. There is an artery that runs along with the nerve. If that artery swells, such as when you are upset or tense or even when there is a pressure system affecting the weather, the nerve will rub more and more of the sheathe off. Some people say its not this, some people say it is. I don't know. This was the closest I had come to an explanation so far and it was good enough for me. Especially if he thought he could stop the pain. You get a little tired of falling to your knees in agony.

Instead of stopping it right that minute as I certainly would have preferred, he gave me the history about how this condition usually affects people 80 or older and is often diagnosed as TMJ, when it is not. It would continue to get worse and worse. There was no cure. Thirty percent of the people who get it, kill themselves. Oh, good. I'm glad I made this trip. The medical community considers it "the most excruciating pain known to medical society today." HOO-HA! That made my day. Damn, Carol, if you are going to get something, have at it. I couldn't get something simple. Why not pick excruciating? Somebody told me that Cher and Bert Reynolds, that guy that starred in Smoky and the Bandits, had it. I knew Mama was up there going, "See, if you had just behaved...but, no. You had to piss the big guy off."

When I told him what had been going on in my life, he told me it probably was brought on by all the stress. I didn't know if he meant Bobby or Sunny Shores or both. It was a toss-up, I guess. One of my looming problems with treating it was going to be I was so little. Not to mention no insurance. I knew that would get on my nerves someday. Literally. I could only graduate to so much medication before I began to overdose. He was going to prescribe a rather high dose to begin with, so I could only double the prescription before I die or kill myself. You notice I got it rather young compared to the norm.

He was going to give me a prescription, but I could not take it until I was back in Morehead because I needed to be where

I could sit down until I saw my reaction to it. It might make me high at first, so I didn't need to be driving. My mind went immediately to flying back, but nobody flies to Pine Knoll Shores, North Carolina. I was going to have to wait three more hours with MaryBeth wanting to hear every word he said. He prescribed Tegretol, a strong, controlled narcotic. There would need to be some time set aside to see how I reacted. I was as okay as I could be because I had heard the pain was excruciating. I knew he had some idea of the pain, and he was going to help. Good enough for me. Hell, I would have tried a seance if it would have done any good.

    I went back into the lobby to deal with a pissed off, pouting MaryBeth. I mean, good grief, I was the sick one here. I told her I would talk to her about everything when we got to the car. I knew MaryBeth. I was glad I did not let her hear that her little sister was going on additive narcotics the rest of whatever life she had left before she killed herself. Especially while we were in the doctor's office. She would have tackled him. I will give her credit, though. She was seriously worried about me. She kept on me about what he said and I kept begging her to let me get out on the open road. We got back on the highway, through the hard traffic onto the major highway going around Raleigh. Once the cars cleared out, I told her what things he said. She went bat shit. Let me say that again. She went bat shit. I don't think she was even touching the car seat. She was bouncing up and down and I was sitting there thinking, "Do you even know the pain all that jumping is doing to my face? Because if you did, you would QUIT IT !" She was screaming at me that she was not going to let me take Tegretol Like she could stop me. She was bleating about it being a terrible medication. She knew. She had tried it one time and it caused the back of her head to catch fire. Damn. Let me say that again. Damn. She was such a reassuring presence. I really appreciated her input. You know, there are some people you just shouldn't carry around with you. MaryBeth was one. She was always, always, not worth the effort. At home, ok. On a road trip. No way, Jose. I don't care where you were going, she made you want to turn around and go home. MaryBeth, you know its true. Maybe it was because I was not Ed. That's another story.

    You know I couldn't wait to take it now. I knew I was going to have to listen to her rant the whole three hours home. She did just that. I tell you this, those suckers were going down the minute I got the chance even if I had to swallow them without water. I didn't care if somebody cut my stomach open, threw them in there and sewed me back up again. As long as they hit where ever they needed to go to metabolize. Head on fire be damned.

    I dropped her ass off as soon as I hit Newport. Off I flew to the pharmacy. Again, thank you, Lord, for giving somebody the idea to build fast cars. I didn't say anything while they filled the prescription because I was scared. They did ask me had I taken Tegretol before. I got a feeling they were looking at me with sympathy or something. When the pharmacist asked me if I had any questions about the prescription, I thought "What the hell?" I asked him, "Hell, yes. Is it going to set my head on fire? If not, what does it do?" He looked at me like perhaps I needed something to handle my psychotic state as well. When he told me it was a drug for epilepsy, I was floored. I told him I had been diagnosed with Trigeminal Neuralgia. I put that in big letters because it was a big deal for me. He said the drug calmed the nerves that were having spasms. He also said it was a very heavy narcotic and a controlled substance. Shit, I had never had anything worse than kidney infections before. I had intentionally avoided permanent use of cigarettes, alcohol and marijuana, and now I was gonna get addicted anyway. I could have gone ahead and gotten addicted to anything I wanted before because it wouldn't have really made a difference. He told me to be sitting down when I took it until I knew the effect it would have on me. Again, that was not reassuring. He said it was a build up drug and that the pain wouldn't be under control for awhile but it would start to help. Oh, and it would make me fat. Thanks tons for that information. I don't think he would have looked at me like he did if I told him the look on his face scared the crap out of me. I could see the concern on his face. I really hated that for the both of us. The epilepsy thing was something I couldn't wait to tell MaryBeth. She would have a field day with that. I wanted to ask him if it would set the back of my head on fire, but something told me that was just a MaryBeth thing. Caused by her experimenting with every drug she could get her paws on.

    So frightened I wanted to pee, I went home like a good girl, got a glass of water and parked my still small butt on the couch. I had told MaryBeth I would call her in an hour. Otherwise, she would have been sitting on the couch right beside me, staring at me. Bobby was home and I told his drunken ass to keep an eye on me in case I weirded out. He stared at me with eyes that couldn't even focus. Oh, well. I went to get the phone so I would have it near me. If anything scary happened, I could call 911.

Bobby still couldn't drive because of the DUI, so he was extremely useless as far as getting me to the hospital, which was twenty five minutes away, minimum. I'd have felt much better if 911 was sitting on the couch with me, but it was not to be. MaryBeth, the bitch from hell, had told me to take the medicine and sit straight up for twenty minutes. I sat up straight, like a good girl, took the medication, and waited for the back of my head to catch fire. I waited. I waited. I got high. I mean higher than I ever got with marijuana. I didn't join the clouds, I think I became one. I wasn't sure if I had fingers and toes. Or a nose, for that matter. I was sorry this stuff was illegal but I actually had a right to use it. Alright! I don't think I would have known if my head had caught fire. Hell, I was so high I didn't care if my head did catch fire. I waited about an hour and then called MaryBeth and cussed her out. She had no right to scare me like that. Fart face.

I got up the next morning and took my medication like a good girl. As soon as I made sure my head hadn't burned off during the night, I started the drive to work. As soon as I pulled out into traffic, I felt like I went into free fall. I couldn't tell the car had wheels. More like wings. It was like I was a trapeze artist who didn't know they had fallen off their rope. I wasn't even worried about hitting the ground. I didn't think I would feel it. My steering was off, too. The lane the car was in and the lane I wanted it in would not synapse. I turned around, went home and had someone pick me up until I adjusted to this stuff. I found out I got high every time I took one but less and less as time went on. Damn it. I started with one 200 milligram every four hours except overnight.

Those were the good old days. Life went on it's painfully progressive way, as they say. Once I got used to the Tegretol, the pain crept back into my face. Sometimes you wondered what it was that makes people want to live with agony. There must be a gene that says you cannot stop living. Its got to be a gene law or a lot of us would opt out. If thinking about it qualifies for an opt point, I had plenty saved up. Maybe when you hit a certain amount of opt points, you lose interest and the gene says go ahead, who cares? I can tell you this. If it wasn't for my owners and renters, I would have opted out in a heartbeat. This shit hurt. I was a tad surprised because I never considered myself someone who cared if they lived or died. I never wanted to live past fifty five, anyway. Especially after Mama was gone.

I went through many extremely painful experiences where it would recede for awhile and then it would come raging back. Ka-

Pow. Sometimes I couldn't even get out of bed. Even with the medication, it never really went away. It just lessened somewhat. I am not telling you this for sympathy. I want you to know there is a damn big, bad thing out there that nobody knows about and it sucks, big time. I ended up with, including the 400 mg overnight pill, getting up at 2:00am anyway because otherwise, I couldn't make it through the night. Eventually, I had to include Neurotin, which is another narcotic, so I am narcotic blessed. I had to take Neurotin because the Tegretol is so hard on the liver. The great high was over, unfortunately. I spent my time wanting to be a cloud. I forgot names and things that happened. Happy days. When my doctor who, in the beginning, knew no more about this condition than I had told him, added the Neurotin because the pain was not being controlled enough to even eat, I was getting ready to go to Charleston. I was giving myself a four day vacation because I had worked so hard for so long. I had worked my way back up from $4.25 an hour to being a part-owner in a successful business. I was making enough money to go to Charleston and stay where I wanted, which was downtown. I wanted to stay in the Francis Marion, a real old hotel that was there when I lived IN Charleston earlier. I knew it wasn't going to have all the luxuries of a fine hotel but I figured that would result in my having more money to spend on me. That was the plan.

    Then, I told MaryBeth. I hate me, sometimes. She started whining about being broke all the time. She used to travel with her buddy, Ed and went all over the U.S. She was far more used to traveling than I was. I have to admit I felt sorry for her. She was grieving. Ed had taken her to Lowe's with him, bought a rope and a ladder but never told her why. She and her boyfriend, Rocky, took a rare weekend off to go to Ocracoke. She says she never went anywhere. I'd never been to Ocracoke. When they got back, she was concerned because Ed neither returned her calls nor called her, so she went over to the apartment she got him when he'd had his heart attack. He was hanging in the foyer. He chose that location for a reason. He knew she'd find him. He made sure. Hope I never piss anybody off that bad. That's mean.

    As always, I gave in and we got started. Well, actually it got started. It being the bitching and fussing. As I said, MaryBeth was incredibly, incredibly dominating, and it was an amazingly bad idea to try it with me. Do not dominate me. I will come out of my cave and kill you with whatever I can get my hands on. Foolish, Foolish person, do not tell me what to do. If you cannot accept just sitting there and letting me do this my way, since it is my money paying for it, then shut up until we get back. It should be as simple as that. Right?

We argued all the way to Charleston, and I was fed up. I was not only fed up, I was higher than ten kites. My doctor had increased the medication to eight Neurotin. He told me I could take them all at once if I wanted, so I did. Stupid, stupid, stupid. We pulled over just before we got to the Cooper Bridge. If you hadn't been on the Cooper Bridge, God liked you just fine, don't push it. You could die on that bridge. If you were not that lucky, you could live, but wish you were dead. Its two very narrow lanes. One going that-a way and one coming this-a way. Some people fly across that bridge. Those are the ones who think if they hurry, it'll be over with in a minute. Like jumping off a sixteen story building. It happened all the time. I know people who throw up from sheer tension once they are over it. Just pull over and hurl. I always wanted to but I never did.

I went over that bridge not knowing who I was or what the hell I was doing. I may have been doing ten miles an hour, I don't know. I could hear MaryBeth screaming, though. Oh well. What I do know is as soon as we got over it, we came to a stop light. Traffic was stopped. I was in the far left lane. Perpendicular to me were eight lanes of traffic that would pass in front of me as soon as the light changed. My light changed first. Being on the far left of our eight lanes, I took a left and pulled right into them. Then their light changed. I thought MaryBeth was going to loose her cookies. Me, I was flying. I didn't realize what I had done until five hundred horns honked at me. I smiled for a second, thinking they were just being nice. Reality would not emerge for several moments while I was getting the car horn concert and wondering why I was facing so many cars. Thankfully, two lanes stopped, like they had a choice since I was in front of them. I knew something was wrong. Hell, my driving was ok as far as I was concerned because I was too high to care if I died. But, I really shouldn't kill my sister. Not in a traffic accident, anyway. Pretty much any other way would have been acceptable. I thought maybe she would shut the hell up if I let her drive. So, I got out and let her drive. Never my first choice. Nor my normal last. She has that way of accelerating, then slowing down; accelerating, then slowing down. It drives me nuts. I wanted to wave to the nice people, but Marybeth was slapping at my hands and I got distracted. Its a good thing we were already in Charleston you would think, but no, hell no. More trouble started the minute we found the Francis Marion. You remember, my choice. I'm paying. Little details.

We pulled into the Francis Marion and the porters came up to the car to help us unload. MaryBeth had a be-a-bitch moment for some reason. She actually pushed the guy's hand away when he picked up her luggage and snarled at him not to touch her stuff. She would do it herself. We're talking about all three hundred pounds of it. I had a Cadillac and she had filled the trunk. I only had two suitcases in the backseat. I let the guy take mine. Especially since that's his damn job and how he makes his money. When we got into the room, I laid into her. I told her I shouldn't have to explain how these guys had to make a living to feed their families. I let her know the next time one of them came near the car, she'd better step aside and let him do his job or I would leave her and her luggage where she stood. Bad manners. Where did they come from? They sure didn't come from Mama's upbringing, I tell you that.

We got to the room. She didn't like it. It was too small, nor did it didn't have all the creature comforts, like chocolate on the bed and all that crap. I admit the bathroom was so small even I couldn't turn around in it, but, hey, we had a bathroom and it was clean. The view sucked. All you could see was the top of buildings. I had asked for a suite and this was it. The closets were those old closets that were only three feet wide and there was one lonely little dresser sitting on a wall all by itself. There clearly was no where for her to put all her stuff, but I didn't care. I wanted old Charleston and I got old Charleston. We were right downtown where I could go to the boutiques that sold petite clothes. You can get mediums anywhere. Look, I am not a tiny snob. I have no problem with people being big. I have to go where I have to in order to find clothes that fit me. Larger people do the same. It is not a contest, for Christ's sake. I have met people actually pissed at me because I was so small. They wouldn't feel that way if they knew water ran down my arms to my elbows if I tried to wash my face. Its very irritating, but the every bathroom I ever met bowl was too high for me. I would be on my toes. Maybe I need a stool.

MaryBeth wasn't happy. Of course not. She never was. I told her we had been on the road for six hours and I wasn't moving. She pissed and moaned and said she was going to find another room the next day. I said "Fine, go ahead. Pay for it while you're at it. I'll be shopping while you let that guy you insulted today move all that damn stuff. And tip him, too." The next disappointment was the restaurant closed at 9:00pm. We got there at 9:30 because she'd been bitching a half an hour. We didn't have a lot of choices that late so we ordered a pizza. I could have had that in Morehead. She grumbled all night like a mountain about to erupt. She snored, too. Loud. Its a good thing I didn't talk in my sleep or she'd have heard what I thought of her. And what I wanted to do to her.

    I popped up like happy toast the next morning ready to go. She was, too. Very first thing she did was get on the phone to talk bitchily to the manager about seeing other rooms. He had six and she wanted to see them all. He advised her they were just like the one we were in, but no, hell no, she had to do her snob thing. I told her she could room shop if she wanted to but I was out of there. I went downtown and wandered about the streets I had so enjoyed before. Alone. Naturally, I hoped I would not run into Charlie . Charlie the girl friend beater, not Charlie the roach.

    I went back to the room after having thoroughly enjoying myself. I asked if she had made any acceptable progress, but she said no. She was not spending another night in that dump. You would think this woman came equipped with balls. It wasn't costing her a damn cent and she was acting like a prima donna. She spent way too much time around rich people, and thought she was one. She had already asked the bell boys to come get our stuff and had already packed up mine, damn it. I am amazed Ed ever took her anywhere after the first time. When the guy came for our stuff, I told her again. She had better not say a damn word. Let him do his job and leave him a damn tip or his next job would be sweeping her ass off the sidewalk in front of the hotel.

    Off we went, riding around looking for a place to stay. She had spent all day talking about not staying where we were, but she hadn't spent five minutes looking for another hotel. We ended up on the road leading out of Charleston and there stood a fifteen story Sheraton. We were completely out of Charleston, on 95 somewhere. Everything I didn't want. We were too far out of town to walk to it and there was nothing around us except what you see every day. Gas stations, fast food and a mall. Great.

    Because she was jumping up and down for joy, I pulled up. Before I got out, I told her to sit. Like a dog. Sit. Don't move until I get back. It was the only language she understood. I wasn't going to let her go in and control everything. She was pissed, but then so was I. I have the ability to get more pissed than MaryBeth. Every now and then I hauled out the pissation and used it like a gun. I aimed and fired it. I can glare better than she can, too. I glared just for overkill. I asked the lady behind the counter if she had a room or a suite with two queens, non-smoking. Bingo, she had a room on the top floor, and it even had a balcony. That made me stop a second and peruse my thoughts. I fired again. I could not help myself. Sometimes I don't care what people think of me. I looked her right in the eye and asked her would they charge extra if I threw my sister off the balcony? She laughed and said she had a sister like that. She gave me the penthouse for ninety nine dollars a night. That was two hundred a night cheaper than the Francis Marion, but I hated it. You've been there, you know what I'm talking about..nothing is different. Nothing is quaint. Just the same old, same old. The balcony view was of the highway, gas stations and mall. If I tossed MaryBeth out in my drug addicted sleep, she would, for sure, hit pavement. I would then have happy dreams.

    I got out to the car and satisfied her, if not me. She couldn't be happier. Yes, she let the guy take her stuff, but she never left his side. You would have thought she was a female Wells Fargo guard and he was handling bank money. He absolutely filled one of those carts with her stuff and then went for help pushing it. As soon as she got in the room, she called the concierge. Damn, won't she quit that? Can't she just sit the hell down or something? Take a bath? Take a razor blade to her throat? But, leave the damn concierges the hell alone. No. Oh, no. She told her in no uncertain terms..she wanted a map. She wanted a yellow, not red, line drawn down the highway directing us to the nearest mall from the hotel and she wanted the line highlighted so she could see it. This was at five o'clock in the afternoon. I wasn't going anywhere. I had wasted a whole day of my vacation. Yes, the Sheraton had a restaurant. Same old, same old. Crap. The garlic mashed potatoes earned their name. You know what I mean? They were like garlic with the potatoes thrown in. When you ate some, your nose filled up with the garlic smell, grease and you couldn't breathe for a minute. Then, you hit the after burn.

    When we got up the next morning, she got on the phone again, immediately. Making sure they had followed her orders. We were going to the mall. Oh joy. I had a surprise for her ass. She was acting way too much like my ex mother-In-Law. She would pay, too. We got dressed and went downstairs to find the concierge busy with someone. MaryBeth waited sixty seconds and didn't just interrupt, but rudely interrupted, stating she was only picking up the map. The concierge politely asked her to wait a minute, she wanted to explain something. MaryBeth ignored what she said and literally ripped the map out of her hand, and said she would be fine. She glanced at it, then interrupted again. She glared at the girl and said in a low, put down, sarcastic kind of voice, "I told you to highlight the directions." When I heard MaryBeth's emphasis on the "told," I told her with the same emphasis, to stop right there. That was it. I was fed up. Chips a-flying. You know, the ones you store up because you want to be a good guy even though somebody's on your last nerve. I'm good when I get fed up. I told her she wasn't to move until I said so. I made her sit while the concierge helped two other people. Damn, I love that. I waited for the concierge until she was finished so I could apologize for MaryBeth's behavior. I made sure I spoke loud enough for MaryBeth to hear. I told the concierge I didn't know where she had learned her manners. Perhaps she had spent so much time with rich people that she mistakenly thought she was Somebody. However, she wasn't. We were white trash from Carteret County, North Carolina. Ask Jimmy's wife. I loved it. MaryBeth turned bright red. Served her right for snatching that map out of the girl's hand and then giving her a hard time for it not being ready.

    We got in the car and now I had a major league pissed off sister sitting beside me. On my vacation, no less. Worse than that, I had a pissed off me. She just wasn't smart enough to know it. When we got to the damn mall, while I was parking the car, she had the gall to tell me I embarrassed her. I embarrassed her, go figure. It was my turn for the slow, put down, sarcastic voice. Our voices are identical, so she heard first hand how she sounded. First, I told her I would not have her treating people the way she had been the whole damn trip. If she kept it up, I would leave her ass in Charleston and go home. I wouldn't even feed or water her. I asked her why she was so hot to find a mall when she told me she didn't have any money. Got a head-down mumbling response for that, which I expected. Then I reminded her we could see the damn mall, road and all from the room. There would be some words starting with a "f" sprinkled to and fro around here but, I am a lady. Then I laid the bomb on her. I told her when she got out of that car, I didn't want to see her for an hour, minimum. Nor did I want to hear her voice and her ass had better run if I walked into the same store she was in. I told her she had an hour to see the things she could see without even leaving Carteret County. Then we were leaving whether she liked it or not. Unless she actually had enough money to pay for a cab to get her back to the hotel. However, if she chose that option, fine. But she wouldn't be sleeping in the room with me and her clothes would be outside the door. She knew I'd do it. I done it in that cute little condo I had with the Murphy bed. Remember? If she kept acting up, she would sleep in the car because I wasn't going to listen to her whine another minute. Then, I laid on her that the hour was starting right that minute so she had better get the hell out of my sight. She knew I was hot. My bottom life was sticking out. She slunk off hunched over and mumbling. That made my up mind for me. I wanted to slug her. Hard. I could out hissy-fit her any day. It would be a sight to behold, let me tell you. Mumbling? I was doing some mumbling myself.

    I wandered around, bored shitless. They did have a store that sold petites, at least. I had been in one just like it a million times in every mall in the country. However, I was on my semi-annual buying trip. I hate to shop so I only do it twice a year and buy everything I could possibly need. I rounded up about $500.00 worth of the same crap that every short person in the U.S. would be wearing when I ran into them. MaryBeth had wandered in while I was there but was staying clear of me. I noticed she kept going up to the counter where I was leaving the clothes I wanted to buy. She had been gone the required hour. Finally, she wandered over and started o-o-ohing and ah-ing everything I was getting. Only when I got to the counter to pay did she start trying on clothes. She was trying on everything I bought, only her size. Everything. The only thing missing was a sweater and she demanded they call all over. They found one ninety minutes from home and an hour and a half the wrong direction from where we were going. Naturally, she assumed we were going to change our route on the way back for her. God give me patience until I got her ass home.

    Let me explain something about MaryBeth buying my style in her size. Our bodies looked nothing alike. I was short, as you know, and weighed about one hundred and five pounds. MaryBeth was three inches taller than me and outweighed me by fifty pounds. Most of the weight that was not in her butt was in her breasts and around the top of her back. She did not present herself well in slender styles, like vests. Because of her humongous breasts, the sides of the vest were around six inches apart and screaming for the sales girl to get 'em off her. I told her if she didn't take the damn vest off, I'd rip it off. The sales girl stood there with her mouth open, then said, "I take it you two are sisters." Smart girl.

    After I paid, they started to ring up MaryBeth's stuff. The her stuff that matched the my stuff. The girl at the cash register stared at her because MaryBeth didn't respond at all. She didn't make a move to pay. She even looked away. I asked her was she going to get them or not? Her answer was classic. This is a woman who had done nothing but get on my nerves. I was paying for the gas, the food, the room, everything. Knowing the girl at the register was staring at us, she looked at me and said she didn't have any money. Out loud. I was rooted to the spot with humiliation. She asked me to "lend" her the not one hundred dollars or two hundred dollars but five hundred dollars. I paid. This was so she could walk out with clothes exactly like mine. Let me remind you, you don't "lend" money to MaryBeth, you give it to her. You might as well eat the money for lunch with a duck sauce. You are never in your lifetime going to get it back. She apparently didn't get that I had "lent" her the whole damn trip to Charleston. I was fried crispy.

    I'd cashed in my last chip. We left Charleston the next day. I never went downtown again because I didn't have enough money to pay for everything I wanted, and everything she wanted which was everything I wanted only a different size. I cut the trip short two days for, obvious to everybody but her, reasons. She bitched all the way back to North Carolina. This was supposed to be a birthday gift from me to me. I hadn't had a real vacation for years. I took her to Wilmington for the sweater. Then I took her butt home. She had rescued me from Lancaster and taken care of Mama when they took her face off. I kept my mouth shut, drove home and sat with nothing to do for the two days I lost. Butthead. I think I mean me.

    The day after we got back from Charleston, it started pouring buckets. I haven't mentioned it before but every time it rained hard at Reefstone, I had to lie sideways on the bed. The leaks in the roof strongly resembled pours. The whole bed would be saturated. Sometimes it would get so bad it would force me to the floor. Then, the next day, I had to haul the mattress onto the deck to dry. Let's guess what the neighbors thought. I needed a new place to live. Bobbyless.

TILT

    I called every rental owner I had and finally found one that would rent year to year to me with what I told her was four animals. I had gotten two golden retriever sisters from my MaryBeth. I had two dogs, Aja and Bobby. Her condo was in Beacons Reach. I couldn't believe I was getting a chance to live in Beacons Reach. I moved right to the oceanfront. Just like at Reefstone, while I was at work, Booby moved in. No, I did not misspell that. I decided this was not going to last. My foot was down. I would have to get rid of him whether he had somewhere to go or not. This was the high rent district and he did not fit in. I knew the neighbors would get a little tired of the cooking on the grill at two a.m. Who do you know who eats ribs every night of the week? Not to mention, every evening after his dinner, he would open the door of my bedroom and cuss me out. Shut the door and pass out. Every night. Who do you think was buying the damn ribs?

Immediately after moving there we had another hellacious hurricane of all hurricanes. This one scared the crap out of me because it was coming at us with one hundred forty five miles an hour winds. Hell, I was only about 150 feet from the Atlantic Ocean. That's a little close during a blow up. When I was growing up and chasing storms with Jimmy and Daddy, we were able to put the beach and the whole sound side between it and where we crouched.

I had been at work all day, slinging keys at my people to make sure the maintenance guys got into the condos and houses to secure them. We always checked to make sure the water was off, the air conditioning cut down, and all the windows and doors secured. Sometimes a hurricane blows out the windows. If the inside doors are not secure, it can create a vortex and can tear the whole place up. Sometimes we boarded the sliding glass doors for the owners, but only once we were finished with everybody else because it could take so long. Its kind of hard to find that many damn boards in one little Lowe's in Morehead. They are sold out the minute the word hurricane is mentioned.

Bobby came in the office to tell me our friends at B.T.'s had gotten a group of rooms at the Hampton Inn. I thought that was great because I sure didn't have time to look for a place and I knew Bobby wouldn't. I was close to Fred, his wife Sam, Dwight and the crowd. Fred and his wife, Sam and Dwight were experienced in the Bobby and me saga. They would all be there. I liked knowing there were people around that I knew. At least it was one thing I didn't have to worry about. I usually stay on the island, but I was now oceanfront and I had not experienced a biggie in a long time. I told Bobby what to get out of the condo and I would be there later. Mr Useless as hell took off. No doubt to find something to drink. I still had plenty to do. This wasn't funny. I was frightened.

Grady was the property manager for most of Beacons Reach. About three o'clock, he came over to tell me it was time for me to get out of there. They were going to close the bridge to trap people either on or off, so it was time to get cracking. I figured that was all he had to say, but I was wrong. He made me stop what I was doing and look at him. He looked me right in the eye and told me to get out of there. Then he said something odd. He told me, whatever I did, to not look out the sliding glass doors. Get my stuff and go. I sure as hell wouldn't forget the medication. This storm could get on my nerves, if you know what I mean.

    That got my attention. I finished up what I was doing and took off for the condo. I had not planned to take the animals. I wouldn't risk their getting hurt. When I got to the condo, I was a good girl and got everything ready to go. I had told Bobby to make sure we got a room of our own in case I took the animals. The first stupid thing I did was look out the sliding glass doors. My God Almighty. The waves were already over the dunes and into the small maritime brush. You could see areas where the waves were cutting right into the dunes, making them look like cliffs. The hurricane wasn't even here yet. If this hurricane came in at the wrong time, with any force, this sucker might come right under the building. We were on stilts, but that didn't reassure me at all. No doubt now, my animals were going with me. I packed up what I could and took off before they closed the bridge. One of the reasons they close it is because the wind is stronger the higher you go, and we now had a high rise unlike when I was a kid. A forty five miles an hour wind on land is one thing, but it is raising hell on the crest of a high bridge. When I crossed it, my car was shaking. Both retrievers had their ears down, and they looked at me like what the hell was I doing. Their antennae were probably picking up my anxiety. But, in a way, it was as much fun as when I was a kid. Sometimes with me, fear and excitement go hand in hand. This day was no exception. Except for worry about the pets. I wanted to get where I was going and stay there until this was over. I couldn't get the picture of that high water out of my mind. Damn. I wish I had never looked.

    I got to the Hampton Inn only to find out Bobby had gotten us a room on the sound side right next to the water, damn it. I had hard sliding glass doors at the condo and now I had a puny, weak looking large pane window to stop a hundred and forty five mile and hour wind. Given enough velocity, it was liable to come right through it. It sure wasn't going to keep out the noise. We were also on the far left of the building next to the parking lot where all the idiots who wanted to see everything would be going in and out. I got the animals settled first, then looked for Bobby so I could give him a good cussing. I found him a crowd he usually hung with.

They were not exactly my best friends. The only thing they brought was beer. Nobody in this crowd brought any food in case this lasted awhile. I had brought animal food but not Carol food except for peanut butter. I always take some when I travel. Bobby was going to hang around with his buddies and he would most likely stay drunk no matter what they did.. It was perfectly alright, as long as I didn't need him. Let me say it again, as long as I didn't need him. Fred and his crowd brought food. I liked Fred, Sam and Dwight, but they would soon realize I wasn't in the mood to party. I was worried about all the properties and my animals. I decided to tuck in and just wait it out. I was not about to leave those petrified pets alone. They'd freak. Maybe Bobby would come back and spell me. Sure.

It seemed to take Hurricane Floyd forever to get here. We had been in the room one whole day, but it sat there off the coast. It had to be ruining the beach. It had slowed down some but was still coming at us with one hundred thirty five mph winds.

Big TV station trucks had started pulling up. At my final count, there were eight of them. Every one was on our side. They started running big cable feeds through the emergency door. The first thing I noticed that would cause problems was they broke the emergency doors so they could keep their feeds going to their rooms during the hurricane. Then they jumped in and out of their cars and wandered up and down the sound side trying to find a breeze or some cat-tails blowing in the wind. There was only thirty miles an hour winds at that point but they were putting it out there like they always do. Get people scared. Get them riled up. That's what sold ads. It had nothing to do with reality, but this was when they made their money so the worst they could put it out there, the more ads they sold. You gotta understand, these people are trained to scare the hell out of you. That's why you see them wandering around on beaches acting frightened while people are laying out there on their blankets. Ads. That's all. Its all about money. They were the ones getting my owners scared shitless.

I went outside and looked way out over the ocean. You could see the mass out there, all dark and menacing. The thick, moving clouds took up the whole sky off the coastline. Lightening would streak through it from time and time and you could tell it was raining like hell right under where ever it was sitting. I couldn't tell how far away it was, but I could see it was moving our way. If a hurricane moves along at fifteen miles an hour with one hundred and thirty five mile an hour winds, that is was too fast for me. My excitement was still there, but my fear was, as well. That room was the last place I wanted to be when Floyd came knocking on my windows asking to be let in. Lord love a duck. Give me enough strength to not pee my pants every time it throws lightning into that mix. I hate it when it hits at night and all you can see is the lightning flashes. If I have to be in one, I want to see it all. That way, if it decides to slap the shit out of me, maybe I'll have time to duck.

    Finally, the rain started to come down in sheets, blowing vertically to the ground. Not a good time to walk dogs, but you might not get a chance for a long time. The TV people started hunkering down in their rooms. In their mass stupidity, they took the broken emergency doors and propped them open for their feeds. This is the door right beside my room. Their rooms were on the street side where anybody of intelligence would be. Being on the water side was incredibly ignorant, but all the rooms were taken. I was stuck. The hurricane had started to move in on us big time, slapping at the beaches, palm trees and signs as it powered by. I was damn glad I was getting my face smacked by that sand. When it hit, Floyd was still one hundred and thirty five miles an hour winds. I wondered what everything would look like when I got back. The wind would take whatever it wanted regardless of your worry. You had your job; it had it's. It was like Floyd was flailing itself at you. Over and over. The nights seemed to last forever.

    Bobby never showed. Fine. I could handle this. What I didn't know I going to have to handle was the wind slamming the emergency doors open and shut. With the tremendous noise that was making, it was getting scarier. The animals were on the bed, staring at the damn window pane, standing on their toenails. I had gotten a parrot and she was screeching to beat the band. I put her in the bathroom because if she actually saw what was happening, she would deafen me. The hurricane was coming right down the hallway on our end because of the emergency doors. Let Floyd right on in, dumbwats. Hells bells!! Then my door started trying to blow open because the wind had found a corridor to party in. Hey, this is different. We get to blow 135 mph down a tunnel and whip these people into massive fright! I already had four inches of water in the room, which was of major concern to the dogs and Aja. I got them on the bed Bobby should have been sleeping in. The lights blew out. It was going to be an all nighter with no lights. I had brought a flashlight and I prayed I had good batteries. We didn't know if we were here for one night or if it would be more. I knew no one would be open tomorrow to buy any more batteries. Hold out, guys. Would you do that for me? Good grief. Now I was talking to batteries and there was a good reason for it. I knew we were headed for the worst part.

With the wind from the tunnel-playing hurricane trying to blow my door open, I plopped my ass down in the water with my back to the door and tried to push against it to keep it shut. It, and the emergency doors, were banging loud enough to wake the dead in the cemetery near the Bridges Street house. We were in finally in the full blown hurricane. At four o'clock in the morning, in the complete dark, I had worked myself into a real snit when, unexpectedly, the air conditioning window unit, that I hadn't noticed, blew right into the room. Because it was dark, I didn't know what made all the racket. I thought the window pane blew in. I can tell you, that pissed me off to no end. I was not having a good time. I think I was so upset, I was downright bewildered with myself. It would have been nice to have the guy in the household holding some of this responsibility. But no, he was drunk. Fine. I was better off without him. At least the animals got to stay dry. They were still on the bed, still on their toes. For once, the cat and the dogs were getting along just fine. I got up from the door and worked my way over to the A/C unit with my flashlight. Rain was blowing as hard as it could into the room through the hole. I hissy'ed. I picked up that A/C unit, oblivious to possibly being electrocuted, found the hole in the dark and slammed it back into the hole. I sat with my back against the bed and kicked that damn unit as hard as I could. It did not come back out, I promise you. I would have beaten it to smithereens if it had. Not to mention, running out of the room, screaming like a demented banshee. Which I am quite sure I resembled right at that damn moment. I needed a pill. Maybe ten. Of course, my pain pills only settled that one nerve. It didn't do jackshit for the rest of the ones firing off every second.

This went on for two more miserable days. Off and on. Fluctuating between fright, worry and excitement, I was over the top. With all the weather pressures flying around, the pain in my face was excruciating, as advertised. I absolutely refused to increase my dosage. I had to save it for when I really needed it. When I, hopefully, got older. For those ladies who worry about such things. My hair was a mess.

Although I had brought plenty of pet food, I had only managed to scoff one pizza off an embarrassed TV guy. He knew what had happened because they broke the door. The water was all over the hotel. The top six floor rooms all had water in them and everybody was worried that the roof might collapse. God, give me patience. The wind would recede to make you think it was over, then pick right back up again. The water had come into the courtyard in front of the hotel. I was lucky that the water never rose above the four inches in the room. I only saw Bobby twice, thank God. His little butt was going to be gone when this storm was over.

    I got all of us over the bridge the minute they opened it. I didn't know where Bobby was and didn't care. I doubted he would be in working mode since he wasn't even on a good day. I was ecstatic to be fast enough to get over the bridge before it backed up with worried owners. Once I unloaded the animals, who went tearing around the condo, undoubtedly frantic about being somewhere they recognized. I rushed off to the office to grab keys, which was my way. I tore off to the beach to get in front of the condos on the ocean side to see what damage had been done. I ran east down the beach towards condos and houses, looking up. You can see a lot of damage that way. I couldn't believe it. Most of the damage was to the beach. It was gone. Low tide was high tide. Our beautiful maritime forest was almost completely gone. It had been there for centuries and one hurricane took it out.

    Its just as well no one was with me because I was rendered speechless. I kept running, crying now, until I reached the houses. The first four houses had no maritime forest at all. The ocean had gotten under them and taken out some of the sewage pipes. That, my friend, is a close call. A very famous author from New Bern, North Carolina lived in the fourth house. I knew his heart would be broken. He might be able to express his sorrow about this catastrophe in one of his novels. His sorrow and that of a lot of other people. Altogether, an unbelievable, devastating blow to our previously pristine beach. As expensive as it is, there was insurance for the houses. What were we to do about the loss of our wonderful beach? I was way past devastated.

    I ran back across the street, still struck by the damage to our beach, to grab another set of keys. Getting on the beach again, I headed west. I went to the far end of the complex where Ocean Grove stood mighty and proud. A great architectural design. I went first to the "A"' building because it was the farthest west. I seldom use the word "stunned", but I was stunned. I couldn't believe it. The "A" building had been undermined. It was obvious that the ocean had come right under it. There were seven units in the building and the first two were only partially supported by sand. If it had been worse, the whole building could have come down. I hated to think how hard this would be when Grady saw it. He had been here since the beginning of the development and I am sure loved it more than I. He had some hard work ahead of him. I didn't think there was much I could do but give him reports of the condos we rented so he didn't have to worry about those, too. It would lessen his responsibility a little. But I knew it wouldn't lift his heart. Poor Ginny, his assistant. She would be on the phone continuously for what seemed like the rest of her life. You couldn't find a better choice to settle the owners. Her calm demeanor was priceless. She always knew exactly what to say. And, like Grady, never lost her temper.

Our dunes. Our poor, destroyed dunes. They were mostly gone. You knew there was going to be a fight before long about how to restore them. All these years, no one ever had to restore sand to this island town. The east side of the island had been getting sand for years. I am one of those who believe when they extended the dredging past Fort Macon, it re-directed the sand from it's natural flow, lessening the amount of replenishing sands that nature meant the island to have. You know. Men messing with God's plan and thinking they are right. He'll let you know who's in charge. He'll throw a hurricane at you to get your attention.

Our town, Pine Knoll Shores was second on the island, from east to west. We sat almost in the middle of the island and got sand from the east tides and sand from the west tides. We ended up losing fifty feet of sand from the water to the dunes. Low tide would continue to look like high tide. Some of the dunes in front of two complexes were breached and the tide came right into their grass boundaries. High tide came way too high. At another complex just down the road, the two end units, closest to the ocean, fell in the water. They were lying there. Upended by a force of nature. Awesome sight to see. Serious action was required.

Whether you believe in building on the ocean was smart or not, it had been done. It had to be saved. It not only represented hundreds of thousands of dollars in investments by the owners, the town would not survive without the taxes. Our town paid 70% of the taxes for the whole county so we weren't talking about restoring for this owner or that one. It was for the good of the town and to prevent the county from going belly up. Sides were chosen. Fights began. But finally, work began. It would take several years to really re-build the beach but it had to be done. Period.

During these trying times, I got a gift from God. Bobby got a chance to get his fifteen year old son. Knowing what he would expect, I refused to be his babysitter every night of the week. I also knew he would take little Bobby to a bar with him every night if I didn't. So, I told him, if that was his intention, little Bobby could not come. He would be better off with his mother. The good news was, Bobby also didn't like living there because there wasn't a bar close enough except the Ramada, where the drinks cost too much. God love him, the love of liquor made him move. Enough about Bobby. I fired him and paid him four hundred dollars a week for three years to not come to work. I had that power. Worth every dime.

After Bobby left, I stayed home for two blissfully quiet years. I didn't go anywhere except to work and get groceries. If I hadn't had the pain, it could have been perfect. However, I was still struggling with the pain/agony. We couldn't seem to get the dosages right. I think I have a fairly high pain tolerance compared to some people I talk to. Like MaryBeth. This thing was kicking my butt. I finally decided I couldn't sit at home forever. I could be in pain out just as much as being in pain in. I knew there would be a time when I would not be going out much at all as it got worse so now was the time to head out. Little Callie was ready. Yee-ha.

I went out my door, hit the dance clubs and decided to go to SOS. This was a big dance get together held every year in Ocean Drive, South Carolina. Tens of thousands of shaggers go for nine days of running into people you haven't seen in years, and dancing your feet off. I would be barefoot, of course. Barefoot or not, I hadn't seen anybody for so long, I was bound to have a good time. I only wanted to go for the second weekend. I got to Ocean Drive in time for dinner. I headed for my favorite restaurant, Rossi's. Yum. Gotta love it. I didn't get a table because I was alone, so I wandered into their lounge. Luscious. Before long, I was munching on filet medallions in a rich wine sauce. Sitting next to me were six guys who looked like golfers by the way they were dressed. They were a lot of fun but almost golfers were there to pick up a girl before they had to go home to their wives. I didn't take their attention seriously. One guy was really good looking and didn't have a ring on, which meant nothing. He said he wasn't married, but who knew? They all said that. He asked me out the following evening. Dumb me, I said yes.

He showed up forty-five minutes late. Smashed. I think I am a drunk magnet sometimes. You know? Its like they can spot me a mile away. There's a good chance he had been drinking the whole time he was playing golf. I knew I was in trouble when he headed down the up ramp in dinner traffic at Myrtle Beach. We made it through alive with horns blaring and people giving us the finger. We swerved all the way to Rossi's. I didn't think I was going to have a very good time because he wasn't near as nice as the night before. I started counting what money I had with me in case I needed a taxi. It would cost a bundle to gt back to the room. I didn't think this night was going to end pretty.

    I was somewhat stressed from the roller coaster ride down the up ramp, so I ordered a B52, which is a shot drink with Kahlua, Bailey's and Grand Marnier. The bartender said I couldn't have it because South Carolina state law said you couldn't have a drink with more than two liquors. It was fine with me and I was ready to order a glass of wine when my date's teeth showed as he snarled at the bartender to "Get the damn lady what she asked for." Oh, great. I'm a damn lady. Hoo-ha. Next thing I knew I had a humongous martini glass filled with liquor. I bet it had a pound of liquor. I hoped the bartender didn't pee in it while he was at it. I thought we were going to SOS after dinner, but apparently not. He seemed to have that much abused "one thing on his mind" thing going. Maybe two things. Drinking and the other. Me? I couldn't wait to get home. However, he fooled me and didn't drink during dinner and seemed very much aware that he was way too drunk to be attractive. When he got me back to the condo without further incidence, he had morphed into a nice guy again. He actually apologized for being drunk. I had never had anybody do that before. He said if I would give him another chance, he would be sober. I did. He didn't even show. I stayed home because I figured I was too stupid to go out in public. I had missed the whole weekend at SOS with this fool. He won't land on my doorstep ever again. Down the up ramp. Great. You go, girl.

    I decided to go SOS Sunday afternoon to see whatever the hell remained, but it was the last day and most people had left. Consequently, only the die hard drunks were there, but not exactly standing. More like tilting. I was standing in Fat Harold's with about five people. All guys. Finally, one big guy came up with a glass of Merlot in his hand and started talking to me. He said I looked like I didn't know whether to run out of there screaming or needed a drink. Therefore, he helped me decide and got me the drink. He asked me to dance, but wasn't very good. You could tell he had a problem with his legs. They acted like they wanted to collapse under him. Since I went there to dance and everybody was gone, I was lucky to get that so I was happy. He told me he had a condo there, but lived in Salisbury near the great golf course, Pinehurst. We talked about golf. We got comfortable with each other quickly. We ended up having dinner. I had an excellent evening. He was very thoughtful and kind. He was one of those guys that open your door for you, but that didn't normally last long. His name was Ray. He was about five ten, about forty pounds overweight, with legs bad enough that he couldn't stand very long or walk very far. He was the big linebacker type, although a preppy dresser. The men in the dancing crowd tended to dress in starched blue or white button down shirts and khaki pants or shorts. He fit that mold. He wasn't not that good looking but reasonably rugged looking. He had mostly gray hair, but so did everybody else at SOS.

  I was very impressed that he was willing to dance with me with legs that bad. I have to say that Ray was an excellent conversationalist. He went from subject to subject with ease and yet allowed me plenty of time to get in my little stories. The relationship survived the trips back home. Every night he could call. We talked on the telephone at work and at home constantly. He would keep me on the phone for hours. The main topic of conversation was how bad he wanted me to marry him. That popped up within two weeks. Hell, he didn't even know me. That was not something that would impress me no more than I knew him. However, it was good to hear someone say something nice to me after all those years with Bobby complaining that I wasn't the drunk he was. Bobby thought that would solve all our problems. Imagine. The relationship with Ray was very casual and easy going. I enjoyed that. I never saw him drunk.

  One of the main topics of conversation, other than Ray's football years at Elon, was Vietnam. He told me he had flown in rescue helicopters in Vietnam. Their job was to pick up the wounded soldiers and fly them back to safety. I don't know what you called them but he sat right behind the pilot. I think he was a gunner. He and his crew were shot down one day. When he opened his eyes, his buddy's head was gone. This was a guy he had gone to high school with. It destroyed him. He told me he was disabled because of his legs and had Post Traumatic Stress Syndrome. He said every year he would freak out on the anniversary of his buddy's death. He had been found wandering around outside condo carrying on about the enemy. The last few years, he had chosen to lock himself in until it passed. Because of the stress and violent feedback, he had to see a psychiatrist once a month. I went with him one time and after awhile I glanced in the room. They were both asleep. Snoring.

  I hadn't slept with him, yet. Nor did I want to go to Ocean Drive that damn bad. Our relationship was allowed to continue mostly because I was willing to drive to Ocean Drive on Monday nights, stay Tuesdays, then Wednesday night I would drive back. He lived in Salisbury and did the same thing in order to be with me. He seemed very easy about the fact that I wasn't the least bit interested in having sex, and if I was going to be there, he had to accept that. If it happened, it happened. If not, he could get tired of it and I would go home, and that would be that. When I was there, we would lounge by the pool and drive around to look at property. He had a nice little two bedroom condo right in Ocean Drive, but he wanted to upgrade to something near the water. I could care less about a water view, but it seemed to matter to everybody I knew. He and I were getting closer and closer. We had a great time together and enjoyed each other's company immensely. It was as comfortable a relationship as I had ever had and I liked that more than the rush to love thing I usually found myself in. At one point, I introduced Jimmy's buddy, Ernie, to him, but they didn't take to each other at all. Ernie and I had gotten very close since Jimmy died, and normally I trusted his opinion. Ernie had talked to some friends who said Ray had left a friend of their's high and dry. Hell, at our age, who hasn't. Of course, I didn't listen. We are talking about me here.

One day, Ray and I ran into the guy who owned the unit between the water and Ray's condo. It was a perfect location and the condo was a gorgeous three bedroom. The architectural design inside took my breath away. The colors and the decor was breathtaking. When Ray saw how much I liked it, he decided he would sell his condo if the owner would sell the three bedroom to him. We found out a couple of months later, the man had decided to sell it but hadn't put it on the market yet. We talked to him and he said he would take $145,000 for it with an $8,000.00 down payment, and he would finance it for us. Part of the payment would be rent and part mortgage. We jumped on it. We also agreed to get engaged. I agreed to pay the down payment and Ray agreed to pay the rent. This all went on in October. The kiss or go home date was November 1st the following year. I was not about to get into this if I was not married by then. And yes, we were having sex. Not great sex, but acceptable sex. A little on the rush side but, hey, I had met very few masters of it. For that matter, except for the rush I knew I gave Gary, I didn't know if I was worth a toot, either. Not to be too modest, I knew my husband was more than happy in that area. Believe me, sex would have been the last thing that broke us up.

My fine, still small, butt was ready to get away from Carteret County. Ocean Drive may be a beach, too, but it is totally different. There are tons of things to do there. It abuts North Myrtle Beach and then you have Myrtle Beach. You can find anything you want, not to mention things you didn't want, but bought. Restaurants are everywhere. It dawned on me, Ray and I only went to cheap ones. I sincerely hate cafeterias. And buffets. He would wash his car at the expensive, high velocity car wash every day and it was a half hour drive into Myrtle Beach. Ok, his priorities are different. I didn't mind cooking, so we ate in sometimes. His food choices were not mine. I hate fatback and will not eat collard greens. Or grits. Little white balls with no taste if you didn't drown them in butter. Then, you wondered why your bowels were in an uproar while you desperately looked for a toilet. If you are lucky, you go to it before your bowels attacked you. They did me, anyhow. Perhaps he ate that way because he didn't have that much income from his disability, so I decided to live with it. Then again, perhaps he just liked country cooking. People do. Not me, boy.

The first thing I did after we signed the paperwork was start shopping for furniture. We got two couches and a dining room set with the purchase, but everything else had to be bought. Since I was doing the shopping, I paid for everything. For the first time in my life, I kept the receipts. I think I wanted to know how much it cost to do it right. When I was done, the condo was a show stopper. It was done in taupes and electric blues. Perfect accessories finished it off beautifully. Just right. It truly was. I had found an awesome painting for a very large, cathedral wall over the fireplace. I had been begging them to lower the price. They finally did. The colors were perfect. I bought a large Sony TV with all the fixin's, as they say. I drove to Ocean Drive as often as I could. I loved the three hour drive and was always excited to get there. Everything had come together. I was so tan I looked like I was from the Caribbean. Sometimes things got in my way and sometimes they got in his, but for the most part, we got together often. We still liked to drive around and look at property and prices, but we were very happy at the condo. He would bring his seventy four year old Dad down and I adored his Dad. I set up the second bedroom just for him. We called it Dad's room and you could tell he loved it. He could see the water the moment he opened his eyes. Sailboats would float by, and people on the boat would wave at him. They were so close, he could tell the breed of dogs they had. Ray would bring his daughter, too. She was a handful and although I could see where she got it, Ray couldn't. He could be a handful himself. Other than that, everything was go. But, I am me, remember?

This went on from November to February and then I began to see little changes. One weekend he came to my beach and I found a barrette down the side of the seat in his Cadillac. He freaked and started carrying on about leaving if I didn't trust him. He was so mad he was spitting. There was all this screaming about trust. If I didn't trust him, there could be no future. A I had to trust or else, kind of thing. I'd had enough fighting in my life so I stayed calm and calmed him down. I don't know when this peace settled in me, but I had a feeling I was never going to fight with a man again. I decided it could be his daughter's, and said so. That was the end of it. I didn't make the fuss over it he was obviously used to. My screaming days ended with Bobby. I had assumed a new persona. How do you like the visual that creates? No hissy fits. Easygoing. That was the new me. Pissy faced Carol is outta here.

Out of nowhere, he started talking about wanting a three thousand dollar tanning bed. Good grief, he lived at the beach, right by the water, in a complex with a pool where we spent all day. I couldn't figure out why he wanted to waste good money on a tanning bed. The days at the pool were our favorite thing. I realized he didn't care what I thought. He wanted me to buy it. No. Ray went on and on about it making his legs feel better. Ok, maybe there was that. The whole idea set me back a bit. We would have to re-arrange the master bedroom since it wouldn't fit anywhere else. That also set me back because I had laid out the bedroom just the way we liked it. The tanning bed was rather large. Not exactly a decor item. There was no good way to deal with it. So, I decided for his comfort, to forget about decor. But. I wasn't buying it.

He let me know he could afford it which was unusual because he usually was very secretive about what he had and didn't have. I knew his Daddy had money, but I didn't have any reason to think Ray had any more than what he could pay for when he was around me. I don't know why, but to justify buying the tanning bed, he told me he received three thousand dollars a month from the government because of the Post Traumatic Stress. Thirty six thousand tax free dollars a year and a Daddy that would throw money at him. I guess he knew what he could and couldn't do. It wasn't my money or my decision, he said.

Just after February, Ray started talking about having a big weekend family reunion at our condo. I was invited, but he wanted me to stay somewhere else because he had so many people. That seemed odd, but ok. Remember my preference for being alone. He had what seemed like twenty sixty people there and some got hotel rooms. We got together, went out to dinner, had catered lunches and a good time was had by all. It seemed to me from the conversation that everybody thought the condo was Ray's, not our's. I foolishly let that go by.

While we were all having such a good time, Ray mentioned his mother's jewelry to his Dad, right in front of everybody at the dining table. Ray had always talked about his deceased mother's jewelry and this time he asked his Dad if he had brought the jewelry down as he had asked him. People, we are talking about gorgeous stuff here. The diamonds were everywhere and the jewelry was truly better than what I had seen in stores. The watch was all diamonds, the ring was a beautiful four carat blue diamond with a platinum mine setting. Very old. My size. The necklace was to die for. I was very impressed. I figured it was worth about fifteen thousand. It was my engagement ring. Ray gave it all the jewelry to me that night, right in front of everybody. He said he wanted to set a date to get married during the summer. He wanted to get married before anything happened to his dad. I was happy, but I didn't think I was in love. Maybe this was the way to go, though. Leave all the emotion that goes with love behind and be happy. Maybe I just wanted it because it would get me out of Carteret County. In front of everybody, I agreed. We decided to set a date.

So, ok, it wasn't the loving relationship women dream of. But, hey, we got along. I tried to forget some of the things that started to occur that made me queasy. One night he came back from Salisbury to tell me he had beaten the hell out of his daughter. Yikes. Ray was very strong and had powerful hands and arms. He told me he was so good during his football years in college, he had a trophy. I had to admit, she was an in-your-face teenager. According to him, she had gone around the bend as far as behavior went. The mother couldn't handle her and had asked Ray to. His daughter was beautiful, but she was mean like Ray could be. I had seen it in how he treated some people or how he talked about black people. I told him I didn't like it, but he didn't care what I thought. I knew where she got it and it always amazed me that he didn't see it. He said there was a screaming fight involving language that resembled that of Mama and MaryBeth. He beat her so badly she wouldn't be able to go to school for a couple of weeks. If a child cannot go to school for a couple of weeks, that was way too bad a beating. I tried to talk to him, because although he seemed ashamed, he would not admit it was wrong. I told him there was a good chance that Social Service might take her away, but he didn't care. It was obvious that he didn't want her. Breaking her down was his solution. I thought about Mama and MaryBeth and how useless that method was for them. Believe me, Mama never did anything to keep MaryBeth out of school for a day, much less two weeks. I thought his child probably had black eyes and I was very worried about the state of her jaw. He must have hurt here where it showed for her to stay out of school. He wouldn't tell me anything. I tried to call her, but he took the phone out of my hands. I was afraid she might feel about her Daddy as I did about mine. This gave me major pause. I was in a high state of conflict, and we argued for the first time. I didn't think it was right, but I also didn't believe you should interfere between someone and their children. Ray had never been the least violent towards me. He said it only came out if somebody pushed him to his limit. Ray seemed to think this anger in him came from his PTSD. Hey, with my history of anger, who am I to judge? Would I ever beat my daughter? No. I know that down to my soul. That's a little rash. Hell, it's a lot rash.

I finally got through to her by phone. She wouldn't tell me what happened but I could hear the hatred in her voice. That is what you accomplish when you beat a child. Hatred. You make a decision to throw the respect your child may have had for you, out the window. There are other ways to do that, like Daddy did, but I think this is worse. As I kept talking to her over the weeks, she settled somewhat. She knew I cared about her and although she was belligerent, she never challenged me. I brought her down one weekend and told Ray if he laid a hand on her, I would call the police. It was restrained, but when she and I got off all by ourselves, we had a ball.

I went down one unsuspecting weekend and by damn, a lock had appeared on the master bedroom closet. He had split the master closet in two, put up a section and put a lock on it. Locked. This whole relationship was getting weirder and weirder. Back to the old Ray said thing. Ray said he brought some valuables from Salisbury that belonged to his Dad and he wanted them under lock and key. The next time I went down, the picture I had taken of myself, at his insistence and expense, was in one of the drawers. You know how badly I hate to have my picture taken. Up to then, it had been front and center on the dresser in the master bedroom. It was in the drawer where I put my underwear. Under my underwear. He said it must have fallen. It didn't fall under the underwear.

Maybe its just me, guys, but isn't this something a man does to hide a picture from whomever he is taking to bed? Other than the person in the picture, I mean. Let me emphasize here, I wouldn't have even had done it if I had known it was to dress up the underwear. How do you drop an 8x10 and not know it? I got the feeling this guy could lie as well as MaryBeth. Maybe as often. I knew something wasn't right here. What do you think? Something smell here? Other than the tanning lotion that he had for his and her's, open, that I had never used. Made sense to me. I didn't pursue it because I didn't feel like going through the fuss, but I had started a filing cabinet in my head. I liked my condo, and I wasn't getting married anytime soon. I had an investment here, but it was time to take notes. Believe me, I would review everything carefully before I went down another damn aisle with somebody bleating about choice vessels.

Everything went along the same confusing route through the end of March. It didn't appear this relationship was going to go the direction I hoped. Ray acted like nothing was wrong but he seemed tense all the time. Nothing like the comfortable, easy guy I had met. Then Ray started talking about the PTSD coming on him the first week in May. He suggested I not come down all of April, in case it came on early. What? He said he didn't want me to see him like that. Six Weeks? Excuse me, did he say six weeks? Believe me, if he wandered through people's yards for six weeks, his last problem would be me seeing him like that. How about the police? Ray kept this line going, saying he would call if he could, but not to expect it. Six weeks? People, we had been going together for two years and had gone any of these May traumas. I had not been asked to not come down nor had I seen much in a behavior change. It was nothing like stay away six weeks. I wanted to remind him I had his mother's jewelry hanging all over me. In case he had forgotten and might want me to bring it back before this terrible trauma took over. Maybe whoever was using the tanning lotion would like it. Perhaps look better in it? Who knows? Yeah, ok, I was getting cynical, but I kept my mouth shut. I figured I would open it soon enough. I may be in an easy going mode, but don't push the cart over the mountain, you know?

His next idea was to try to convince me his stress may blow because of the problems with his daughter. It hadn't seemed that big a deal to him before. I thought he was crazy, but I figured he knew himself better than I did and even though I didn't believe a damn word he said, I was also very concerned that he might be right and hurt himself, because he was so wigged out all the time. It was like he was looking over his shoulder or expecting a nasty surprise. He made this whole annual event sound even weirder and scarier than he had in the beginning. But, I agreed. Why not? I figured I would sit back another couple of weeks to see how the curtains fell. See whose fireworks are better than mine when its all over. After all, I had the jewelry and half the condo. I didn't think, in his state, he had focused on that in a very long time. It was starting to become my only focus. *I was conflicted.*

A couple of weeks went by and I didn't even hear from him. I didn't know what was happening and, in spite of the cynicism, I was still very worried. Weird and all, I wasn't going to stop caring about Ray until reality was slammed in my face. It hadn't yet. However, my face had taken a couple of shots. Worry was affecting my ability to work. Finally, one of the men who had worked with the mentally ill in his pre-Realtor years, sat me down to tell me this was stupid. No shit. Pat, my muse, told me I needed to go down there and put my eyeballs on him. I needed to make sure he was ok, then turn around and come back. Worked for me. I wanted to see if he was wandering the neighborhood, shooting cats. For all I knew, he could have been arrested and was sitting in jail somewhere. I didn't want to pass judgement with no information. I headed to Ocean Drive not knowing exactly what I was going to find. If I had known, I would have still gone.

When I got to the condo, Ray wasn't there. Neither was his car. He was very predictable, so I headed out to check out the three places he went every day. He had to go to the post office, the gas station and Kroger's, Oh? Do you reckon he didn't do that in a traumatic state? Down, cynicism, down. Maybe he was at Lowe's because he had to piddle with things until they were right. Maybe Kroger's. He needed to eat. Right? Just as I was coming into Kroger's, stopped at one of their parking lot stop signs, he came out the main doors. He had a woman with him. She saw me, clearly knew who I was, and started to laugh. I wasn't more than twenty feet from them so she had a full head shot of me sitting in my car. I wasn't quite sure what was so damn funny. Unfortunately, I thought I knew. I didn't recognize her, but I assumed she had seen my picture in the condo. You know, the one in the bedroom drawer. Ray kept his eyes down, so I couldn't say with any clarity that he had seen me, but when he grabbed her arm and dragged her to his car, it became a touch suspicious, don't you think? She leaned over in the car and whispered in his ear. Even in his car, he did not look up, ever. How did she know me unless she had seen my picture or knew my car, or both? It certainly would explain his stress, I dare say. I stayed at the stop sign. I wanted to see what he would do. I knew I could have pulled in behind him and trapped him or pulled up beside him and demanded an explanation. No. I like head games. It was more important for me to see what he would do. He could do the unlikely and walk over like everything was natural and she wasn't giggling her head off. I checked her out, no, she wasn't younger than me. She was as old or older. I figured he would either back out, go around and come beside me, roll the window down and introduce me to his friend. He could keep going right past me which would pretty much tell all. This would be interesting. I couldn't wait. He backed up, went around and came straight towards me. He didn't stop. He went right past me, as fast as the speed bump right beside me would allow, without looking at me. She was still giggling. I wanted to shove her voice box into her brain. But, she wasn't my problem, was she? I had made it to my fifties before a man ran on me right in front of my eyes. I felt like Mama that day she saw Daddy at Bud Dixon's Texaco. I wanted to ram My Cadillac into his Cadillac. But, I wasn't Mama and I wasn't at Bud Dixon's Texaco. I was at Kroger's, for Christ's sake. Does that suck or what?

  I couldn't believe it. I could believe he was running, but I couldn't believe he wouldn't just say so. Shit, I wasn't Genghis Khan. I wasn't going to lop his stupid head off, regardless of my feelings. I went through the lot, turned around and got behind him at the stop light. Simple flow of traffic. I didn't kill myself to get there. Again, I was curious what he would do. Perhaps he would head back to the condo and expected me to follow him. Sure. Boy, did I ever get an answer to that question. That light turned green, the man took a right, away from the condo, and kicked it. I mean kick-ed it, into overdrive. Down a road that would take him outta there unless I went after him. By now, we both had eight cylinder, sport model Cadillacs. His was black, mine was the pearl white he always wanted. Kick ass cars. The man left skid marks going around the first curve he encountered while in 35 mph downtown Ocean Drive. Do you reckon he was in a hurry? I didn't know what I felt, at the risk of stating the obvious. I couldn't believe it. Did he think, for one minute, that I was going to chase him? I don't think so. My mind went back to the sleazy motel Daddy and Jackie were in. Thank you, God, for sparing me that. The relationship came to an end the minute he passed me. On top of that, he ignored me sitting there in a car he had always wanted. A hard to miss car. Oh. Excuse me. His came equipped with a giggling idiot. Sorry, I didn't get that accessory with mine. Everything that had confused me made all the sense I knew it would. Oh well, shit happens.

I went back to the condo, and walked around. Looking at what I had so enjoyed putting together that was now lost to me. There was no way I would end up with this condo. I didn't have the money. I knew Ray could whip it up just by asking his father. I figured since he knew I was in town, and knew what he was doing, he would scope the place out for my car before he came home. Since I had not been expected, there was the ladies sun cream with the tanning bed. It had been used more than the last time I had been there. There were ladies clothes in the closet. My God, she was living there. I was stupefied. Running out on me was one thing, but she was by damn living there. That's what the lock on the closet was for. Its not like she didn't know about me. What the hell did he do with her when I came down? I got what I needed from the condo and got a room at the Hilton just down the road. I was not blubbering, but I was not in the mood to drive three hours home either. I sat on the bed and couldn't think of anything to do, but sit there. Run on me, yes. However, I couldn't believe the shock of her living there. That train of thought took about a minute and a half. Of course, I could believe it. How many clues would it have taken for my stupid brain to tell my mouth to open and say it? How could he let her live there? What was he thinking? Did she come with his Daddy there? I don't think so. His Daddy was not the liar Ray was. Unless Ray came up with a great lie for us breaking up, his Daddy was going to be really pissed. He would also know I had not done anything. I realized this was the real truth about the PTSD crap. I fluctuated between anger and confusion about her living there, but I was not hurt. I don't think women whose men run on them should be hurt, they should be mad. Like Mama. Like me. Calmed, I was not in the mood to be destructive. I had been a lady most my life and I was not stopping now. But, don't push me any farther.

Finally, around seven he tracked me down by phone. I didn't know if I wanted to ever speak to him again. However, good sense said I needed to open the lines of communication. I had all his mother's jewelry and I knew what happened would kill his Daddy if he didn't get them back. And back they would go, but I had invested good money in that condo. It was not going to end without conversation. After he said, "Carol, will you talk to me?" I didn't answer. For a few minutes, neither of us said anything. I didn't know what to say and I reckon he didn't either. Maybe, he was used to being cussed out and figured it was my call. I don't know, but I wasn't expecting what he chose to do. He started to cry. All I could manage was "What were you thinking?" I don't mean running out on me, but her living there while he was running out on me. I don't usually date men so stupid. Why would he want a relationship with me if he wanted her to live there? Why did he keep it going? I didn't believe for a moment that he truly wanted both of us. Why didn't he just get out when I found the barrette? It was a perfect time to walk away. Why not go then? All he did was cry and say he was sorry. I asked him if he loved her and he said no. Hell, that's always a great excuse for being an idiot. I didn't know why I asked because I really didn't care. But no, of course he loved me. Ray, the liar. He wanted to come see me to talk. I'll bet my ass and the toilet paper that goes with it, he didn't tell her he loved me. I'll also bet this was a rare night where she was not sitting right there. He was sobbing, I got tired of listening to him. Hell with it. I hung up.

Well, sorry folks, I was weirded out. This day had to end sometime. It had been a long, damn day. I wasn't going to lose any sleep over this guy. After I hung up on him, I wrapped the covers about me and promptly fell asleep. When I got up, I had a good breakfast. Feeling refreshed in more ways than one, I decided I would head home and didn't want to have a little get together. This boy needed to give me space before I even wanted to talk to him again. Maybe one hundred and twenty miles of space. Hey, I had the power. I had the jewelry. I didn't plan on keeping it, but I thought it was worth the wait to see what lie he told his Daddy. I had a feeling his Daddy wouldn't buy this one. Instead of talking, I felt like breaking his back. Or his bad legs. Or his dick. Hey! Great idea. Which, by the way, was tiny. I wasn't going away quite yet, until things got unwound. I was on the lease until October 31st. He could not legally throw me out. The romance, as it was, was a done deal. No going back. He knew it was a mantra of mine. If I got in a relationship and the guy runs on me, he's a done guy. Fried crispy. No more, not ever. I don't have the second chance gene in me.

When I got home and told everybody my story, I was surrounded by the "I told you so's." These are people you can't get to talk to you for a year, but break up with somebody and you are flush with them. Hey, I had my doubts, ok? Geez, its not like I was heartbroken here. I hadn't married him. I really never thought I would make it to the altar with Ray. There was the issue of child beating that I never ignored. I didn't want to get married again in the first place. I didn't mind walking around with all this jewelry in the meantime. What was beyond me was why in the world would this guy ask me to marry him, give me around fifteen thousand dollars worth of his mother's jewelry, introduce me to about fifty people he was related to, to simply run out of me? Why would he not only watch me get close to his father, but knew his father and I adored each other? Why would he do that? Why would the neighbors downstairs not tell me. I was never close to them, but we socialized at the pool. Wouldn't the neighbor lady want me to tell her if her husband did this? The one who bitched all the time about her husband's faults. Sorry, if I had known he ran on her after fifty years of marriage, I would have told her. Period. She obviously didn't return the favor. Neither did her husband who rubbed up against me every time I was at the damn pool. I was one confused female. What about all the money I had tied up in this? What about the down payment of eight thousand dollars and all the furniture I had purchased? How was I going to get all that back? Damn!

    I figured the best way was to go about it. I called Ray and told him we needed to work together to end this thing. I needed to come down and get my stuff and we needed to talk about my investment in the condo. I need to get my stuff and work out getting his jewelry back to him. He wouldn't listen. He wanted a second chance. I have to admit, I wanted to keep going to Ocean Drive. I liked my condo and all the dancing. I told him we could leave things the way they were, but I wanted to come down. If I came, he and giggle face pie had to go. He needed to accept that she was who he was going to end up with because it sure as hell wouldn't be me. He had a hundred places he could go, so I didn't care about that. I made it clear I didn't want her shit all over the place when I got there. He had made her a closet, so I told him to put her crap in there when I was coming and lock it up He was used to doing that, so it shouldn't be a hardship. He agreed. Hell, it should be easy. He'd been doing it that way for months By the way, I wasn't the shredding type. I wasn't interested in taking hurt feelings that I never had out on her damn clothes. Or anything else for that matter. I didn't know how many months this had gone on and didn't want to know. He said he would agree because he could talk to me when we were coming and going. I made it clear to him he had to be gone and the condo clean when I got there and he couldn't come back to the condo until I had left. It was either that or I would show up unexpectedly and since I was on the lease, he couldn't kick me out. I could kick her out, have her arrested and her stuff removed. I'll bet his life would be hell then. I had done my homework. That gave him pause.

This went on for the summer and it worked out well for me. I still got to go to Ocean Drive on my days off and I had the condo to myself. He had enough class to have her stuff out of the way for the most part. I think she intentionally left little cards she had sent him with all this love stuff all over them. You have to think its intentional if somebody leaves postcards in the kitchen drawer with the knives and forks that said "I love you all over it." Postcards from places they went when I came down. Ray grinning stupidly. So she could do what? Mail it to themselves? Got me. Stupid stuff. All this and he was still on the phone with me all the time trying to make up while I knew she was still living there. All this time, he lied about even dating her. He didn't know it didn't matter what he said.

From May to July, I had been going down every other week. It was about the end of July when Ray asked me if I could skip a week. He had some biker friends from Salisbury coming down and needed all the beds. I didn't care, so I said fine. The week after his biker buds were there, I went back down. When I walked into the master bathroom, there was a brilliant blue, silk nightgown hanging on the back of the door. Size 4. My size. Oh my. A gift, I don't think so. It was scraggly. I wouldn't wear anything that looked that scrungy. At least he hadn't lied about liking little women. I pinned a note to it saying it was old and bedraggled and she needed to get cheapskate Ray to buy her a new one. I added, it was disgraceful. I ran into the neighbor lady on my way out for the evening and very graciously told her to kiss my ass. I do be a lady. I'm glad I found out the way I did. Watching him run from me was a hoot. Once the weekend was over, I left the condo but decided to dance some more and hung around. Later that afternoon, my cell phone rang. It was Ray. He wanted to know if I was gone and did I leave it clean? I took some umbrage to that since I usually left it clean but I verified both. I told him I was still in town, but I had vacated the condo. Then I had to say it. I told Ray he needed to tell his four hundred pound biker bud he left his size 4 blue nightgown on the back of the bathroom door. I was sure he would miss it terribly. I sincerely hoped he enjoyed the hot tub. There was this long silence. I snickered. Snickered again. Ray had told me she was gone because he wanted to get things right with me. Right. I told him, "In that case, she needed stop by and get all those precious love note postcards she picked up while they were on the trips they took when I was in the condo. She had left them in the kitchen drawer with the forks and knives. The kitchen, Ray? I didn't know you were that stupid. Are you that dumb? Won't work, sweetheart. I have to give a shit first." I told him the next time he asked me not to come down, my answer was going to be "No, sir. I am on my way. Take her ass on a trip."

By September he actually realized I wasn't coming back to him, so we entered the "I want my stuff" stage. The condo had to be bought the end of October, and I wasn't buying it. I didn't have the money. I already had an attorney tell me I probably wouldn't get my eight thousand dollars back. She told me this kind of stuff happened all the time in Myrtle Beach. That, I must admit, was humiliating. I had never seen myself as an old woman picking up a gigolo. Hell, he was older than I was. She felt I could get the furniture and all I had bought because I had receipts. Ok, I was going to get my furniture, by God. Especially that Sony TV he loved so dearly. It cost sixteen hundred dollars and I knew it would kill him to have to spend that. Whether or not he was going to buy the condo was his business, but he was going to get it mostly empty. Let her furnish it so he can then run on her. Where I would put all this crap was another story. But, I had to be steadfast and not give in or allow myself to be bullied. I can do the steadfast thing damn well. Ask Ray. I told him I wanted what I paid for. He refused. He told me he was keeping everything. He refused to give me the furniture or the money because we were going to get back together. He liked the condo the way I had decorated it. Why would any intelligent person think otherwise? Too bad, Chad.

My answer was to drive to the police station while I was down to find out what I should do. In South Carolina, you contact a magistrate, you file a claim explaining your problem to him, and a date for a hearing is set. Both parties had to be in court on the date set to see if he could make a determination. If he can, its done right then, right there. Worked for me. I took Conrad, my right hand, and another couple of guys for the heavy lifting. We jumped into a van to head south. Hey, hope for the best, you know. We got there and there was Ray. I was very nervous about it. It was the first time I had seen him face to face since KROGER'S. Standing in front of judges was not my idea of a good time, either.

The magistrate finally called us. He asked both of us to come stand in front of him. He asked me to tell my story first since I filed the claim. I got the distinct feeling he hadn't read it beforehand. He listened to me, looked at Ray, noted the size difference, then asked for the receipts. When I laid a million of them in front of him, he turned to Ray. Ray never got to say a word. Bless that little magistrate's heart, he took one look at Mr. Ray and said, "Give the little woman her stuff. All of it. You might also want to find four thousand dollars fast or I just might get mad. The police will accompany her and each piece must be properly packed and identifiable. If everything on her list is not there, you will be brought back here. Period." He had his clerk set a date and that was it. I got it all. Ray never got a chance to say squat. He, of course, was going to get the condo. I got Carteret County. Is there no justice?

AN APPLE AND A CALLIE

I decided to take another trip. I had been talking with Pauly Brown, a lady I worked with, about going somewhere, but I didn't know where I wanted to go. But, I knew I needed to get away. Somehow New York City came up in the conversation. My first reaction was absolutely not. I would be going alone. Remembering the assertiveness program and being afraid to go out the doors in New York didn't help. Our company had done well in 2005 so I had the money to go if I wanted. I put it off, but it was in the back of my mind. I was going somewhere. Destiny stepped in. I received my first American Orchid Society magazine since 1989 in the mail. I had just gotten my first orchid after fifteen years of refusing to even think about them. The largest ad in the magazine was about the World Orchid Conference to be held in Rockefeller Center in April 2006 for four days. I saw this ad in March. I made an instant decision. I was going. I didn't care if I was going alone. I wasn't that girl anymore and I wasn't afraid. I was only worried about my pain, which had not abated at all, going nuts if there was a pressure issue from flying. Nonetheless, I was going to give it a go. I would carry buckets of medication. I was not about to be caught short on an airplane if it kicked in. Don't even think about it.

I thought about getting a room at the Waldorf Astoria, but put it off a day. The next day, when I finally convinced myself, there were no rooms available. I was bummed. I ended up with a room in a hotel called the "W" which was situated on 56th and Lexington. It was real modern and classy. I would be within one block of Park Avenue, two blocks from Madison Avenue and eight blocks from the Rockefeller Center. I had a flight from Wilmington that went straight to LaGuardia. The hotel limousine would take me to the hotel. It all just fell into place. I had gotten a travel agency to put everything together. I would get a night at the theater if I wanted, but there were no shows I wanted to see. I had wanted to see "Cats", but it was no longer on Broadway. Then I opted for an opera, but although Phantom of the Opera was playing, it was sold out. I could go to the Metropolitan Museum of Art. Good enough for me. I got all my breakfasts and a dinner a day at restaurants they offered. These were not junk restaurants. These were the real New York thing, you know. One was a Italian restaurant near the theater district. It definitely looked like somebody could get shot there. The other choice was Tavern on the Green. Ho-ha. I was going.

  The flight only took two hours. No pain. That was great. I'm surprised I didn't set it off from sheer tension. Once we got to LaGuardia, the van picked us up. It was a van for a lot of hotels so we went all over the place before we got to the hotel. I was really frightened that the hotel would not be as advertised, it was small, but perfect. I understand now that most of the rooms in New York are small. Why hadn't I thought of that? Duh

  I checked in, threw the luggage in the room and hit the streets of New York running. I did. I did. I went everywhere. I must admit, I had no fear of danger at all on the streets of New York City, and it was just as busy as it appeared on TV shows. Before I went back to the room that night, I had carved out an eight block square and knew I wouldn't get lost within those eight blocks. I could expand while I was there. Pretty much everything I wanted to get to during the day was within reach. Hot damn. When I got back to the hotel, it was dinnertime. Off I went to one of the offered New York-looking Italian places and indulged in awesome lasagna. I hadn't wanted to eat in the hotel restaurant since the Italian meal was in the plan I purchased. I must say, the hotel had something much more exciting than a good restaurant. They had a spacious, open room with soft, comfortable looking conversation pieces in earth and sienna tones, grouped around a massive, blazing fireplace. Was I in love or what? There was a small bar at the back and two very discreet looking waitresses. The real bar was on an open loft above. You didn't get any noise from it though it was packed. The acoustics must have been great. I ran to my room, grabbed a good book, then climbed into one of the chairs. It swallowed me. I sat close to the fireplace and snuggled in. I think the book kept any men away who might have wanted to approach. Good enough for me. I didn't go back to my room until three a.m. Apparently, the bar was open much later than that. The city that never sleeps. I didn't want to either, but that warm, cozy fire had put me to sleep.

The next day I took off on foot for the Rockefeller Center. You hear about the Big Apple but you have no idea how big it is until you are standing in front of it. Its truly surprising how many of the buildings in New York City are beautiful. This Center was one of them. Truly remarkable. Once I got down in the bottom level where the Conference was being held, my mouth didn't just drop open, it stayed open. You can't imagine how big a World Conference can be. I couldn't believe it was all on one floor, and there were so many floors to go. There were orchids as far as my eye could see. All of the exhibitions were professionally designed for them to appear in their natural habitats, so the entire Conference level of the portion of Rockefeller Center we were in, looked like a jungle. It even had waterfalls. For an orchid lover, it was orgasmic. The judging was taking place, but they wandered around like everybody else so your enjoyment was not restrained in any way. I took a million pictures. I had never taken pictures on a trip in my life. But then, I had never seen so many beautiful orchids before in one unbelievable setting. An amazing amount of these orchids were rare and I might never get another opportunity to see them. This Convention put Longwood Gardens to shame and I adore Longwood Gardens. As I wandered around I realized The Center had massive conventions going on in other areas at the same time. I mean important ones, with other countries, and there was no telling how many people were in the building.

Ok. Now. The question was, how in hell would I get orchids back to North Carolina? I knew I could take a small bag on the plane, but with this abundance of orchids, I wanted more than would fit in a small bag. Not to mention, they were in full bloom. You can't exactly cram an orchid with a four foot inflorescence in a bag. The prices were unbelievably low because of so much competition and the choices were mouth watering. I was on a mission. Everybody in New York better get out of my way. I raced through the streets of New York eight blocks to get back to the hotel for advice. They told me to find a Kinko's. They would ship them for me. I found one about four blocks away and met a really cool manager. The first thing she said was she would not ship them for me or anybody else. New Yorkers are very direct, I learned. No how, no way.

I stood there, mournful looking and hauled out my famous Pout. I slipped into that brogue naturally, wanting the manager to think she was dealing with someone unable to do anything for herself. That bottom lip was dragging the ground. Mama would have had a field day with it. Most New Yorkers never have to deal with somebody from Down East. Down South maybe, but not Down East. We don't quit until we get your first born if we want it. I started asking questions with a dumb, unhappy look on my face like I couldn't understand, and I wouldn't leave her alone to do her job. I worked my way into making her feel like she would have done this for someone else, but not poor, little pitiful me. The word please must have come out of my mouth a hundred times. I think my being polite and so bereft surprised her. She was more used to being pushed around. Finally, she said she would cooperate if I would compromise. Hell, yes. That's my middle name. She could not ship them because she was not allowed to pack them. If I would be responsible for their condition upon arrival, and if I would pack them myself, she would ship them. She offered the packaging and the popcorn to ship them in. We were instant friends. I dropped the ignorant act immediately, which she found hilarious. We bonded.

    I tore back to the Rockefeller Center. I stopped only long enough to eat at the Rockefeller Café, which was on my itinerary, and I would kill to go back there. There must have been a thousand people in there, yet I got excellent service. I had an Asian salad with an oriental dressing and roasted almonds. So good. Then I sprinted back to the Conference where I bought eight huge orchids. Covered in orchids and carrying a box bigger than I was, I stumbled through eight blocks of New York back to Kinko's. On the way, I had to stop several times to re-adjust something that was getting away from me. Every time I stopped, someone stopped to help me. I slipped into a florist shop long enough to get the manager of Kinko's a red rose. She loved it. She also gave me a box big enough to bury myself in. Good Lord, female. I only needed one about four feet, but I got one six feet long and two feet wide. Then she gave me ten million pieces of shipping popcorn. It took me four hours to wrap the orchids and fill that damn box. When I got done, she said she hoped they got home ok. I was going back to the Conference. She clearly thought she had done her good mission for the day. I told her I hoped she had more popcorn, smiled, and off I went.

    Getting my own box this time, eight more orchids were on their way by the end of the day. I had walked all over the New York from 56th St to the Rockerfeller Center, around and back. I headed back to the hotel for another night at a well known restaurant. This time one in the theater district. Even though I wasn't going to the theater, they sat me at a window so I got to see people walking and running to get to the theaters in time. You could tell some we cutting it too close, because the men would be practically carrying the women and going at a dead run. Some were dressed in true finery and some were in rags. At seven thirty the theater traffic was dead. The plays were on. Time for me to concentrate on food.

I ordered a 12 ounce prime rib, medium rare. I had to order something big because there was nothing small on the menu. I could see a couple with a plate of spaghetti where the plate looked like it was fourteen inches across. When they served my prime rib, I was looking at a piece of the biggest, thickest slab of meat I had ever seen. The prime rib hung over all four sides of the plate. It didn't hang down, because it was so thick. It just hung over. I felt like they thought they were serving Frank Sinatra's daughter. I ate my heart out. My dinner was juicy and cooked to perfection. Spices on it brought out a sumptuous flavor without destroying the taste of the meat itself. I had asked the waiter to pick the wine, and oh what a choice. Delicious. When I had eaten all I could, I paid then asked would he order a cab for me. While we were waiting for the cab, the waiter told me he was an "actor" on Broadway when they had a part for him. He was tall, thin and as distinguished as anyone could possibly be. A perfect host. Maybe he was playing a part? Who knows? When the cab arrived, I gave him the open bottle of wine and bought a full bottle. He probably owned the place. Great restaurant, great meal with an altogether memorable day. I was exhausted, so I headed for the soft furniture, a book and the fire.

The next day I decided to get to know a fourteen block square. I wasn't going to wander too far off the path. The Orchid Conference was still on, but my orchid spree was done for, thank God. I couldn't afford any more, but I had relished it. I meandered around Park Avenue and Madison Avenue. You could tell how much money some of the people who live on Park Avenue must have by how expensive everything looked. Those huge condos must cost millions. And yes, there were cabs everywhere. Horns blew constantly, but it all seemed to work. There were black limos everywhere. They were "high end cabs" by appointment only. There was Sac's Fifth Avenue, Armani; all the to die for stores. The travel agency got me twenty five percent off coupons, but I had spent my money on orchids. I was happy. I was back with my first love. I wandered in and out of stores looking for little gifts to bring back to the people I worked with. There was a man selling scarves on the street that were luscious so I invested in them. One for all the girls.

That evening I got all prettied up and headed off to the Tavern on the Green. This was to be my last night since the Orchid Conference closed that day, so I was looking forward to an elegant time. Can you believe it? I got a cab driver who did not know where it was. Perhaps he did, but he acted like he didn't. Apparently. he wasn't smart enough to think of a way to find it, either. No friends in New York? I finally told him I was not going to pay him to wander around, so either I was going to get out and pay him nothing or he needed to call somebody. We had been wandering around New York for twenty minutes. I told him I was going to find a policeman if he didn't get it on. I did say it nicely because I had no idea what nationality he was. We could barely communicate.

I had reservations for seven with only had fifteen minutes to get there. He asked me whether it was on the West Side. Hell, what did I know? Why would I know? He finally went through what seemed like a tunnel and poof, out of nowhere, there was Central Park. Central Park caught me off guard. Hell, I would have been willing to pay separate for it and here I got it for free. The sun was still up but going slowly down, so I saw the Park for the first time in the early evening. It was as lush and as active as you hear about. People were walking their dogs, playing football and soccer and they all appeared good looking, young and disgustingly healthy. The grass was a luscious green and all the trees looked as healthy as the people. Although I was seeing only a small part, it looked monstrous. I could see at least five football fields of the Park. If anyone was not having a good time, I missed them. It is amazing, as immense as it obviously was, that New York was wrapped around it. Suddenly, I was at the historic Tavern-On-The-Green.

Even though there was a long line, it moved nicely and I was seated in only a few minutes, still before seven. The restaurant was vast, but unbearably classy because it was set up in what I would call parlors. I do love that. It was like The Pink Room in Savannah and The Mills Hyatt House in Charleston, where I got slugged. None of the parlors looked very large, but as you were seated, you traveled from room to room and it seemed to go on forever. It also looked like it had been there for centuries. The host asked if I had a preference of where to sit like I had been there a million times. If he thought I was a Southern cracker, he was kind enough to hide it. I asked if he had a seat where I could continue to see Central Park. That's where he put me. Once he seated me, there was no rush like you get at a Ruby Tuesday's or the like. I can tell you this, I was certainly not dressed like some of the people there. However, I had worn my finest, so I felt comfortable with my choice. I watched the people play in the Park while I enjoyed a delicious wine. I had asked for the steward's recommendation and he chose a fifty-five dollar bottle of Henry's. The meal was never to be forgotten. The wine was so good, I bought a bottle to bring home. I still have it. I also have the one from the Italian Restaurant. I got everybody at work another gift, making sure they were all inscribed with Tavern on the Green, then headed back to the hotel.

  I still had some orchids I would be carrying that had to be dealt with in order to get them on the plane. I unpacked them and spread them on the floor in the very, teeny, tiny bathroom so they could get some humidity. My seemingly innocent decision would lead to a Calamity Jane move later that evening. Had I but known. Once done, my book and I headed for the cozy fireplace.

  I found a comfortable seat close to the fireplace and snuggled in. As always, I was alone and no one bothered me. After ordering a glass of wine, I expected a quiet night. It was, with the exception of a girl of about twenty five who kept striding back and forth between the fireplace and me; obviously agitated and argumentative. She had a "I'm somebody" headset on. She continued to wear the carpet down with her pacing. She was clearly highly agitated. This girl had a dire need for "relax lessons." I had seldom in my life been more relaxed. She passed me once then gestured like "Can you believe this?" with her arms gesturing and an irritated look on her face. It was ten at clock at night. This female needed to quit working. I remembered when I had to work that hard and missed a good forty years of normal, quiet solitude. One thing I brought back from New York were cozy nights with good music and a good book. At night, relax. It was now embedded in me. Relax at some point before you go to bed. In between what must have been fifty separate phone calls, she passed by me again. Hoping to help, I spoke up, saying, "You don't know how to relax. You should hang up that phone and cut it off. You need to learn how to relax more than anybody I have ever met." I said this very languidly because that is how I felt. Like I had melted in a bowl. No nerves allowed. She stared at me and for a minute I thought I had offended her, but suddenly she asked me what I meant. I told her that first she should take off that damn headset; second she needed to cut off the phone; third, she needed to get a drink and fourth, she needed to sit down with someone who was already relaxed. She did it all but cut the phone off. It was amazing.

We became immediate friends. She was a wedding planner in town for a planning conference with four scheduled weddings coming up in Conway, South Carolina. Obviously the cause for her stress. There was also her boyfriend who had obviously been putting her down, and was absolutely livid that she was in New York City, since she was gorgeous. I kept my mouth shut. After he called her four straight times, I asked her to hand me the phone. I told him I was a female from North Carolina, and for his information I was neither a lesbian nor a con artist. If he would be kind enough to leave her the hell alone for at least an hour, she might be able to relax enough to speak with him without being so strident. I said I was tired of hearing him upset her. Then, I cut the phone off. He must have gone nuts. Great grits. Just do it. Shove him off a cliff in a bag. You can haul him up later. Sandy was a warm, caring, snickering kind of female. She could spread laughs a mile in any direction. I would have wanted her for my wedding planner if I didn't hate the damn things. Weddings, not planners. I told her about my wedding dress and she howled.

All the nights I had been in the lobby, I hadn't had much to drink. However, this night I had imbibed drinks at dinner, coupled with the few I enjoyed in the lounge by the fire. Without being aware she must have been replenishing my wine because we laughed and drank together until one o'clock in the morning. Then, I did something that threw me over the edge. I had forgotten my noon dose of narcotics. I had also forgotten my six o'clock pill. And was late for the ten o'clock one. Therefore, I thought I should take a double dose of my ten o'clock major pill. Dumb move. Suddenly, and I mean suddenly, I couldn't stand or walk. I could communicate just fine. I just couldn't hold my balance and lurched like John used to when he bounced off walls. She got worried, too, because it came on me so quickly. Thinking I was drunk, she was kind enough to get one of the porters to help me to the room. I couldn't find my legs. I knew what was happening because it had happened once before when I drank too much and then took that dosage. I should never have done it, especially given what happened.

Sandy came into the room with me to make sure I got in alright. I explained to her what was going on with me while on the way up in the elevator. Of course, she wanted to hear the whole story about my so-called condition. You can't tell people you have trigeminal neuralgia. They look at you like they're asking should they run. You don't want to talk about it at one o'clock in the morning when you have an eleven o'clock flight out. Sandy had been incredibly nice, and I hated to see her go. So, I started telling her about it. I could think fine. I could even speak clearly but then there was that unfortunate falling down thing. Once in the room, I made another cataclysmic decision.

I needed to go to the bathroom. I made it into the tiny bathroom, but had those damn orchids all over the floor. Unable to find anywhere to place a foot, I lost the oh so important balance that I had been trying so desperately to keep, and toppled. The following events happened in separate episodes that seemed to take forever to end. First, I hit the hardest ceramic sink known to man, with my chin. I hit it so hard that my head ricocheted off it like it had bounced off a trampoline. In mid-bounce I slammed my head into the hard, wooden door. About to pass out just from that, I fell and slammed my head against an unbelievably rigid Spanish tile floor. After that, I couldn't get my vision or my balance back. I can't imagine how I must have sounded from outside the door after hitting everything so hard and so damned often. Sandy was screaming so I my hearing was ok. She somehow got me out of the orchid forest without destroying anything. She held me up, and duck walked me to the bed where we both were trying to decide how to get me on it without my rolling onto the floor. I was conscious but belonged on the damaged aisle.

I had to give her credit for sitting with me awhile to make sure I was ok. She was still sitting there when I entered the land of doze. Before I went out, she left me her number to call if I needed her. I could hear her like she was already back in Conway and I was still in New York like through a bad connection. Hell, I didn't know if I needed her or not. I felt like I had just killed myself but hadn't died yet. At least my hearing hadn't. The rest of me you could take away. I had a new cure for alcoholism and a new way to commit suicide. Put 'em in that damn bathroom.

At four a.m., I woke up. I had some balance but I couldn't seem to get that world famous shit together. I took another dose. Had to. I had screwed up the two o'clock and was off schedule. If I missed the major dose, major shit could happen. Like it hadn't already. I took these suckers every four hours all day and all night or the ramifications are far, far worse. I do not abuse them, but once you have taken one, you sort of lose touch with reality and are subject to making bad decisions. Like the one I had just made. With that pill, I was back in La-La land. I was disoriented and couldn't think, much less focus. I was trying to decide if I knew anybody who would fly up here to get me, but that only wasted valuable time. I managed to get packed, paid my bill, and yes, they did look at me like I was the talk of the hotel, hailed a cab and got my ass to LaGuardia. Once there, I couldn't figure out how to get where I needed to go. I kept asking people. I heard their answers but couldn't seem to assimilate the info. The feet, the hands and the brain were out of whack. I remember thinking, maybe I was hungry. I asked a lady at the security lane if there were anywhere to eat. Sustenance, that was always Mama's answer to a problem. I was concerned because I realized if I was so high I couldn't straighten up. I couldn't believe the pills wrecked me so completely.

    I went where I thought the security lady said to go. She said, "Check your luggage through, take a left. All the restaurants are at the end." I turned around and went back the way I had come. When I couldn't find a restaurant, I re-traced my steps, but I had lost my luggage. I went back and there she was. She looked at me like I had recently been released from an institution. She probably thought I was a heroin addict or something. She held my bags when she saw me walk away. This time, she escorted me through security, all the while holding my arm. When we reached the other side, she walked me to the food court. She must have been used to brainless people in New York, she was so good at it. Maybe I looked like I was not used to being a junkie. Who knows? I knew on some level how kind she was being. Before she sat me down, she told me how to find my plane. Everybody I had encountered in New York was nice to me. Maybe I looked helpless. If you go, try that. I ate, but didn't feel any better. I had nothing left to do but wait for the plane. I managed to find it. I managed to get the orchids stowed. I managed to fall asleep. I also managed to sleep until the stewardess woke me up. The plane was empty. We had landed.

    I got into the Wilmington airport and got my butt through the baggage mess, I even found my big white Mercedes among the morass. I got behind the wheel and sat. I didn't know whether to try it or get a room for the night. Sandy called while I was sitting there to ask if I was alright. We talked about an hour or so. By the time we hung up, I felt better. Still woozy though, I got on the road and realized I had must have had a concussion from that fall. Most likely I broke my damn skull when I hit that tile floor. What ever happened to vinyl flooring? I had really hurt myself. It took me three days to get back to normal. How's that for a memento?

    After the glow of New York City started to wear off, I was ready to go dancing again. I threw myself back onto the dance floor. Ernie, who was my very best friend, welcomed me back from

New York with open arms. Instead of going to Ocean Drive on my days off, I headed to Raleigh. To stay with Ernie. We would always go to a place called Red's, which is a shag institution there. The only good night during the week was on Wednesdays. I would head up Tuesday night and drive back on Thursdays. Sometimes Ernie would dance; sometimes he wouldn't; so I got better at asking people to dance with me. Hell, I would go up to a guy and ask him had he ever thought about what knowing me could be like. You know. Like? If his answer was yes, I would tell him he had to dance with me. I never promised anything except fun. Then I would lose him at some point. I always knew I was a lot of fun. Not too many guys had a bad time around me so I didn't feel bad about it. That's what they were thinking if they had asked me on their own. I could get into a real "let loose" mood. I felt more like Mama than I had in years. Ernie would walk up to guys he thought were good dancers to tell them they ought to dance with me. He would tell them I was special in the shag world and they'd eat it up. I ended up in the best shape I had been in for a long time. It got so I was dancing on Tuesdays, Wednesdays, Fridays and Saturdays. A good time was had by all. We went to the spring and fall SOS's. Guys would try to pick me up but I told them I was closed for the season. This went on from the end of the Ray Era til August of the next year. I never forgot bouncing off a bathroom floor in New York City.

A LAST HURRAH? LET'S HOPE SO

Summer being over was the platform for the Labor Day Party at Memories. I always enjoyed the day parties more than the nights because the nights didn't start until 10:00 pm or even later. I got bored waiting for it to come around. Half the time, I would say the hell with it and stay home.

This particular Labor Day Party had all the old regulars, glad handing each other like we hadn't seen each other in years when we had all gotten together the week before. I sat outside on a picnic bench with Ernie to listen to music and waited for Sophia to arrive. She was always gorgeous because she dressed to the nines. Every day. You would usually see her in some form of black or black and white. Whatever she was in, she was always well worth the wait. Sophia had that Italian appeal that can be so striking. She had style. She wore her black hair in between a bob and a Cleopatra style. All the same length and curling slightly around her chin. Her eyes were always done perfectly, as were her nails, toenails, the heels of her feet and every thing else. She stood very erect and emoted that well brought up persona. Her head was held high, showing her long, lovely neck and her arms were almost always in motion when she saw someone she liked. When Sophia looked you in the eyes, she could be riveting with the bright, bright blue contacts she had that were so striking against that black hair. After about twenty minutes, she arrived in her black dress with the sparkling blue and white rhinestone jacket and a big, blue hat. As she approached the rest of us, she waved and worked her way over to us. Most of the women were jealous of her because she looked great all the time. I think they also hated her because she can actually pull the prima donna thing off with panache. I loved it and I respected someone our age who cared enough herself enough to keep her style, looks, clothes and dignity in place. After speaking to several people, she sauntered over to me for a moment, then went on her way. She liked to everybody and enjoyed spreading a positive attitude. I couldn't do that. It wasn't in me. Find me a spot where I can see over people's heads and I am like concrete. I ain't moving.

    About an hour later, I was sitting on one of the rails, finally able to see, listening to the music. I didn't have anyone to dance with but I loved that rhythm. I had to put my foot down on every beat even when standing still. I had noticed when I watched Michael Jackson dance, he did the same thing but, of course, he had a talent and precision I certainly don't have. However, they didn't call me the Fastest Feet in the East for nothing. Sophia came over and we spoke again. When she stepped away, a scrumptious guy started talking to her. He was about 5'11", had exquisite snow white hair, a very trim silhouette and was very well dressed. I could tell by the way he held himself erect that he had been raised with good manners. Posture, you know. How often do you see it these days? He had on black slacks, not jeans, and a pure white button down shirt. That "country club" style of dress. Like Gary did. When he stepped away, I grabbed Sophia and demanded to know who was that gorgeous man she was talking to. She said his name was Carlton. She became all enthusiastic about introducing us because she thought we would make a great couple. I had not known Sophia loved to be a matchmaker among her friends. She had apparently been successful a few times. She kept going on and on about how good we would look together. I thought so, too.

    She spoke to me later to tell me Carlton told her he was too plastered to meet anyone. He had seen me sitting on the rails and didn't want to make a bad first impression. He did, however, ask for my phone number. Sophia was delighted. I sat alone the rest of the day and went home intrigued about Carlton. In my fifties, I was past the age of most men wanting my phone number. I wondered if he would call or if he was merely being polite.

Since I was bored for something to do, I decided I wanted to try another trip. A year had passed since I went to New York and I was trying to go somewhere, preferably within driving distance each year. This time I decided to go to Savannah. Alone. I wanted to have the trip I couldn't enjoy when I went with somebody else. I made reservations the East Bay Inn. I knew it was very old, but respectable. It was also one block from the Olde Riverfront. This was going to make up for the disaster when MaryBeth and I went to Charleston. I packed what felt like a hundred books and headed out. It was not my way to spend a lot of evenings out partying on vacations. I was happiest with peace and quiet. At work, I spent my whole day listening to people talk and talking back. At night I didn't want to say a word. I didn't want to have to listen to anybody, either. Solitude. Damn right. Hide me.

I was still driving a big ass, sport Mercedes. I had been driving Cadillacs because Mama would rattle on about "You don't look successful" until I could scream. I didn't know it was a look and I didn't want to do it, but I had this bad habit of doing what I was told when it was Mama doing the telling. My Mercedes E320 Sports Coupe was a joy to ride in. However, I had only gotten to Wilmington when the unthinkable happened. I stopped at an intersection and when the light turned green, I tried to accelerate. I had eased into the middle of the intersection when the car just plain ceased to function. Nothing happened. Nothing. I was blocking major traffic here, guys. The car wouldn't move. I couldn't get it to crank, change gears or anything. After listening to people scream about me being a dumb blond, I found two guys willing to push me off the road and look at the car. Neither could figure out what it was. They called a tow truck who wanted to tow me to the local Mercedes dealer. I waited an hour in a convenience store where everybody seemed to think it was funny, but me. My worst problem had to be it was Friday at 6:00pm. Service would be gone for the weekend. No car and I was on my way to Savannah. My tow truck came and we headed over to the dealer while I tried to decide what to do. I opted for spending the night in Wilmington because it was 8:30 pm by the time we got everything done. I found a great suite and settled in. I enjoyed a delivered pizza and spent a peaceful night. Not fine dining, I daresay. I determined I would not grouse. Things happen. I only needed to find out what had happened, how bad it was and how damn much it was going to cost. No matter what, I was going to have a good time.

    I called the Mercedes place the next day and spoke to one of the salespeople who told me he knew what the problem was. It was a $2,000 problem. Good God Almighty, people. Two Thousand Dollars, and I had not gotten ninety miles from home. I didn't know whether to rent a car and go home or rent a car and take the trip. Hell, I opted for the trip, but the two thousand put a real crimp in my spending. If you can call that a crimp. Damn, I hadn't planned to spend that on the entire trip. I was going to Savannah and no damn body was going to stop me. It was my trip and I was going to enjoy it. I kept telling myself that through the deluge of rain. Six hours of soaking, pounding highway rain. Sometimes I wondered who the hell it was that pissed God off. Perhaps He didn't want me to go? Couldn't He have sent me a sign during the pizza? I was struggling, but still optimistic. With this start, the trend had to change. Didn't it?

    I found my East Bay Inn without any trouble Then got drenched trying to get the luggage out of the car. Once I did, I was told the only parking was a parking garage one block away. I was going to have to pay for parking the whole time I was there. They credited me two days because they realized I was about to have seizures right there in the lobby. I drowned walking from the parking garage back to the Inn because I didn't plan on needing an umbrella. The people at the Inn were very charming Southern people. They did the best they could with the rules they had to follow. Very informative as well. As I headed to the room, they mentioned my room was haunted, and hoped I wouldn't mind. Hell, what did I care? I'd been ready to die for quite some time. I just didn't want it to hurt. If he strangled me in my sleep, what would it matter? I don't know if they told me that for local color or if they really believed it, but they had been repeating it long enough to give the ghost a name. As far as I knew, it was the only ghost in the inn, I guess I should be honored to be the chosen one. I wondered if they told everybody that and snickered or if they thought I needed a pick me up. It was actually the best news I'd had since I left home. At least he wouldn't be talking to me. His name was Charlie. Do you notice how that name keeps popping up and its never a good thing? I figured when I died, and they were looking for something meaningful to put on the cemetery marker, just put Charlie. I'll know how to find myself. Even in the dark.

I unpacked first, then did the old tourist meander to the river. I found a great restaurant and ordered eggs benedict. You do not get eggs benedict for breakfast at home. I fully intended to eat in fine restaurants despite the car. I intended to throw myself into that whole Savannah ambience, and thrive on it. I planned to return home looking, acting and speaking like I was from Savannah.

That evening, after I wearing myself to a foot frazzle, I went back to the room to find light classical was playing on the radio. I called down and they said Charlie did that all the time. They hadn't cut it on. I had never been too fond of light classical, but it was on every station I tried. However, it fit the environment in Savannah perfectly so I chose a good book, relaxed in a wonderfully comfortable chair, pulled over an antique lamp with soft lighting and solituded out. I fell in love with light classical music that night. The room, the music, the book, even the chair I was sitting in, was perfect. I was happy for the first time since I'd left home. I intended to stay that way the whole trip. I said hello to Charlie and thanked him for allowing me the use of his room and radio. I told him he could make all the noise he wished while I was up, but would he please hold it down during the night? He was a very considerate ghost for the most part. He only got rambunctious about five a.m. I knew he was really there because the hair stood up on the back of my neck around then. Here was another ghost I could actually feel. Spooky, but not that scary. He didn't throw things and he didn't say a word so I was cool with it. He went well with the music, let's say.

Digressing a minute but staying with the ghost topic, something happened just before I left home. About two weeks before my trip, I was asked to meet with a lady who was considering allowing us to manage her property. I took to her right away. What you saw was what you got. I was floored when she told me she was Warren Buffet's sister. She gave me a tour of her house, and we were really getting along. She was extremely pleasant to be around. When we entered her basement, the hair not only stood up on my neck, I got nervous tingles up and down my arms. I asked her if she knew she had a ghost? I was surprised when her response was "How did you know?" Most people think you're nuts when you say that. She told me her cleaning lady would not go into the basement. I asked her was her cleaning lady black and she nodded. No surprise to me. Black people in our community were known to be afraid of ghosts. I asked her if she knew who the ghost might be. She thought it was the great grandmother of her husband, who had lived in the home. I didn't tell her that I thought her ghost was definitely not Casper. This was the first ghost I had ever encountered that threw off very scary vibes. I didn't think this was a happy household. There was an aura of anger. We weren't close enough for me to dare ask. Whoever this ghost was and whatever he or she was mad at, I would take my Charlie any day.

    The next day, I wandered to the river front again. Because of the cost to fix my car, I was not able to buy the presents for my friends at the office that I wanted to, but I made sure I got each and every one of them something. I can't enjoy myself on a trip if I am not taking something back that reminds them I was thinking of them. That's why I like to travel. The memory is forever. I only remember fine food and restaurants if they were out of town. As I was wandering, I went in and out of several art shops. Most of the art was way too expensive for me, but I had never bought art and decided it would be the special gift I would get for myself. I decided then and there that would be my goal. Savannah was slam full of art. It was on the sides of buildings. I was almost close enough to downtown to walk. I decided to do some major walking. When I was tired, I'd head back.

    After I a scrumptious lunch, I took the opportunity to read in one of the wooded squares that Savannah is so noted for. People are so polite. You can sit in one of the squares, read a book and there is no noise whatsoever. People leave you alone like you are not even there. My kind of people. Invisible is how I like it. I found the house that had been in the "Midnight in the Garden of Good and Evil", one of my favorite books. I learned the history of the musician who had built the home. I bought a statue of the girl on the cover of the book. She would go among the orchids.

    One day I wandered downtown only to end up in a music store. I had been intrigued by some art he had on the walls. I found what I considered a treasure. The owner had what resembled a four foot tall waiter entirely made of a thick, black wire. He was real cool. He stood there, with a English bowler hat on his head, tipping his hat to you. He also had an extended arm where you might hang a small napkin like waiters do. He was a cocky looking kind of guy with his head only slightly off center. With wire pieces strung to look like one eye, a nose and a mouth, he looked at you like he knew he was special. Twelve bottles of wine fit between his spread legs. This baby was a keeper. I had to have him. I bought him but I had to leave him there because I didn't want to haul him all the way back to the room, which was about seven blocks away. Four feet tall of him and five feet tall of my trying to carry him through traffic, was not a pretty picture. I talked the owner into holding him until I was ready to leave town.

    I went back to meandering and found myself right in the middle of an area that was dedicated to art, food and wine. Lord God Almighty, I had died and gone to heaven. I took a moment to thank heavens I had not let anybody come with me on this trip. I had about six more city blocks that were blocked off so no cars could drive through. There was everything art-wise that you could think of. I really got a kick out of going into these high faluting places knowing damn well they knew I couldn't afford anything in there. But, I made them acknowledge me. I asked questions and they were gracious enough to answer me once they realized I wanted to learn. Sometimes you were climbing stairs and sometimes you were heading into basements. It was great. I found myself climbing stairs at one point and found this very interesting artist. He had been to the Wilmington area, where my car was on vacation, and really liked it. I loved his style. All of his work was very colorful. A style to which I was seriously drawn. He was comfortable to talk with and showed me around his studio. He asked me what I liked and when I said color, he showed me some pieces but didn't try to force anything on me. I found two ten by twelves of the specific area where I was standing right that moment. The buildings were painted all different colors and they were of the carriage houses so very conspicuous everywhere. When he wrapped my art, he painted the wrapping for me and signed it. He spent about forty minutes painting the wrapping of these small pieces of art. Wonderful. I couldn't have been more impressed. Maybe this is normal, but it wasn't for me. It was heaven on earth. Believe me, Carteret County is nothing like Savannah. All they do there is drink and fish. Neither are particularly beautiful.

    I had spent way too much money and had to cut the trip short so I could pick up my car on Friday. My last night there I ate at the Pink House where they actually played parlor music. It reminded me of the Tavern on the Green in New York City with it's ambience. The entire evening was like being back in the time of gracious men and women like Jane Austen and the writers of her genre. Although I sat there alone and was not going to leave the tip an entire table would, my waiter treated me like I was royalty. No wonder that restaurant is a legend. The next morning, on the way out of town, I ran by and got my little man wine holder. He took up the entire back seat of the car and was much heavier that I had thought. I was damn glad I hadn't tried to haul him across town. I was on my way out of town and I regretted it. Savannah is a dream compared to most places. People are polite. What a concept! I prayed this would not be my last vacation.

I was grateful to Deborah and Pauly for holding down the fort. Deborah was one of those people who was amazingly willing to carry someone else's load. She looked after my cats, watered my orchids, whatever I needed. And she did it without complaint. Pauly Brown was someone who always personified the word lady. You enjoyed working the days that Pauly worked. She was kind, sincere and pretty much liked everybody. Great people. Allen and Darlene were so much fun to be around. They were huge animal lovers. I liked to think about the people I was coming home to. Its really great to know someone was worth coming back to.

As warned, the car cost two thousand dollars, plus. That was a crappy end to a great trip. I am glad, when faced with the choice, I didn't miss Savannah. It was worth it. Especially since I got to do it by myself. Well, Charlie and me.

SHOULD HAVE HAD MY BRAINS APPRAISED

After I got home from Savannah, it was back to work time. One night after work, my phone rang. Surprisingly, it was Carlton, from the Labor Day party. He said he wasn't much of a talker, but somehow the call lasted a good hour. I got a favorable impression and was reassured by the number of acquaintances we had in common. Although I liked what I heard, I had gotten several boo impressions from friends who said he drank too much. Hell, when did I ever let that ruin a relationship? Just about every time. Being me, I decided to keep an open mind. I hate it when other people make up my mind for me. After that first call, he would call every couple of days. During the flurry of calls, it came to our attention that we both loved golf. I didn't know about him, but I was really reluctant to start another affair. I had a feeling that the next one, if there were a next one, would be my last and then I was slamming the damn doors forever. But, I'd talk golf with anybody. We made plans to meet at Morehead City Country Club late in October for a round. It had been years since I played and I didn't even have clubs anymore so the intent was I would ride around with him. That lasted three holes until I grabbed his seven iron and played the whole rest of the course with the it. Did a really poor job of it, too, I must say. I must have made a decent impression of my willingness to make a fool of myself because he asked me to dinner. He did say I had a nice swing. After dinner, we both drove to my condo on the ocean to walk the beach. I liked him because he was very well dressed, had good manners and was a good looking man. He was a total delight at a dinner table. By occupation, he was a real estate appraiser. It would be nice to date someone after all those years who actually had a job. You know? All in all, he'd been in real estate about twenty five years. He was kind of quiet but clearly intelligent so it wasn't from lack of good sense. I hate to admit it, but he still reminded me of Gary. Only in the Country Club thing and how he dressed, though. Nothing else.

      He drove down from Raleigh about every two days for weeks. I couldn't believe it. I wouldn't let him stay the night or have sex, but he kept coming. One night we made out some on the beach and I told him in no uncertain terms that there were a lot of girls on the island who would jump at the chance to have sex with him the night they met, but I wasn't one of them, so he was taking his chances running back and forth to Raleigh.

      I was still going to Raleigh several days a week to see my good pal, Ernie, but so far we hadn't run into Carlton. Then, one night at Winston's, there he was. I was dancing my butt off and I must say, I did look good. I must have danced with ten guys but it didn't seem to turn Carlton off. He said he liked to watch me dance. He also like to tease me about being in the "Hall of Fame" at Memories. That night he ended up going back to Ernie's with me and the next morning we slept together for the first time. After that, the three of us went everywhere together and Carlton and I grew closer and closer. Played a lot of golf, too. Naturally, the day came when he wanted me to stay over at his house instead of Ernie's. I really felt bad about that but I also felt bad about abusing Ernie's friendship by making him put up with someone who was my friend if he didn't want to, although he had never said anything. I think he liked having people around and I know he liked to see me having a good time. He hated the whole Ray thing and felt he didn't push me enough to look into what he had heard. Ernie still didn't get that I had to learn for myself. Unfortunately.

      I won't go into the condition of Carlton's apartment. No, it wasn't dirty but you couldn't see the top of anything either. He worked more and harder than anybody I had ever met. He would get up at six in the morning, and head into the kitchen where he had his "office" set up. He generally let me sleep until about eight and then he would make me breakfast. Great guy, huh? It wasn't until one very special morning when he hollered for me to get up that I learned he often surfed naked ladies on the Internet instead of working. Now look. I can understand that appraising can be boring. This particular morning, he woke me to show me his favorite porn star. Obviously, he was a man who was drawn to very petite blonds. This lady was standing on her head, stark naked. The naked girl was from North Carolina and is now on national TV, all cleaned up. Unfortunately, I am someone who is gargantuanly (not a word) turned off by this. He had been honest enough to tell me that he lost two wives running on them and had just broken up with his last girlfriend, but he hadn't mentioned this part. Apparently he saved some of his favorites in his documents because he told me I was not allowed anywhere near his computer. Worked for me. He didn't know I was not someone who surreptitiously looked through other people's stuff. I was smart enough to know there was a good chance I'd see something that I didn't want to know. Somehow, I miss the draw in that. I had done the drawer surfing often enough when I was younger, but I had learned my lesson. I'm telling you, stay out of other people's stuff. Its for your own good. You know, like finding a naked female standing on her head. Therefore, there wasn't a chance in hell I was going to touch his computer. Right after we started dating he told me he was "off the market" and I took that literally. Foolish girl. I didn't know what he meant, but it sure wasn't what I thought. So much for being crazy about me. A man doesn't get it that showing a girl another naked girl lies somewhere in the area of ridiculous? Fellas, don't do it. Ever. And another thing, do not sit there and tell your girl what it is about the naked female that you like. Stupid move. Huge.

On top of the upside-down naked girl at Carlton's, jolly events were going on at work that had unseen repercussions. I had recently gotten a new computer and bought a ream of paper just for my own use. A guy named Roy was my current mentor. Only he and I knew how to use the computer. We spent the day setting it up and getting it understood by everybody else that they were not to touch it until I felt comfortable with their training. When I came in the very next morning, all the paper was gone. Five hundred pages. I got pissed and started looking for what happened. Since Roy was the only one trained, I went straight for his desk even though I didn't expect to find anything there. I thought perhaps he had taken some of the paper out because the printer was too full. Another naive move from this baby child. There were some printed pages from the tutorial on his desk, but that was all. Since I wasn't expecting anything nefarious, I thought maybe he had printed the whole tutorial and opened his top drawer. Normally, not one to go through other people's stuff, it came as a complete shock (told you, didn't I? Don't do it) to me that about 475 pages of the missing pages were in his drawer. Every single had naked women. Every damn one of them. Some of them were doing some real butt-ugly stuff to each other. Ew!

It was a good bet that Roy didn't know I was aware of the cool little History button on the web. I hit it and started wandering through the naked women sites he had been looking at the night before. You would have thought the sumbitch didn't go home at all. My favorite was "Café Flesh." Nobody should ever see this site. It was gross. Roy didn't know it, but he was gone. Outta there. If it had not been near Christmas, I would have fired him that day. We closed December 16th, two days after I found this trash. I waited until we opened the 3rd of January and fired him at five o'clock. And, told him why. Since I had thrown away 475 sheets of naked women, he probably had surmised that I knew about them. He lost his job and 475 of the women. Wouldn't five or ten have been enough? I might have let that go. I doubt it, though. Good grief.

Getting back to the romantic side of events, several things happened in quick succession that were guideposts not to be ignored. Of course, I did. One was the night Ernie stopped by and wanted to go for a drink. Carlton said he couldn't go, but the two of us could take a run to his favorite restaurant and bring him back something to eat. That was cool and I had missed Ernie so off we went. We were having our second drink and they had just put Carlton's dinner in front of us when he came in the door, furious. Didn't we know he was starving? Lord, he acted like we had intentionally just sat there and let his food get cold. Hell, I paid as soon as they put his plate down and didn't even have my change yet. When I told him that, he grabbed his food and left. Very angry. I have to admit, I had second thoughts. It was very uncalled for behavior, and he embarrassed me in front of Ernie and the bartender. Ernie and I just looked at each other without saying a word. I was humiliated. No doubt it was a defining moment in the relationship, but I was too stupid to know what the definition was. If he was crazy about me, it didn't show.

I jumped into the car, red faced with either humiliation or anger, to head back to Carlton's. I knew Ernie wanted to snatch me right out of my car and drag me home with him. He wasn't really big on guys treating me like that. It must have been a difficult moment for him. One part of me felt bad and the other was furious with Carlton. Why can't love crap always stay in the getting to know you stage when everybody is behaving? Why the hell do we have to meet the real thing? I am sure Carlton felt the same way, damn it. All my clothes were there. I would have to go back to get them and probably hear how rude I am all over again. Trying to go back and get things in order, I missed my turn. I didn't know where I was. I hadn't driven there in the dark before so I was not sure what turns to take. The next thing that happened, while I was turning around, confused, was my cell phone went off and Carlton cussed me out, wanting to know where the hell I was. I didn't know where the hell I was. I was so mad I could have chewed my front teeth to a nub. I am sure he didn't think I was mad, because he settled down and gave me directions. When I got to the house, he sat me on the sofa and lectured me on behavior. It was obvious that he didn't know me that well. Bad move. Feelings shifted. I could literally feel the shift. This was the first catalyst that changed the whole relationship. All of a sudden, he had assumed power. In his mind. I also gave it to him. However, I did not give him power over my mind. That's different. It was just a matter of time now.

Still stinging somewhat from that little behavior correction, the next guide post to disaster was one day when we were driving from house to house for one of his appraisals. He brought his last girlfriend into the conversation. He mentioned he was still talking to her. I just kept my mouth shut and let him bury himself. He was talking about her having mental problems. Not that she was crazy, but that she couldn't handle emotional relationships. He indicated she was very jealous, in love and wanted to get married, but her boyfriend didn't and she couldn't handle it. This whole conversation was taking place only about six months after Carlton broke up with her. She had only been dating her new boyfriend for twelve weeks. I found it odd that a woman would talk about marrying a guy she hadn't known more than three months to a guy she dated for five years. But, that's just me. I kept my mouth shut and let him keep talking. Let that string lengthen until it's long enough to hang them, I say. Finally, he said that they had lunch from time to time and he tried to help. I couldn't have possibly gotten any quieter. What happened to the "off the market" thing? Why would someone get upset about me being with my best friend if they were still seeing their old girlfriend? How many standards do we want to apply to this pot, huh? I knew Carlton well enough that if he was still seeing her, there was a good chance it was sexual. He had mentioned to me one day that the "only" reason he drove back and forth from Morehead to Raleigh so much was I was his best bet of getting some. He didn't put it that way but that's what he meant. Maybe, while I was still saying "no", she was his best bet. Something to think about, huh? THIS PISSED ME OFF. I had gotten tired of ranting and raving with men and have adopted a new attitude. It's called having an ATTITUDE.

    I waited until we got to his house, went in, started putting my crap together, got into the car, cranked it and pointed that car's front end toward Morehead. He was following my every step, literally begging me not to go. When I pulled out, he started running behind the car. He kept hollering, "Didn't I know he was crazy about me?"I lost sight of him when I took the curve but he was still there until then. It reminded me of the movie, Shane. That movie broke my heart. Once I couldn't see him anymore, I felt terrible about his running down the road behind me like that. I had never had a guy try so hard to keep me from leaving. You know what I mean, they always pull the "don't let the door hit you in the ass routine." Carlton was devastated and showed it. Why don't guys always act like that? Naturally, being the dumbwat I am, I turned around, and there he was, still standing in the road. I drove back to his house and decided to wait until five o'clock to make a final decision. He went back to work, and we never discussed it again. But it was a catalyst. You can only survive so many of them in a relationship. I have learned once they start, they come one after another like waves on the beach. I do not operate well in the tumbling cycle. Once I get back up on my feet, I usually start walking. Away.

    Just to further confuse the issue, I learned he wanted to use me before I could use him. He started pushing to move to the beach; obviously in with me. I had always wanted to move to Raleigh or somewhere to get away from here. I, too, now had someone to move in with, and tried to get him to let me move in with him but his heart was set on moving to the beach. I felt at this point that I was not "in love" anymore, but still had a relationship. I was pretty sure it had been about moving here all the time, not about me. The dinners and the wine were conversation not romanticism. But, at worst, we had become good friends. I think Carlton thought I was still in love, but I wasn't nor was I implying it. I did expect respect as long as we were dating. Love was a wrong assumption. The catalysts had taken care of that. I let him move in with my two golden retrievers, my cat and my parrot. He didn't like animals, smells or hair. Who would have thought it would ever work? Not me. Let him learn. I didn't have anything to lose. I had been fussed at before.

I tell you what, though. I gotta give the guy credit for giving awesome Christmas gifts. One year he gave me a whole set of Callaway irons. To me, Callaway is the best in the business and these were brand ass new. It breaks my heart every time I have to cut about seven inches off a set of new clubs, but what are you going to do when you are a munchkin? I had never in my life had someone give me a gift of true value. His gifts were not only monetary, but he cared enough to give me the very best. It wasn't a Hallmark card or red roses. He knew how I loved Callaways because they were his clubs. I still have them. I will always have them. If they weren't so damn uncomfortable, I'd sleep with the damn things.

Another year, he gave me an Alan Cheek painting. Alan Cheek was our "famous" local painter. Carlton had been taking me places because he wanted to make up for the fact that I had never seen what the County and the area I was born in had to offer for so many tourists to want to come here. This man was kind enough to introduce me to the county in which I was born but never had the money or means to explore. He didn't get that I didn't give a damn about seeing it prior to meeting him and that finally wanting to see it was mostly because he was so impressed with it. One weekend, he took me to Ocracoke. I have to admit I liked Ocracoke. Everybody does. At one point, we drove down a narrow lane where he showed me a quaint shack that sat out in the water. This painting was of that exact spot. It's called Crystal Lake and it was reproduced on canvas. It was another gift I didn't know he had in him. It is so well done that the water seems to change colors with the sunrise and sunset. It's just beautiful. Feeling as grumpy as I did, I wondered why he would be so generous with his spirit. Carlton was at his very best when it came to Christmas gifts. He always said later that when he gave the Alan Cheek to me, it was our's. That sucker is mine.

But, despite everything, the pets continued to be a problem. Bacall was my parrot. She had been an absolute delight to me for six years. I kept her in the office and the tourist kids loved her to death and ran to my office to see her when they arrived. I didn't let anybody touch her because she was in complete control and would take pieces and parts off you if she wanted to. The people who sold her to me said she was trained, but, darling, this was not a trained bird. I started working with her because I had trained birds before, but never one so intelligent that you could tell she knew exactly what you were saying. She made it clear when she was not in the mood for you. I had paid fifteen hundred for her and twelve hundred for the cage. She was an investment, people, but I loved her too. She had florescent blue wings and her underside was a scarlet red. Bacall had eyes that would look right at you and let you know if you were boring her to damn tears.

One morning, I went into the office to work with her awhile. She was talking well and seemed to be a happy, but pugnacious bird. She was about eight to nine inches long and known as an Eclectic. I was going to get a male and name him Bogie after Mama's favorite movie stars. In my research, I found out males are much more gentle and responsive. That didn't matter to me because she was so beautiful, I didn't regret getting her first for one moment. Until that morning. I opened her cage because she liked to stand on the door. She seldom got off the cage, but if she did, she would quickly run back to it if I came after her. This particular morning, I opened the cage and reached in for her food. She was already on the door and I got too close to her without begging her to be nice. She leaned over and grabbed my top lip. Damn, just like Mama used to. Only this time her top beak went through my lip and her bottom beak met it halfway. I had a full size parrot attached to my face. She would not let go. They don't, you know. I was standing there with a bird holding onto my lip and not moving. Blood was running from my lips down my face and onto my clothes. I was having a major "OW!" moment, but couldn't speak because I had a bird dangling there. Panicked and in pain, all I could think of was they always told us not to hit a bird, and I really didn't want to but she was coming close. I couldn't say anything or move either. If I moved, her whole weight would be dangling off my face. I don't know why she let go, I think it was the taste of the blood. Her head was only an inch from mine when she got this confused look on her face. She let go and started licking her lips, For Christ's sake. All in all, it had lasted about three minutes, I think. I took off for the office refrigerator and grabbed a bag of frozen Hunan Chicken and slammed it up against my face. What would you have done? It was the only thing available and I knew my lip was swelling. I had blood all over the front of me. I could envision what I was going to look like when everybody got there in the next few minutes. Charlie, my Irish salesman, suddenly walked in the door. I swung around in surprise, still holding my chicken bag to my lip when he took one look at me, started to say something, but thought better of it, I guess. He promptly turned around and left. He told me later he couldn't handle blood. No kidding. Me either.

I had her for six years when we started having a serious health issue. She started chewing on her foot. She had been doing it for two years, but it got so bad, she took skin and pieces from her foot. One day, she finally chewed one "toe" almost off. Needless to say, she must have been in deep pain and was a very, grumpy bird. Mean bird, really. The people at the pet shop where I got her, my Vet and I had been desperately trying to save her foot. For those two years, we tried everything. One vet told me she was psychotic and prescribed haldol, or something like that. It was for people on the fourth floor of Dix Hospital. The only people on the fourth floor of Dix are mental patients at their worst. To make it even scarier, when I went to have it filled, instead of the prescribed .05 mg, the pharmacist filled it at .5mg which would have killed her. I had decided on the four hour trip home that I was not giving my bird that medication. No how, no way.

The next move was to take her to the NC State Veterinarian Hospital. This place was not cheap, let me tell you. We tried everything. Finally, the decision was made to take off her toes. Over time, it became her foot and then her leg up to what is comparable to our knee joint. She was living in the bottom of a cat litter box because she could no longer climb. She was pissed and would take it out on the Vet students. My heart was broken. And so was my wallet. When she wasn't being taken back and forth to Raleigh to the vet hospital, I was taking her back and forth to the shop where I bought her so we could change her bandages. She was so mean from the pain that one person had to hold her while another changed the bandages. The owner told me she would not charge me for the food Bacall ate while she was there which I thought was great. She knew how much I was spending taking her back and forth to the Vet Hospital. Finally, when we took her leg to the knee, we seemed to have corrected whatever it was. The day they took part of her leg off and I saw her hopping around, I cried like a baby. It didn't seem to bother her at all. Probably because she wasn't in pain anymore after it healed. They finally decided she must have had a bone infection that had been there for years for it to have gotten that bad. She was one year old when I bought her she probably already had it. Hell, those shop people had been so good to me, I didn't hold it against them. From beginning to end, this took three years of stress and strain on her part and mine.

We then incurred another problem. I noticed she was much happier when the guy at the shop was around than when I was. You just know his name was Charlie. No kidding. I let her stay at the shop when I went to Raleigh. I knew she loved me, but she was happiest with Charlie. She deserved to be happy after all she had been through and I think that came with being with Charlie, not me. He had put her box right beside the cash register and most of the time, she had his full attention. At the office, she screamed all day because she wanted the same attention and I couldn't give it to her. There was also the sad fact that he was the only one with whom she was truly tame. She adored him. She loved being at the shop which was full of birds and noises and bird calls. I finally went over there one day and gave her to him. I told him I wanted visitation rights and to let me know if she got sick again. I never went there again. I think of her all the time but I miss her most when I drive by the shop. Someone who went there told me Charlie eventually took her home where he had three birds. Scratch one bird who cost six thousand dollars overall. I didn't mind losing the money so much because it was over a period of time. But, I lost Bacall. Broke my heart. Her leaving made Carlton happy but he saw what Bacall and I went through trying to get her healthy, and he clearly had felt sorry for both of us during that very difficult time.

    I still had my darlings, the golden retrievers. These babies and I had loved each other for twelve years. They were awesome pals. I dearly loved the natural smiles given to them by God. When I would come home from work, I would fix myself a glass of wine, grab a good book and park my butt on the couch. The minute I got settled, Ginger would come over with that "party time" look on her face that could not be denied. She also showed up with a disgusting tennis ball in her mouth. These sweethearts were fun and easy to please. They could have more fun in a house than I could outside. One of our rituals was when I would sit on the couch, one dog to my left, one dog to my right and the coffee table in the center. I would throw the ball off to the right into the hallway and off they would go. Whoever got it was determined by the bounces of the ball and what it might bounce off. However, whoever got it would return and sit on my right, the other would run around the coffee table and park herself on my left. Then I would throw it again. If the previous loser got the ball this time, she would head to my right and the other would head to the spot on my left. They did this automatically. They almost always shared the ball equally but never showed that was their intent. They went after it with a vengeance, but most of the time, one got it every other time. I certainly had never taught it to them. This happened every time I threw the ball. It was their favorite game. They liked it more than the water which worked for me because a wet, salty, sandy golden retriever is a sad sight to behold. It's also something you don't want on your carpets.

These doll babies were sisters; given to me by my sister, MaryBeth. Ginger was the large, soft, fluffy one with hair everywhere. She had the fur of a lion and her head looked like that of a lion. Sandy colored, with streaks of soft white running threw her coat, she had that big smile on her face and that "I love you" look in her large, sienna colored eyes. Ginger was a goof ball. She reveled in being a silly dog. Not stupid, just silly. The clown of the house. I worshiped her. Cinnamon resembled an Irish Setter more than a retriever. She was tall, with beautiful red with feathers under her torso and below her tail, which was always pointed straight back. She held herself very erect, with her head high. Cinnamon always looked like she was either listening to you or avidly waiting for you to say something. You never failed to have her complete attention. She was extremely intelligent and knew exactly what you were thinking before you said it. Cinnamon craved love and attention and was devoted to me. She was always staring in your eyes to see what you wanted so she could make you happy. They were very funny and sweet and I loved them without restraint. I didn't give a damn about the hair all over the place. I didn't care what Carlton thought. They were there before he was. They didn't put me down, either. At night, Ginger would lie on my side of the bed with her head lolling over the surface of the mattress, so she could look at me. Cinnamon would be on the side beside Carlton. I knew he loved it but he wouldn't say so. I think he always favored Cinnamon because of it. Aja would also be on the bed, but not close to anyone.

After Carlton had been there about a year full of a whole lot of bickering, I began to notice Ginger had a swelling on her left hip. She had always had it, but it looked bigger. When I took her to the vet, she told me not to worry about it, it could be arthritis. It had gotten bigger and bigger over the years and except for a small limp it never seemed to bother her. I was always concerned that it kept growing. I had never seen anything like that without it being a problem. But the vet said not to worry. Ginger still acted so good natured, running around without holding back so I did what I was told. Something I am not known for. When they were thirteen, though, she seemed less able to exercise freely without limping harder so I took her back to the vet. Understand, this issue came up every time we went to the vet and I always got the same answer, "don't worry about it." On this trip, the vet seemed troubled about something she saw. For some reason, she focused on Ginger's mouth. She thought Ginger might have a tooth infection and she wanted me to bring her back the next day for a simple tooth operation. I hardly thought that would make her limp less but perhaps the tooth problem was worse.

When I went to pick her up, the vet said when she cut into Ginger, a smell hit her that was overpowering and rotten, so she sewed her back up. Apparently, that lump on her leg must of been cancerous and was clearly beyond her help. This from a vet I questioned constantly about that leg. I was furious. I could not believe that in all that time, she didn't take one single x-ray of my dog's leg to make sure she was alright. Ought to be a law that vets like that be put away for life.

When Ginger came into the room it was like she was in a daze. She looked like she didn't know where she was. She clearly didn't know who I was or that I was in the room. This from a dog that always, always ran straight for me when she saw me. Ginger, this time, did not even sense my presence. The vet said she thought should have been Ginger should have been over the anesthetic, but felt she would be over it soon. I paid my $400.00 for an operation she didn't do and took my sweetheart home.

At no point did Ginger come out of it. I began to feel like she was brain damaged. That's how I felt about it. Dread settled into me. That night she fell going down the steps to the ground level. I had to carry her the last four or five steps. I had to almost pick her 80 pound, limp body up to get her to the elevator to get her back into the condo. Once I got her back upstairs, I sat on the floor with her, wrapped my arms around her and just sat there. I still didn't think she knew what was going on around her. That included not recognizing Cinnamon with whom she had bonded since she was a puppy. Cinnamon sat back and watched her with a worried look on her face. This from a dog. She knew. I knew. I told Carlton I didn't think she would make it through the night. When I went to bed, she was in the hallway, panting hard, but not moving. She wouldn't eat or take water. I could not go to sleep. I got up at two a.m. to check on her. She wouldn't move or respond to me although she was able to look at me one time. Just one time there seemed to be a glimpse of recognition. I brought out a blanket and coaxed her onto it. Once I had her on the blanket, I gently pulled it into the back bedroom. I didn't want Cinnamon to get up and see her dying. And she was clearly dying. I laid down with her, wrapped my arms around her and hummed to her until she quit breathing. About four in the morning, Ginger died in my arms. I fell completely apart. I couldn't breathe for crying. It was like I had no breath in my body and I was starved for it. I could hear Cinnamon scratching at the door, wanting to come in. It killed me to think how it would affect her.

    I kept the door closed because I didn't want Cinnamon to get in. Closed or not, Cinnamon would not leave. When the office opened, I called Conrad, my maintenance man and right hand. While I took Cinnamon in the other bedroom, he came and took Ginger to be cremated. When I got her back, I spread her ashes over the small maritime growth left by Hurricane Floyd between my condo and the ocean. That way, every time I looked out the window toward the ocean, I would see her and know where she was. I didn't realize it would make me cry so often but I wouldn't have done it any differently. It was Easter when I lost Ginger.

    Whoever "they" are, they say that dogs that have been together all their lives will mourn the other when it dies. They were right. I never believed it until I saw it happen. Cinnamon was destroyed. I don't know if she could pick up the death smell or just missed her, but she kept going to that bedroom door and lying down. There was none of the peppy alertness she always had even at thirteen. She would look at me like she wanted me to say something she could understand. She started to go downhill quickly. It started with her not wanting to eat or drink. She only did it to please me, her favorite thing. I took her back to the vet, but the vet said she was probably still in mourning. I mentioned that perhaps she needed to be checked over. Maybe x-rayed, for Christ's sake, but the vet said no, it wasn't necessary. About two weeks later, she wouldn't stand, wouldn't go out, wouldn't eat or drink. She was getting emaciated. I knew my beautiful retriever, Cinnamon, was dying. We took her to the vet. I didn't want her to die on the floor not knowing who I was, like Ginger. She showed no response while we did the procedure except, like Ginger, she looked at me just before she died. They were both gone. Cinnamon only lasted six weeks after Ginger died. It killed me. I threw her ashes over the maritime forest where Ginger was so they would be together forever. Carlton watched me grieve and I can cry for months when I lose an animal. Two and it tears me apart. It was Memorial Day. Now I only had Aja, my cat. She was already nineteen. I was traumatized.

I'd had Aja since I was married to Dave. She was the only link I had left of Lancaster and all the memories from there. Dave had brought her home one night after his midnight shift. He found her on the side of the road beside her mother, who had been hit by a car. Neither Dave nor I were cat lovers, being all about dogs, but what were we to do? She worked out well because she simply made a home for herself. All I had to do was get used to the cat box. Other than that she settled right into a house with seven dogs and a parrot. My first parrot had died right after we moved home. She never got in the way, scratched the furniture or caused any trouble. She just became more and more beautiful as she got older. I never let her out because I didn't want to lose her. She was clearly a full blue-point. Having varying touches of sand colors in her fur, she had a touch of siamese with big, beautiful blue eyes. When I had gone to see Mama, I always took Aja and Tuborg.

For years, the most irritating issue with Aja was she had never been interested in me or anything I did. She was not affectionate the entire first ten years I had her. After I lost the dogs, she started coming into my lap, purring and rubbing against me like she had been doing it forever. It was quite a culture shock. Perhaps she could never get to me for the dogs before. I had always had them. Until now. She had always slept on the bed but now she curved up against the back of my knee, a warm presence all night long. I wouldn't move at night for fear of making her move. I didn't care if Carlton liked her or not, she was all I had left. Because she was seventeen, and I was spooked about losing my retrievers, I found a new vet and had her checked. He said she was good to go, especially for her age.

About this time, Carlton and I had a chance to move into a house of three thousand square feet on the sound side of Beacons Reach. We jumped at it. I think I forgot I didn't have all those animals to fill it up now. But that's ok, because they were right across the street. I could visit any time I wanted. They would have loved it. I admit, I had been wanting to get away from the ocean after Hurricane Floyd's waters were practically right at my feet and I had all my animals to worry about. We moved to this big, gorgeous house, fully furnished for twelve hundred a month. It had porch for the orchids and enormous decks for my plants. It was less than a half mile from work. No mileage on my car. Worked for me. It was a steal. However, the owners were happy because I had Conrad and if anything needed any kind of maintenance, I offered to do it free as long as it was something Conrad could do.

Soon after moving in, I felt the hair standing up on the back of my neck. It was odd because this time I did not get the usual friendly ghost feeling. I told Carlton there was a ghost in the house. Being smarter than me, he scoffed at me. I waited for it to show me what it was about. I started hearing noises above the master bedroom coming from the very large office above. It was in the office at night. Carlton scoffed. He did that often.

I found out the house had been built by the mayor of the town. His son, who was in his forties, had moved home because his marriage was falling apart. Apparently, the father and son had a very nasty argument about the son needing to put his life back together. Easily said, but not always easily done. Instead, the son walked over to the beach, sat down, and shot himself in the head. A couple of months later, the father died, without warning. We were the first to move in after this. My queasy feelings did not tell me the ghost was in the office during the day. As we moved our things in, I got to go from room to room and felt comfortable in each. I even felt ok in the office, although somewhat cautious. Carlton put his appraisal stuff in the office and looked perfectly comfortable there.

I was alone at home one day, still looking for places to put things. It was time to move miscellaneous items that weren't used often that I wouldn't throw away. Namely junk. I decided to move these into the attic. It had one of those doors that had that long sqe-e-e-ek when you opened it. Like in a movie about ghosts and Halloween. You know the sound. After hearing that and feeling jumpy, I entered the room. I stopped in my tracks. The most eerie feeling came over me. It was a feeling I had never experienced and I didn't like it at all. I felt pure evil emanating from that attic. It was the worse response to a possible ghost I had ever had. I fled. I mean it. I ran out of there and I didn't plan on ever going in there again. It had a lock on it. Every now and then, I would check it and it would be unlocked. Carlton swore he hadn't done it. I got so bad, I wouldn't even enter the adjoining bedroom.

A few months after we moved in, I was doing some yard cleaning when I discovered a dead dogwood tree right in front of me. It was only about six feet tall so I knew it had been planted in the last year or so. It was odd because dogwoods usually flourish in this area. Hell, they grow wild. It had a stone marker in front of it inscribed "Scott's tree." Scott was the son who had killed himself.

Dead son, dead tree. Is somebody trying to tell me something? Weirded me completely out. Look people, weird or not, I didn't put that tree there and I was not about to dig it up nor would I throw it away. Somebody else could, but I wasn't.

Within six months, I could tell Carlton wondered about things. It wasn't long after that Carlton was with me in bed one night when he said, "We really do have a ghost here, don't we?" Sure do, fella. He had become a believer. It was hard not to in that house. We heard sounds every single night that sounded like someone was walking around in the office upstairs. Not some nights, every night. They didn't keep you awake, but if you were awake, you couldn't miss them. Just walking across the floor, that's all. Heavy steps, like a man would make. That didn't bother me because whoever or whatever it was, was upstairs, not standing beside me. It didn't seem to scare me unless I approached that attic. It was like we had two ghosts. The son, trapped in the attic; The father, trapped in the office. Woo-woo.

I have to admit life was not so good with bad boy Carlton. He was a nice guy and very thoughtful. Unfortunately, that seemed to be to other people, not me. I felt he had contempt for me for the very reasons I told him he would if he moved in with me. I am what I am. I was never rich. I was never sophisticated. Even worse, I couldn't seem to do anything right. Of course, when he first started dating me, he told me I was the first woman who cooked for him in sixteen years. Then, it was more like "can't you cook anything else?" Christ, the guy had been eating out all his adult life and had his choice of a million restaurants, chefs and menu choices. How was I supposed to compete with that? Who wanted to? Not me. Not anymore. Then he screamed at me, literally lost it, because I dried his towels. His towels! He told me if his towels were in the washing machine when I needed it, to take them out, put them in a plastic bag and he would dry them when he got home. Good grief, guy. Oh, then there were the odors. He freaked when one of my cleaners used Pine Sol on the very large tile floor. He demanded the cleaners never use chemicals with odors, including Clorox. And he meant me, too. I do realize some people have more sensitive noses than others, but at the time, to me it was just one more thing after another. Lord Almighty, I was still grieving. I was really not in the mood for the crap being thrown at me. Working together? Oh that was hell, guys. He and I were at complete odds. I wasn't quite sure why he thought I could afford his suggestions, but wouldn't say so. He kept telling me what to do without realizing that I almost never do what people tell me to. Damn it, I can't help it. Its in my genes. There was the lack of money to do the things he wanted, but he couldn't accept that, either. To him, it was me being obstinate. Not at all. I thought some of his ideas were excellent, but when I didn't implement them, silence, cold shoulder, contempt.

  The relationship was in melt down. I felt he got what he wanted which was to have a way to move to the beach until he established himself. I am sure a lot of it was my fault because with my parrot going away, my goldens dying one behind the other, I was not up to trying at the time. My grief tends to hang around. I had always had a dog since Denny gave me Tuborg. I had seven dogs at one point. Now I had none. I tried as much as I was capable, having a kiss my ass attitude and having to give away and lose my pets. What chance did this relationship have? Nada, Vada. She was going to be seriously disappointed.

  His two kids, Peter and David, came down from Raleigh to see him. It was the first time I had met David and I wanted desperately to make a good impression. Peter and I already got along very well, as far as I knew. I was striving to put on my best behavior. I forgot that their dad seemed to like to get drunkest when one of his kids came around. Why? I don't know. We went to dinner at Peter's favorite restaurant and Carlton sure didn't change his spots that night. I have to say, he is a happy drunk. His second wife told him he should get drunk more often. Now that I think about it, she had a point. But, he had some unpleasant habits while drunk that were hard to overlook.

  On that night, he decided he wanted to find Peter, who was dateless, someone to be with. He picked the waitress. Not quite drunk yet, he started to sing along with the music. To her. Then, he started to wiggle to the music while seated. Before long, up he got, like no one else in the restaurant might mind. Well, some did. Namely me and probably Peter, who was squirming more than I. Eventually, Carlton was boogeying beside the table, The waitress came over and joined him. Pissed me off. I kept asking him not to embarrass me in front of his sons. So much for crazy about me. I wonder why I was the one embarrassed?

  We finally got out of the restaurant, without the waitress, who promised to meet us. Oh joy. We headed to Memories, the resident shag club on the beach. Peter, David and I went no further than just inside the door, tucking ourselves against the wall while Carlton danced off to the bar. He was already smashed. Those of us huddled in the corner knew this was not going to be a night to remember. I take that back. Maybe it would. I was already pissed about the waitress and looking for trouble. He came back and out of the blue, he did something really stupid. He would have never in hell done it sober. He grabbed my ass. Hellfire flew through me. These were my friends in this club and nobody, but nobody was going to be seen grabbing my butt and getting away with it. I had never even left this club with someone I didn't come with. I was not some nasty slut. Man needed a lesson. Somehow, I grabbed the last two fingers of his right hand and twisted them so hard I got him down on his knees. I didn't know what I was going to grab, but it was going to be something and I planned to hurt it. It worked. He begged me to let go, which I agreed to only if he would never do it again. I let go. He grabbed me again. You know where. I got the fingers again. This time I wrenched them. The next thing you know, he's on the floor again, squirming with pain. I really hated that this was going on in front of his sons, but, hell, it was his choice. Maybe I was embarrassing him. I sure hoped so. After he begged and I got myself in a position where he couldn't get to it, I let him up. For years after that he bitched about me hurting him and embarrassing him in front of his kids. It never crossed his mind that it was my ass and who grabbed it was my decision. You can't grab me on a good day and after the restaurant fun and games, he was last on my list. He was pretty much last on all my lists by then. He didn't want to be my boyfriend by then, anyway.

While the tension grew in the house, I came home from work one day and couldn't find Aja anywhere. I searched for her for three days. I cried, I screamed, I walked the floors at night. I searched the house, the garage, the attic. If she was in the garage, it was ninety degrees in there. I knew she hadn't eaten or had anything to drink for three days. You know how scared I was of that attic. But I searched it. Three days after I started looking, I went into the garage again. I cried for her. Suddenly, there was this very low mewling sound. I cried out again and heard nothing. I started tearing things apart trying to see if she was out there. In a bag of clothes hangers, where she had fallen to the bottom and couldn't get out, was Aja. She was twenty years old. I ran her to the emergency vet where they told me she was severely dehydrated and probably wouldn't make it through the night. I asked them if she was in pain and should we put her down, though it would kill me to get a yes. They wanted to see how she would be in the morning. Of course, I went along with it, but she seemed so weak.

The next morning, they called. She had made it. They couldn't believe it, especially at her age. The vet told me the whole vet staff was amazed and involved with working with her. He said he couldn't believe, sick and all, she looked about five years old. She did, too. He told me most of them cried when they saw her alive the next morning. Next, he told me we had to put her down, anyway. It was time. She was tired and weak and didn't have the strength at her age to come out of it. It was his guess that she was looking for somewhere to die and found it. She would start to suffer. I knew he was right. I drove up and we did it.

I couldn't drive back. I sat in his parking lot for hours trying to stop crying long enough to get home. When I could at least see through my swollen eyes, I drove the forty minutes it took to get home. I went out into the room I used to read in with Aja on my lap and I stayed there. I couldn't eat. When Carlton tried to talk to me, I couldn't speak. The stress of losing all of them was more than I thought I could take. After a few days, I tried to go to work. I went into the office, then into my office, closed the door and just sat there. A glass office, like in next to Mr Stanache's. It seemed a good idea up to then. Everybody left me alone. It took me months to get over the loss of Aja. She's buried in MaryBeth's backyard. My sister, God Love her, got her a marker with her name on it. That's all I can say.

I still cry today when I think about Muff, Tuborg, Ti, Honey, Aja, Ginger & Cinnamon, or Bacall. That is in the order in which I got them, not necessarily the order in which I loved them. When people talked to me about getting a new pet, I said I couldn't do it. MaryBeth and I figured out that it had been forty years since I had not had a dog, cat, bird or something to keep me company. Sometimes anything that is an animal or bird that could breathe was better than people. I was simply not good at the people part.

Truly not in the mood to party, a set of Carlton's golfing buddies came down. I will say this, no matter how badly we were getting along, he kept me in the golfing part. He was always willing to call me and have me join the guys in the bar after the game and they always seemed to welcome me. Often we would go out to dinner either alone or with friends. Good times. The night his buddies came down, I had been melancholy all day, but I met them for drinks and then we went to Memories. Carlton had told me in the past he didn't like a woman to hang on him. When he went out, he wanted to talk to his buddies. Ok. Fine. I didn't want to hang on him, anyway. When I got there, I grabbed every damn guy I could get my hands on and danced song after song. And drank. After forty minutes of not hanging on him, all he did the entire time was talk to one girl, not his buddies. I had run out of guys to dance with, so what was I supposed to do? I walked up to say hello. I decided to try being nice. Maybe this was a really good friend of his he hadn't seen in awhile. It happened all the time at the beach. Once I walked up, he said hello to me with a blank look on his face. Like he didn't know me. Or want to. After a minute, he took her by the arm and walked her over to the guys to introduce her. Left me standing there. Oh, and he hadn't introduced her to me. When he introduced her to the guys, I realized she was the girl that kept calling him in Raleigh even after he and I started dating. She called one night when I was there and he told her he wasn't dating anybody else. Apparently, he didn't see fit to tell her that I was the girl he had been talking about or that I still existed. I would have found it hard to believe that in the four years he had lived with me, he hadn't heard from her. Maybe if I had been in better spirits. Maybe this, maybe that. My defenses were all over the place.

    I had a hissy fit. In public. Damn, I hate that. Right there in front of God and everybody, I cashed in my chips. I had been carrying the grabbing my ass crap, the cooking crap, the dryer crap, the not loving my animals and me not having them anymore to love crap and all of it and laid him out. Loudly, as they say. And, it was an in your face lay out. Then, I left him there to do whatever the hell he chose because it sure as hell didn't matter to me. The last catalyst had rolled into this relationship. There wasn't anything left he could do to affect me. It was clear I didn't interest him anymore, in bed or otherwise. It was clear I was not interested in him anymore. Just like with Bobby, we just lived together. Period. A day getting along here and there isn't enough. I know Carlton had his version, but he ain't writing this. This is my story and I am sticking to it. He told me about old cows. I had become an old cow and was damn ecstatic about it. Chew on that cud, why don't you?

    If you have never heard of the old cow theory, I sure as hell didn't come up with it. I don't know who to thank for it but it's simple to understand. If you have a guy who's never been to bed with you, you have his interest. Consequently, you are a new cow. Pretty much the minute you go to bed with him, you are an old cow. Men are geared to want the one they have never had. Listen to them deny it. If you believe them, you deserve what you have coming. Maybe it's a left brain/right brain thing, I don't know. Nor do I care. I do find it frightfully right on. Women, for the most part, are not geared to wanting the new bull. They will stick with the old bull through thick and thin. They grieve for damn years when he lets them down; knowing he is going to let them down; knowing they are an old cow who is never going to be a damn new cow again. By the time the woman walks out, she's worn thin. Once they are out, they stay out. They do their grieving before they go out the door. The guy's grieving just starts. And people wonder why we can't all get along? One's going out and one's coming in, that's why. I'm an old cow and I don't give a damn. Door's shut.

    Like I said, things had been going down at the hacienda. Being good? Don't even think about it. The only thing I had left to offer was good manners, which I put into play. He had moved upstairs. Polite was the order of the day. I was done going out with Carlton. Especially to Memories. He only went when he was drunk so everybody there, and I mean everybody, including my friends, thought he was a full time drunk like Bobby. It wasn't fair. He wasn't. During the week, he didn't drink anything except two glasses of wine at dinner. He got a bad rap. We didn't get along but he was certainly not as bad as the type of drunk I was used to. Come the weekend, he would let loose. Especially when the summer crop came in. All the guys did. It was like when summer hit the beach, their dicks needed new cows. The drinking was so bad on weekends, when he wanted to go to Memories, even his son, Peter, began to refuse to take him or pick him up because he hated to see his dad like that. Peter didn't even drink. Carlton should have shown him more respect. Me? I was getting to be too old a cow to even consider taking him to bed. He asked me one night."How about one for the good times?" My answer was." They were too long ago to remember."

    I was still grieving over Aja, but I had decided that I needed something in my house that loved me. I didn't care if Carlton threw a fit or not. That had to be an animal because I just couldn't seem to give people or get from them, the kind of pure affection I shared with animals. Nor had I ever met anybody willing to love me like an animal could. I couldn't have a dog, so I went looking for a cat. I surfed the Internet until I found a Himalayan. The lady who had them had had a set of nine kittens and had put pictures of them on her web site. They were gorgeous. I fell in love with one right away and got in touch with her. I had to describe the picture because she never named them. She let the one who took them do that. They were only four weeks old so she wouldn't let me have her until she reached twelve weeks. Every week she took the most interesting pictures with the kittens in poses to send to me. I don't know how she did it. They would be on little beach chairs and stuff. Posed. Have you ever tried to get a cat to pose? Not me, boy. You couldn't help but love them. One picture just took my heart away. It was a little male. The next thing you know, I had picked both and am off on the Internet searching for names. I wanted to name them something relative to their ancestry so I went looking for Siamese, Persian and Himalayan names. I ended up printing 5,000 off one site. I was hooked. These babies were going to be named something regal and ancestral.

Waiting for my kittens to get to twelve weeks was killing me. I decided to take a trip to Ocean Drive for my birthday. The owner let me come play with them on the way down and said I could pick them up on the way back. Was I excited or what? I don't even remember what I did on the trip except look for two cat carriers. Three days lost to my mind except getting those two carriers. They were good looking and deserving of two good looking Himalayan kittens.

These two kittens took my hurt away. They were absolutely precious. Eventually, I ended up with names for them based on how they acted. The female I called Sassy, because she was. She loved to roll around in sinks and bathtubs. You didn't have to call her, she followed you everywhere. I used to be like that with Mama. She always said I was "too sassy". I often called her Aja by mistake because, except for having three times the coat, she resembled her. The male was called Shyguy, because he was. He hid if anyone came into the room. I tried to make them more ancestral so eventually they became Sasi and Shigi. They settled my grieving heart and made me smile again.

Shortly after all this excitement, another set of pals came down. Lord knows I'm not going to ever be able to relax. Do I get the normal invitation to join them at the nineteenth hole? Did I want to? Hell, no. Nohellno. That's one word. This particular night they stayed at the nineteenth hole until time to go to Memories, which opened at ten p.m. That tells you the drinking was well into play before they got there. I had long since accepted all those phone calls to join them simply made me the sober driver. Nothing else. All I know is it was a night when the rain in North Carolina was coming down viciously. I got up around two a.m. to take my normal pill and sat up to watch the rain and lightening coming down over the sound. Carlton wasn't home yet and I didn't give a damn. I didn't even expect him to come home anymore. I knew they took a cab to Memories because Carlton will not drive drunk so I assumed he was at least safe. I often thought about how much time and gas I had spent driving men to their cars the day after a big drunk. Somehow, I knew they wouldn't have done it for me. I was still awake about three when he stumbled in. Note, Memories closed at two. I asked no questions, wanted no answers. He put his head around the bedroom door and motioned to me. I followed him into the kitchen. Smashed, he was. Really, totally smashed. But, friendly as always when he was drunk. I wasn't worried about him wanting to have sex with me because one: I wouldn't and two: he couldn't. He had been sleeping upstairs since we weren't close anymore, but I couldn't carry him up a flight of stairs. I hauled him to my bed and threw him on one side. Once I got into bed, he put his arm around me and got Chatty Cathy. He wanted me to know about his night. When Memories closed, they had called a cab and waited until almost three in the pouring rain for it, but it never showed. Right. They walked to a convenience store about a block and half away in the still pouring rain and were going to call again, but they met two girls at the store. They offered the girls twenty bucks to take them home. Giving the level of rape these days, not much of a brain in those two girls. But hey, who cares? These very kind ladies took the other guys first and they invited the girls up to visit. Carlton stopped and looked at me, surprised, then with that kind, gentle Carlton look I had once found so attractive, and with his arm around me like we were pals, said, "I can't believe what I was getting ready to tell you." He rolled over and went to sleep.

We once had a pact that we would never run out on each other as long as we lived in the same house. I don't know if he broke it that night or not, but he might as well have. Or any other night for that matter. I was already past done. If I had been a steak, you would have had to either throw me away or feed me to Mac. To my way of thinking, its not if a man might have run out on me. To me, its over if he wanted to. I had felt for some time that Carlton was more than ready.

This was the last year I experienced a good year in real estate. It went to hell and stayed there. I wanted something to do. I was bored. One of the Realtors, Sarah had started painting to try to make money. I have to admit she got me interested in trying it. She sounded like she was having so much fun with it. In August 2008, bored tearless, I decided to give it a try. Spurred on by the support of the people in the office, I ended up extremely prolific. By April 2009, I had done eighteen. I joined the local Adopt an Artist group and in May-June seven of them went out. In July-August, all seventeen went to our local history place. This is a great place to hang paintings for the summer because of the tourist traffic. Pat, from the local library asked me could I put them in the library for October. I was real tickled about that because October was my birthday month. The next thing I know, I hear that AanA has committed me to the local senior citizens place for September-October. I called Pat back and told her seventeen were going to the senior center, but by then I had eighteen more. She took them. I was painting my little heart out, I tell you. They did seem to be getting better. Most of all, it was so relaxing when things were so scary otherwise with real estate being so bad. I saw scary financial times ahead. I sold four..can you believe it?

COSTA RICA, BABY

Cognizant of our relationship, Carlton found a lot in Morehead where he wanted to build a house. He asked could he live upstairs until his house was built? Loving the fact that I would not be his biggest nightmare at the end of this relationship, I told him fine. He lived there another year, then left. He asked me if I wanted to go with him, but I knew he didn't want me to say yes. I cried the day he left. There was so much about him that I truly disliked. And, so very much I did. It was sad. I would have liked it to work. Control issues? Maybe. But, both of us were guilty of it.

After another year, while trying to survive a life without dogs and the terrible years in real estate, my owners told me they wanted to move down. I had to leave Beacons Reach. It broke my heart. Except for the people at work like Deborah, Pauly, Allen and Darlene, Sherry and Conrad, I wasn't getting much juice out of life. The lady I mentioned before, Sarah, appeared to dislike me intensely so I stayed away from her as much as I could, not wanting to argue. She didn't see how much I respected her work ethic, her energy and how she dove into stuff without fear. But, she didn't like me. I was flummoxed. I needed something to do to make me happy. The cats did, but I needed a trip. Carol needed a trip fix.

Life had pretty much sucked and I was pretty much broke when I saw an ad for Costa Rica in an American Orchid Society magazine. The trip was all about orchids. There would be a World Conference of Orchids, a trip to the hacienda of an aristocratic Spaniard who owned more orchids, and more rare orchids than anybody in Costa Rica. A visit to her greenhouse with a man who was promoting nationally the preservation of the rain forest. A trip to a simple couple's home, the only place where we could buy orchids. I thought about it from January to March. I spoke to the agent hosting the trip and reserved it. I was going to Costa Rica. It was going to cost $1500 for the trip. I had to pay extra for the flight from Wilmington, NC to Atlanta to Miami. I wanted a single room and would have to pay for that. He paid for breakfasts and some buffets but anything else was going to be on me. It didn't take but a couple of minutes to figure out I couldn't afford it. And who would take care of the orchids and the cats?

From December to January, I looked for a place to live while the agent badgered me to go. I finally backed out completely. I still needed a home. I was packed and ready to move with no where to go. A week later the travel agent called me back and said he had a deal. I was still interested enough to want to hear it. He would pay for the trip from Wilmington to Miami and all meals, and he would let me have the single room. There were only eight people going because seventy dropped out because of the economy. It got me thinking. I had found a place and was to move March 1st or so. Deborah said she would take care of the orchids and the cats. Sherry and Conrad said they would finish moving me. Everybody was encouraging me to go so, what the hell. I was going to Costa Rica. Heavy, huh? I needed a passport. How cool is that?

On March 1st, I started moving. On March 13th, I left for Costa Rica. The flight from Wilmington to Atlanta was easy, but I was supposed to run like hell for the flight from Atlanta to Puerto Rico when I got my bags in Atlanta. What I did instead was grab a guy with a cart, paid him twenty bucks and let him do everything. And he did, by God. We flew through the Atlanta airport like we had wings. He took my ticket to the counter, got me checked in, did everything. Then he left me, went to get us some coffee and something to eat while we waited to be called. We sat there an hour and talked liked we had been friends all our lives. Great guy. Before I left, I got his cell number so I could call him when I came back through. And, I gave him a big tip. He deserved it. After all this running around, I still sat for two hours waiting for the flight. However, it was Atlanta, for Christ's sake. That's exciting in itself. I hadn't been to Atlanta since a weekend with Michael. What a weekend with Michael. Oh well.

In Miami, I hooked up with the other guys and off we ran to get our connection to Puerto Rico. The flight was fast and easy and we weren't in Puerto Rico long enough to even think about it. I could see how beautiful their beaches were from the plane and would love to go there sometime.

When we got to this teeny, tiny airport in Costa Rica, we hopped into a van driven by Roberto, who was going to be our driver for the whole week. We introduced ourselves once everyone was picked up. I was the last to arrive and apparently, everybody else had taken the opportunity to gamble while waiting for me. There was a couple from Miami who grew orchids on a large scale, but not commercially. They had two greenhouses and another one being built while they were on the trip. A couple from Hawaii, who only grew cut orchids, came with us. Coming along on the trip was an older gentleman from Ft Lauderdale who had recently fallen in love with orchids and there was a gay fellow named Wes from Clearwater, who was very knowledgeable. I didn't care who was with us. I had never been out of the country before. Yee-ha. I was back in the game.

Off we went at what seemed to be a million miles an hour. For two hours we climbed a mountain to the first hotel. The hotel was better than those at home, as were the rooms and we got there just in time to go to sleep, thank heavens. I really hadn't expected something nicer than places I had stayed in the U.S., but it was far and above your chain hotels. I missed dinner and I was too excited to sleep so I got a good book. Ecstasy.

The next morning we got our first taste of how long we were going to spend in the damn van and how bad our butts were going to hurt before the trip was over. Only the town streets were paved and we weren't going to spend much time in town. Okey-dokey. Off we go. Keep it coming. Nothing's going to get on my nerves. Absolutely nothing. Make it an adventure, I always say. We headed to a cattleya plantation that a man had owned for forty years. Cattleyas are what most people think of as prom orchids. The big, showy ones. The story behind Julio's plantation was kind of quaint. When the British pulled out of Costa Rica, they gave the country to the people. The people formed a democratic government. That government gave four acres each to everyone Costa Rican in the country. Some still had them, some had sold out to the bigger plantations.

Julio still had his. When he first got his four acres, Julio, a poor man, but one who loved orchids, walked into the rain forest and pulled one pink cattleya off a tree. They grow naturally on trees. He took it home and planted it on the side of a tree at the very front of his property. His particular orchid was the national orchid of the country of Costa Rica. Given that orchids can pollinate through the air, he now had four acres of pink cattleyas. Thriving, healthy orchids. Everywhere. Every possible square foot had an orchid on it. In addition to what was hanging off his house and his trees, he had eighty tree stumps planted eight feet tall, eight feet apart, ten rows of them and the orchids grew up and over them so much they were attached from stump to stump. What's a better word than awesome? I use it too much, but what's a soul to do?

Julio was an older man and very shy. The tour guide told us he loved to have his picture taken, so please take his picture. My batteries were dead, so I could only pretend. However, since I have a flirt gene for great guys, for good measure, when we were leaving, I went over to him and kissed him on the cheek. Gave his Costa Rican cheek a big smack. A Down East smack. If somebody gives you one of those, you know you have been smacked. If he had been a dog, he would have been pawing at the ground in delight. I saw him blush. Before I got in the van, I gave him a wink. He blushed again. He loved it. He waved at me until we were out of sight. The guide frowned at me. He might not have liked it, but Julio did. If he thinks that's all I have in my repertoire, he's got another think coming.

The next morning we jumped into the van and headed off for the couple's house where we were going to be able to ship orchids back home. Apparently, the government makes it difficult to ship orchids out of the country because they do not want the orchids to be ripped right out of the trees for money. Therefore, they removed the incentive of profit. It was easier to get papers as an individual than it was for a company. The trip to their house took two hours of up and down, up and down, jostling and we were seemingly doomed to die on the road .

The people in much of Costa Rica live in what we think of as shacks, but they are normal living quarters to them. They only average six hundred dollars a year. We were to leave a lot of tips because tips were very important to these people. Tips can make the difference between starving and an education for their children. Therefore, Mario and Pela's home looked like a shack. There were magnificent orchids everywhere, even in the yard. They were adorning every room, including the kitchen and bathroom, decorating the squalor beneath. It was wondrous to be wandering around this little yard and through the house. On what you and I would think of as a second level, was their "greenhouse." It was open to the sun except for netting. They had rafters running from side to side with orchids hanging from them. You had to climb up rickety railings placed one horizontally and one vertically to get up there. The Costa Rican people are blessed with perfect weather and perfect humidity so, with some light protection, they can leave the orchids outside. Like what I used to do with the area that joined my house in Pennsylvania to the carport, but I had to hose the lattice on mine to create the humidity. We were there three hours choosing our orchids and giving them the information about where to ship them. I know you may not get that excited about orchids, but I was orgasmic, guys. Damn near everything was in bloom.

When all that excitement was over, we rode the seven hundred hours back to the hotel for the second snooze at the hotel. No. Really. I was fine with it. If my butt could take it, I would be good to go. I wandered through the spacious, lovely gardens around the hotel until dark. Everybody, but moi, went gambling. Believe me, that is no way to lose good money. I came here to buy orchids. I'll throw my money away that way, not on the crank of a lever. That's weird thinking to me. On my the way to the buffet dinner, I saw this beautiful artwork on the walls. Huge pieces. They had the same artist's work throughout out the hotel and I went from piece to piece taking pictures. By the way, I hate buffet. I walked into the fine restaurant. The only person there. I made friends with the host and he and I had dinner together. He could barely speak English, but that was ok, I could barely speak Spanish. Kidding. I couldn't speak Spanish at all. However, I could point to the most delectable chocolate desert I had ever seen.

The next morning at breakfast, the other guys were all whining about the money they lost. Boo-hoo. If you don't want to lose it, try not throwing it down a metal box or on blackjack. Since the Buzz incident in Charleston, I knew all I needed to know about how the house was stacked. You didn't stand a chance. If you won, they gave it to you. They, would, however, take it the hell back if you kept sitting there. Win? Get your ass outta there.

Right after we ate, we rode the seven hundred required hours back down the same damn mountain to check into the second hotel. If you are in Costa Rica, you are either up the mountains or down them, no in between. Or we weren't, anyway. We were going near San Jose, the Capitol, for the rest of the trip. First thing I noticed was this hotel had the same artist's work displayed, but all different pieces than what I had seen before. So, picture taking came first. Then, we spent the day wandering on our own. This is a really stupid concept since not one of us spoke

Spanish and couldn't go anywhere or do anything. But, the hotel was wonderful. The people, the rooms, everything. I spent my time telling the people behind the desk how wonderful their country was and how friendly the people were. I tried to learn their names, but since I couldn't pronounce half of them, I used the North American way and just didn't use their names after that. Instead I cranked up that Southern accent and dropped "dear" and "sweetheart" and "baby" around like they were seeds. I was so entranced, I planned to keep all my information because if I ever came to Costa Rica again, I wanted to stay at that hotel. As luck had it, Wes, the gay guy, and I came up with a breakthrough for the times between the ass kicking rides. It was called the bar. He found it first. Then, the doll baby ran up to my room, hollering for me. He wasn't into gambling either. Actually, I think I was the only one who didn't give a damn if he was gay or not. Polite is good enough for me. Off we went to the bar, introduced ourselves to the bartender, who spoke a little English. We said "Rum." He understood the word rum. It was awesome. I had two and absolutely had to go to sleep. Out like a candle that ran out of wick. Either that or see if the hotel had a local male prostitute. I figured sleeping was better because I hadn't studied up on Spanish genital diseases. Sorry, but you do have to think of these things. Especially when you're drunk. Don't think for a minute that these Spanish men are not good looking. Hoo-ha. But, I'm doing the mantra thing. Money is for orchids. And rum. And whatever it was he put in there with it. Good Lord, that was good.

    The next morning, we climbed into the van and spent another half a day going up another mountain on the other side of the country. Now we were headed for something I was most interested in. Mainly, because I couldn't believe it. We were going to the home of Ileana and Dominique, the Spanish aristocrats. Think about it. Aristocrats. Me. From Carteret County. My Dean of English could have made me write it on the board a hundred times and I still wouldn't have believed it. On the way up the mountain, I noticed all these white cottages with blue roofs that we passed from time to time on the way up. I asked the guide were they where the coffee plantation workers lived. He explained that a lot of the aristocrats in Costa Rica believe in sharing the joy, so to speak. They provide housing, clothing, food and education for their workers. They even throw parties for them. It was pretty obvious that having people work your fields for you in Costa Rica was not quite like having slaves. I was already surprised enough that these ultra rich, sophisticated, people would let eight strangers walk through their home and orchid greenhouse. Try getting someone in the states to let you do that. Talk about a whoosh. Excuse me. We have some rich people in the U.S. Do we have aristocrats? Real ones? I don't think so. There might be some who think they are, but not the real deal, you know.

After the van climbed and climbed this mountain, one lane by the way, we finally pulled in front of a home that we still had to look up to see. It could have been an English castle but it was near the top of a mountain, surrounded by a rain forest that grew right up to the front steps. Exquisite. We climbed moss covered steps, in high humidity, to the front door and when we walked in, the whole back side of the house was the mountain, with a waterfall in the living room. A waterfall in the living room!! A real one. Not one installed for effect. This estate had been there one hundred and forty five years. That's how long ago someone climbed to the top of this mountain and thought, "A waterfall would look nice in that living room." Think about it. Try that, Home Decorating Network. The front of the estate was all windows overlooking the mountains and valleys we had spent hours driving through. This was the "clear day, you can see forever" stuff. Absolute lushness abounded. With my love for trees, plants and all of nature's bounty, all the richness of the landscape you could see, was such it took my breath way. I was in overload. I could not conceive how far away things could actually be. Ileana had not been introduced to us yet, but when I turned back to the living room from the windows, Ileana happened to be watching me. She clearly understood my reaction. I looked at her and we didn't need Spanish to communicate. I knew this woman did not take this beauty for granted.

Our guide told us this coffee plantation had been in the family for one hundred and forty five years. Imagine. Do you even know who your ancestors were one hundred and forty five years ago? Do you even care? For most of us in the U.S., the answer would be, of course not. It was unbelievable. To me, this was worth the whole trip. Within an actual rain forest, attached to one side of the home was the greenhouse, on four levels made possible by carving steps out of the mountain itself. Unbelievably, you could still see rain forests as far as your vision would take. Ileana took my hand. MY HAND, PEOPLE, and we entered her greenhouse. The back of the greenhouse was still the mountains, with another waterfall, and the most mouth watering orchids you could ever imagine. On benches, attached to walls and hanging from above. She didn't even have to hose them down. It rained periodically. Just enough. Naturally, the humidity was such you were immediately soaking wet. Most importantly, I felt four feet from God. It was a sensory overload. I have to admit, they had to drag me out. Ileana was with me the whole way. When we left, she took my hand and smiled. I wanted to say something, but neither of us could communicate. Then she disappeared. The others? They had already figured out when we went somewhere with orchids, to look for me when they were ready to go. I'd be the first in and last out.

They herded us back into the living room to meet someone who is trying to teach the children to honor their rain forest heritage. He showed us a fifteen minute video that is shown to the children of Costa Rica, in different format, throughout their education. I could not have been more impressed.

We jumped back into the van to head down the mountain. This time we were going to the same people's other home, but this little hacienda was only 40 years old. These people of rich, historic backgrounds, were now going to feed me. Me. Was I impressed? Hell yes. They didn't have to. My Mama couldn't even do that and these people, who didn't even know anything about me were willing to. The party was to consist of Ileana, Dominique, the judges from the orchid conference and us. I was going to meet judges from a Word Conference of Orchids. Somebody hit the overload button. I'm toast. I can't stand anymore. This was better than speeding down a highway with a statie on your tail. Better than him putting a gun in your face. Much.

When we got there, they had prepared themselves, a buffet for the stars. They served us, not the staff. I never saw any staff. I saw rich food and wonderful wine. We ate by the pool and then wandered through the grounds. Did you know bamboo grew fifty feel tall? I couldn't believe how tall everything was. I had to look straight up even when I wasn't right under something. There were cliffs that went straight up, or down, if you were on top, covered with moss and overgrowth and orchids blooming naturally. They lived in the rain forest in this house as well. I was still speechless. It was worth the whole trip if I died that night. I was way past overwhelmed. I didn't want to ever go home. Please, please, please. Can I stay here? Do I have to go back to all the strife and discontent. Mine mostly? When we headed for the van to leave, Ileana came looking for me. She took my hand. She had the softest hands I have ever touched, and I have shaken some hands in my lifetime. She looked at me with soft, brown eyes and with what I considered a moment when two people bond, she asked me, carefully, because she didn't speak English well, how would she get in touch with me? She said she would love to have me back. Can you believe that? What do you think the chances are I'd ever be able to go back? Right. But I had that moment. I had that day. I had that beautiful, sophisticated woman in the cross hairs of my mind where she will never leave.

Later that night, I focused on the day. I wanted it burned into my brain so I would remember this trip no matter what. Some people never get the chance to ever travel. I decided I should not whine about never having a chance to go back, but to thank God I ever got there in the first place. And, I thank those at work who encouraged me. You will never be forgotten. You had seen me go through tough times and you knew I needed a break. You have no idea the depth of the gift you gave me.

The next day was the World Orchid Conference. I was squirming like a lizard to get on with it. On the way over, one of the women on the trip asked me why the hell I dressed the way I did? Why do people act this way? I don't see t-shirts as fashion. I wear good clothes. Good quality. Was I supposed to suddenly change and want to look like hell. Not me. The clothes I took were the ones I wore to work. I owned them and I was close to broke. I didn't invest in a ten t-shirt wardrobe to go to Costa Rica. Personally, I thought the people in Costa Rica liked the way I dressed. I wanted to ask her why the hell she dressed the way she did since she apparently thought, with a husband, that it was ok to show up in rags with hair that had never seen a brush. I didn't. I politely said I dressed the way my Mama taught me. I would never go out in public not put together nicely. I added that I assumed she dressed as her mother taught, as well. Nudge, nudge.

Unfortunately, we showed up a little late for the Conference. Like a day late. The judging was the day before. The judges hadn't mentioned that. Perhaps they had. Since we didn't speak Spanish, what did we know? I really didn't mind missing the big day because it had to have been a lot more crowded. We had been told that we couldn't buy anything because the government would not give us permits to ship them back nor would the U.S. let us bring the orchids in without tearing the boxes open and comparing plants to invoices. In other words, major hassle. The others in the group got bitchy because they couldn't buy anything even though they were told, so they wanted a day just to run around. You know them. The ones who want to find a Wal-mart to buy another t-shirt. Not me, boy-o. I went there to see orchids and orchids I planned to see. Wes and I decided to stay. We would take a cab back. The hell with the rest of them. I figured they could afford to take orchid trips all the time so this meant nothing to them, and it showed. Well, it meant the hell something to me. I dove into it like it was water and I was a drowning duck.

    You make friends so easily and quickly in Costa Rica. Before I knew it, I was chatting, in English, with a guy who used to be a boat captain and had actually been to Beaufort. I really enjoyed his orchid display and, I have to admit, was a little bummed that I couldn't get any. He explained it was just too hard. I was seriously considering smuggling. One of the other women on the trip planned to smuggle some flasks in her suitcase. Then, I ran into Wes and he had made friends with another guy, but heard the same thing. So be it. We decided to spend our time taking our time. While we were still gawking at the displays, the guy Wes had met came running up to us to tell us there was an official there who he had talked into letting us buy some orchids. We tore through hundreds of people, looking for the judge, who we were told was dressed "as a government official." Of course, we didn't know what that meant, so we ran back to get Wes's friend. Sure enough, he took us to the guy who was in full dress uniform. That was ok because now we had a translator with us. The official was a darling. He would let us both buy a limited amount of orchids. The magic number was eight each. We had to do everything he said, though. He said he would be there until two o'clock. It was twelve. There were papers that needed to be filled out. Bring it on!!

    We tried not to act like "westerners," not to mention rude people, but it was hard because there was so much to go through and so little time. SO LITTLE TIME, PEOPLE !!! We finally decided since Wes wanted one species and I wanted another, we would go our separate ways and meet up when we had eight each. Once we got back together, we sprinted back to the official. Wes was going first because he was pushier than I was, but found out we had to have our passports. Yee-ha. I had mine. The official said he would wait for Wes to get back if he wanted to go all the way to the hotel to get his. Was that polite or what? Wes kept whining like he thought the official would do it anyway. But he was wasting his valuable time and mine so I got in his face and convinced him to shut up and go get his damn passport. The damn man was willing to wait. That's all the official was asking for, and he had to have it. The information from it must go on the form. Period. It wasn't gay bashing, damn it. There was nothing to argue about. GO.

The taxis there are unbelievable, too. They wait for you. Wherever you go and however long it takes. Wes went all the way back to the hotel, got his passport, raced back and the taxi was going to wait until both of us were done to take us back to the hotel, orchids and all. Would they do that in New York City? I don't think so. And they don't ask to be paid until you are through. They don't come looking for you. When you go back out, there they are, a bunch of them, lazily relaxed, ready to help. Amazing.

I had taken my time filling out the papers just in case Wes was late but he made it in record time. When we were done, it was two thirty. Then, in spite of the fact that he had planned to leave, the official took us on a private tour of the exhibition where we were allowed behind the cordoned off areas to take pictures. I had, of course, donned the whole Southern Belle demeanor hoping to stall for Wes. Finally, orchided out, I asked him a key question. I asked was getting his permission the hard part or getting the permit to take them out of the country? He said he was the hard part. Oh joy of joys. Back to the hotel we flew on wheels that had become wings. Now, we had to wrap them for shipment just like they were to be wrapped when they hit the U.S. All we had to have next was the permit. Supposedly, the easy part.

At dinner that evening, the rest found out we had gotten orchids at the Conference. We were cussed out in English and Japanese. There was a whole lot of bitching going on, but I had no sympathy for them, nor did I feel bad that we got our orchids. We had schmoozed. Then we had schmoozed again. We earned them. This was an orchid trip. They went to the damn mall. In Costa Rica. Can't they wait until they get home to go to a mall? Imagine. Going all the way to Costa Rica to go to a mall. Lord, save me.

The next day we were supposed to go to a coffee plantation to see how they work. I had zero interest in that so I sat it out at the restaurant and the market place at the plantation. I got a few more gifts. The exhilaration of Ileana and the Conference was having to hold my interest, because this wouldn't. We had visited a wood factory on the way to the plantation where I had gotten presents, so this was a perfect opportunity to get the rest. When everybody got done walking through a dead hot coffee plantation, the tour guide had cut the rest of the trip short to give Wes and I time to get our Cites Certificates, the only thing left to worry about except Customs. While everybody grumbled like they had lost their first born, we walked in and were done in twenty minutes flat. The guide couldn't believe it. He had been doing these trips for twenty years and had no idea it was that easy. He had never tried. He had never schmoozed. Tough luck. Wes and I went back to the hotel to finish the wrapping, since they unwrapped everything we had done, we also had to make sure the invoices matched up to the Cite Certificates and the little bill of sales the merchants gave us. Then we hit the bar and that damn fine rum drink the bartender made. Everybody else went shopping, for Christ's sake. Again? Go figure. Not me, boy.

The guide told us if Customs took the invoices, or if the other forms didn't match, they would confiscate the orchids and throw them away. They would probably burn them. Heaven forbid. Some of these were orchids grown only in Costa Rica. I was one nervous orchid freak, I tell you.

The next morning was all our's. Another useless free day. In the three days we had been at the hotel, I had made friends with the telephone girl and the kids at the front desk. You have no conception of the word friendly until you meet people who are so anxious to please you. Age did not matter. Everyone. So anxious to make you happy. So anxious to make sure you love their country. To meet people so in love with their country, you can see it on their faces. And no, they are not running for office with a million bucks of sordid money behind them. Not to mention the bartender. Loved that rum. Tell you a secret later. No, I'll tell you now. It's a sugar liqueur. Yum!

As best I could, not speaking Spanish, I asked the kids at the desk to get a taxi for me. I needed to buy a book. They couldn't figure out what I wanted. I finally just asked to go to a Hiper-Mas, or a Hyper-Mas, whatever. I knew there was one close by. I'd seen it running back and forth in the van. They told him where to take me and he did. When we got there, he gestured for me to tell him what I wanted. I said I wanted a book and then put my palms together and opened them, you know? Nothing. I finally went into a bank, figuring someone would speak English. Nobody. I went back out and the cab driver had found someone who did. They walked all over the mall looking for a bookstore, with me trailing behind like a lost puppy. Hallelujah. God is good. A bookstore. They even went in with me to make sure this is what I needed. They stopped what they were doing and waited for me..what a concept. They found me the book store so I thought I was on my way. Well, guess what? All their books were in Spanish. Duh..so I gave up and went back to the hotel. All in all, the trip cost me five dollars. Try that in the U.S.

One of the people at the desk during the three days I had been at this hotel, had been a girl I thought was so beautiful I had to tell her so. She had long black hair with blue highlights running through it. Like Mama's. Only Mama's wasn't long all of the time. Her eyes were black and sultry, but there was no make up or pretense. Her face was one you would expect to see in the movies on women who are famous. Or on a model in the finest magazines. Not behind the counter of a hotel. I had already found out how hard it is for the people here to even get a job. Without college, and consequently English, they would go nowhere in Costs Rica. I had already been told if they could not speak English, they had not been "educated." The first time I told her how beautiful she was, a gentleman at the desk had to interpret it for her, but she picked it up from that point on. She would blush and blush. Prettily, I might add. I have absolutely no problem telling another woman I think she is beautiful. It is a gift from God and should be acknowledged. Understand, even the "interpreter" found it difficult to translate. No one spoke English easily. These people struggled with it.

I could not accept it was over. I was completely distraught. Don't make me go home. The day I was to check out, heartbroken, my beautiful hostess behind the desk came around the counter, put her arms around me softly and said, in English, " I will miss you, Car-ol." The gentlemen behind the counter told me she had asked him to teach her that. I was so very touched. She started to cry, then went back behind the counter and said it over and over as I was paying my bill. She then reached across the counter touched my earring and said "Beautiful." They were my favorite earrings. I also knew someone had to teach her to say that so she loved them enough to ask them to. Without a second thought, I took them off and gave them to her. She would have had to work for years to pay what those earrings cost. It was a truly remarkable gift for her and I felt the better for doing the giving. I made sure she understood I wanted her to give my gorgeous blue straw hat to the telephone girl, then climbed into the van for the trip to the airport. I knew they wouldn't remember me very long with all the tourists they had to handle. What they didn't know was I would remember them as long as I am on this earth. Julio, the old man with all the cattleyas. Roberto, our van driver, who needed a really big tip for driving me around for seven days up and down mountains for hours at a time. How the hell do you even calculate that? I hope I did ok. I remember Ileana, Dominique and the kids at the hotel. You may not know it but you burned your way into my heart, never to leave.

When we got to the airport, the only hurdle was going to be the orchids. We had been warned and warned by our guide The customs agents didn't even look at them. I carried them on the plane, which I had been told they wouldn't let me do. They didn't even look at them, either. I flew to Atlanta and called my buddy to help me. He was off, but he had told a friend about me and he helped me get on the plane for home. I drove home to the strange house I moved into March 1st and continued to unpack, not only from the trip but from life's accumulations. Believe me, I am so glad I didn't give up on that trip. Spent way too much money, though. I wouldn't have if I couldn't have bought orchids. Mixed blessings.

I learned something on that trip you might not have grasped. The people behind the counter got to know me more than the people with whom I shared that van. I realized, in the general scheme of life, the one most concerned and perhaps the one most hurt, is the one least considered. Like dust on a shelf. It's an irritant. Brush it away. Hire someone to get rid of it, if necessary. Just make it go away. I chose to make myself known to those who wanted to know me. Oddly, most people are comfortable dealing with the problem maker. Strength against strength. They banded together and openly cast Wes and I from their world. No interest in another unless they go along. What a concept.

The only reason I always had to make a noise was because no one would listen to me. It never crossed anyone's mind that I was anything but dust to brush aside. Even I knew better. How sad to have people see you other than you truly are. How long did that go on? Most of my life? Probably. I believed it even in my own mind. I also learned the times I find serenity is when it is quiet and peaceful. I won't forget it. I will seek it with a vengeance.

CLOSED

With my newfound wisdom, and the serenity that went with it. I went back to painting. Deborah, the woman so supportive of everything I did, wanted four giclees so I let her have them for the cost the lady charged for making the giclees. Two of them were my favorites, Kenny's Coral, named after her recently deceased husband, a really great guy, and Big Daddy. It should come as no surprise that Big Daddy was named after my Daddy. It looked nothing like him, of course. Actually, it was the smart ass look on the face of the Big Daddy fish that did it. I got a little kick out of naming a fish after Daddy. Wonder how he would have liked that? Like I give a damn. Up yours, Dad. I have to admit they were two beautiful coral scenes done in reds and corals with modeling paste which has a build up you can feel to give the coral texture. I was learning every day. I painted a small eight by ten named Windswept Hair. She had that kind of hair I always wanted, but MaryBeth got. Breasts? Hair? You have to wonder if there is a God. Its several shades of blond, long and thick hair. Shortly after, Farrah Faucette died and I figured this looked like my rendition of Farrah, but because of MaryBeth, I kept the name. She was my initial inspiration, after all. I did, however, do one like Jacqueline Smith, with darker, windswept hair and one focused blue eye, like mine. I even put gold highlights around the iris. I named her Windswept's Sister. I kept painting and painting until I did Blue Coral Paradise which was a large 24"x30" canvas with a lot of tropical fish and blue coral in it. Deborah asked me for one of flamingos. I asked her how many flamingos she wanted and she told me she would be happy with one. When I was done I ended up with sixteen on the canvas. It looks like a find the head puzzle.

  I did a Babe on the Beach with a back view of an undoubtedly beautiful woman who wrote "I love the Beach" in the sand. After that, I did Exotica which was my very first face, hands and feet. Exotica was the first to be a person filling the canvas instead of a lot of ocean and sand.

  A friend of mine sent me an email with what he called Awesome Photos. One of the photos was a beautiful woman with long black hair with blue highlights in it. I remembered the girl behind the desk in Costa Rica. I never could get what her damn name was. I had her clearly in my mind although this was now late December. Deborah had just been to see Cher in Las Vegas. I took all this, my Mama, Jimmy's eyes, the girl in Costa Rica, and the photo in the email as inspirations and painted a whole canvas with a pure black background. Then I filled with only her looking over her shoulder with her blue-black hair hanging down. When I tried to paint her eyes brown, as in the photo, it just didn't cut it. I ended up painting the eyes the same color as the blue highlights in her hair, like the girl in Costa Rica. They started out small but got bigger and bigger until they were mesmerizing. Before I was done, I realized they looked like Mama's eyes. Her deep blue, beautiful eyes.

  Six terrible months later, broke and deeply in debt, I went to the office and closed it forever. The building had gone into foreclosure while I had tried to maintain my serenity. The loss of

Pauly, Deborah and all the others with whom I worked will never leave me. I had so enjoyed Alan and Darlene and their two standard poodles, though they might not know that. I will sincerely miss Deborah calling me twenty times a day when I was home. I have a feeling, after awhile, no one will be calling. I decided I needed to finish my book about Mama and my life, With the grace of God, you will see her eyes on the cover of my book.

Mama. It hurts just to think about her sometimes. Times like when she is not as close as the phone. Times when I see Bogey and Bacall. I haven't forgotten Mama. You don't forget your Mama even if she wasn't a wide open female like mine. When I sit down in front of a canvas now, I think of painting Mama. I have a picture she had done when she was younger and she is beautiful. I know I am not a good enough painter to do her justice. I also know I couldn't do it because she wouldn't be the screaming, hollering so mad she'd spit at you kind of Mama I knew. I don't need to paint her because I have her pictured so clearly in my mind. If I tried, would she come right out of the earth and take my ass apart just for fun? There was only one Anna in my life and she wasn't on a canvas. She'd be standing in front of me or it isn't good enough for me. When I was young, she was alive, so very alive. I don't want her on a canvas, I want her standing in front of me, alive, damn it.

You know, when you look back sixty two years, given all that has gone on in your life, what is the one thing you would change if you could? I wish Mama were right here. I wish she would ask me again to get on the pony. Anything. I would promise not to cuss her. I would take her drunk and all. Anything.

I wish she could see my paintings. Hug me. Laugh with me or at me if she wanted to. I'd even settle for the walk to the water if I had to. I don't want to live my life over. The only thing I hate when I think of death is my memories of my mother will be lost forever. What if I am the last one to remember her? What happens to her then? Does she disappear, like she never existed? They say you touch people in your lifetime and your life goes on. Bullshit.

You might say, "Hell, what does she care? She'll be dead." I'm talking about me here. You see, I don't fear death. What I do fear is my trigeminal condition. It hurts more every day. I was pretty much down to no days at the office because of it. I always figured I wouldn't last long after I quit working. Deep down I don't even mind that. I tell myself, the worst is finally over. Nothing I can think of can hurt me now. I can become invisible. Disappear. What I do mind, to this day, is I can't imagine never seeing Mama again in my mind,

not to mention talking to her right out loud. I do think she could have done a better job with me if she had a second chance. Or even easier circumstances. But hey. What are you going to do? Obviously, I don't hold her circumstances against her, like the others did. I was right there with her when she was doing all she could to teach me manners and how to dress, not to mention how to eat. How did she continue on do that when we had no clothes or food even for the two of us? How did she hold her head up? She not only held it up, she held it up high, people. Never forget that. Don't think badly of her because of her faults, whether they be a result of her circumstance or her weakness. I don't give a damn. Its all a little amazing that she did what she did. Put her down and I will take you down. Simple as that. Did I turn out ok, as they say? Hell, I don't know. I turned out Mama's child, that's all I care about.
    Yee-ha.